A Study of
Spinoza's *Ethics*

A Study of Spinoza's *Ethics*

Jonathan Bennett

HACKETT PUBLISHING COMPANY

The paper in this book meets the guidelines for permanence and durability established by the Committee on Production Guidelines for Book Longevity of the Council on Library Resources.

Printed in the United States of America

Cover and jacket design by Ken Farnhill

Interior design by James N. Rogers

First edition, second printing 1988

Library of Congress Cataloging in Publication Data
Bennett, Jonathan Francis.
A Study of Spinoza's Ethics.

Bibliography: p.
Includes indexes.
1. Spinoza, Benedictus de, 1632–1677. Ethica.
2. Ethics—Early works to 1800. I. Title.
B3974.B46 1984   170   83–18568
ISBN 0–915145–82–0
ISBN 0–915145–83–9 (pbk.)

Contents

CONTENTS

Contents

Contents

Preface

This book expounds and argues with Spinoza's *Ethics*, in the hope of drawing into the argument philosophers who have not previously brought Spinoza into their work as an energetic collaborator or antagonist. My aim is to tell them what some of his main doctrines and arguments are, and to help them read his text for themselves and use it for their own purposes.

I taught a course on Spinoza in 1952, studied him in a seminar of Stuart Hampshire's in about 1954, and since then have taught at least two courses on him at each of three universities. I have been working towards the present work for a quarter of a century. In a project stretching across such a long period one accumulates too many debts to be fully remembered or properly acknowledged; but I can say that while at Cambridge I was richly helped in my Spinoza work by Michael Tanner, and that at the University of British Columbia Peter Remnant's influence stands out. Although my philosophical education at Syracuse University is in the charge of all my colleagues, the Spinoza work owes most to Bill Alston, Larry Hardin and José Benardete. I have also learned from Syracuse graduate students: I make acknowledgments in the text, but there are doubtless some borrowed ideas in the book which I liked so immediately that I forgot their provenance. I do not attempt to acknowledge the intellectual debts that I know I have to students at Cambridge and UBC.

The work was finally revised during a 1982 Summer Seminar for College Teachers which I directed at Syracuse under the auspices of the National Endowment for the Humanities. I am indebted to the NEH for that opportunity, and to the members of the seminar for all they did to encourage, challenge and improve my thinking and writing about Spinoza. The few mentions in the body of the book do not do justice to my debt to Harold Zellner, Roderick Stewart, Jonathan Schonsheck, Stanley Riukas, Anthony Murphy, Phyllis Morris, Richard Miller, Ronald Messerich, Robert Carnes, William Brenner, Jonathan Bordo, and Jesse Bohl. I am also grateful to George Bealer, Edwin Curley, Harry Parkinson and Margaret Wilson for reading and commenting on parts or all of the work.

Although I don't know much Latin, I have not had to rely on earlier translations of the *Ethics* because for about five years I have worked with successive drafts of Edwin Curley's forthcoming English version of Spinoza's works. My greatest single debt is to Curley for giving me access to his translation (see my note on it in the Bibliography) and annotations.

1

PREFACE

When I depart from one of his renderings, as I quite often do, it is usually on the basis of an understanding of the text which I got from him in the first place; and it often involves my taking some slight liberty which is permissible in a commentator but not in a translator.

The Social Sciences and Humanities Research Council of Canada, and the Senate Research Committee of Syracuse University, helped to defray secretarial expenses in producing certain drafts of the book; I am grateful to both. I am also glad to acknowledge that parts of the book have appeared in different form in *The Journal of Philosophy*, *Midwest Studies in Philosophy*, and *Syracuse Scholar*.

Readers who find slips and inaccuracies of the sort that might be set right on reprinting are asked to tell me about them.

A few dozen small corrections have been made in the second printing.

Syracuse, N.Y.   J.F.B.
November, 1987

Abbreviations

In the text I use what is becoming the standard method of referring to items in the *Ethics*—the method according to which '2p7s' names Part 2, Proposition 7, Scholium, and according to which 4d2 names Part 4, definition 2. In a context where there is no possible ambiguity, I sometimes drop initial numerals from references, putting 'p7s' instead of '2p7s'. In these references a comma means 'and'. Thus the expression '5p23,d' refers to Part 5, Proposition 23, *and* its demonstration.

References to passages within long scholia, prefaces, appendixes, et cetera are given through page and line in the Gebhardt edition of Spinoza's works. Thus '1 Appendix 80/9' refers to the passage in the Appendix to Part 1 which *begins* at line 9 on p. 80 of the Gebhardt edition, volume II. Where a reference of this kind is to any work but the *Ethics*, it is given with the volume number first—e.g., 'Letter 4 at IV/14/15'. This system is at last widely usable because Curley's forthcoming edition of the works in English will, happily, provide Gebhardt's page and line numbers in the margin.

In footnotes and Bibliography, I use the following abbreviated names for certain works which are mentioned a number of times:

Alquié:	Ferdinand Alquié (ed.), *Oeuvres philosophiques de Descartes*, vol. 1 (Paris, 1963), vol. 2 (1967), vol. 3 (1973).
Descartes's Principles	Benedict Spinoza, *Parts 1 and 2 of René Descartes's Principles of Philosophy, Demonstrated in the Geometrical Manner.*
Edwards	Paul Edwards (ed.), *The Encyclopedia of Philosophy* (New York, 1967).
Emendation	Benedict Spinoza, *A Treatise on the Emendation of the Intellect.* I have used Curley's forthcoming translation

of this work, and my references are based on his section numbering.

Essay	John Locke, *An Essay Concerning Human Understanding.*
Ethics	Benedict Spinoza, *Ethics Demonstrated in Geometrical Order.*
Grene	Marjorie Grene (ed.), *Spinoza: A Collection of Critical Essays* (Notre Dame, Indiana, 1973).
Gueroult	Martial Gueroult, *Spinoza*, vol. 1 (Paris, 1968), vol. 2 (1974).
Hessing	Siegfried Hessing (ed.), *Speculum Spinozanum 1677–1977* (London, 1977).
Kashap	S. Paul Kashap (ed.), *Studies in Spinoza: Critical and Interpretive Essays* (Berkeley, 1972).
Kennington	Richard Kennington (ed.), *The Philosophy of Baruch Spinoza* (Washington, D.C., 1980).
Linguistic Behaviour	Jonathan Bennett, *Linguistic Behaviour* (Cambridge, 1976).
Loemker	Leroy E. Loemker (ed.), *G. W. Leibniz: Philosophical Papers and Letters*, second edition, (Dordrecht, 1969).
Mandelbaum	Maurice Mandelbaum and Eugene Freeman (eds.), *Spinoza: Essays in Interpretation* (La Salle, Illinois., 1975).
New Essays	G. W. Leibniz, *New Essays on Human Understanding*, translated and

ABBREVIATIONS

	edited by Peter Remnant and Jonathan Bennett (Cambridge, 1981).
Principles	René Descartes, *The Principles of Philosophy.*
Shahan	Robert W. Shahan and J. Biro (eds.), *Spinoza: New Perspectives* (Norman, Oklahoma, 1978).
Treatise	David Hume, *A Treatise of Human Nature*, edited by L. A. Selby-Bigge (Oxford).

1

A *Character Sketch* *of the* Ethics

The central topic of this book is Spinoza's one indisputable masterpiece, the *Ethics*. In my first chapter I shall say what sort of work the *Ethics* is, what sort Spinoza took it to be, how it relates to the rest of his work, and in what spirit I intend to approach it.

§1. *The place of the* Ethics *in Spinoza's corpus*

1. Setting aside Spinoza's grammar of the Hebrew language and his two works on politics, which I do not find helpful in understanding the *Ethics*, we are left with six substantial items. Four of these were finished or abandoned by the time Spinoza was 31 years old, and the other two occupied him intermittently between then and his death in 1677 at the age of 44.

2. Of the four earlier works, I shall not attend much to the *Short Treatise*. The manuscript of this, written in Dutch by a hand other than Spinoza's, came to light only in the nineteenth century. It seems clear that it stems from Spinoza somehow; but its status is dubious, its content confused, its fit with the rest of his work uncomfortable. These factors and its probable early date make this work a feeble aid to understanding Spinoza's mature thought.

The *Emendation of the Intellect*, a treatise about ways of acquiring knowledge, avoiding error, and vanquishing scepticism, is largely epistemological, although its announced purpose is practical:

> After experience had taught me that all the things which regularly occur in ordinary life are empty and futile, and I saw that all the things which were the cause or object of my fears had nothing of good or bad in themselves, except insofar as the mind was moved by them, I resolved at last to try to find out whether there was something which . . . , once found and acquired, would continuously give me the greatest pleasure.

The discrepancy is explained by the fact that *Emendation* is an unfinished work, presumably abandoned in favour of the fresh start that Spinoza was making at about that time in the *Ethics*, to show that durable happiness may be reached through the cultivation of intellectual virtues—the emendation of the intellect.

Spinoza's practical or ethical aims in the *Emendation* contrast strikingly with the project that launched Descartes into his *Meditations*:

(1) A CHARACTER SKETCH OF THE *ETHICS*

It is now some years since I detected how many were the false beliefs that I had from my earliest youth admitted as true, and how doubtful was everything I had since constructed on this basis; and from that time I was convinced that I must . . . commence to build anew from the foundation, if I wanted to establish any firm and permanent structure in the sciences.

Leon Roth's observation that 'Descartes' ultimate interest was in the "true"; Spinoza's, in the "good" ',[1] captures accurately the contrast between their ultimate targets. But we shall see that on the way to his practical conclusions in the *Ethics* Spinoza traverses oceans and continents of theory—metaphysics, biology, philosophy of mind and of matter—not only because they project into territory that lies directly between him and his practical conclusions, but also because he loved the philosophical problems and his own solutions to them. Much of the present work will be devoted to those discussions, which are some of the most instructive and nourishing things in early modern philosophy.

The *Emendation* is a risky guide to the thought in the *Ethics*—not because it is merely a start, but because it is a false start. Let us remember that Spinoza dropped it and started afresh. Still, the work is not entirely negligible by us: although Spinoza left it unfinished, he did, late in his life, include it with the works he wanted published posthumously.

3. The remaining two early works, unlike any others described in this section, were published during Spinoza's lifetime. They are *Descartes's Principles* and, tacked on as an 'appendix' to that, *Metaphysical Thoughts*. The former work claims to present in Spinoza's way the main content of the first two Parts of Descartes's *Principles*. It throws helpful light on Spinoza's own thinking; but because much of its content is Cartesian doctrine which Spinoza confessedly does not accept, it must be handled warily. So, too, must the *Metaphysical Thoughts* which, although it has Spinoza more often speaking for himself, carries in its Preface a claim to 'express the opinions of Descartes' which are not always Spinoza's. These two works were published only at the urging of friends, one of whom wrote the Preface; most of their content was written originally to help a pupil whom Spinoza would trust with Descartes's ideas but not with his own. Nevertheless, just once in the *Ethics* Spinoza obliquely refers to something in his *Descartes's Principles*, and in §24 I shall show that this reference is brilliantly illuminating.

4. Of the two works that stretch out to the end of Spinoza's life, one is his *Ethics Demonstrated in Geometrical Order*, a product of labours which extended, albeit with interruptions, across sixteen years. We have no early drafts of the work—an astonishing fact, as versions of it were being read in Holland and in England many years before Spinoza's death. Still, a

1. Roth, *Spinoza*, p. 234.

book cannot go through as much revision as this one did without leaving traces of how it developed, and some of these will be mentioned in due course. Also, after Spinoza's death most of his works were published both in the original Latin and in Dutch translations; the Dutch version of the *Ethics* was probably based on an earlier Latin version,[2] and numerous small differences point to changes in Spinoza's thinking.

Further clues come from the other partly late body of work by Spinoza, namely his letters. We have about fifty of these (the numbering runs higher because the standard edition includes letters *to* Spinoza); they spread across the years when the *Ethics* was being written, often replying to questions from friends who were reading drafts of the work. In the first of them (Letter 2), written before *Descartes's Principles* was published, and at about the time of the *Emendation*, it is clear that Spinoza has already promulgated certain of the basic doctrines on which the *Ethics* is founded. So the letters can help us.

Often, however, they are disappointing. When a correspondent confronts Spinoza with a profound, central difficulty in his work, the response is seldom satisfactory. It is often an outright snub, especially towards the end of Spinoza's life; but even in the earlier years, before he became sick, his replies tended to be unsympathetic and evasive. The source of this behaviour is more intellectual than moral, I believe. Spinoza was not at his best in correspondence because his mind, although deep and powerful and tenacious, was rather slow; which may also explain why his best work is the one which occupied him for the longest time.

5. Although Spinoza had at an early stage some of the seminal ideas of the *Ethics*, I am sure it underwent steady changes, mostly of a deepening and broadening tendency, throughout the last third of his short life. We should take the chasm seriously: on the one hand, the works Spinoza finished before he was halfway through his philosophical lifetime; on the other, the great, baffling masterpiece which he had begun on the edge of the chasm, but which, in its present form, is the fruit of its author's maturity.

§2. *Why is it called 'Ethics'?*

1. The work contains three elements that belong to 'ethics' in some normal sense of that term.

One is a thesis in the metaphysics of morals: there are no properties of goodness and badness that states of affairs can inherently possess, and no properties of rightness or wrongness that can inhere in actions.

The second is an account of what is actually going on when the plain man judges things to be good or bad. Ordinary 'ignorant' people think

2. For a dissenting view see F. Akkerman, 'L'édition de Gebhardt de l'Ethique de Spinoza et ses sources', *Raison présente* no. 43 (1977), at p. 43.

that goodness and badness are objectively out there in the world, Spinoza says, and he explains why:

[Good and bad] are nothing but modes of imagining, by which the imagination is variously affected; and yet the ignorant [a] consider them to be chief attributes of things, because . . . they [b] believe all things have been made for their sake, and [c] call the nature of a thing good or bad, sound or rotten and corrupt, as they are affected by it. (1 Appendix, at 82/16)

Like much in the *Ethics*, this is tough and interesting in ways that will be missed by a fast reader who overlooks the word 'because' in the passage, or an inexperienced one who does not know how amazingly condensed Spinoza's writing can be. Let us try to understand what he is saying here.

It has the general form 'a because b and c', which is ambiguous. I think its meaning is analogous to that of 'She hit him because he insulted her and she became angry'; that is, b explains c which in turn explains a. Here is how the connections go.

We (b) put ourselves at the centre of the universe, taking it that everything is 'for us' because made for us by a loving God. This encourages us not merely to *care* most about how things suit us, but to think that what *really matters* about things is how they suit us. (A little earlier, at 81/25, Spinoza said: 'After men persuaded themselves that everything that happens, happens on their account, they had to judge that what is most important in each thing is what is most useful to them.') And so we are willing (c) to abbreviate 'This is good for me' into 'This is good': the 'for me' goes without saying, and so it plays no role in our speech or thought, just as the tip of my nose plays no role in my visual field. And this practice of characterising things in the monadic language of property attribution ('This is good') leads us (a) to think that there are value properties corresponding to our talk.

On that account of Spinoza's views, he sees an intimate connection between (a) a certain metaphysical belief which he attributes to plain people and (c) the way in which they use words like 'good' and 'bad'. If he thinks that (a) somehow infects (c), so that when uninstructed people call a state of affairs 'good' they *mean* that it has a 'chief attribute', i.e., is objectively and inherently good, then he should conclude that all the plain man's value judgments are false. Alternatively, he might hold that when an ignorant person calls something 'good' there is an outer crust of metaphysical error and an inner core of meaning that is confused but not downright false. There is no way to choose between these two accounts of his position: what separates them is the distinction between 'what he means when he says . . . ' and 'what is going on in his mind when he says . . . ', and Spinoza had no such distinction in his conceptual armoury.

Anyway, Spinoza deplores the way in which ordinary value judgments are made, and in Part 4 of the *Ethics* he offers something better. In brief, he proposes to call 'good' whatever is useful to mankind, and 'bad' whatever hinders the good (see 4d1,2,p39). This is an improvement on ordinary value judgments in two ways. (i) It makes the relative nature of value judgments fully explicit: we are now to understand that 'x is good' really stands in for something of the form 'x has relation R to y', so that our apparent subject-predicate language will no longer seduce us into thinking that goodness and badness are properties. (ii) Taking it that 'x is good' means something of the form 'x is conducive or favourable to y', Spinoza offers us a better y. An ignorant person will call x 'good' so long as it suits *his mood then*, and those three words correspond to three inadequacies in his position. Spinozistic value-judgments on x depend upon whether x is favourable to everyone's interests in the long run. Not just mine but everyone's, not just feelings but real interests, not just for now but for the future. In the later parts of the *Ethics*, then, where Spinoza puts his own sort of value judgments to work, we are given an account of what is 'good' in the sense of being conducive to survival, stability, health, happiness and clarity of mind (Spinoza argues that these stand or fall together).

Why is that better than basing value judgments on one's immediate reaction to the thing being judged? How, indeed, can any total theory of value be *better* than another? If the judgment that B is superior to A is based on standards established by B, then the judgment is trivial; but if it is based on standards lying outside both A and B, then B is not after all a comprehensive theory of value.

2. The answer lies in a theory of Spinoza's about human motivation. He argues that any person who clears his mind, and looks both at ordinary value judgments and at Spinozistic ones, must be swayed by the latter and not the former. Although Spinozistic judgments are really a manual for survival, happiness, et cetera, they are entitled to be expressed in the language of value because they relate in the right manner to human motivation: they ought to hold sway, in the sense that they must hold sway if our minds are not clouded by error and confusion.[3] Spinoza's reasons for holding all this will appear in due course, mainly in chapters 10 and 11.

That, then, is the third of the ethical elements which I mentioned earlier. The first was the negative metaphysical thesis; the second, the description of ignorant people's value-judgments; and the third is an extensive, detailed, substantive morality.

The action-guiding parts of the *Ethics* are sometimes stated without using the language of value: humility does not arise from reason; a free man does not brood on death; you'll have more power over your emotions

3. For more on this, see Curley, 'Spinoza's Moral Philosophy'.

if you grasp that whatever happens is inevitable; someone who truly loves God will not try to get God to love him back (4p53,67, and 5p6,19). There is no problem about how nonevaluative statements can *influence conduct*. We are familiar with that phenomenon: 'There is a dead elk in the water fifty yards upstream', 'The dried fruit is at the bottom of my pack'. But Spinoza would be prepared to associate any part of his manual for survival and happiness with a *value-judgment*, on the grounds that his sort of value-judgment is the best possible—the most informed and rational and clear-sighted—that could be salvaged from the muddled value-judgments of the man in the street.

Although the later parts of the *Ethics* are meant to be action-guiding, Spinoza does not emphasize that aspect. When he does use value-language, he does so coolly rather than with urgency. This is partly a matter of personal style, but it also reflects doctrine: Spinoza has theoretical reasons for being suspicious of the very concept of intention or purpose, and thus for playing down his own purpose of influencing his readers. But he certainly has such a purpose. When he refers to 'one who desires to aid others by advice or by action so that they may enjoy the highest good together' (4 Appendix 25), he surely means himself.

3. Some systems of morality assume little about human nature. Kant's was one of those and in our own day Hare's is another. Spinoza's is at the other extreme: his normative material *is* a doctrine about certain aspects of human nature. More specifically, in Part 5 and the last nine propositions of Part 4 Spinoza describes the causes and effects of the state of being which he favours—one of pleasure (in a broad sense), rationality, prudence, and stability—while the rest of Part 4, heavily supported by Part 3, presents the contrasted state of anxiety, confusion, inner turmoil, and impulsive rashness. Thus, we are shown first a 'bad' way of life, and then a 'good' one, in Spinoza's senses of those value-terms.

The bad way of life in Part 4 is dominated by what Spinoza calls 'affects'. These include all the emotions, and also certain motivational drives such as ambition and the craving for alcohol. In the good way of life of Part 5, the affects are controlled through the use of reason. Thus, Part 4 is entitled 'Of Human Bondage, or the Strengths of the Affects', while Part 5 is called 'Of the Power of the Intellect, or of Human Freedom'. I cannot find any significance in the switch in the ordering.

Are we being offered an intellectualist ethic? Yes, in a way. Spinoza does think that the best way of life involves the guidance of reason, and that this is also the way of knowledge, of understanding, of relative freedom from error; and he would have agreed with Locke that nobody is so enslaved as he who is so in his understanding. But Spinoza seems to value knowledge and understanding less for themselves than for their effects.

In the *Ethics* as in the *Emendation* the centre of the target is not knowledge but happiness.

4. To achieve his ethical purposes in Parts 4 and 5, Spinoza must convince the reader not only of what the contrasted ways of life are like, but also of certain theses about what causes people to follow one rather than the other. That brings in his Part 3 theory about the causes and workings of the 'affects', i.e., those emotional turbulences and dominating drives that are said to bind, agitate, depress, and confuse us.

§3. *How Parts 1 and 2 fit in*

1. The conceptual repertoire of the later, strictly ethical Parts mainly comes from Parts 1 and 2. These also help to set the scene. The ethic is totally medical or psychotherapeutic: to improve yourself you must understand your mechanism and then intervene in it so as to reduce your propensity for feeling and thinking and acting in ways that make you ill and unhappy. Three of Spinoza's earlier doctrines help to remove possible cramps or inhibitions or distractions from this programme.

If the programme were combined with a belief in objective, intrinsic goodness and badness, it would immediately lose its bearings. For then the pursuit of stability, survival and happiness—which are understandable and amenable to scientific treatment—would be replaced by the pursuit of *goodness*; and from where are we to get our scientific understanding of that?

In Part 1 Spinoza vigorously denies that there is a personal God. If he had accepted a traditional Judaeo-Christian kind of theology, this would have inhibited his psychotherapeutic programme. There is no straight conflict between the two, but it is hard to see how someone can both deeply believe that he was created by a God who loves him and whom he should love, and think that the principal route to self-improvement is to study one's own pathology and deal with it intelligently.

Third, the strict determinism launched in Part 1 is negatively felt all through the therapeutic material. One need not be a determinist in order to study and manipulate causes; but someone with an interest in self-improvement, if he also thinks he has 'freedom' in some radical sense which involves rising above causal influences, will be apt to think that self-improvement should come partly from uncaused moral effort; and Spinoza could only regard that as a distraction. If asked about exhortation to moral effort, he would say: 'That is one way of acting causally upon a person, but not a notably efficient one.'

2. So much for the rejection of value properties, of a personal God, and of radical freedom. What about more specific doctrines, corresponding to numbered propositions in the early Parts of the work? Plenty of those are

13

(1) A CHARACTER SKETCH OF THE *ETHICS*

invoked in the formal demonstrations later on, but often the invocations amount to little. In 3p6d, for instance, the mentions of 1p25c,34 have a dubious role in the argument. In other cases, Part 1 or 2 is brought in quite genuinely, but only in proving something marginal to Spinoza's ethical position.

I can find only one important specific doctrinal link between Part 1 and the last three Parts; I shall present it in §52.1. There are two solid links between Part 2 and the rest, which I shall now explain.

Part 2 is called 'Of the Nature and Origin of the Mind'. The most striking thing Spinoza says about the human mind is that it contains representations of whatever happens in the human body, and contains nothing else (2p11,12). Combine this with his doctrine that there can be no causal flow either way between mind and body (1p10, 2p6), and you get a picture of a person's mental and physical aspects running in harness without either acting on the other. That lets Spinoza treat 'affects' as phenomena which are at once mental and physical (3d3), without having to discuss how the two aspects are interrelated. His interests in human affects are largely curative, and he has some cures to propose, but he is faced with no problem of the form 'Should this condition be cured through the mind or through the body?' His doctrines would allow him to ask 'Should this condition be cured through psychotherapy or through drugs?', for he can regard the condition—the affect—as physical, and can view psychotherapy as a physical process, a way of causing medically helpful vibrations in the patient's eardrums, vocal cords et cetera. But the question of mental versus physical therapy would be an absurd one for Spinoza to raise, given his parallelism doctrine in Part 2.

Also, Part 2 advances a view about the nature and sources of error (see for instance 2p35). This hovers about Part 3, and is prominent in 4 and 5, where it generates Spinoza's thesis that Part 4's bad state of being, unlike 5's good one, essentially involves a proneness to error. Not needed for Spinoza's route to happiness, Part 2 is needed for his claim that the route to durable happiness is also the route to secure knowledge. This is the aspect of Part 2 which lies closest to the *Emendation*.

Those are the only large, integral ways in which Part 2 conditions the ethical parts of the work. But Part 2 also provides a kind of frame for what follows. Spinoza was by temperament a broadener and deepener, and it is typical of him that his account of the human condition should rest on a psychology that is linked to a biology which is based on a physics; and all of this occurs in Part 2.

3. Part 1 is a metaphysic—an account of the basic structure of reality, so general as to be consistent with any physics, biology, psychology, or ethics. But it is solidly relevant to Part 2 through a doctrine in the latter which I have not yet mentioned. Spinoza's view about how people's minds mirror their bodies comes from his more general thesis that the entire physical realm is mirrored, event for event, by a mental realm (2p3,7): without this, Spinoza would have no basis for what he says about the human case in particular. And this is where Part 1 most visibly tries to come to the aid of Part 2.

Spinoza purports to derive the general thesis directly from an 'axiom' which stands at the head of Part 1. But that derivation is not what I am looking for, since it jumps across Part 1's entire argumentative content. Of more interest in our present context is the Part 1 doctrine that the only thing that meets the strictest conditions for being a substance, or absolutely thing-like thing, is the whole of reality. This one-substance doctrine is used in support of the thesis that the physical realm is mirrored by a mental realm: the argument for that depends on assuming that the two realms are different 'attributes' of a single 'substance' (2p7s).

Help for parallelism is indirect help for Spinoza's approach to human emotional health and sickness, in which both mental and physical aspects are acknowledged but the difference between them is not allowed to generate any details. This whole line of support, tenuous as it is, marks the only transmission of weight from the ethical doctrines back down to the argumentative core of Part 1.

4. No careful reader of Parts 1 and 2 could doubt that Spinoza is pursuing them for their inherent interest as well as to help the rest of the work. There is abundant evidence, not only within the *Ethics* but also from the letters and the early *Descartes's Principles* and *Metaphysical Thoughts*, that Spinoza acquired early and never lost a deep interest in metaphysics, epistemology and philosophy of mind. We shall follow these interests through Parts 1 and 2 without caring much about how they bear on the rest.

5. Inevitably, Spinoza inherited most of his problems from previous philosophers. The one who looms largest is his older contemporary Descartes, the only philosopher named in the *Ethics*. I shall make much of Descartes as a bequeather of problems which Spinoza tried to solve, and of Leibniz as another of Descartes's legatees, tackling many of those same problems in vividly and instructively different ways. Descartes died when Spinoza was eighteen years old; Spinoza died when Leibniz was thirty years old.

Of course the background goes further: there are ancient and medieval philosophers who influenced Spinoza and would have to be considered in an intellectual biography of him. But I am not writing biography. I want to understand the pages of the *Ethics* in a way that will let me learn philosophy from them. For that, I need to consider what Spinoza had in mind, for readings of the text which are faithful to his intentions are likely to teach me more than ones which are not—or so I believe, as I think

15

him to be a great philosopher. And one can be helped to discover his intentions by knowing what he had been reading, whose problems he had been challenged by, and so on. But this delving into backgrounds is subject to a law of diminishing returns: while some fact about Maimonides or Averroes might provide the key to an obscure passage in Spinoza, we are more likely to get his text straight by wrestling with it directly, given just a fair grasp of his immediate background.

I am sure to make mistakes because of my inattention to Spinoza's philosophical ancestry; but I will pay that price for the benefits which accrue from putting most of one's energies into philosophically interrogating Spinoza's own text. I am encouraged in this by the massive work in which Wolfson places Spinoza in a densely described medieval setting: the labour and learning are awesome, but the *philosophical* profit is almost nil.[4] Such philosophically interesting readings of Spinoza as are contained in Wolfson's two volumes could all have been arrived at without delving into the medieval background.

§4. *'Demonstrated in geometrical order'*

1. Much of the *Ethics* consists of smooth expository prose, in portions of half a page or more in length; these are Spinoza's prefaces, appendices, and scholia. Their literary standard is high: although Spinoza employed a fossilized academic Latin, drained of warmth and colour, his writing could still have virtues of elegance and dry pungency; and some of the prose passages are lively, entertaining and a good source of epigrams.

In contrast with that, the remaining sixty percent of the work consists in a charmless apparatus of 'demonstrations'. Spinoza himself implicitly apologizes for the prolixity which these force on him (4p18s), but he clearly thought the trouble was worthwhile. His remark that demonstrations are 'the eyes of the mind, by means of which it sees and observes things' (5p23s), though vague and metaphorical, clearly assigns them some important epistemic role. Let us see what it is.

When Spinoza says that his propositions are *demonstrata*, that ought to mean that they are rigorously, deductively proved—that being the main seventeenth century sense of the Latin *demonstrare* and the English 'demonstrate'. And the phrase 'demonstrated *in geometrical order*' invites comparison with that most celebrated of all deductive enterprises, the *Elements* of Euclid.

Euclid began with 'postulates' involving spatial concepts, and 'axioms' concerning magnitudes in general (not just spatial ones), and some initial definitions. Whatever his own intentions were, his system came to be viewed by many people as a direct convincer—proceeding from unassail-

4. Wolfson, *The Philosophy of Spinoza.*

able starting points, through irresistible argumentative moves, to theorems which are thus equally unassailable. It did directly convince Hobbes:

Being in a gentleman's library, Euclid's *Elements* lay open, and 'twas the 47th Proposition of the first Book. He read the Proposition. By God, said he, . . . this is impossible! So he reads the demonstration of it, which referred back to such a Proposition; which proposition he read. That referred him back to another, which he also read. [And so on, until] at last he was demonstratively convinced of that truth. This made him in love with Geometry.[5]

On the face of it, that is how things are supposed to be in Spinoza's *Ethics*: the only fresh material that is explicitly added in the later Parts consists of definitions, axioms and postulates; they could all have been given at the outset, so that the entire work would seem to flow from its opening two or three pages; and the material in those pages would all, apparently, be offered as self-evident, undeniable.

2. If the *Ethics* was intended by Spinoza as a direct convincer of that sort, he must have been madly optimistic about the plausibility of the initial definitions and axioms. I don't believe it. No doubt he thought that the definitions are correct, and the axioms true; but he cannot have expected them to impose themselves on the mind of someone whose course of Spinozistic study was just beginning.

Consider 1d7, for instance: 'That thing is called free which exists from the necessity of its nature alone, and is determined to act by itself alone.' If this claims that that is what people in general actually mean by 'free', then it is obviously false. It would be true, or anyway unassailable, if it were merely stipulative—an announcement meaning 'This is how I shall use the term "free" in the pages that follow'. Many of Spinoza's definitions are worded as though they were mere warnings about his own idiolect: 'By cause of itself I understand . . . ', 'By substance I understand . . . ' and so on. But the wording misleads. Spinoza means his definitions less tamely than that, offering them as saying how he will *and how everyone should* use the defined words. Although this is not controversial, I shall present a bit of evidence that Spinoza is not offering his key technical terms in the spirit of: 'This is how I shall use these words, and I have nothing to say in justification of these uses.'

It concerns 1d1, which I shall abbreviate to: 'By cause of itself I understand that which is F'—never mind what F is. This is used in 1p7d, as follows:

> By cause of itself I understand: that which is F.
> Substance is cause of itself.
> ∴ Substance is F.

5. John Aubrey, *Brief Lives*, 'Thomas Hobbes'.

That is valid. A definition licenses replacing the definiendum by the definiens, which is just what that argument does. But from where does the second premiss come? Well, 1p6c says that substance is not caused by anything other than itself, and Spinoza assumes that everything is caused by something; from which he infers that substance is caused by itself. That is valid if 'caused by itself' is used in its normal meaning. What is not valid is the move from 'Substance is caused by itself', understood like that, to 'Substance is cause of itself' when this is taken in the sense given in 1d1. An argument using that definition should involve *only* the sense of 'cause of itself' which the definition ceremonially confers on the phrase; and it must not be assumed that only what is 'cause of itself' in that sense is 'caused by itself' in the phrase's ordinary untechnical meaning.

The only way to clear Spinoza of this charge of malpractice is to suppose that 1d1 is not intended stipulatively, and is rather meant as a substantive thesis linking 'that which is F' to at least some aspects of the ordinary meaning of 'cause of itself'. And that provides some evidence that 1d1 was intended in the latter way, though of course the evidence is not conclusive.

When Spinoza's definitions are not stipulative, we must take them—as he says in Letter 9—to be 'propositions' which are acceptable only if they are 'true'. That kills any attempt to use the *Ethics* as a direct convincer, for such definitions as 1d1,7 cannot possibly count as unassailable starting points unless they take refuge in a plea of stipulativeness.

Why would Spinoza disguise a proposition as a definition? I think he does this when the proposition is partly about common meanings of terms. This can be seen in 1d7, Spinoza's definition of 'free'. I think he means this to embody a doctrine which he will defend later on, namely, that the common idea of freedom as involving uncausedness is indefensible, a piece of bad thinking which careful philosophy will rectify. We should take 1d7 as saying: 'I am going to use "free" as equivalent to . . . , and if you want to give the word a meaning as close to the ordinary one as possible without falling into error or confusion, you will use it like that also.'

3. What about the axioms? Only someone who approaches Spinoza in a spirit of stultifying piety could regard the axioms as immediately certain, or their contradictories as impossible or unthinkable. When Spinoza says things like 'Everything which is, is either in itself or in something else' (1a1), our first problem is to know what he means. He is inviting us to adopt and employ a certain way of thinking and talking, and we cannot know whether to comply until we know what we would be getting into. So we, at least, must regard the axioms as something to be accepted provisionally in order to see how they work out in the sequel. 'These first definitions and propositions can be properly understood only in the light of the propositions which follow them in the order of exposition; they form a system of mutually supporting propositions.'[6]

Spinoza addressed himself to an audience who were more familiar with his terminology than we are; but I am sure that he offered his axioms to them, too, not as immediately compelling but rather as the first bricks in an edifice which was to be tested as a whole. In one place he says: You won't like what I have just said, but please suspend judgment until I have gone somewhat further (2p11cs).

4. So when Spinoza says that his results are *demonstrata*—demonstrated or rigorously proved—presumably he is talking about the logic and not the psychology of his procedures. That would be reasonable: if one has a logically valid argument with true premises and conclusion P, this is a 'demonstration' of P even if it would not convince anyone of P's truth because the premises are not obviously true.

Sometimes, indeed, Spinoza uses 'demonstrate' more weakly still. The full title of his *Descartes's Principles* says that it presents Cartesian doctrines 'demonstrated in the geometrical manner'; yet Spinoza insists that much of this 'demonstrated' material is false. The Preface implies that the work will be based on 'propositions so clear and evident that no one can withhold his assent from them, provided that he has understood the terms'; but Spinoza did not write the Preface, and that bit of it must be mistaken. It would be much more in character for Spinoza to offer the premises as partly false—which he must do if he is to reject some of the conclusions while claiming that the deductive moves are valid.[7] Presumably, then, he is willing to call something 'demonstrated' if it is validly derived from false premises. It is easy to believe, then, that in the *Ethics* he took his conclusions to be 'demonstrated' in the sense of validly derived from premises which, though true, are not always immediately convincing. (In the seventeenth century 'demonstrate' et cetera could mean 'display' or 'exhibit'; but that is irrelevant here, for Spinoza's demonstrations are certainly arguments.)

As for 'the geometrical manner' or 'geometrical order', this must point to the likes of Euclid's *Elements*, but it is not clear what its precise implications were in Spinoza's mind, if indeed it had any. He may have been in a slight muddle about the notion of doing things geometrically. Of 'those who prefer to curse or laugh at the affects and actions of men, rather than understand them', he says: 'To them it will doubtless seem strange

6. Hampshire, *Spinoza*, p. 30.

7. This is well argued for in Barker, 'Notes on the Second Part of Spinoza's *Ethics*'.

that I should undertake to treat men's vices and absurdities in the geometrical manner, and that I should wish to demonstrate by sure reasoning things which they declare to be contrary to reason.' (3 Preface at 138/6.) This seems to refer to that 'geometrical' demonstrative procedure which is my present topic; but the sequel shows that Spinoza chiefly has in mind his view that men's affects can be causally explained through the laws of nature, and are therefore fit subjects for scientific study. His point, which would have been better served by a comparison with physics, has nothing to do with handling the affects through an apparatus of axioms and logical derivations.[8] Spinoza may not have been clear about this in his own mind.

§5. *The hypothetico-deductive method*

1. It is best to view the *Ethics* as a hypothetico-deductive system—something that starts with general hypotheses, deduces consequences from them, and checks those against the data. If they conflict with the data, something in the system is wrong; if they square with the data, the system is not proved to be right but it is to some extent confirmed. That is a widely accepted story about the abstract structure of scientific method, though in recent years it has been challenged. I shall keep out of that dispute.

In a hypothetico-deductive procedure, there are entailments running downwards, so to speak, and weaker confirmation relations running upwards. The two are related, but not as simply as this: if P entails Q, then Q somewhat confirms P. Let P be 'My bicycle is rusty and Mt. St. Helens will erupt in 1997' and let Q be 'My bicycle is rusty.' In this case, P entails Q, but it is unsatisfactory to say that Q supports or partially confirms P.

The further requirements for confirmation are probably complicated and may not yet be fully known by anyone. But Leibniz made a strong start on them, which will do for now. He entertained the objection that one should not 'undertake to discover the unknown by assuming it and then proceeding by inference from it to known truths'—which neatly describes the hypothetico-deductive method—on the grounds that 'this is contrary to logic, which teaches that truths can be inferred from falsehoods'. In reply he said that this procedure 'sometimes yields great likelihood, when the hypothesis easily explains many phenomena which otherwise would be puzzling and which are quite independent of one another'.[9] That is a good nutshell: the hypotheses must explain, and must unify, if they are to gain strength from the truth of their consequences.

2. In recommending that we view the *Ethics* as hypothetico-deductive,

8. On this point, Wolfson is useful: *The Philosophy of Spinoza*, vol. 1, pp. 45–55.

9. *New Essays*, p. 450.

I am implying that Spinoza would have endorsed this. Perhaps an approach to a text could be profitable even though sharply at variance with the author's own view of it; but it is not likely, and I would be uncomfortable with my approach if I thought Spinoza would reject it.

He was certainly no stranger to the hypothetico-deductive method. In the introduction to Part 3 of *Descartes's Principles*, where he seems to be speaking for himself, Spinoza says that a 'good hypothesis' is consistent, simple, intelligible, and 'permits the deduction of everything which is observed in the whole of nature'. That last requirement is extravagant, and Spinoza would certainly not claim so much for the starting points of the *Ethics*, which I am taking to be his 'good hypotheses'; but he would defend them as consistent, simple, intelligible, and entailing a lot of important truths.

3. It sounds as though Spinoza, according to me, thinks he has found a set of sturdy hypotheses—ones we can retain until they fall foul of the data and/or are supplanted by more satisfactory rivals. That was not his attitude. In Letter 76 he says: 'I do not assume that I have discovered the best philosophy, but I know that I understand the true one'; and that dogmatic tone permeates the *Ethics* also. However, that can be reconciled with a hypothetico-deductive view of the work, as follows. Spinoza could—and I think would—say that although his system must work on untutored minds in a hypothetico-deductive manner, when the tutoring is completed the reader will see the starting points to be certain, indubitably true, beyond question. Something like that is implied in Descartes's remarks on this topic, late in his reply to the Second Objections to the *Meditations*, by which Spinoza is known to have been influenced. And perhaps we can charitably take it to be implied when Spinoza, having claimed to know that he understands the true philosophy, adds this: 'If you ask me how I know this, I shall answer, in the same way as you know that the three angles of a triangle are equal to two right angles.'[10]

But there is a problem. What is supposed to be happening to us as we work through the *Ethics*? We are to entertain its definitions and axioms as hypotheses, to follow through their consequences and find that they square with the data, and to finish up in a state of mind where we see them as self-evident. But how is this change to be wrought in us? It is to be assumed that it is not like swallowing a philosophical tranquiliser, a pill to make sceptical doubts dissolve. What we must demand, and what Spinoza will agree that he should supply, is an account of rational procedures whereby a careful study of the *Ethics* could convince us of the truth of its doctrines.

We might look for help to a passage in the *Emendation* where Spinoza

10. For more on this, see the note on 'known through itself' in the Glossary-Index of Curley's forthcoming edition of Spinoza's works in English translation.

says that 'When the mind attends to [something false], considers it carefully, understands it, and deduces from it in good order the things to be deduced, it will easily bring its falsity to light' (§61). This shows him as willing to combine a hypothetico-deductive approach with absolute confidence in its results. But *why* will that method 'easily bring its falsity to light'? Spinoza's answer to this is supposed to be gatherable from *Emendation* §§61–65, but I can get nothing useful from that material.

4. Fortunately, we can find something better to say on his behalf. I shall state it abstractly at first.

Suppose we want to test hypothesis H by deducing consequences from it and then observing whether those consequences are true. If we have deduced a number of consequences and found all of them to be true, that may give some support to H. But if there is a rival hypothesis H* which also has those consequences, our testing of H so far does not support it as against H*. For that, we must find a test which discriminates between them. Let us suppose that H entails something which H* contradicts, and that we perform an experiment which shows this proposition to be true. That leaves H still standing while it knocks out H*. If we test a wide variety of consequences of H, each test that it survives may eliminate rival hypotheses; and a test can eliminate a rival which has never been thought of or formulated, but which exists in logical space and threatens H's claim to truth.

Some philosophers have thought that confirmation *is* just the procedure of making H ever more secure by reducing the number of unrefuted rivals to it. Others have objected that there are infinitely many hypotheses at the outset, and each observation eliminates only finitely many of them, so that we cannot make the slightest dent in the number of unrefuted rivals to H. If they are right, then *a fortiori* we could never establish H as our only unrefuted hypothesis.

Spinoza would say that such critics are wrong, that one could be left with only one surviving hypothesis, and that in the *Ethics* he achieves just that. He holds that most of our general terms are unsuitable for serious theorising, and that only a very limited stock of concepts are fit for use in metaphysics and science; so he could argue that at the outset there is really only a small number of considerable hypotheses to be dealt with, which makes it credible that by the time his hypothesis has shown its paces all the others have fallen by the wayside. That could be grounds for untentative confidence in his axioms and definitions—a system I have called his 'hypothesis'. For if no other system is true, then Spinoza's must be, he would conclude; for he would never entertain the thought that no system is true, i.e., that reality is not fundamentally orderly (see §8).

I would be willing to argue that a given hypothesis has only finitely many considerable rivals, but I would not use as a premiss Spinoza's doctrine about theoretically respectable general terms. That doctrine, so far from expressing deep insights into reality, merely shows how thoroughly Spinoza was a child of his time. But he does hold it, and I have sought to show how it could help him to maintain his absolute confidence in his results while still permitting us to see the *Ethics* as working in a hypothetico-deductive manner.

5. Opinion is divided on what the job of an hypothesis is, independently of the debate about what proportion of the rivals can be eliminated. Some philosophers think that an hypothesis cannot do more than 'save the phenomena', that is, imply all the lower-level truths and no falsehoods; and they reject as senseless or at least unprofitable the question of whether the hypothesis, as well as doing that, is actually true. That line of reasoning is utterly foreign to Spinoza, and may have been what he meant to reject when claiming for his philosophy not that it is 'the best' but that it is 'true'.

§6.   *What are the data?*

1. The hypothetico-deductive scheme has mainly been explored as a rational reconstruction of what natural scientists do: they devise high-level theories, deduce predictions about how experiments will turn out, and then experiment to see what happens. In this scheme of things the ground floor is occupied by particular events in laboratories: *that* is the touchstone of the truth of the 'propositions' and thus of the degree of confirmation for the 'axioms' and 'definitions', i.e., the theories at the top level of the system.

How can we apply that picture to the *Ethics*? Against what data are we to check Spinoza's propositions?

Some of the propositions are answerable to empirical fact. When Spinoza says in 4p57 that 'The proud man hates the presence of the noble', it is relevant to check this against the actual attitudes of people who are indisputably proud; and Spinoza would not deny this. We shall see in chapter 5 that he at least flirted with the idea that every truth, 4p57 included, is absolutely necessary, so that this is the only possible world. But that does not imply that every truth can be known *a priori*; and I am inclined to believe that Spinoza always distinguished truths which can be established by conceptual analysis from ones which we can know only by looking at the world. Some of his starting points are evidently offered as things everyone knows from observation—for instance 2a4 and the postulates preceding 3p1.

2. The *Ethics* is noted for playing down experience in favour of reasoning; but this emphasis does not falsify what I have been saying. In 2p40s2 Spinoza presents three kinds of cognitive process of which the first, much frowned on by him, is said to have two sources of input: hearsay, and *experientia vaga*. The principal meaning of the Latin *vagus* is 'inconstant' or 'wandering', and in Spinoza's use it means 'random'. In the *Emendation* he speaks of 'random experience, that is experience which is not controlled by the intellect' (§19). Presumably, what is frowned on by Spinoza, as a source of confusion and error, is the jumbled sequence of sensory states which one would gain by roaming the world with no sense of epistemic direction.

This contrasts with the orderly, controlled experience which comes through attending to experiments which have been deliberately contrived to test some prior hypothesis. Such a methodology was memorably advocated by Kant a century after Spinoza's time: 'Accidental observations, made in obedience to no previously thought-out plan, can never be made to yield a necessary law', he said, and went on to say that although we 'must approach nature in order to be taught by it', we must 'do so not in the character of a pupil who listens to everything that the teacher chooses to say, but of an appointed judge who compels the witnesses to answer questions which he has himself formulated'.[11]

3. Spinoza nowhere discusses *experientia non vaga*. So far as hard textual evidence is concerned, we could attribute to him the view that all experience is *vaga*.

But that cannot be right. Several times in the *Ethics* he appeals to something which he says 'experience shows'; all those could be appeals to unrandom experience, i.e., to the experience of someone who puts to nature questions dictated to him by Spinoza's philosophy,[12] and it is hard to see what else they could be.

Why, then, is Spinoza so silent about intellectually controlled experience? Perhaps he thought there was nothing to be said about it until more is known about how the senses function. In the *Emendation* he mentions the senses as needed for knowledge of particular things, but he does not theorize about them because that *can* be left until 'the nature of our senses has become known to us' (§102). That makes best sense if we take Spinoza to mean that a treatment of the senses *should* be left until more is known about how they work; and that would express a scruple which could also explain the silence about unrandom experience in the *Ethics*.

4. Much of the *Ethics* is philosophical rather than scientific, i.e., is answerable to conceptual analysis rather than to empirical observation. These propositions might be evaluated by how well they fit in with material which *can* be empirically tested; but that is not the only way to do it, for the hypothetico-deductive method can be used where the terminal propositions are closely related not to experience but to logical or conceptual truth or falsehoods.

11. I. Kant, *Critique of Pure Reason*, B xiii. See also F. Bacon, *Novum Organum* I, 100.

12. This line of thought is developed by Fløistad, 'Spinoza's Theory of Knowledge in the *Ethics*'.

Much philosophical analysis is like that. For instance, we may evaluate a proposed analysis of propositions of the form 'If A had happened, B would have ensued' by deducing from it conclusions of the following form: 'In a situation of kind K, if A had happened B would have ensued', which are then checked against the intelligent and careful person's intuitions. If an analysis implies 'Whatever the actual states of mind and body of the people on the scene, if Sirhan Sirhan hadn't shot Robert Kennedy at the moment he did, someone else would have shot him a moment later', that is powerful evidence against the analysis. We look for an analysis which doesn't entail anything that we and our friends intuitively judge to be false. But usually we cannot find such an analysis, which is one reason why good philosophers sometimes say things which appear to be dazzlingly false. When we cannot rescue all our intuitive judgments, it may be hard to decide which to relinquish. There may be different alternative trade-offs and no short, sharp procedure for choosing amongst them; which is one thing that makes philosophy difficult and wonderful.

In trying to evaluate the *Ethics*, then, we can appeal not only to how we find our world to be, but also to our sense of which propositions of logic, broadly so-called, are true and which false. When Spinoza offends against this sense, we shall be caught up in the harder business of evaluating the trade-off he offers us, that is, his reasons for saying that we must embrace his strange conclusions to avoid ones which are stranger still.

§7. *The invalidity of the demonstrations*

1. From the upward relation of *support* we now come to the relation of *entailment* which is supposed to run downward through the official demonstrations. Many of these are not valid as they stand, and we must decide what to think about this fact.

Sometimes we should treat a defective argument as a valid one with a premiss left unstated. Sometimes a defective argument of Spinoza's can be non-trivially rescued by adding a premiss which we know, on other evidence, to be accepted by him. We have met one example already, namely, the move in 1p7d from 'Substance is not caused by anything else' to 'Substance is caused by itself'. We can make this valid by adding the premiss 'Everything is caused by something', which Spinoza does accept and presumably employs here.

Other invalidities can be repaired by plausibly supposing that Spinoza did not say quite what he meant; as when he infers P from Q on the strength of 'If P then Q', where he clearly meant 'If and only if P, then Q'. Sometimes, again, we have trouble because he doesn't give a word the meaning we would give to it, as in the use of 1d6 in 1p14d, where Spinoza in effect moves from 'Infinite[ly many] Fs are G' to 'All Fs are G'. Using 'infinite' as we do, that is invalid; but we shall find independent evidence that Spinoza gives to 'infinite' a meaning different from ours. This argument itself is evidence for that, but is far from decisive. To treat it as decisive would be to adopt the axiom that all Spinoza's arguments are, when properly understood, valid.

2. So there are two sorts of demonstrations that can be regarded as valid but not perfectly realized on the page. Some others, however, cannot be thus rescued.

Still, they are not negligible. Even when an argument cannot plausibly be saved by addition or reinterpretation, its premisses may give *some reason* for accepting the conclusion. I have no crisp theory about the conditions under which, if P and Q are logically independent, P gives some reason for Q. We might start with the thought that P gives some reason for Q if there is a probably true R such that Q is entailed by (P & R) but not by either conjunct alone; but that cannot be the whole story. Still, even without such a theory we can sometimes reasonably judge that one proposition gives some reason for another, and many of Spinoza's putative demonstrations can be viewed in that manner.

Much of the structure, then, is really hypothetico-*supportive*, with many downward as well as upward relations being less than entailments. The difference between (weak) confirmations and (strong) entailments does not coincide with the difference between the two directions of flow.

3. The inferential structure of the *Ethics* is not wholly contained in its demonstrations, officially so-called. Argumentative movement also occurs in the scholia, where Spinoza's comments on his demonstrated propositions sometimes involve drawing conclusions from them. In §3.3 I mentioned the important attempt to bring the one-substance doctrine to the aid of the thesis that the physical realm is paralleled by a mental realm; this attempt is entirely confined to a scholium, 2p7s, making no appearance in the official demonstrations. So we must often consider arguments of the informal kind which most philosophers employ most of the time, as well as ones purporting to be rigorous.

Spinoza sometimes offers more than one demonstration for a proposition, or indicates how a second one could be given; and in yet other cases we shall find alternative demonstrations without help from him. There can be many Spinozistic routes to a single doctrine.

That is a strength in the work, and should not occasion surprise or complaint. What does invite comment is that, of the argumentative routes to Spinoza's conclusions, some which we are left to find for ourselves are stronger than the ones he marks for us. For example, his demonstration that there is only one substance or ultimately thing-like thing (1p14d) is a creaky, leaky affair which cannot be fully salvaged. There are much better reasons than that for accepting the one-substance doctrine—reasons that Spinoza has but leaves unexpressed.

This can be explained. It seems that Spinoza's demonstrations are not meant to indicate the reasons which first led him to his conclusions, or even necessarily the principal reasons which he now has for retaining them. The demonstrations are supposed to give reasons—good enough ones, indeed—for the conclusions; but they are also meant to enable Spinoza to lock his doctrines together into a rigid, logically unbreakable structure. Some of his more powerful reasons are unsuitable for that because they are not sharp and hard enough to be handled demonstratively, even by Spinoza's standards of rigour.

Because there are different routes to a single Spinozistic conclusion, when the inferential thread is broken at a given point we are not always compelled to relinquish everything depending on it. Even if the break is total, leaving not so much as a weak support relation let alone an entailment, there may be other threads to take the weight.

4. I do not credit Spinoza with conceding that some of his demonstrations are not valid, or side with those who hold that the work's deductive surface was not meant to be taken seriously. There is room for debate about why Spinoza chose to present his results in that manner;[13] but whatever else he meant his demonstrations to do, I am sure that he did offer them as strictly valid, intending them to achieve a tight interlocking of his principal doctrines, and expecting that a proper study of this structure would eventually enable us to respond to it as though it were a direct convincer. I also think that he would agree to its being viewed, first time through, as hypothetico-deductive. But not as hypothetico-supportive: that change in the story is mine, based on my seeing something that Spinoza didn't see, namely, that many of the demonstrations are invalid.

How could someone as supremely able as Spinoza have been satisfied with demonstrations so many of which are invalid and unrescuable?

To begin with, he was dealing with some of the hardest problems there are, and elementary slips and oversights are easier when the matter is difficult. Also, when an argument depends on concepts which are dizzyingly abstract, basic, general, one is not much helped by a firm, reliable, intuitive sense of how the argument should go.

Second, it is relevant that Spinoza's demonstrations do not represent his own order of discovery. When he 'demonstrates' R by deriving it from P and Q, it is not that he accepted P and Q and wondered what they entailed; rather, he accepted R and wondered how best to derive it from a mass of other accepted doctrine including P and Q. In these circumstances, and given strong confidence that it could be done somehow, it is natural that

---

13. Wolfson offers four conjectures about that (*The Philosophy of Spinoza*, vol. 1, pp. 57–9). An interesting further suggestion is propounded by Efraim Shmueli, 'The Geometrical Method, Personal Caution, and the Ideal of Tolerance', in Shahan.

(1) A CHARACTER SKETCH OF THE *ETHICS*

Spinoza should have been uncritical about the derivation he actually came up with. I speak from experience.

Third, Spinoza was not good at close, rigorous reasoning. Leibniz, who is ordinarily charitable about others' intellectual failings, sometimes comments on Spinoza's central demonstrations in terms of casual contempt,[14] and I think that Spinozistic studies are best served by facing the fact that deductive rigour was not Spinoza's strong point. This is not to deny that his thinking was considerable and valuable (it didn't stop Leibniz from taking him seriously[15]), but it is to say that he was not skilled at constructing strictly valid arguments or at criticising invalid ones.

Perhaps this fact about Spinoza's mind is linked with his being somewhat slow. This thought was prompted by the double contrast with the nimble, razor-sharp Leibniz, and is confirmed by my own experience of my contemporaries: those whom I find to be faster on their feet than I am are also those who are better at rigour than I am. I would add that although agility and sharpness are enviable, they are not everything. Spinoza was a greater philosopher, and also a better philosopher, than most of those who could think faster and more tightly than he could.

In addition, Spinoza was interested in logic only for the good it could do him. Had he cared more about it for itself, he might have used it better in doing philosophy, just as a carpenter might be saved from some failures if he chanced to be interested in glue for itself as well as for its service in holding things together. Leibniz was, among other things, a connoisseur of glue: his *New Essays*, for example, are full of his pleasure in logical relations as an inherently interesting topic of study. There is nothing like that in Spinoza.

14. Loemker, pp. 532, 555.

15. Loemker, p. 663.

2   *The Cast of Spinoza's Mind*

In this chapter I shall present five aspects of Spinoza's thinking which lie deeper than any of his argued doctrines and are so influential in his thought as to deserve special attention.

§8.   *First aspect: rationalism*

1. Spinoza is customarily classified, along with Descartes and Leibniz, as a 'rationalist'. This can mean various things, of which at least three are true of Spinoza.

The term comes from the Latin *ratio*, meaning 'reason'. Like all philosophers who have been called rationalists, Spinoza is impressed by what he takes to be the superiority of reason to the senses. This has a large effect on the *Ethics*, but I shall not discuss it here. It is a matter of explicitly defended doctrine, and can be treated when its turn comes.

Other strands in Spinoza's rationalism concern 'reason' not as the name of a cognitive faculty but rather as involved in the notion of a *reason for* a belief or a *reason why* something is the case—this notion also lying within the scope of the Latin *ratio*.

2. Spinoza assumed that whatever is the case can be explained—that if P then there is a reason why P. I call this 'explanatory rationalism'. It is the refusal to admit brute facts—ones which just *are* so, for no reason. As between this and the opposing view that there are brute facts, the latter will always have a certain advantage—it can produce various facts and demand 'How could that be explained?', and it will not always be easy to answer; whereas the explanatory rationalist cannot make similar trouble for his opponent. If he demands to know how a given fact could be inexplicable, the answer may be that it just *is*; and that answer, since it leads nowhere, must be safe. I believe that the explanatory rationalist's problems are insoluble, and that his position is therefore untenable; but I admit the discomfort of this stand, and proclaim the attractiveness of the idea that everything can in principle be explained. So I urge that disbelief in explanatory rationalism, though perhaps it may be carried out of our study of the *Ethics*, is not something to be carried into it.

3. In addition to explanatory rationalism, Spinoza seems to have accepted causal rationalism.

At least since Hume it has been widely thought that what is causally possible is only a fragment of what is logically or absolutely possible:

a kind of event which *cannot* happen, given the causal laws by which the actual world is governed, may nevertheless be logically possible—e.g., fully describable without overt or covert contradiction. It is causally impossible that the moon should spontaneously veer away from the earth towards the sun; but one could tell a consistent story—in fine detail, with every gap plugged, every question answered—in which the moon did just that. Or so Hume implied, and most of us agree. Before Hume, some philosophers distinguished causal from logical necessity; but others did not, and most were unclear or indeterminate about it.

Spinoza does not make the distinction: he thinks that a cause relates to its effect as a premiss does to a conclusion which follows from it. When he speaks of 'the reason or cause why Nature acts' (4 Preface at 206/26), he thinks he is talking about one relation, not two.

It is not that he sees logical links as weaker than they are; rather, he sees causal ones as stronger. He sometimes uses the *language* of causality in discussing logico-mathematical topics, as when he says that 'the properties of a circle' should be approached through 'the cause of a circle'; but by 'cause' here he means 'method of construction', this being thought of not as a concrete event involving compass and pencil, but rather as a mathematical item, a procedure or method which necessarily exists even if no one ever implements it. (That is *my* description of what happens in Letter 60, not Spinoza's.) So this passage does not bring into mathematics anything we would call 'causal'.[1]

On the other hand, Spinoza's thinking about the matters which we would call causal is much influenced by his not distinguishing causal from absolute necessity. For example, after describing the effects on behaviour of despondency he adds: 'These things follow from this affect as necessarily as it follows from the nature of a triangle that its three angles are equal to two right angles' (4p57s). There are many other such turns of phrase.

Because I think that logical (or absolute) and causal necessity are distinct, I believe that Spinoza was in error about this. But that is not to accuse him of an elementary blunder. It is a theory of ours, these days, that causal necessity is weaker than absolute necessity; it is not trivially or obviously true, nor has it been well supported by arguments based on clearly good accounts of the two sorts of necessity.[2] So we are not well placed to be condescending about Spinoza's causal rationalism.

1. The opposing view is vigorously argued in A. Wolf's introduction to his edition of *The Correspondence of Spinoza* (London, 1928).

2. The only argument I know of against causal rationalism is a Humean one given in my *Locke, Berkeley, Hume: Central Themes* (Oxford, 1971), §61, using a premiss about the nature of absolute necessity which few philosophers today would accept.

4. It is, indeed, virtually forced on Spinoza by his explanatory rationalism. I now explain why.

An F event occurs, and causes a G event. Why did a G event occur just then? Because an F event occurred just before. That throws up two further why questions. (a) Why did an F event occur just before? This promises to launch an infinitely long series of why questions, each answerable by mentioning a still earlier event about which a new why question can be asked. The rationalist may be untroubled by this. He may say that this backward running series is infinite: each of its answers throws up a further question, but each of the questions has an answer; so it poses no challenge to explanatory rationalism, he may say. That is not the end of that issue, however, and I shall return to it in §28. I mention it here only in order to set it cleanly aside. (b) Why does the occurrence of an F event explain the occurrence of a G event? This is the question I want to confront.

The answer will adduce a causal or natural law according to which F events cause G events. Now the rationalist must step with care, for he needs an account of the status of the causal law which will let him cope with the question 'Why is that law true?' If he must allow the question, he must think it has an answer, or else his explanatory rationalism collapses. Let us consider his options.

He cannot adopt Hume's view that the causal law states a general brute fact. According to Hume, that F events are followed by G ones is simply the way it goes, and there is no more to be said about it except for some doctrine—irrelevant here—about our psychological attitude to such sequences. On that view, a causal explanation of a particular event handles one brute fact merely by putting it in with countless others. That does not meet the explanatory rationalist's need because it answers a small why question only by leaving a bigger one unanswered and, if Hume is right, unanswerable.

The explanatory rationalist might take the causal law linking Fs to Gs to be stronger than a mere brute fact, though less than absolutely necessary, thus invoking the notion of a *causal necessity* intermediate between absolute necessity and mere brute-fact generalization. But this familiar and perhaps useful notion will not serve the rationalist's turn. Consider the question 'Why are F events *always* followed by G events?' or 'Why was the F–G law operative on this occasion?'—either will do. If it is not absolutely necessary that F events are followed by G events, then it is legitimate to ask *why* the F–G sequence happens when it does. The question is not self-answering. Nor is it met by saying that there is a less than logical necessity at work here, i.e., that F events have some sort of G-making power by means of which they force G events to occur. For we can still ask two questions:

(2) THE CAST OF SPINOZA'S MIND

> Why does every F event have a G-making power?
> Why is a G-making power, whenever it is present,
> operative?

If either is answered by appeal to some deeper-lying causal law, then the question arises again about that; and even those who accept an infinite horizontal series of events will jib at the idea of an infinite vertical series of ever more basic causal laws. So the questioning has to be stopped; and that requires saying that my why questions are both self-answering, i.e., answerable on the basis of logic alone. That is to say that it is absolutely necessary *both* that every F event has a G-making power *and* that whatever has that power is followed by a G event. This, however, makes it absolutely necessary that every F event is followed by a G event; that gives absolutely necessary status to the causal law in question, which is to take the causal rationalist line about it.

That is how an explanatory rationalist is pushed towards causal rationalism. Causes help to explain events; but if causal laws are less than absolutely necessary then a causal explanation always leaves something unexplained, and the infinite regress of laws which this generates is not acceptable. I should perhaps mention that 1a3 can be seen as conjoining causal rationalism with a version of explanatory rationalism: causes necessitate, and nothing happens without a cause. But if that is what the axiom is saying, then Spinoza is wrong to say that the first conjunct is the converse of the second.

§9. *Second aspect: theism*

1. Spinoza was a pantheist, in that he identified God with the whole of reality. Thus he agreed with the atheist that reality cannot be divided into a portion which is God and one which is not. Although pantheist and atheist may seem to be poles apart, with one saying that everything is God and the other that nothing is, in the absence of an effective contrast between God and not-God we should not be quickly confident that there is any substantive disagreement at all.

It depends on what Spinoza means by 'God'. Is he a genuine theist, or rather a mealy-mouthed or perhaps an ironical atheist? The answer must depend on why he selects 'God' as a name for the universe. If his reason hasn't enough to do with the concept of God as ordinarily understood, then Spinoza's uses of that word do not express a theology, and we can view him as an atheist. Well, then, why does he choose the word 'God'?

A pantheist might be abundantly a theist because his position is reachable by starting with Christian theology, say, and deleting the non-God part, i.e., contending that the 'created world' is an illusion and that all there is is God. But that is not a usual form for pantheism to take, and Spinoza's position

32

[handwritten: Joachim's + Hegel's interp. of S.]

is nothing like it. He does not hold that the everyday world is unreal, the only real thing being a God lurking behind the illusion of galaxies and comets and lizards and grocery shops and hopes and fears and headaches. On the contrary, what he calls 'God' is the familiar, everyday, natural world. *[handwritten: not exactly,]* If Spinoza and the atheist each pointed while saying, respectively, 'That is all God' and 'None of that is God', they would point to the very same world. *[handwritten: see my]*

Some writers have disagreed with this; for example Caird, who said that *[handwritten: obj. (2)]* Spinoza's metaphysic of God proceeds from his belief in the unreality of the given world.[3] But these days no commentator as able as Caird would say such a thing. It has become clear that Spinoza was, in Wolfson's happy phrase, 'no mystic, no idealist of the kind to whom everything that kicks and knocks and resists is unreal'.

2. Spinoza's main reason for liking 'God' as a name for the entire natural *[handwritten: interesting sugg.]* world is that the world comes closer than anything else to fitting the tradi- *[handwritten: but prob.]* tional Judaeo-Christian account of God. If God is to be infinite, eternal, *[handwritten: but prob. wrong]* not acted on by anything else, the ultimate source of the explanation of everything, and not susceptible to criticism by any valid standard, then God must be Nature as a whole; or so Spinoza thinks.

Of course, if God must be a *person* who is infinite, eternal, et cetera, then Spinoza has no candidate to offer. The most Godlike item he can find is Nature; but it does not completely fit the traditional account of God, and, in particular, it is not 'a man, or like a man' (2p3s; see also Letter 23 at IV/150/1). Many theologians in the tradition Spinoza is attacking *[handwritten: wh. one ?]* would agree that God should not be conceived in an anthropomorphic way, and some held that *no* general term is true, in a single sense, of God and of human beings. But Spinoza wants a larger retraction than that. When he says that God is not 'like a man', he thinks he is in conflict even with the theologians who warned against anthropomorphism, and I believe he is right. If asked 'Are we helped to understand the nature of God by being told that God is, in some broad but not empty sense, a person?', those theologians would answer Yes and Spinoza would answer No. I know of only one passage in the *Ethics* that might suggest the contrary. Between 2p13 and 14 Spinoza presents a theory of 'individuals', meaning something like 'organisms'. Near the end of that he says that one individual can be part of a larger one, which in turn is part of a larger, and so on to infinity, so that 'we easily conceive the whole of Nature to be one individual' (102/11). *[handwritten: but S.]* If this means that the entire universe is a sort of organism, then it implies *[handwritten: does not]* that God has something closer to personhood than I have allowed. The *[handwritten: say here Nature = God!]*

3. Caird, *Spinoza*, pp. 20–25. According to Parkinson's 'Hegel, Pantheism, and Spinoza', Hegel accused Spinoza of being committed to believing, and of actually believing, that the familiar given world is unreal. Parkinson defends him against both charges.

remark is suspect, and Spinoza certainly rejects that implication of it, e.g., when he implies that to credit God with 'will' and 'intellect' in anything like the normal senses of these terms would be as a great a mistake as expecting Sirius (the Dog-star) to bark (1p17s at 62/34). Not that he is well placed to take this line. To argue cogently that the universe is not a person, he needs something he does not have, namely a satisfactory account of why a human being is a person.

It is a nuisance that English has pronouns which are always used for people and not freely used for anything else. We use 'he' for God, thinking of God as a person; if we came to think of God as impersonal, we should switch to 'it'. No such choice faced Spinoza, because none of his half-dozen languages has personal pronouns. In Latin, for example, he had to use a masculine pronoun for God, to agree with the masculine noun *Deus*; but this masculinity is grammatical only, and implies nothing about the nature of the object. Whereas in English we must use 'he' in referring to a man and 'it' in referring to a pebble, in Latin a single pronoun serves for both, since *homo* and *calculus* are both masculine. As for 'his', 'hers', and 'its': there is a single Latin word for all of these, whatever the gender of the relevant noun.

In translating Spinoza into English, then, it is inaccurate to use 'he' and 'his' where God is in question. But it would be misleading to use 'it' and 'its', since that would get the tone wrong, implying that Spinoza keeps reminding his readers that the item in question is not a person. The problem is insoluble for a translator into English; but a commentator can step delicately around it, and I promise that it will give no trouble in this book, except of course in direct quotations from Spinoza.

3. So Spinoza holds that the natural world answers to many traditional descriptions of God; but not to all, and in particular not to the description 'a person'. Isn't that sufficient to atheize Spinoza's use of the name 'God'? It was commonly thought to be so in his own day. Leibniz reports Arnauld's opinion that Spinoza was 'the most impious and the most dangerous man of this century', and adds: 'He was truly an atheist, that is, he did not acknowledge any Providence which distributes good fortune and bad according to what is just.'[4] If that is all it takes, then Spinoza was an atheist. But there is more to be said.

Spinoza had another reason for using the name 'God' for Nature as a whole—namely his view of Nature as a fit object for reverence, awe, and humble love, i.e., for the attitude traditionally reserved for God. While viewing Nature as an inexorably unfolding system of mental and physical

4. G. W. Leibniz, *Sämtliche Schriften und Briefe* II.1 (Darmstadt, 1926), p. 535.

events, rigidly controlled by necessary laws, and while having no hope that it could 'love him in return',[5] Spinoza could still be genuinely awed by its extent, grandeur, complexity, and ultimate orderliness. He could thus regard Nature not only as the best subject for the metaphysical *descriptions* applied to God in the Judaeo-Christian tradition, but also as the best object of the *attitudes* which in that tradition are adopted towards God alone. In Pollock's words: 'The Mosaic conception of the one God of Israel wedded to the Lucretian conception . . . of the one and inflexible nature of things; such is the mood Spinoza would have us bring to the questioning of the world, such the majesty and gravity of nature in his eyes.'[6]

I conclude that Spinoza's position is a kind of theism rather than of atheism. No doubt Santayana is right when he says, in his wonderful essay on Spinoza's religious aspect, that as compared with 'some other masters of the spiritual life [Spinoza] was more positivistic by temperament and less specifically religious'.[7] But Spinoza did accept pantheism as a kind of religion, and apparently did not think of himself as an atheist. Although as a young man he was expelled by the Jewish community, he remained permanently preoccupied with God's nature and relation to man. If he was not 'drunk with God' (as the poet Novalis said), he was obsessed with God. I am sure that he thought of himself as discovering things about God rather than as revealing that there is no God.

Not that the issue affects my engagement with the *Ethics*. Even if Spinoza saw his work as growing out of his early religious education, what he says about God in the *Ethics* is always to be explained by philosophical considerations, never by his having detoured to rescue something from the Judaeo-Christian tradition. He is awesome in his combination of strong religious concerns with great penetration, courage, and imperturbably cold-blooded honesty in his views about God. From my standpoint, which is concerned not with Spinoza's mental biography but with getting his help in discovering philosophical truth, it would make no difference if he saw himself as an atheist.

§10.   *Third aspect: naturalism about mankind*

1. Spinoza could not regard humanity as specially favoured by a personal creator of the universe; so he lacked one common support for the view that humans have features not found elsewhere in the universe. He had indeed

5. 'He who loves God cannot try to get God to love him in return.' (5p19)

6. Pollock, *Spinoza*, p. 143.

7. George Santayana, 'Ultimate Religion', in I. Erdman (ed.), *The Philosophy of Santayana* (The Modern Library, n.d.), p. 588.

no patience with that view. His thinking is firmly grounded in the conviction that there is nothing fundamentally special about mankind as compared with chimpanzees and earthworms and cabbages and rivers; for Spinoza, man is just a part of Nature.

He offers to prove that each person is 'a part of Nature' in the weaker sense of always being at the mercy of his environment, never causally insulated from it (4p4). But what I call his 'naturalism' is the stronger thesis that what happens in any human being is fully explicable through the same laws that explain everything else. A good part of this is captured by 2p13 which says that our bodies are ordinary material systems, and 2p48 which applies determinism to us. But none of Spinoza's demonstrated and numbered propositions adequately expresses his profound conviction (not that he puts it this way) that the whole truth about human beings can be told in terms which are needed anyway to describe the rest of the universe, and that men differ only in degree and not in kind from all other parts of reality.

None of my formulations of Spinoza's naturalism quite captures it, however, for they all fit Leibniz's theory of man too, yet I would not call it naturalistic. When Leibniz says: 'The foundations are everywhere the same; this is a fundamental maxim for me, which governs my whole philosophy',[8] Spinoza would applaud. But Leibniz's 'foundations' are what you might get by starting with mankind and forcing your whole metaphysic into that mould. According to him, the only things that there ultimately *are* are 'monads', sizeless substances, which include human minds; they are all on a continuum with minds or 'souls', and that is our main conceptual handle on them. For example, the varying states a monad is in, says Leibniz, are its varying 'perceptions' of the rest of the universe. I do not count this as 'naturalistic' because although it tells a uniform story about people and pebbles, it starts with people instead of at the other end. That makes my use of 'naturalism' a little vague, but not harmfully so.

Spinoza's naturalism about mankind is eloquently expressed in 3 Preface, where he protests against those who 'conceive man in Nature as a dominion within a dominion' because 'they believe that man disturbs rather than follows the order of Nature'. And a little further on he says in effect that there is no pathology *of* Nature, and that any pathology *in* Nature must be perfectly natural and fully explicable. He reverts to this theme later on, when theorizing about certain affects. He says that pride and despondency are bad from the standpoint of 'human advantage', but adds a warning that that standpoint is a parochial one:

8. *New Essays*, p. 490.

But the laws of Nature concern the common order of Nature, of which man is a part. I wished to remind my readers of this . . . in case anyone thought my purpose was only to tell about men's vices and their absurd deeds, and not to demonstrate the nature and properties of things. For, as I said in the Preface of Part 3, I consider men's affects and properties just like other natural things. And of course human affects, if they do not indicate man's power, at least indicate the power and skill of Nature, no less than many other things we wonder at and delight in contemplating. (4p57s at 252/31)

This invites us to extend the range of things we can wonder at and delight in contemplating, by enlarging the scope of our understanding. Anyone will rejoice in the outer appearance of a live butterfly, but even the innards of a dead and dissected one may engender 'wonder and delight' as one learns how the organism functions—the complex, orderly processes which constitute the life of the butterfly. Anyone may delight in a fine waterfall, but more humdrum movements of water can also interest someone studying how mountains take water from the sky and then return it. It is a familiar line of thought, which Spinoza invites us to extend to human beings. He wants us to see that we might study the aetiology of pride or despondency— or of cruelty, cowardice, vanity, stupidity, or whatever—and find 'wonder and delight' in the intricacy and inevitability of the mechanisms that are involved.

2. He doesn't hold that we should relate to our fellows only as students of biology and psychology: 'But I continue to note concerning the affects', he goes on, 'those things which bring advantage to men, and those which bring them harm.' Each human, Spinoza believes, has special reason for concern with things which are 'good' or 'bad' in the special sense of being conducive or inimical to the welfare of humans; this is because he thinks he can prove that self-interest is inevitable, and further that the real interests of any individual are tied to those of the rest of his species. But this special human concern of ours is, though natural and inevitable, also parochial. It is a domestic matter, with no metaphysical importance.

3. Other philosophers, such as Hobbes and Hume, have tried to carry through a naturalistic account of humanity; but Spinoza may be unique in how thoroughly he abides by his commitment to naturalism, refusing to slip back into treating humans as special in some basic way. Unique, that is, until our century: there are many unblinking naturalists now, because naturalism is easier now than it was in the seventeenth century, partly because of the nineteenth century science which suggests that *Homo sapiens* is a species of animal and the twentieth century science which suggests that animals are chemical systems.

4. Someone who thinks that the whole truth about humans can be told using only concepts which are necessary to describe the rest of the universe should want to tell enough of the story to satisfy us that the rest could be told without stepping over the line. That is what Spinoza tries to do.

He fails, however, in at least two ways, and probably in three. His account of us is impoverished: it positively excludes some large aspects of human nature, such as our ability to act because we have purposes. Also, some of what it includes is misconstructed out of the basic materials. And —the third possible failure—Spinoza's list of concepts for describing the rest of Nature is probably too long: he credits reality as a whole with a feature that seems to be confined if not to its human then to its animal fragment. I allude, of course, to the doctrine (mentioned in §3.3) that there is a mental realm which precisely mirrors the physical realm.

If Spinoza did not have that doctrine of panpsychism, his naturalism would commit him to some kind of materialism: he would have to show how a mostly nonmental world could generate small pockets of mentality through the same physical laws that reign throughout the rest of Nature. As things are, he lets himself off from that task by introducing mentality as a basic feature of the entire universe. Still, he does not shy away from specific problems about the mind: for example, he does not simply help himself to the concepts of perception, memory, pleasure and unpleasure, and belief; rather, he works hard to earn his right to employ these concepts. Unlike Leibniz, who was catapulted across much of the philosophy of mind by his doctrine that all substances are comparable to human minds, Spinoza keeps his feet on the ground, despite his panpsychism: he travels overland, the hard way, and we can learn a lot by following his steps.

Let me be clear about this. I do say that Spinoza's total naturalistic programme fails at both ends and in the middle; as though he undertook to build a sturdy mansion all out of wood, and achieved only a rickety shack using bricks as well as wood. But his attempt was a work of genius; and a thorough, candid study of it can be wonderfully instructive. The failures have at least as much to teach as the successes, if one attends not only to *where* Spinoza fails but *why*. I shall add a few words about this at the end of my next section.

§11. *Fourth aspect: conceptual minimalism*

1. A philosopher embarking on a programme which is 'naturalistic' in my sense must start with a small stock of basic concepts—ones which are needed all through the description of the universe—and any others that he needs should be explained through these. Conceptual parsimony and constructive ingenuity, then, will be marks of any serious attempt to give a naturalistic account of the human condition.

Spinoza's parsimony, however, is not purely a result of his naturalism. He *likes* to work with exiguous raw materials, that being part of what I mean in calling him a conceptual minimalist. The tiny stock of basic concepts in the *Ethics* reflects Spinoza's intellectual temperament as well as his naturalistic programme.

2. It also has a basis in a doctrine of his which is sometimes wrongly called nominalism. He writes at times as though he were a nominalist, allowing existence only to particulars. In the *Metaphyical Thoughts* he writes that 'Universals do not exist, and have no essence except that of particulars' (I/263/5), and echoes of this linger on in the mature work. Some commentators have held him to this, trying to explain away the strands in his thought which go against it. They have said, for instance, that what he admits into his ontology is not really the universal *extension* but only *the extended realm*, which is a vast particular. That interpretation, although wrong, is plausible; but other doctrines of Spinoza's cannot be given plausible nominalistic readings. Most notably, in 2p40s2 he says that reason involves knowledge 'of the properties of things', which would be odd (to put it mildly) if he denied the existence of properties. Other facets of his work, too, become strange if they are combined with nominalism.[9]

The chief passage that looks nominalistic is 2p40s1; but most commentators agree that really it is not. Its topic is not the metaphysics of all general terms, but rather the semantics of some of them. Spinoza is arguing that general 'notions' of a certain kind are unfit for serious theoretical use because of how they are formed in our minds:

Those notions they call *universal*, like Man, Horse, Dog, etc., have arisen . . . because so many images (e.g. of men) are formed at one time in a human body that they surpass the power of imagining . . . to the point where the mind can imagine neither slight differences of the particular [men], such as the colour and size of each one, etc., nor their determinate number, and all it imagines distinctly is whatever is common to their effects on the human body. . . . And the mind expresses this by the word *man*, and predicates it of infinitely many particulars. (2p40s1 at 121/13)

The 'imagining' spoken of here includes perception. When I see you, your body acts causally on mine, creating in it a physical 'image' of your body; and the mental counterpart of that is my 'imagining' of you. Now, my universal notion of *man* results from a piling up of these imaginings, and so it will be a fuzzy mess except to the extent that my imaginings of men have been alike. (In fact Spinoza thinks that each separate imagining is a mess, but he is not pressing that point here.) This alikeness, however, depends not on whether the men have been alike but on whether they have had like effects on my body, and that depends on thousands of coincidences.

9. For a good survey of them, see Haserot, 'Spinoza and the Status of Universals'. Friedman, in 'An Overview of Spinoza's *Ethics*' at pp. 89–90, puts clearly the view that Spinoza was a nominalist.

Spinoza is making the metaphysical point that a 'notion' formed in that way cannot be expected to carve up Nature at a real joint.[10] He is also making a point in social semantics, namely, that my universal notion of *man* is bound to be unlike yours, because my body differs from yours in how it has been affected by men and in which of those effects have stuck in the memory. 'These notions . . . vary from one mind to another, in accordance with what the body has more often been affected by and what the mind imagines or recollects more easily.'

This is not a metaphysical view about all general terms, but only an aetiology and a criticism of some of them. It is not nominalism, but rather a rejection for theoretical purposes of sense-based universality. We shall see later that it is accompanied by a welcome for 'rational universality',[11] that is, for general notions coming from reason rather than from the senses.

And so, as I said, Spinoza has grounds in addition to his naturalism for confining himself to a skimpy stock of basic concepts; for in an enterprise such as the *Ethics* no weight should be carried by any of the sense-based notions treated in 2p40s1.

3. Spinoza thinks that nobody's general notion of *man* is fit for serious use. How then can he write his treatise on human freedom and human bondage? Since he did not regard himself as bound by the meanings of words, he could have given 'man' and 'human' new meanings, divorcing them from the cluster of general notions by which they are backed in ordinary language. In fact, he performs no such manoeuvre; the *Ethics* contains no redefinition of 'man', explicit or implicit; and in §64 I shall explain how Spinoza does get the term 'man' into his theorising without putting onto it a load which, according to 2p40s1, it cannot carry.

4. Back now to conceptual minimalism. Although we have found two theoretical grounds for Spinoza's economy in basic concepts, I still see his minimalism more as a fundamental aspect of his cast of mind than as forced on him by other opinions and attitudes.

And a second strand in the minimalism could not come from either of those theoretical sources: I refer to Spinoza's evident liking for drastic simplicity in his conceptual constructions. Of course when philosophers go wrong they usually oversimplify, and Spinoza often goes wrong; but that is not the whole story. Nor is it just that he likes to express himself in brief, pithy utterances, offering the reader dense little wads of philosophy to be

10. This is confirmed in 2p18s at 107/9. In drawing this conclusion Spinoza is implying that what kind or property is picked out by a general term is determined purely by what is in the mind of the term's user. That is probably false, for reasons given sketchily in the *New Essays* (e.g., p. 345) and re-presented in a more disciplined fashion in our own time by Kripke and Putnam.

11. Haserot's phrase—*op. cit.*, p. 53.

chewed on for hours. In addition, he takes pleasure in starting at a dizzyingly abstract level and moving in about two short steps down into the thick of everyday life. I cannot illustrate this before expounding details in the *Ethics*; but examples will come in due course.

At the end of §10 I spoke of how much we can learn from Spinoza's successes and, especially, his failures. It is his minimalism that makes his work so instructive. If you set a mechanical genius to build an automobile engine out of a Meccano set, you won't get a working engine from him, but as you watch him fail you will learn a lot about automobile engines.

§12.   *What is dualism?*

1. Because most of Nature seems to be mindless, any naturalist (in my sense of that term) is likely to hold that human beings are fully describable in physical terms—that mental terminology may be brought in through definitions but is not needed on the ground floor.

That was not Spinoza's position, however. He never questioned the truth of a doctrine that I shall call property dualism, which says that the properties of things can be cleanly split into two groups, mental and physical, with no property belonging at once to both groups; this being so understood as to rule out any defining of mental terms through physical ones.[12] When I speak of Spinoza's dualism, I allude to that doctrine which he shares with Descartes. He rejects Descartes's stronger substance dualism, which adds to property dualism the thesis that no one thing can have properties of both kinds—so that a human being is not one thing but two, e.g., a worried mind and an emaciated body.

Spinoza, then, thinks that a person's mental aspects are part of the basic story about her; this, combined with his naturalism, leads him to say that all of Nature has mental aspects. I shall discuss later his case for this bold hypothesis; my present topic is the dualism which lies in its background. I want to get clearer about what the dualism is: my statement of it above, though no worse than most in the literature, is too vague to support a proper study of the *Ethics*. We need a formulation which is tighter and clearer, yet still in touch with Descartes's thought and with Spinoza's; and it should not make dualism come out as obviously true or as easily demonstrably false.

2. I shall approach dualism by way of a thesis about a split through a certain range of concepts, rather than properties; that is, abstract items in logical space rather than universal items in the contingent world. But be-

12. To avoid the ugly words 'mentalistic' and 'physicalistic', I speak of properties, concepts, and words as 'mental' or 'physical', meaning that they *pertain to* the mental or the physical.

cause the end-point is a thesis about properties—and indeed about properties which some things could have and some things could lack—many of our concepts can be kept out of range of the split. For example, the split has nothing to do with the concept of existence, for if that corresponds to a property it's a property which necessarily everything has. Nor do tautologous or contradictory concepts come under the axe.

More generally, our entire apparatus of logical concepts, and everything we can construct out of them alone, should be kept out of reach of the dualist divide. Conceptual dualism is supposed to be a split within a scheme which has some kind of unity, but if the very logic is split there is no unity left. Anyway, who would want a mental/physical dualism that cut so wide and deep that it involved a mentalistic logic and a different physicalistic logic? Let us, then, exclude from the dualist split all our logical concepts and, for similar reasons, our numerical concepts.

There will have to be other exclusions as well. But first let us take a preliminary look at the dualist split.

3. In expounding it, I shall speak of concepts as entailing one another, borrowing this from entailments between the corresponding propositions. Thus, F entails G just in case 'Something is F' entails 'Something is G', and R entails S just in case 'Something has R to something' entails 'Something has S to something', and so on. I am speaking only of entailments which hold by virtue of the nature of these concepts. Spinoza has general metaphysical views that imply that whatever is thinking must also be extended, but I do not want to commit him to holding that thought entails extension; and I head off that implication by stipulating that for F to entail G there must be between the corresponding propositions an entailment which holds because of the nature of the concepts themselves and not by virtue of any more general metaphysical thesis. This is unsatisfactory, and I hope it can be improved on, but at present it is the best I can do.

Two bits of technical terminology, to be used briefly and then discarded: two concepts are logically 'in touch' if either entails the other; and two concepts are logically 'connected' if they are the termini of some sequence of concepts each of which is logically in touch with its immediate neighbours. Thus, *cubic* is connected with *spherical*, because each is in touch with *shaped*. And *jealous* is connected with *aware of danger*, because the former is in touch with *in an emotional state* which is in touch with *afraid* which is in touch with *aware of danger*. Notice that the relations I have defined are symmetrical, although they are defined in terms of entailment which is not.

Now, property dualism rests on the idea that all our concepts fall into two great groups—call them 'categories'—such that each concept is connected with every member of its own category and with no member of the other.

Can we put every concept into one category or the other, apart from those we have set aside as belonging to logic or arithmetic, or as being tautological or contradictory? No. If dualism is to have a hope of being true, we must exclude some more concepts from its range. If F belongs to one category and G to the other, then the concept *F-and-G* is connected with both, thus contradicting dualism as I have formulated it. For example, the concept *happy and strong* is logically connected with both the mental and the physical. But it is easy to modify dualism so as to avoid this difficulty: instead of saying that all our concepts can be segregated into the two categories, we can say that they can all be *resolved into* concepts each of which belongs in one category or the other.

This will trivialize our dualism unless some constraints are laid on the notion of 'resolving'. I propose a very strong constraint: a concept F can be 'resolved' into concepts $G_1, \ldots, G_n$ only if F involves no concepts except $G_1, \ldots, G_n$ and concepts which are explicitly excluded from the scope of our dualism. Thus, our explicit exclusion of logical concepts, on any reasonable understanding of what that means, will cover the relations used in constructing *strong and happy* and *strong or happy* out of *strong* and *happy*. But there are other combinations—such as *strong when happy* and *strong because happy*—which are still making trouble for us. These will easily succumb, however, if the concepts of time and cause are put out of reach of the dualist split.

4. The dualist is certainly under pressure to treat temporal concepts as transcategorial, i.e., to protect them from the split. Because there is no way of resolving the metrical *brief* or the topological *before* into components which divide between the two categories, we must either make temporal concepts transcategorial or else assign them en bloc to one category or the other. But either assignment seems arbitrary. How could we decide between treating *brief pain* as a mixture of physical *brief* and mental *pain*, and treating *brief storm* as a mixture of mental *brief* and physical *storm*? It might be argued that our temporal metric is essentially rooted in measures of duration, which must be based on regular kinds of physical process, so that the physical category is indeed the home ground of *brief* and its kin. I am not convinced that this is right; but in any case it can be no help with topological concepts such as simultaneity and beforeness. One might in desperation suggest that words expressing temporal topology are ambiguous—e.g., that ' . . . occurs before . . . ' expresses a different concept in each category. But then what could we make of temporal relations between mental items and physical ones? And are we to say that the argument 'The headache preceded the storm, which preceded the flood, so the headache came before the flood' is fallacious through ambiguity? Surely not!

So there will be trouble if temporal concepts are not pushed out of reach of the dualist split. But we can also give independent reasons for this. Just as the dualist needs a transcategorial logic if his two categories are to be held together within a single intellectual system, so he also needs some nonlogical transcategorial concepts if his categories are to apply to anything he can regard as a single *world*.[13] Now, I contend that a multitude of items can be taken as pertaining to a single reality only if they belong to a single temporal scheme: the reality must not only be temporal but must involve *one* time. For temporal concepts to be transcategorial, they need only be applicable within each category; but to secure the unity of the world, temporal topology must apply between the categories, in such statements as 'the pain stopped before the sun went down'. I base this on some thoughts of Kant's, and especially his thesis that we cannot envisage a personal inner history which does not occur in a single time-series, and cannot apprehend any reality except by somehow embracing it within our own inner histories. But I cannot follow that up in detail: it ranges too far into unSpinozistic territory. Anyway, even non-Kantians would agree that an intending dualist should keep temporal concepts out of reach of the split.

5. Now for causal concepts. One who holds that physical events alone have causal powers may be able to locate causal concepts purely within the category of the physical, though he may have problems if he allows that mental events, although powerless, can be caused. But Spinoza, for whom the situation is symmetrical with regard to causal concepts, must treat them as transcategorial.

A Kantian justification could be given for this too: Kant argued powerfully that any conceivable reality which we could know about must be held together causally, because temporal order presupposes causal order.[14] It is not maintained, this time, that there must be causal flow between the categories, as there must be temporal relations between them; but at least there must be causal laws operating within each category, and so causal concepts must be protected from the dualist split.

Spinoza, however, would say that he needs no such justification, since for him there is no need to *add* causal concepts to a transcategorial list which already contains our full equipment of logical concepts. His causal

13. I am here guided by John Passmore, *Philosophical Reasoning* (London, 1961), ch.3.

14. The most accessible version of the Kantian argument is in my *Kant's Analytic* (Cambridge, 1966), §54. See also C. Peacocke, *Holistic Explanation* (Oxford, 1979), p. 186.

rationalism equates causality with logical entailment, and that was pushed out of reach of the split right at the outset. Oddly enough, if he held causal laws to be general brute facts, he would again be spared from adding causality to his transcategorial list. For he would then be holding that the concept of causality can be analysed in terms of *true* and *universal* and *many instances* and the like, and these all belong to that logical and numerical apparatus which was the first thing to be declared transcategorial.

6. We have been establishing the class C of concepts whose members consist of our logico-numerical apparatus, purely temporal and causal concepts, and nothing else. And the notion of 'resolving' which I introduced in .3 now becomes: F can be resolved into $G_1, \ldots, G_n$ if and only if F involves no concepts except $G_1, \ldots, G_n$ and members of C. With that in hand, we can formulate dualism as follows:

> All our non-tautological and non-contradictory concepts which do not belong in C can be resolved into ones which fall into two categories, the mental and the physical, such that every member of each category is logically connected (a) with every member of that category and (b) with no member of the other category except through non-logical members of C.

Notice that C is referred to twice—once to keep *brief* etc. out of both categories, and once to allow *brief fight* in one category and *brief worry* in the other, although they are logically connected through *brief*. Of course *brief worry* can be resolved into *brief* and *worry*, according to my definition of 'resolved'; but we can't handle this sort of difficulty by supposing that the members of the categories have been 'resolved' down far enough to contain no temporal or causal implications. I am sure that all mental and physical concepts have temporal import, and probably causal import as well.

An untrivial dualism requires a complete *list* of the kinds of concepts that have transcategorial status—a list such as I have tried to provide in specifying the contents of the class C. If we specified C merely as containing 'whatever concepts it has to contain to make dualism true', that would trivialize the position. Is my list of sorts of transcategorial concepts complete? Well, if you want a unified theory about a single world, you will make a pretty good start if you have a unified logic and universal applicability of temporal and causal concepts; but I cannot prove that there are no other concepts that must be transcategorial if dualism is to have a hope of being true, although I do know that my study of Spinoza won't force any more on us.

For a while I thought that the concept of aboutness must be transcategorial, so that the two-legged concept *thinking about a rose* could be resolved into *thinking* and *rose*, and that this would prevent that concept from counting against my version of dualism. But really there was no need. Although *thinking about a rose* does in a fashion involve the concept *rose*, it is not in my sense 'logically connected' with it: 'Something is thinking about a rose' neither entails nor is entailed by 'Something is a rose'.

Am I in trouble from the concept *ambiguous written word*? A written word is physical; ambiguity is having more than one meaning; and many of us think that meanings are mental. It would be miserable if I had to add to my transcategorial list a concept of *having* which could relate words to their meanings! I think that can be avoided, however. With great labour and at the expense of some complexity we could resolve *ambiguous written word* into concepts belonging to the separate categories, with the aid of nothing but logical, temporal and causal concepts, i.e., ones already belonging to C. Here I rely on the general approach to meaning taken in my book *Linguistic Behaviour*.

It has been suggested to me that the concept of *part/whole* is transcategorial. I think it must be. We have the notion of the parts of physical things, and it is not obvious that we don't also have the concept of parts of thoughts and sensations; in addition to which we do speak about temporal parts (of events) and logical parts (of propositions or concepts). I would be reluctant to handle all this through a plea of multiple ambiguity. On the other hand, I am not sure that part/whole has to be added to the existing membership of C; perhaps it is already in C, as part of our logical apparatus. My unsureness about this is a sign of unclarity about the scope of the 'logical', which brings an admitted softness into my formulation of dualism.

7. Descartes sometimes alludes to transcategorial concepts, giving two laconic lists: 'substance, duration, number, and other such things',[15] and 'being, number, duration etc.'.[16] I have already dealt with *being, number* and *duration*, and also with *cause* which is inexplicably absent from Descartes's lists. There remains *substance*, about which I should say something.

The root sense of 'substance' in early modern philosophy is just that of 'thing', or 'subject of predication': there are properties or qualities or attributes or modes, and there are substances that have them. When 'substance' is used in that manner, the concept of substance is involved whenever there is predication; and that suffices to include *substance* in that logical apparatus which we have already protected from the dualist split. If the latter is to cut only through properties, then certainly substance

15. Meditation III, in Alquié, vol. 2, p. 443. The Latin version says ' . . . and any other such things as there may be'.

16. Letter to the Princess Elizabeth, in Alquié, vol. 3, p. 19.

must be kept out of its reach somehow, for there cannot be a property of substantiality: if there were, it would be the property of being-a-thing-that-has-properties, which leads to absurdity.[17]

In Descartes's hands, and even more in Spinoza's and Leibniz's, the term 'substance' takes on a richer meaning. Spinoza, for example, denies the title 'substance' to ordinary physical things, reserving it for ultimate, basic, irreducible subjects of predication; and, as we shall see, he thinks that these must be very special indeed. However, the specialness of a 'substance' in this rich sense consists in its being logically and causally self-sufficient, and in its lasting for ever; and this is all provided for by concepts already assigned to C. If C needs to be enlarged, therefore, it is not because of anything in Descartes's lists.

8. My formulation of dualism throws no light on what it is for a concept to be mentalistic. It says merely that our concepts can be split into two groups, to which it gives the labels 'mental' and 'physical'; but unless we already have meanings for these, all I have presented is the thesis that *some* dualism of concepts is true. That is to be expected: the formulation is too abstract to help with any such concepts as those of mentality and physicality. How much this matters for our understanding of Spinoza will appear shortly.

§13. *Fifth aspect: dualism*

1. Spinoza assumed a dualism like the one I have been developing: he thought there was a deep logical split through most of our concepts. That would forbid him to accept philosophical behaviourism, according to which mental concepts are logically derivable from physical ones; and it would rule out phenomenalism, as that allows entailments running the other way.

Dualism as so far formulated implies that there is no *logically* true conditional whose antecedent uses only concepts from one category and whose consequent uses only ones from the other. (I here ignore conditionals with impossible antecedents or necessary consequents.) For Spinoza, that is equivalent to saying that there is no *causally* true conditional—no causal law—with the antecedent confined to one category and the consequent to the other. On the reasonable assumption that all mental and physical properties have concepts corresponding to them, it follows that there is no causal flow between the two sorts of property—e.g., a fact about an entity's physical properties can't be explained by reference to any entity's mental properties.

Spinoza uses the term 'attribute' for what is common to all the prop-

---

17. The point is developed in my *Locke, Berkeley, Hume: Central Themes* (Oxford, 1971), §11.

erties in one group. Thus, mentality and physicality are attributes. In calling them distinct attributes, Spinoza is saying more than is asserted by mere dualism about them, in my sense. Dualism implies that neither is reducible to the other and there is no third item to which *both* are reducible; but Spinoza holds further that *neither* is analysable in terms of anything else. According to him, each is a basic, irreducible way of being.

He seems to hold that there are many attributes in addition to these two; indeed, he speaks of 'infinite attributes'. Fortunately, our two are the only ones that play a significant part in the *Ethics*, so that 'dualism' is an acceptable label for what actively goes on in that work. Furthermore, in developing dualism in §12, I have stated it in terms of a split through 'our' concepts, and that keeps my formulation well clear of Spinoza's notion of 'infinite attributes'; for he does not think that we have concepts of any attributes other than the famous two. Still, because others are being theoretically allowed for, we find Spinoza speaking of the causal quarantine not between the mental and the physical but more generally between attributes.

He states this explicitly in 2p6, according to which all causal flow is confined within the attributes and never goes across from one to the other. That is derived from 1p10 which says that each attribute is 'conceived through itself', meaning that you can't get at it conceptually through anything else, which entails that the attributes are not logically connected with one another. In the shift from 1p10 to 2p6 we can see Spinoza's causal rationalism silently at work.

2. Where I speak of physicality Spinoza speaks of the attribute of 'extension'. That reflects an important doctrine about the metaphysics of matter, namely, that the fundamental spatial reality is space, and that what we loosely treat as things *in* it are really intermittent thickenings *of* it. On this view, the difference between matter and empty space, ordinarily so-called, does not belong to basic metaphysics—it is merely the difference between stony regions of space and airy ones, so to speak. In chapter 4 I shall say more about how this part of Spinoza's doctrine works. In the meantime, we can say that it answers the question of what there is on that side of the dualist divide. The category of what I call the 'physical' has in it every property whose corresponding concept includes the concept of extension; and if you want an explanation of 'extension', Spinoza and I will refer you to Euclidian geometry.

3. What about the other side of the dualist split? We might try to explain it simply as what is left over when the physical is subtracted;[18] but that would not be acceptable to Spinoza, for he certainly held that

18. That account of the mental is suggested in Matson, 'Spinoza's Theory of Mind', p. 51.

there could be more than two attributes, and that forbids us to define 'mental' as 'not physical'. He has no other explanation of mentality either, apparently thinking that this concept lies too deep to be capable of analytical explanation.

We can, however, get some light on his view of the mental by noting that his word for this attribute is 'thought'. In this, as in his use of 'extension' for the category of the physical, Spinoza follows Descartes, largely for Cartesian reasons. It seems odd to us to use 'thought'—or the Latin *cogitatio* or the French *pensée*—to cover the whole range of the mental. It may reflect a tendency to use 'thought' more broadly than we would find natural, but it also, more certainly, indicates a narrowed emphasis within the range of the mental. Although Spinoza allows that mental events include sensings and feelings as well as thinkings, his stress is mostly on the latter.

4. I have described Spinoza's dualism as a fundamental aspect of his cast of mind, rather than as explicit doctrine. He has plenty of doctrine based on the view that thought and extension are basic and mutually irreducible ways of being; but that view itself is an undefended assumption. In 3p2 he says that there is no causal flow either way between body and mind, but his argument for that runs back only to 2p6, which says that there is no causal flow between attributes; the argument merely assumes that body and mind pertain to different attributes.

We might see Spinoza as arguing that thought is an attribute, and pointing to a similar argument for extension, in 2p1d. But the argument is no good. It amounts to this: 'Particular mental events occur within Nature; so Nature must have some attribute within which they all fall; therefore thought is an attribute of Nature.' This assumes that mental events—thoughts—are a natural class and not a mere ragbag like the class of surprising events or nuisances or obstacles; and it also assumes that there are attributes, i.e., that the notion of a basic way of being is not a mistake. But granting both assumptions, what follows is only that thoughts fall under *thought* and fall under *an attribute*; it doesn't follow that thought is an attribute. For all this argument shows to the contrary, thought could be a special case of something more basic, of which extension is another special case. I don't think Spinoza was capable of asking whether thought is an attribute of Nature, as an addition to the question of whether thought is instantiated by Nature; and the wording of 2p1 is evidence for that. As I said, his dualism is assumed rather than defended.

5. A few words about property dualism in Descartes. He accepted the underlying concept dualism, but he was not enough of a causal rationalist to infer a causal barrier between the two categories of property. In some of his works, indeed, interaction is freely allowed, and I shall be discussing Spinoza's criticism of that in §32. Usually, however, Descartes was uneasy about allowing causal flow between thought and extension, and many of his followers rejected it outright. This was because they held that causing consists in one thing's giving a property to another, handing over part of its own resources. That is plausible enough if you think of transfers of motion, of heat et cetera, but as a general account of causation it is probably false and certainly disputable. But the Cartesians thought it was true. As Descartes said, 'Where else can the effect get its reality from if not from the cause?'[19] And from this, together with concept dualism about mind and body, they inferred a kind of causal dualism: a causal law whose instances are *transfers* must have some concept occurring in both antecedent and consequent, to represent what the cause loses and the effect gains; which implies that the antecedent cannot belong wholly to one category and the consequent wholly to the other. So there can be no causal transfers, and thus no causal influence, between mental and physical.

We find this thought in Spinoza also. In Letter 4 he writes: 'Of things which have nothing in common between them, one cannot be a cause of the other. For if the effect has nothing in common with the cause, whatever it receives [in the causal transaction] it would receive from nothing.' Whether this line of thought was at work in his later years, encouraging his view that if one thing has nothing in common with another it cannot be its cause (1p3), I do not know. But that view was certainly supported, in his case, by causal rationalism.

§14. *Psychology and logic*

1. Spinoza's dualism involves a logical and causal split between extension and thought—between physics and psychology, as one might say. But there is a way of taking his term 'thought' which divorces it from psychology, and makes his position different from the property dualism of Descartes. I don't quite say that Spinoza conflates these two senses of 'thought'; but both are perceptibly at work in the *Ethics*, and are not explicitly confronted and sorted out.

I shall approach the second sense by focusing on Spinoza's Latin word *idea*, which means something like 'particular item belonging to the attribute of thought'. We translate it by 'idea', and think of it as mental—for someone to have an idea, we assume, is for a mental event to occur or a mental state to obtain. And we take it that my idea of Socrates is a different particular from your similar idea of Socrates: one is an episode in my mind, the other in yours.

But there is a way of taking 'idea' in which ideas are not mental at all. In this second meaning, there is an idea of Socrates which you and I might both have before our minds as an *object* or *content* of our thoughts. This

19. Meditation III, in Alquié, vol. 2, p. 438.

is to use 'idea' to mean what 'concept' means in philosophy these days: an 'idea' is a logical item, a constituent of propositions, something thinkable by many people. Much of the time Spinoza takes ideas to be propositionally structured, i.e., to be of the form 'that P', where P stands for a sentence; and then on the psychological reading an 'idea' is a state or episode of believing that P or the like, while on the logical reading it is just the proposition that P.

A single propositional content can occur in beliefs that are not only numerically distinct, because occurring in different minds, but also vastly dissimilar from one another. My belief in determinism is intermittent and tentative, while yours is fervent and continuous, but what we believe is the same.

2. Whether there really are such items as concepts and propositions is an old topic of debate amongst philosophers. A resounding affirmative answer is given in Frege's 'The Thought',[20] which powerfully argues that if someone believes that grass is green, this involves not just a thinking but something to which the thinking is done. Frege calls it *ein Gedanke*, which, though inevitably translated as 'a thought', is not a thinking but rather the possible object of a thinking, as a football is a possible object of a kicking. Since this item is not a (mental) thinking or a (physical) sentence, Frege says, we must move from dualism to trialism: 'Thoughts are neither things of the outer world nor [mental things]. A third realm must be recognized.'[21]

Surely he is right that 'thoughts' in his sense—propositions and concepts—must be distinguished from both mental items and physical ones. Those distinctions are needed for it to be true that two people share a belief; that there is a concept which Smith did not grasp until last week; that the entailment of *Grass is coloured* by *Grass is green* did not come in with the English language; and so on. But that is not necessarily to endorse Frege's making this a matter of basic metaphysics, his postulating 'a third realm'. The concepts of *concept* and *proposition* may be constructible out of mental or physical concepts—e.g., a proposition may be a special class of sentences, or a concept may be a special class of mental episodes. But even if the so-called third realm can be constructed out of the other two, it will not be a construction by simple identification. Whatever the ultimate metaphysics of the matter, we are not entitled simply to ignore the differences between concepts and propositions on the one hand and mental episodes or linguistic expressions on the other; and we can applaud Frege's

20. G. Frege, 'The Thought: a Logical Inquiry', translated by A. and M. Quinton in *Mind* vol. 65 (1965), pp. 289-311.

21. *Ibid.*, p. 302.

warning about that, even while suspending judgment on his third-realm metaphysics. When I speak of 'third realm' entities, I mean entities of the sort Frege would put into the third realm.

Spinoza does ignore the difference between mental items and third-realm ones. He does not argue that belief-contents are constructs out of believings, and that logic really comes down in a complicated way to psychology. In fact, he says nothing about logic except for the passing remark that logic is normative for psychology, laying down rules for how one ought to think (5 Preface at 277/13). But from time to time he makes his psychology double as a logic as well, taking the term 'idea' to stand indifferently for a mental item and for a concept or proposition.

3. If this seems like such a crass error as to make Spinoza unworthy of further attention or my account of him incredible, let me plead in his defence or in mine.

He was not alone in this tendency to conflate logic with psychology. Leibniz was also guilty of a subtle form of it, and it is less subtly present in the work of Locke, who is led by it to put elementary logical truths into the same box as psychological self-descriptions, on the grounds that each can be known by inspecting one's 'ideas'.[22] This should not be confused with Locke's better known conflation of the sensory with the intellectual. He thought that when (a) a sensing occurs, the mind is cognitively related to (b) an inner object, an image or sense-datum or sensory 'idea'; and that when (c) a thinking occurs, the mind is cognitively related to (d) an intellectual 'idea'. Now, the conflation of psychology with logic is a smudging of the line between (c) thinkings and (d) concepts or propositions which are their objects or contents;[23] whereas Locke's sensory/intellectual conflation is a smudging of the line between (a)–(b) on the one hand and (c)–(d) on the other. It is extremely unsatisfactory to describe the latter, as I have done, as Locke's propensity to use 'idea' to cover 'both sense-data and concepts', and then, on the same page and purportedly on the same topic, to speak of his 'assimilating the sensory far too closely to the intellectual'.[24] Those two phrases pick out two entirely different philosophical mistakes: one, shared with Leibniz, about the nature of the subject-matter of logic; the other, of which Leibniz was innocent, about the internal geography of the mind. The difficulty that some of us have had

22. For textual and other details, see the abridged edition of the *New Essays* (Cambridge, 1982), pp. xxi–xxiii.

23. There is no comparable mistake of conflating (a) with (b). The mistake there is to believe that (b) exists, i.e., that when someone is in a sensory state his mind has an inner object.

24. J. Bennett, *Locke, Berkeley, Hume: Central Themes*, p. 25.

in coming clear about this is some measure of the temptingness of the conflation of (c) the psychological with (d) the logical.

There have been two main alternatives to the view of logic as psychology. One sees it as physics. This view, different forms of which have been defended by Mill and by Quine, has the merit of providing an answer to the question 'How can anyone have reason to believe that it is necessary that P?' Locke has an answer to this question, namely, 'Since the necessity of P stems from relations between our ideas, we can know about it by introspection'; and Mill and Quine have a different answer: 'For P to be necessary is just for it to be true and scientifically well entrenched; and we can have the same grounds for believing that as we can for any other scientific belief, namely, that it stands up well to the battering it takes as we continue with the scientific enterprise.' So there is a possible epistemology for logic as psychology, and for logic as physics; but for the currently popular view of logic—according to which necessary truths are about 'possible worlds', items belonging to Frege's 'third realm' between the mental and the physical—there is no coherent epistemology at all. We speak of being guided by our 'intuitions' about what is possible, but third-realmery allows us no explanation of how such intuitions relate to their subject-matter or, therefore, why they should be trusted. This should warn us against being too smugly condescending about the seventeenth century assumption that necessary truths are at bottom truths about one's own mind.

4. Some writers on Spinoza seem not to have noticed that he has logic jumbled up with his psychology. I know of only one, Balz, who has contended that Spinoza is offering only a logic and no psychology at all:

Spinoza's problem is not set in terms of the relation of psychical ideas in a spiritual substance to modes of a physical, extended substance. Nor does Spinoza split existence into halves, things of the mind and things of extension. Idea means for Spinoza what essence had denoted in scholastic philosophy. It is a logical entity, and in explicated form and verbally expressed, it is a definition.[25]

The flavour of Balz's vigorous working out of this theme is conveyed by his treatment of two terms which are usually thought to be mental, namely *anima* (soul, but connected with 'animated') and *mens* (mind). According to Balz, one belongs to biology and the other to logic; psychology, in the sense of the theory of what is 'psychic or spiritual', is squeezed out.

This is not a mad view of the *Ethics*. It has in its favour many remarks about 'thought' or 'ideas' which make better sense as logic than as psychology, and occasional places were Spinoza seems to say outright that ideas are logical entities. In deploying his doctrine about 'ideas of ideas', for instance, Spinoza says: 'The idea of an idea is nothing but the form of the idea . . .'

25. Balz, *Idea and Essence in the Philosophies of Hobbes and Spinoza*, p. 30.

(2p21s), and 'form' is sometimes a term pertaining not to psychology but to something like Frege's third realm. And there is precedent for this way of using the term 'idea': Descartes sometimes adopted it, saying that 'ideas themselves are nothing but forms'.[26] The word 'idea' was given to philosophy by Plato, for whom ideas were not mental, but were objective, mind-independent, third-realm entities.

As for doctrines which go better as logic than as psychology: Balz mentions as a prime example Spinoza's doctrine that corresponding to every idea there is an idea of it, and an idea of the latter, and an idea of that, and so on *ad infinitum*.[27] These infinite sequences do indeed seem implausible as psychology and all right as logic: there is the proposition that P, the proposition that the proposition that P is true, . . . et cetera.

Yet Curley, who construes 'the attribute of thought' purely logically through most of Part 2 of the *Ethics*,[28] switches to psychology precisely at the point where 'ideas of ideas' come in, taking the latter to be a doctrine about self-consciousness. This is natural too. For although the doctrine itself is easier to swallow when understood logically, Spinoza's justification of it, namely, 'For as soon as someone knows something, he thereby knows that he knows it, and at the same time knows that he knows that he knows, and so on to infinity' (2p21s), reads so much like psychology that one cannot think it was intended as logic. If Spinoza meant only to make a logical claim concerning propositions about propositions, how could he hope to convey it in words like 'as soon as someone knows something'? On passages like this, Balz is prudently silent.

The Balz thesis is not supportable, and in chapter 6 I shall also argue against Curley's restricted version of it. There is too much in the *Ethics* that must be read psychologically, and Balz is forced to misrepresent these passages.[29]

---

26. Reply to the Fourth Objections, Alquié, vol. 2, p. 673.

27. Balz, *op. cit.*, p. 71.

28. Curley, *Spinoza's Metaphysics*; see for example p. 124.

29. See for example Balz's p. 52 for an attempt to give a third realm reading to Spinoza's phrase 'action of the mind'.

3 *The One Substance Doctrine*

This chapter will expound Spinoza's official argument for his doctrine that there is only one substance. There is some preliminary explaining to do.

§15. *Substance in the rationalists*

1. To begin to understand Part 1 of the *Ethics*, one must grasp its concept of substance. The root idea is that of what has properties or is a subject of predication; but that is too thin to be useful, since anything can be a subject of predication—his honesty is pleasing, but honesty is not a substance. In Aristotle, to whom the seventeenth century use of 'substance' runs back, the concept of substance is thickened in two ways.

One is in the *Metaphysics*, where substances are items that can be subjects of predication and can undergo change, i.e., they can maintain an identity while having mutually contradictory properties at different times. Aristotle's paradigm substances in this work are organisms, because they change a lot and thus support a rich and contentful notion of diachronic identity.[1]

This notion of substance links with Aristotle's distinction between *matter* and *form*. An organism consists at any given time of matter which is shaped, formed, organized in a certain way; and it can be made up of different matter at different times, because it can metabolize—taking in, processing and releasing matter without loss of identity. Notice that on this account most of the stuff in the world does not consist of substances, or groups of substances, but merely of relatively unformed puddles and lumps and heaps. The genuine substances are those rare bits of the world that are highly 'formed' or organized and persist through radical change.

That is in the *Metaphysics*. In the *Categories*, Aristotle enriches the concept of substance in a different way, adding to 'subject of predication . . .' the clause '. . . which cannot be predicated of anything else'. This amounts to using 'substance' to cover everything on one side of the great divide between things and properties. Thus, a person's honesty, though it can be talked about, can itself be predicated of the person and therefore is not a

---

1. I am here guided by Montgomery Furth, 'Transtemporal Stability in Aristotelian Substances', *The Journal of Philosophy* vol. 75 (1978), pp. 624–646, especially pp. 644–6.

substance; whereas the person is a substance because he is not predicable of anything else.

The *Categories* seems to hold that everything is either substance or property, whereas the *Metaphysics* seems to imply that many items—e.g., pools and heaps—are neither. I am not equipped to discuss this as a problem in understanding Aristotle: I have invoked him merely to help me present two influential ways of using 'substance'.

2. The use of the term by Descartes, and even more by Spinoza and Leibniz, derives from the *Categories*, but something happened to it along the way.

In a nutshell, substances came to be, by definition, items which are causally self-sufficient or indestructible. Descartes remarks that by this standard only God counts as a substance, because everything else owes its existence to the Creator who could take it away; he copes with this by proposing a weaker sense for 'substance' in which a substance depends causally on nothing except itself and God.[2] I shall not discuss this supposedly weaker sense of 'substance', or Descartes's indecisive handling of questions about which particular items are 'substances' in the weaker sense. All I want is the fact that in his thinking, as also in Spinoza's and Leibniz's, 'substance' is tied to causal self-sufficiency. How did this come about?

I do not know what route 'substance' and its cognates followed in the long journey from Aristotle's *Categories* to Descartes's *Principles*. But Kneale has pointed out a philosophical connection between the two senses of 'substance', which probably figured in the history of the term's development.[3]

It starts from a view held by some philosophers such as Aristotle, though denied by others such as Plato, namely that the existence of a property depends on its being instantiated—i.e., that there cannot be squareness unless something is square, or honesty unless someone is honest. This suggests that there is a relation of dependence running from properties to the things that have them, and not conversely. The dependence would be logical: the thesis must be that 'existent but uninstantiated property' is conceptually defective, not merely contrary to physics. Thus, one mark of a genuine thing, or substance, is its not being *logically* dependent for its existence on anything else.

Put that into the hands of a causal rationalist and it becomes the thesis that a substance must not *causally* depend on anything else for its existence —i.e., the thesis of Descartes's *Principles*. I do not offer this as clearly ex-

2. *Principles* I. 51–2.

3. W. C. Kneale, 'The Notion of a Substance', *Proceedings of the Aristotelian Society* vol. 40 (1939), pp. 103–134.

plaining Descartes's taking this view of substance, as he was not straight-forwardly a causal rationalist. But I do submit that the line of thought I have taken from Kneale helps to explain the prevalence in the seventeenth century of the idea that a genuine substance must be causally self-sufficient.

In presenting it I am not agreeing that there is a one-way logical dependence of properties on things. That seems to be a mistake, even if properties cannot exist without being instantiated. Granted that the redness of my face could not exist unless *something* were red—the redness does not need *my face* in order to exist. And that establishes a symmetry: my face cannot exist without *some* properties, but it does not need *this* property. It may be objected: 'In saying that the redness doesn't need this face, you are taking the redness to be a universal which can be equally present in several particulars. But there is a property-instance that needs this particular face; if this face didn't exist, this *case* of redness wouldn't exist.' Such an objection presupposes that in addition to the face and the redness, there is something called a redness-instance which is particular like the face and yet is a property rather than a substance.[4] I deny that there is any such item: the only sense I can attach to 'instance of redness' is that of 'red thing'; and then the instance of redness doesn't depend on the face because it is the face.

3. What of the original idea of substances as subjects of predication? Did the seventeenth century philosophers forget about that? Descartes probably didn't, and Leibniz and Spinoza certainly didn't. Leibniz indeed used that idea as a basis for arguing that ordinary physical things are not substances: he does not talk about their being causally vulnerable to things outside them, but rather about their not being 'simple'; and he maintains that that disqualifies them from counting as, by strictest and most serious standards, subjects of predication. I shall explain.

Consider whether an army is a substance. What makes it an army—its 'essence', as Leibniz says—is the fact that a number of men are interrelated in a certain way. All there is to the army, Leibniz holds, is the relations among the men, so that the whole truth about it could be told in the form $F(a_1, a_2, \ldots, a_n)$ where each a_i refers to a soldier, and there is no substantival reference to the army: 'What constitutes the essence of an entity through aggregation is only a state of being of its constituent entities; for example, what constitutes the essence of an army is only a state of being of the constituent men.'[5] Quite generally, the thesis is that the reality of

---

4. For a valuable treatment of this and other matters, see Kenneth C. Clatterbaugh, *Leibniz's Doctrine of Individual Accidents*, *Studia Leibnitiana* Sonderheft 4 (1973).

5. H. T. Mason (ed.), *The Leibniz-Arnauld Correspondence* (Manchester, 1967), p. 121.

any collection or aggregate consists in its parts' being interrelated in certain ways—by spatial proximity or chain of command or whatever, depending on the sort of aggregate. From this, Leibniz infers that no aggregate is a substance.

Leibniz sees himself as working here with the concept of substance as that which is not predicable of something else, and as drawing out a previously unnoticed implication of it. When Arnauld accuses him of wilfully replacing the Aristotelian definition of 'substance' as 'that which is not modality or state' by a new-fangled one of his own, namely, 'that which has a true unity',[6] Leibniz replies that an aggregation is a 'state of being' of its constituents, thus implying that his definition follows from Aristotle's rather than replacing it.

That seems wrong. The army itself is not predicable on the soldiers: we cannot identify *it* with the relations amongst them, for those relations cannot be armed, deployed, disbanded, and so on. The Aristotle of the *Categories* probably would not have denied that an army is a substance, at least not for Leibniz's reason. (Because an army is highly organic, with matter flowing through it as recruits are ingested and casualties excreted, it is a good substance by the standards of the *Metaphysics*.) Still Leibniz has a point. Even if an army is not literally a property or relation, it is something which can be handled predicatively; it can be exhaustively treated without any substantival reference to *it*; and it has that in common with such clearly nonsubstantial items as blushes and roundnessses and heroisms. For a blush to exist is for a face to be briefly red; for an army to exist is for some soldiers to be related by chains of command.

Next, Leibniz infers that nothing with spatial parts is a substance. Any thing with parts is just a more or less tightly bound aggregate or collection, he thinks, with differences in tightness of bonding having no metaphysical significance. A diamond is on a par with a flock of sheep—it's just that to scatter the diamond you have to bark louder.

Add to that the view, then widely held, that whatever is extended has extended parts which could be separated, and you reach the conclusion that no extended thing can be a substance. This argument for the conclusion may, for all I know, have been accompanied in Leibniz's thought by a different one, namely: whatever has parts can be destroyed by scattering, and so fails to be a substance because it is not causally self-sufficient.

4. It would not be in character for Leibniz, having concluded that physical things are not strictly substances, to decide that they are unstrictly substances and to leave it at that. He holds that reality must be composed of substances, rigorously so-called; so he has a problem about how to bring

6. *Ibid.*, p. 107.

the concept of substance to bear on the world of extended things. He denies that the latter are composed of unextended parts: the size of an extended thing must be the sum of the sizes of its nonoverlapping parts, says Leibniz, and if none of them has any size then neither has the whole.

He therefore declines to apply the concept of substance to the extended world in any way at all. But he is not banishing that concept from his account of basic reality; rather, he is banishing the extended world from it! According to Leibniz, the spatial world is not ultimately real; there is an underlying nonspatial reality which appears to us in a spatial guise.

Leibniz thought this was an exciting and enriching philosophical move. He says that by getting straight about the 'real unities' which underlie aggregates one is transported into a new world—the world not of appearances but of fundamental reality.[7] I think the move was a disaster. It contrasts poorly with Spinoza's pursuit of a metaphysic that will make unapologetic sense of the given world.

5. How could Leibniz have avoided his calamitous conclusion that the extended world is not real? He might have postulated that there are *atoms*, i.e., extended things which could not be pulled apart by any natural process. Such atoms might pass the causal self-sufficiency test for being substances, since they might be invulnerable to any outside forces. I suspect, however, that Leibniz would regard them as still failing the other test, holding that even an unsplittable atom is still an aggregate, although a tightly bound one, of its parts. Anyway, he would not have tolerated for one moment, any more than Descartes or Spinoza would, the idea that the extended world is composed of atoms.

The other possible escape is to say that reality does not consist of ultimate things at all, and that the concept of *a substance* should give way to that of *substance.* Instead of having individuatable substances, on this proposal, we shall only have substance, stuff, the material of the universe. This is to shift from 'substance' as a count term to 'substance' as a mass term, the difference being like that between 'pebble(s)' and 'porridge'.[8] This is a possible metaphysic: extended things are real, and are in principle divisible into ever smaller extended things, but there is no worry about 'where it will all end'. It won't end, any more than the series of fractions $\frac{1}{2}$, $\frac{1}{4}$, $\frac{1}{8}$, ... will end, but all along we shall be dealing with ever smaller quantities of stuff.

6. Spinoza's use of 'substance' is marked by all the features I have been discussing. The *Ethics* is deeply committed to the view that any thing other

7. *New Essays*, p. 378.

8. For a helpful introduction, see W. V. Quine, *Word and Object* (Cambridge, Mass., 1960), §§19–20.

than the one substance is adjectival upon it—is a property or state or (Spinoza's favourite term here) 'mode' of it. Evidence for that will emerge in due course.

The notion of a substance as logically or conceptually independent is much more explicitly prominent. Indeed, Spinoza's definition of *substance* says, primarily, that a substance is something 'conceived through itself', which he explains as meaning that 'the concept of it does not have to be formed from the concept of something else' (1d3). Although 'conceived' sounds psychological, 'concept' can be logical, and there can be no doubt that *substance* is here being defined in terms of some kind of logical independence or self-sufficiency.

A little later Spinoza offers two arguments running from 1d3 to the conclusion that 'a substance cannot be produced by anything else' (1p6c). Neither looks much like an appeal to causal rationalism, but I shall contend later that in this stretch of the *Ethics* Spinoza's arguments do not point accurately to the structure of his thought. Anyway, whatever Spinoza's route to it, causal self-sufficiency is clearly part of his concept of substance, and he seems to take that as implying not only that a substance cannot be created or annihilated but that it cannot be acted on in any way by anything else.

We shall see in due course that Spinoza also connects substantiality with not having parts: he is at pains to insist that God, the one substance, does not have parts, apparently thinking that substantiality requires this. It is not clear whether this is because he thinks that things with parts must be causally vulnerable, or because he thinks, with Leibniz, that such things are adjectival upon their parts.

So there it is: we find in Spinoza a reason that Leibniz certainly has for denying that sticks and stones are substances, namely, that they are aggregates; and Spinoza has another reason which may also weigh with Leibniz, namely, that middle-sized physical objects are not causally self-sufficient since they can be created by assemblage, and annihilated by dispersal, under the influence of things outside themselves. Leibniz concludes that such things are too large to be substances because they have size at all, whereas Spinoza thinks they are too small because their size is finite. Objection: 'If a pebble cannot be a substance because it has parts, how can something bigger, which somehow includes the pebble, escape having parts?' I shall expound Spinoza's answer to that in §21.

§16. *Attributes in Spinoza*

1. We have seen that according to his definition of substance, Spinoza regards substances as *things*: they have that logical independence which is supposed to belong to what lies on the thing side of the thing/property divide. In contrast with this, modes are *properties* of things: 'By mode I understand the states of a substance' (1d5), to which Spinoza adds that a mode is 'in something else' and 'is conceived through' that something else. This is meant to put modes on the property side of the line: modes are in or of other items and conceptually depend on them, as a blush is supposed to depend on the face that has it.

But not every predicable item is a mode. The absolutely basic and irreducible properties—the ones corresponding to the categories in the dualist metaphysic—are called 'attributes'. An attribute for Spinoza is a *basic way of being*—a property which sprawls across everything on one side of the dualist split, and nothing on the other side. It follows that, setting aside the special transcategorial concepts, there is no logical connection between one attribute and another, as Spinoza himself says: 'Each attribute . . . must be conceived through itself' (p10). I am suspicious of the argument he gives for this and prefer to see it as following directly from his intention to use the term 'attribute' to mean something like 'basic and irreducible way of being' or 'most general property' or the like.

2. That intention is expressed, though not with ideal clarity, in his definition of *attribute* (1d4). Skipping over a complexity, to be picked up shortly, let us take 1d4 as saying that an attribute is the (or an) essence of a substance.

That forces us to look at the term 'essence'. Spinoza uses it freely from d1 onwards, and only in 2d2 does he condescend to define it! The definition is poorly stated, but it is clear what Spinoza means it to say: the essence of x is that property which must be possessed by x and cannot be possessed by anything else—it is a qualitative necessary and sufficient condition for something's being x. (Spinoza's definiens, which omits 'property' and 'qualitative', implies that the essence of x is x, so that 'the essence of' means nothing.)

I do not think that 'essence' means 'necessary and sufficient condition' in d4. If Spinoza were defining 'attribute' so as to secure that if x has attribute A then nothing else can have A, he would not have needed a later, intricate argument for the conclusion that no two substances can share an attribute (p5d). Perhaps the notion of a necessary condition is present in d4, for it seems inevitable that if x is *basically* an F then it could not have been a non-F; e.g., a diamond could not have been a fear, a headache could not have been a number. But I think it would have been better if Spinoza had left the word 'essence' right out of his definition of *attribute*, defining the term directly through the notion of a basic, logically irreducible and unanalysable way of being.

That is the notion Descartes captures when he says that 'there is always one principal property of substance which constitutes its nature and essence, and on which all the others depend'.[9] Here, as in Spinoza's d4, the term 'essence' is used without carrying much seriously considered meaning. In each case, the weight is on the notion of a basic way of being. Spinoza, incidentally, would not say '*one* principal property' since he thinks that a single substance can have more than one attribute. So it is best to read d4 as speaking of an attribute as 'an essence' of substance rather than 'the essence'; the Latin leaves us free to choose.

3. Now let us pick up that complexity which I have passed over: in d4 Spinoza does not say that an attribute *is* an essence of a substance, but rather that it is what an intellect perceives 'as constituting an essence of a substance'. This is one of the most puzzling passages in the *Ethics*. It seems to define one of Spinoza's basic metaphysical concepts in epistemic terms, i.e., in terms of thought; that means that one of the attributes has a special place in the definition of 'attribute', which creates a lopsidedness in Spinoza's system which he does not mention, could not explain, and should not have tolerated.

There is another trouble with this definition. Does it entail that an attribute of x *is* an essence of x? Apparently not: we are told only that an attribute of x is *perceived as* an essence of x, which seems to leave room for misperception. But it is odd—to put it mildly—to define 'attribute' in terms of how an attribute seems to relate to its substance rather than of how it does. If on the other hand the definition says that an attribute is an essence of its substance, then we must prevent the notion of 'what an intellect perceives' from making trouble. So we shall have to take the definition to be saying that an attribute is what an infallible and omniscient intellect would perceive as an essence of a substance. This is like defining *triangle* as what an infallible and omniscient intellect would perceive as a closed plane figure bounded by three straight sides. Why should Spinoza go through such a circumlocution?

4. Some help in escaping from this labyrinth is afforded by Spinoza's explanation of 'attribute' in Letter 9, which predates the completed *Ethics* by many years: 'I understand the same by attribute [as I do by substance], except that it is called attribute with respect to the intellect, which attributes such and such a nature to substance.' (IV/46/3) The clue to understanding this is the fact that Spinoza often uses psychological language to make logical or conceptual points (see §14). I think that here he is saying that substance differs from attribute only by the difference between a substantival and an adjectival presentation of the very same content. If we look for how *that which is extended* (substance) differs from *extension* (attribute), we find that it consists only in the notion of *that which has . . .* extension or thought or whatever; and that, Spinoza thinks, adds nothing

9. *Principles* I. 53.

to the conceptual content of *extension*, but merely marks something about how the content is logically structured. As I did in §12.7, he is rejecting the view that a property bearer is an item whose nature qualifies it to have properties, in favour of the view that the notion of a property bearer, of a thing which . . . , is a bit of formal apparatus, something which organizes conceptual content without adding to it.

According to this view, there is an emptiness about the difference between substance and attribute. But not in the difference between thing and property generally, e.g., the difference between Mt. Robson and its colour. We can say plenty about *the thing which has* the colour—it is a mountain with a certain size and shape and consistency and so on. With any one of those properties we can again contrast the property with the thing which has it; and Spinoza, I believe, sees this as one step in a journey in which we have ever more of the properties behind us and thus have increasingly empty concepts of 'the thing which . . .' ahead of us. The journey at last brings us to the point where our 'thing which . . .' is just a region of space: I shall show in chapter 4 that Spinoza regards a mountain as basically a region of space with certain special features. Now, we can identify the region only by its size and shape and location; and to the question 'What *has* that size, shape and location?' no contentful answer can be given. The difference between size-shape-location (or for short, *extension*) and the thing which has those properties (that is, *extended substance*) is not one of content but just of logical form. Not that Spinoza would ever adduce an example such as a mountain, since he doesn't think that anything merely finite can be a real substance. For him the point would have to be illustrated through its only example, namely the whole universe, but the smaller item may serve to bring out what the point is.

That, I submit, is what is going on in Letter 9. Spinoza means: 'I mean by "attribute" the same as I mean by "substance" except for a difference in logical form: we use the concept of substance to think of what has the attribute, and we use the concept of attribute to think of what the substance has; but it is the same conceptual content in each case.'

5. But can that explain d4? I suppose the term 'intellect' in d4 echoes the line of thought of Letter 9; but that does not explain the phrase '*perceived as an essence*' in d4. Taking it that 'essence' is here being used as a loose pointer to the Cartesian notion of an irreducibly basic property, d4 seems to define an attribute as an item that is *perceived as basic*. My explanation of the Letter 9 passage goes no way towards explaining that. In §35.3 I shall offer an explanation; it involves many things that must be explained first. In the meantime let us proceed—as most commentators do—on the assumption that d4 has laid it down that an attribute actually is, in the Cartesian way, a basic property of its substance.

6. The line of thought expressed in the remark from Letter 9 is also at work in the *Ethics*, for here too we find Spinoza reminding us that the concept of a 'thing which . . .' is empty, and thus that there is only a difference of logical form and not of content between substance and attribute. Occasionally, perhaps even in Letter 9, he carries this too far by implying that attributes are substances. One can indeed argue from Spinozistic premises that attributes are substances: if substance x has attribute A, then A is the essence of x (d4); if A is the essence of x then x is conceived through A (2d2); a substance is conceived only through itself (d3); and so if substance x has attribute A, then x = A.[10] My biggest doubt about this arises from the assumption that 'essence' means the same in d4 as in 2d2. Anyway, something must be wrong with it: Spinoza clearly holds that there are at least two attributes and only one substance.

Yet Spinoza undoubtedly talks sometimes as though he did not distinguish substances from attributes: he uses the phrase 'substances, or what is the same thing (by d4), their attributes' (p4d), and makes certain attributions to 'God or all of God's attributes' (p19,20c2).

One or two scholars have tried to square this with there being only one substance and at least two attributes, by supposing that Spinoza was using a notion of 'relative identity' which Locke employed and which is currently in favour with a few philosophers. Armed with this, Spinoza is supposed to hold that thought and extension are substances and are attributes, but although they are the same substance they are distinct attributes. That makes the count come out right, but at what a price! There is no independent evidence of Spinoza's entertaining the implausible relative identity thesis; and the examples that have recently been adduced to support it— e.g., 'This is the same piece of glass that was on the table last week, but not the same vase'—cannot be brought to bear on Spinozist substances and attributes.

More promising is Curley's view that Spinoza 'identifies substance . . . with the totality of its attributes',[11] which seems to be confirmed by the definition of 'God' as 'a substance consisting of an infinity of attributes' (d6). But we don't know just what Spinoza means by 'consisting'; and this interpretation is at best a stop-gap. Curley wants to do justice to the passages that treat attributes as thing-like (there is another of them in p14c2), while keeping the count of substances and attributes right; and so he supposes that for Spinoza a substance 'consists of' the numerous thing-like items which are its attributes. But the only sense we can attach to this involves treating the substance as an aggregate, a collection with members or a complex with parts; and Curley would not attribute to Spinoza any

10. Thus Charles Jarrett, 'The Logical Structure of Spinoza's *Ethics*', pp. 21–23.

11. Curley, *Spinoza's Metaphysics*, p. 16.

such view of substance as that. So what he is offering is not a complete interpretation: it uses some ordinary language, won't let us understand it in the ordinary way, yet does not provide an unordinary understanding either. I think it better to back off from Spinoza's use of the language of identity and of 'constituting' as between substance and attribute, taking these to be exaggerated expressions of his view that the difference between substance and attribute is formal rather than contentful, in the sense I have tried to explain.

Anyway, neither the relative identity thesis, nor Curley's view, still less the strange position that Gueroult wishes onto Spinoza,[12] provides any foundation for the line of thought I shall develop in chapter 6, purporting to solve a cluster of the stubbornest problems in Spinoza scholarship; whereas the required foundation is provided by my interpretation of Spinoza's treatments of substance/attribute. Any success the chapter 6 line of thought has will therefore indirectly support my interpretation. It is not only mine of course. It has been the usual view among Spinoza scholars, and only recently have a few been willing to take at face value Spinoza's apparent identifications of substance with attribute.

7. One of those apparent identifications occurs in p10s. This is an important passage where Spinoza says that just because two attributes are distinct basic ways of being, it does not follow that they are possessed by two substances, one each. Unfortunately, he puts this first in the language of identity between substance and attribute, saying that it does not follow 'that they *constitute* two substances'. Further on, the point is better expressed: Spinoza says it is all right to 'attribute' several attributes to one substance, and speaks of the attributes which a substance 'has'. Because this is his main statement of the biggest difference between his metaphysic and Descartes's, it is a pity that the waters should be muddied by the suggestion that substances are attributes. I still like the suggestion I once made,[13] that we get comfortable with 1p10s by translating *constituere* by something which does not imply identity. Latin dictionaries permit this by associating the verb with 'fix', 'define', 'determine' and—almost—'stake out'. Donagan proposed a rival way of pushing substance-attribute identity out of the scholium, namely, by taking 'constitute' as an ellipsis for 'constitute the essence of'.[14] That would do the job, with 'constitute' still implying iden-

12. Gueroult, vol. 1, see pp. 237–9. For a useful canvassing of the issue about substance-attribute identity, see Gram, 'Spinoza, Substance, and Predication'. Gram's own view seems to me nearer right than anything else in the literature.

13. J. Bennett, 'A Note on Descartes and Spinoza', *The Philosophical Review* vol. 74 (1965), pp. 379–380.

14. Alan Donagan, 'A Note on Spinoza, *Ethics* I.10', *ibid.*, vol. 75 (1966), pp. 380–2.

tity; for essences are properties, and so on this reading no identity would be asserted between the attribute and the substance itself. I find this puzzling, however. There is no *need* to suppose the passage to be elliptical, and Donagan offers no evidence that such an ellipsis is even *likely*, e.g., by adducing other indisputably shortcutting passages. However, the issue between us is about translation only, not doctrine. Take your pick.

The important gulf is the one separating Donagan and myself from Curley. His translation retains 'constitute', but he does not understand it elliptically. In line with his whole interpretation of this part of Spinoza's doctrine he thinks that 'constitute' is just right—that Spinoza does regard a substance as somehow made up of thing-like attributes—and that it is 'misleading' of Spinoza to suggest, further down, that 'attributes are properties of substance and distinct from it'. Notice that although the usual view implies that certain passages are misleading, so does Curley's unusual view. He would also have to say that when a friend of Spinoza's, in Letter 8, moves smoothly from 'constitute two substances' to phrases about how the *nature* of a substance is constituted and about attributes which a substance *has*, Spinoza ought to have corrected this misunderstanding in Letter 9. No such correction occurs. On the contrary, in Letter 9 Spinoza himself speaks of 'attributing' attributes to a substance. It is true that in that letter he also seems clearly to imply that a substance and an attribute are 'one and the same thing'. All in all, the textual situation on this matter is difficult, forcing us to take some passages more literally than others: the disagreement concerns which to give most literal weight to.

§17. *No shared attribute*

1. 1p5 says that there could not be two substances sharing an attribute, which will help in demonstrating that there could not be two substances at all (1p14). In this section I shall explain the arguments leading to the 'no shared attribute' thesis.

Notice that if any attribute is the substance which has it, it follows trivially that two substances cannot have an attribute in common. The fact that Spinoza argues elaborately for the latter conclusion is thus evidence that he does not hold that form of the thesis that attributes are substances. But it is not evidence against Curley's view that Spinoza takes each substance to be identical with the totality of its attributes; for it is not trivially obvious, and would therefore have to be argued, that a single attribute could not belong to two such totalities.

2. We start with p4, which says that two things must be made distinct from one another—must be made *two*—by a difference either in their attributes or in their states, i.e., either in what basic kinds they belong to or in some nonbasic qualitative way. That is Spinoza's version of the identity of indiscernibles. His official argument for it unfortunately involves the identity of substance with attribute. The most conservative, uncreative version of it that I can understand goes as follows: If there are two substances, what differentiates them must lie (i) sheerly in the substances themselves, or (ii) in their attributes, or (iii) in their states; but because substances are attributes, (*i*) *collapses into* (*ii*); and so really the only alternatives are that the substances are differentiated (ii) by their attributes or (iii) by their states. Q.e.d.

Accept that as it stands, if you will. I won't. I prefer to take it as an imperfectly controlled gesture towards a line of thought depending on the subtler position I attributed to Spinoza in §16.4—the view that there is no conceptual content in 'thing which is extended' except that of 'extension', and similarly for all other attributes. That makes it plausible to suppose that nothing could distinguish two things which had all their qualities in common. And so, given the three initial possibilities, *we knock out* (*i*) and are left with (ii) and (iii), as in Spinoza's argument.

3. The conclusion that two substances must differ in either their attributes or their states is a premiss in 1p5d, which runs as follows. Two distinct substances must be unalike in respect of either attributes or states; so 'if the states are put to one side' the difference must be in respect of an attribute; Q.e.d. What makes it all right to 'put the states to one side'? Spinoza says he can do this because 'a substance is prior in nature to its states'; but he does not say what he means by this or why it entitles him to put the states to one side. Here is Gueroult's suggestion about that:

If one tries to distinguish them solely through the differences in their respective states, one will not be able to do it because, since substances are prior to their states (1p1), we must abstract from the latter in order to conceive the former, in themselves, according to their true nature [*selon leur vérité*].[15]

That sounds good, and stays close to the text, but what does it mean? I find this, like most of Gueroult's philosophical offerings, to be too vague and soft to help me in my thinking about Spinoza. To get something with hard edges to it, we must dig deeper and speculate about what Spinoza is up to.

I cannot rescue this argument of Spinoza's. The best I can do for it involves one dubious move and one invalid one. Still, I suspect that this reconstruction of the argument is right. Here is how it runs.

The proposition that 'A substance is prior in nature to its states' (p1) has been derived from the equation of 'substance' with 'what is in itself and conceived through itself' (d3) and of 'state' with 'what is in something else through which it is conceived' (d5). If we take this to entail that any state of a substance is accidental to it, i.e., that a substance could have lacked any of its actual states, then we get the following argument. Distinct substances

15. Gueroult, vol. 1, p. 118.

must be unalike in respect of some properties which they cannot lose; for if they were unalike only in respect of their accidental properties they could become perfectly alike, and so, by the identity of indiscernibles, become identical. It is obviously intolerable to suppose that two substances could have been—or could become—one. So between any two substances there must be an unalikeness in respect of nonaccidental features, i.e., of attributes.

As will be seen in chapter 5, it is not clear that Spinoza allows that things have accidental properties, although it is also not clear that he does not. I think he does in some places, and that 1p5d must be one of them. If it is not, then I am wrong about why we are invited to 'put the states to one side', which leaves me with no idea at all of how the argument is supposed to work.

4. One dubious move in p5d is the inference that a substance's states are accidental to it. In this context 'state' has to cover everything not covered by 'attribute', i.e., everything which is not basic in the sense explained in §16. But I cannot see that Spinoza has any strong reason for supposing that nothing is essential to a substance, i.e., unlosable by it, except its most basic properties. No doubt they are all essential to it: Spinoza can reasonably assume that an extended thing could not become unextended, for instance; but the assumption that *only* they are essential, i.e., nonaccidental, needs defending. If we try the assumption out on such items as a fundamental physical particle, it clearly fails: it may be essential to such a particle that it has mass M, yet this is not a basic property of it, since 'having mass M' entails but is not entailed by 'being physical'. Spinoza would reject the example, no doubt, though it is hard to decide whether he is entitled to at this stage in the *Ethics*. When I consider this matter in terms of examples he would accept—e.g., thinking about which properties of the whole of space are essential to it, and which accidental—I fall into confusion. Let us move on.

There is a flatly invalid move in the argument I have attributed to Spinoza in p5d, namely, the move from 'x and y are unalike only in respect of their accidental properties' to 'x and y could become exactly alike'. From the premiss that (Fx and possibly Fy) it does not follow that possibly (Fx and Fy). That move is an instance of the notorious modal fallacy of inferring from (P and possibly Q) that possibly (P and Q): to see the invalidity, take the case where Q is not-P.[16]

This too can be illustrated through physical particles. Spatio-temporal location is an accidental feature of a particle, yet two particles may be distinguished by that alone. If x has location L, it could have been the case

---

16. This modal mistake of Spinoza's is endorsed in Charlton's otherwise useful 'Spinoza's Monism' at pp. 514f.

that y had L but then x would not have had L. Again, Spinoza would reject the example; but that does not alter the fact that the argument is fallacious.

5. Even if I have been wrong about p5d—indeed, even if Spinoza's argument so far is perfectly sound—it cannot yield more than the conclusion that two substances could not have all their attributes in common. But Spinoza concludes that they could not have any attribute in common; and one wonders how he could overlook such a gap in his argument.

Not until p9 does he allude to the possibility of a substance's having several attributes. Until then he is thinking in terms of the concept of a one-attribute substance, a concept which explicitly appears in p8d. If one-attribute substances alone were in question, that would close the gap in p5d: analogously, if I don't share all my fathers with you then I share no fathers with you. But are we to suppose that Spinoza intended his argument in that way, and simply forgot to review it in the light of his later thesis that substances can have more than one attribute? That is not credible, given how the pivotal p14d depends on combining 'There is a substance which has every attribute' with (p5) 'Two substances cannot share any attribute'. Surely in *this* context Spinoza could not just forget that p5d assumed that no substance has more than one attribute!

Wallace Matson has pointed out to me that the argument could be rescued with help from a certain reading of 1p2: 'Two substances which have different attributes have nothing in common with one another.' I think that that means 'Two substances which have *no* attributes in common have nothing in common'; but if instead it means 'Two substances which differ in respect of *any* attribute have nothing in common' then it implies that there cannot be two substances which share some but not all of their attributes; and that would nicely plug the gap I have pointed out in 1p5d.

There may be a Spinozistic way of closing the gap. For example, Spinoza may be able to argue that if x had only A_1 while y had both A_1 and A_2, the demand of his explanatory rationalism to know why x did not have A_2 as well could not be satisfied.

Explanatory rationalism is certainly at work in another argument Spinoza gives for p5, at the end of p8s2. In it Spinoza says that if there were n substances with attribute A, for some value of $n > 1$, something would have to explain that fact; and Spinoza thinks he has shown that the explanation must come from A itself, i.e., from what he here calls the 'definition' which lays down what A is. But he has maintained earlier, plausibly, that 'no definition expresses any certain number of individuals, since it expresses nothing other than the nature of the thing defined'. And so, he concludes, if there were (say) two substances each having attribute A, there could be no explanation of why there were precisely two; and that would be intolerable from the standpoint of explanatory rationalism. We can evade the force of this argument by accepting that there are brute facts. We can also wonder why, if the argument is sound for n > 1, it is not also sound for n = 1. I guess that Spinoza would say that if (i) there must be at least one thing with A, and (ii) nothing could explain there being more than one, those two facts *do* explain why there is exactly one. This is suspect, to put it mildly. Not that it matters much. Spinoza's chief use of p5 is in an argument which has plenty of other things wrong with it. It is 1p14d, to which I now turn.

§18. *Spinoza's monism: the official argument*

1. When Spinoza is called a monist, either of two things might be meant. One is a comparison with Descartes: faced with the question 'How many substances does it take to instantiate two attributes?', Descartes answers 'Two' and Spinoza answers 'One.' From now on, however, I shall use 'monism' to refer not to that but rather to Spinoza's answer to the question 'How many substances are there?', to which he says 'One' and Descartes says 'Indefinitely many'. My topic is a monism of Spinoza's which does not contrast with any dualism I know of.

In this section, using materials already assembled, I shall expound Spinoza's official argument for his monism. It is a poor thing, and I shall be glad to get to his better reasons for monism in chapter 4. But the official argument must be studied, because its component parts can affect our understanding of the *Ethics* as a whole.

The argument in question is p14d. Its bare outline is easily grasped:

> There must be a substance with every possible attribute;
> There cannot be two substances with an attribute
> in common;
> ∴ There cannot be more than one substance.

Assuming that there cannot be a substance with no attributes, the conclusion follows. And I have finished with the 'no shared attribute' thesis which is the second premiss. What remains to be understood is Spinoza's acceptance of the first premiss.

2. His official case for it rests on p7,11 which I shall expound jointly. Together they make up a version of the so-called 'ontological argument' for God's existence. Briefly, the argument takes it to be a necessary truth—a matter of the definition or concept of God—that God has every property in some domain of properties of which existence is one of the members: the domain may be perfections, or kinds of reality, or whatever. From this it is inferred that necessarily God has existence, i.e., that necessarily God exists.

It is widely agreed now that the existence of a concrete object—something other than an inhabitant of the third realm—never follows from a definition or from a description of a concept. In particular, you cannot infer the existence of something from the premiss that existence belongs to its essence or its definition. To say that F is of the essence of x is to say that x could not have existed without having F, which means that Fx in every world where x exists.[17] Now let F be existence, and let x be you: you could not have existed without having existence, i.e., you exist in every possible world where you exist! The moral is that if we allow existence as a property at all then it belongs to the essence of everything. That is one core idea in Kant's criticism of the ontological argument.

That does not show that there is no necessarily existing concrete object. The proposition that a certain concrete object exists at every possible world, its nonexistence being absolutely impossible, is not self-contradictory or nonsensical. It must not be derived from an error about the powers of definitions, or about existence belonging to the thing's essence; but that doesn't mean that it is not true. Plantinga thinks that one such proposition is true, namely, that there must be a maximally excellent being. Although he does not regard this as belonging to 'the stock of propositions accepted by nearly every sane man', he denies that there is anything 'improper, unreasonable, irrational' about accepting it and thus regarding as sound a very short argument to the existence of a maximally excellent being.[18] He supports this by some general remarks in defence of allowing unsupported yet controversial beliefs into philosophy, adducing Leibniz's Law as an example.

I agree with van Inwagen that those general remarks are unconvincing,[19] but I would go further and argue positively that it is unreasonable to believe that there must be a maximally excellent being. Plantinga notes that if his thesis is possible then it is true. (In the most widely used systems of modal logic, any proposition of the form 'Necessarily P' is true if it is possible.) And this contributes to his sense of entitlement to believe it. Why, after all, should he give up his view that it *could* be true that there must be a maximally excellent being? Leibniz made a similar point about the premiss which he added to Descartes's ontological argument, namely, that there could be a being which fits Descartes's definition: 'One is entitled to presume the possibility of any Being . . . until someone proves the contrary.'[20]

17. Here and elsewhere I use 'F', etc., to stand for names of properties ('redness') and for predicates ('is red'). This makes for brevity and seems to do no harm.

18. Alvin Plantinga, *The Nature of Necessity* (Oxford, 1974), pp. 219f.

19. Peter van Inwagen, 'Ontological Arguments', *Noûs* vol. 4 (1977), pp. 375–95.

20. *New Essays*, p. 438.

(3) THE ONE SUBSTANCE DOCTRINE

That principle about the onus of proof looks right. But properly used it counts against Leibniz and Plantinga, not for them. Someone who says it is possible that there must be an F being is basically asserting that there must be an F being, and is thus asserting an infinity of denials of possibility: of every world description which excludes the existence of an F being, he is saying that it is impossible for there to be such a world as that. So if F is maximal excellence, he will say that there could not possibly be a world in which the only concrete objects were time and space and portions of matter. I reply that I am entitled to presume the possibility of such a world until someone proves the contrary, and I add that it is not reasonable to believe in the impossibility of such a world without having positive reasons for doing so.

In that argument I have assumed that the proper topic of debate is 'There must be an F'. Admittedly, that is equivalent to 'It could be that there must be an F', which seems to fall under Leibniz's principle that we are entitled to presume anything to be possible if there is no evidence that it is not. I hold, however, that that principle is correct only in application to possibilities that do not themselves have modal concepts nested within them. It applies therefore to 'Possibly there is only space, time and matter', but not to 'Possibly there is something divine at every possible world'. I confess to having no argument for my view about the scope of Leibniz's principle.

3. Still, even if no ontological argument can succeed, there are things to be learned from Spinoza's in particular.

His form of it is peculiar. Like most ontological arguments, it starts from a definition, but it is unlike any other in *how* it gets 'existent' into the definiens. Some ontological arguers such as Descartes have in effect defined 'God' as

> Being which is . . . and existent and . . . ,

and others such as Norman Malcolm have defined it as

> Being which is . . . and necessarily existent and . . . .

Spinoza instead defines it as

> Substance which is . . . ,

and takes this to be sufficient for a proof of God's existence, because he holds that 'substance' should in effect be defined as

> Item which is . . . and necessarily existent and . . . .

Let us see why Spinoza holds that necessary existence is part of the very concept of substance.

His reason stems from his view that any genuine substance must be causally self-contained, not owing its existence to anything else (see §15.6). Add to this the explanatory rationalist idea that everything has some cause—for otherwise there would be something whose existence could not be explained—and out rolls the conclusion that a substance must be the cause of its own existence. The idea that x might cause x's existence is hard to square with any notion of causation that we would find natural today: how could anything *push* itself into existence? No doubt a thing might *keep* itself in existence, but that would not explain why it existed in the first place. David Lewis has pointed out that if there were temporally backward running causal influences, then x might be self-causing by being a cause of a later y which causes the earlier x. But even this does not yield the sort of self-causation Spinoza needs—not merely because he wants it for substances which are not in the required way temporal, but also because it does not meet the needs of explanatory rationalism. As Lewis says: 'Why did the whole affair happen? There is simply no answer. The parts of the loop are explicable, the whole of it is not.'[21]

4. For the causal rationalist, however, the question 'Could x cause its own existence?' is the question 'Could x logically necessitate its own existence?' And a logically self-necessitating thing would presumably be one whose nature or essence had to be instantiated. If there were such a thing, the question 'Why does it exist?' could be fully answered, raising no further why question, without looking beyond the thing itself—its own nature would contain all the materials for the answer. Thus Spinoza in p8s2, which is expanded in p11d2 (the second demonstration of p11).

That is how he argues that a substance must exist necessarily. In d1 he offers as a definition of 'cause of itself' something that is really a substantive claim—namely, that if we are to make sense of the concept of self-causedness we must take it to be the concept of 'having a nature which must be instantiated'. This is then used in p7d: a substance cannot be caused by anything else (and must be caused by something), so it must be the cause of itself, which has to mean that its nature is necessarily instantiated.

I do not see any way of making *better* sense of 'cause of itself' than by equating it with 'necessarily existing'; but like most philosophers today I deny that anything is 'cause of itself' in this sense, i.e., that there are any necessarily existing nonabstract objects. In saying this I implicitly reject explanatory rationalism: if no nonabstract objects exist necessarily, then the whole of reality does not exist necessarily, in which case there is no answer to the question why it exists. Still, given that Spinoza was an explan-

---

21. David Lewis, 'The Paradoxes of Time Travel', *American Philosophical Quarterly* vol. 13 (1976), pp. 145–52, at p. 149.

atory rationalist he needed necessarily existent objects, and his causal rationalism made the phrase 'cause of itself' a perfect label for something with a necessarily instantiated nature.

Incidentally, Spinoza's equation of self-causation with necessary existence is not a mere shift from causal to logical. He takes himself still to be using the concept of cause, as is shown by his linking of necessary existence with the paradigmatically causal notion of *power*. There is an instance of this in p34, and a vivid one in p11d3. It is not a good argument, but its opening remark, 'To be able not to exist is lack of power' shows that Spinoza sees a thing's having a nature which must be instantiated as its being *powerful* enough to cause its own existence.

5. Spinoza defines 'cause of itself' as 'that whose essence involves existence, or that whose nature cannot be conceived except as existing' (d1). Two defects in that definition should be mentioned in passing.

One is the use of the vacuous phrase 'essence [which] involves existence'. This phrase is passed down from d1 to p7d and thence to p11d which is Spinoza's real ontological argument; and it is also echoed in a7, which is the falsehood that the essences of contingent things do not involve existence. But none of this matters greatly. Spinoza is really operating with the notion of a thing whose nature must be instantiated; the fact that phrases about a thing 'whose essence involves existence' do not properly express that notion is a mere nuisance in coping with the text.

There is another minor nuisance, which starts in d1's clause 'that whose nature cannot be conceived except as *existing*', when Spinoza must surely mean 'that whose nature cannot be conceived except as *instantiated*'. The same mishap occurs in p7 and elsewhere.

This illustrates a general tendency in Spinoza to neglect the difference between natures and the things that have them. I suppose his rationalism is ultimately responsible for it: to the extent that a philosopher tries to handle everything in terms of strictly logical relations, to that extent he will confine himself to relations amongst universal items at the expense of particulars. Spinoza's tendency in that direction may help to explain his sometimes identifying attributes with the substances that have them. That tendency is certainly at work in an astonishing episode in the moral philosophy which I shall expound in §69: assuming that if something is good or bad for *me* that is because of how it relates to *my nature*, Spinoza infers that whatever is good or bad for me must be good or bad for people who resemble me, i.e., who share my nature. From this premiss he derives a morality of community of interest.

6. Back now to the main thread. God is by definition a substance and therefore—for reasons I have expounded—God necessarily exists. But it is also built into the definition of 'God' that God has every attribute. Conjoin that with the 'no shared attribute' thesis, and you reach the conclusion that God is the only substance.

A natural and proper first reaction to this argument is to gasp at its impudence. If one can thus prove the necessary existence of an all-attribute substance, why can one not prove the existence of an F for *any* consistent value of F—attribute or state—just by defining some term as meaning 'Substance which is F'? This is the familiar 'floodgates' objection to every form of the ontological argument: it was raised against Descartes[22] and against Spinoza (Letter 3 at IV/10/12). They answer it in much the same way, saying that the challenged definition does not present a 'fiction' or mere conceptual contrivance, but rather a 'clear and distinct conception' (Spinoza at 13/10), or a 'true and immutable essence' (Descartes), something given rather than invented.

What is the difference? The only answer I can get from Spinoza is this: 'A fictitious being is nothing but two terms connected by a sheer act of will, without guidance from reason.' (*Metaphysical Thoughts* at I/236/12) But that cannot affect validity. The validity of an argument depends on what the relevant conceptual structures are, not on the psychological methods used to construct them. So even if Spinoza's way of defining 'God' is unarbitrary, that does not close the gates against absurd existence proofs. Still, the definition *is* unarbitrary, and that matters. I now explain why.

§19. *Are there more than two attributes?*

1. In expounding Spinoza's argument for monism (p14d), I gave it the premiss that God has every possible attribute. But Spinoza actually says that God has 'infinite attributes'. We would not ordinarily interpret that as entailing that God has all the attributes: the infinite set of numbers > 9 does not contain all the numbers. Yet p14d collapses unless it has the premiss that there is no attribute that God lacks.

This is not a blunder on Spinoza's part, but a reflection of what he means by 'infinite': he often takes infinity to imply totality, and does this so immediately and openly as to make it a semantic fact rather than a logical mistake. For example, p16 contains the phrase 'infinite things . . . (i.e. all things which can fall under an infinite intellect)', which I take to mean about the same as 'all logically possible things'. And in p17s at 62/16 we again find 'infinite things . . . , that is to say, all things'. There is also evidence in Spinoza's explanation of his definition of 'God' (d6), where he equates 'infinite attributes' with 'everything which expresses an essence and involves no negation'. Not a pellucid phrase, but it does clearly in-

22. First Objections to the Meditations, in Alquié, vol. 2, p. 517. Descartes's reply is on p. 535.

volve a universal quantifier (*quicquid*, everything which), and so confirms that Spinoza takes 'infinite' to entail 'all'. Again, when he says 'By a part of a substance nothing can be understood except a finite substance' (p13cs) he is saying that incompleteness entails finiteness, and so by contraposition infinity entails totality. And then there is 2p3d, which includes, in scattered form, this: ' . . . can think infinite things, or (what is the same) can form the idea of all things'.[23]

Three centuries ago there were no well understood obstacles to using 'infinite' in that way. Spinoza would probably deny that there are infinitely many numbers > 9, because he thought (i) that there are more numbers > 7 than there are > 9 (see Letter 81); and (ii) that there cannot be an infinite number greater than another (see p15s at 57/36). Mathematical developments in the nineteenth century, spearheaded by Cantor, imply that (i) is false, and that there are exactly as many numbers > 9 as there are > 7; there is a sound mathematical theory which includes this theorem, whereas Spinoza and his contemporaries had no rival theory but just muddles and puzzles. The particular muddle I have pointed to might explain why Spinoza thought that infinity involves totality: if it didn't— he may have held—an infinity could be surpassed, which is absurd. Actually, it is not absurd, but the reasons for that lie far off my present path.

Nobody doubts that Spinoza takes infinity to entail totality. I now offer a second thesis which, though not original to me, is more controversial.

2. It is that Spinoza used 'infinite' as a virtual synonym for 'all': he took 'God has infinite attributes' not merely to entail 'God has all attributes' but to be equivalent to it. Each of the cited passages linking infinity with totality, taken literally, implies an equivalence; and often, starting as early as d2, Spinoza shows that for him the concept of the infinite is the concept of the unlimited, the not-cut-short, what 'involves no negation' (d6 explanation; see also p8s1). Although this is a vague idea (Spinoza's thoughts in this area are nothing if not vague), it points to a concept of infinity that is just an elevated version of the concept of totality, the whole, nothing omitted.

If that is right, then when Spinoza says that God has infinite attributes, he means only that God exists in every possible basic way. This does not entail that God exists other than as extended and as thinking, i.e., that there are more than two attributes.

It is on that reading of 'infinite attributes' that Spinoza's definition of 'God' is least arbitrary, because best supported by the theological doctrine which he was trying to capture. There was a strong tradition making God the *ens realissimum*, the entity with the most possible reality, and Spinoza hints that he has that in mind when he pauses to say in 1p9—which is

23. For further evidence, see Kline, 'On the Infinity of Spinoza's Attributes'.

not mentioned anywhere in the *Ethics*—that the more real a thing is the more attributes it has. This lets us go from a traditional account of God—without appeal to Spinoza's d6—to the conclusion that God has every attribute, that is, exists in every basic way in which something can exist. But nothing is implied about how many basic ways there are. The concept of the *ens realissimum* involves totality or supremacy, but not cardinality.

Spinoza would never build a concept into his edifice, or at least not one carrying as much weight as d6 does, merely because it picks up something in the tradition.[24] He has a philosophical reason for holding that every basic way of being must be instantiated by the actual world; the core of it is in the second half of p11d2, and it goes as follows. Suppose that attribute A is not instantiated, and then ask: Why isn't it? No explanation could come from attributes which the universe does have, since explanatory flow between attributes is ruled out—that is what makes them basic. And if the explanation lay within A itself, that would mean that A on its own was the sufficient reason why nothing instantiates A; but that could only mean that A is inherently impossible, and therefore is not an attribute after all, since an attribute is a basic way things *could* be.

So there are two strong pressures on Spinoza, one traditional and one theoretical, to say that every attribute is instantiated.[25] There are none on him to say that more than two attributes are instantiated, and there is nothing structural—no twists of argument or nuances of doctrine—anywhere in the *Ethics* that reflect the view that there are other attributes. Add those facts to the textual evidence that Spinoza equates 'infinite' with 'all (possible)', and you get a case for interpreting the *Ethics* as not containing the doctrine that there are more than two attributes.

3. I do not say that Spinoza thought there were only two attributes. He refers to 'the attribute of extension, or the attribute of thought, or any other attribute' (2p7s at 90/14)—a phrase which could hardly be used by someone who was sure there are only two. Also, in Letters 63 and 65, in which he is challenged to explain why if there are more attributes we know nothing about them, his answers take the question seriously, conceding that he has something to explain. Still, in his two responses, only one clause actually entails that there are other attributes; discovering it is left as a quite difficult exercise for the reader. Apart from that one clause,

24. The tradition has generally denied that God is extended, whereas Spinoza's version affirms this. But I shall show in chapter 4 that that is a disagreement about extension rather than about God.

25. Not to say that one substance instantiates them all, however. That must await the establishment of substance monism.

the letters hint, suggest and presuppose that there are more than two attributes but stop short of saying that there are.

Spinoza's attempt to explain our ignorance of a third attribute is profoundly unsatisfactory. The problem is not to find something to say, but to find something consistent with the metaphysics and epistemology presented in the *Ethics*. Without that constraint he could fall back on the sort of thing we find in the suspect *Short Treatise* at I/17/45 which says that we are on the line with the other attributes but have a bad connection: 'It is the infinite attributes themselves which tell us that they are, without however telling us what they are.' But the mature Spinoza, his *Ethics* virtually completed, cannot say things like that. He now has a basic metaphysic which implies that if there is a third attribute A_3, then my mind has a certain relation R to an item falling under A_3; and his epistemology implies that my knowledge of the extended world is fully explained by the fact that my mind has R to a certain extended thing, namely my body. Put those together and you reach the conclusion that if A_3 exists I know something about it. In the two late letters he tries to avoid this conclusion by a move which is so abrupt, ad hoc, and unexplained that we cannot even be sure whether it is a retraction of the metaphysics or of the epistemology. I shall not go into the details. That Letters 64 and 66 just won't do will be clear to anyone who carefully reads Parts 1 and 2 of the *Ethics* or my chapters 3–8. Incidentally, it was in a note on these letters that Wolf first suggested that Spinoza's use of 'infinite attributes' does not commit him to there being more than two.

4. The situation regarding the proposition that there are more than two attributes is this: Spinoza was under no pressure to assert it, nothing in the *Ethics* unquestionably means it, none of the work's structures reflects it, and if it were added to the *Ethics* and fully developed it would create an impossible problem for Spinoza's epistemology.

Those are four reasons for reading the *Ethics* as consistent with attribute dualism. Should we read it as entailing dualism? The reasons do not work as well in support of that, though the fourth is still powerful: the difficulty of explaining our ignorance of further attributes is a positive reason for denying that there are any. Spinoza could have argued for dualism like this: 'The universe must exist in every possible basic way, of which the only two we know about are thought and extension. My views about what we are, and about what knowledge is, make it seem impossible that there should be attributes which we do not know. So probably thought and extension are the only possible basic ways of being, though I cannot see why this should be so and cannot make it look self-evident.' The modesty and caution of that were foreign to Spinoza's temperament, however. He said nothing like it, and probably thought nothing like it.

I have no idea what Spinoza really thought about how many attributes there are. My central claim is not about his mind but about the text. It is that if he took 'infinite attributes' to imply 'more than two attributes', then that extra implication is negligible because in the *Ethics* it is idle.

4
Extended Substance

§20. *The need for partless substances*

1. Spinoza's official argument for substance monism, to which I have devoted chapter 3, is not cogent. If its premiss that something has all possible attributes is to be given a decent foundation, it will have to come neither from the theological tradition nor from definitions of 'God' and 'substance' but rather from a naked appeal to explanatory rationalism: there could be no explanation for any attribute's not being instantiated. And not even that will rescue the claim that the attributes are instantiated by a single substance. We must also invoke explanatory rationalism to cover the chasm between 'Two substances could not share all their attributes' and 'Two substances could not share any attribute'; and Spinoza has not even argued well for the former of these, because he has not shown that two substances could not be differentiated merely by their accidental states, nor has he shown that whatever is not an attribute is accidental.

If there were no more to be said for monism than that, it would hardly merit our close attention. But I doubt if p14d represents either Spinoza's route to monism or his reason for staying with it. In any case, he has better grounds for holding that there is only one substance. They can be dug out of the *Ethics*, but Spinoza does not parade them as an argument, presumably because he could not see how to shape them into demonstrative form.

The better reasons support first the thesis that there is only one extended substance and then the further conjecture that the extended substance is also thinking. In crediting Spinoza with this line of thought I am implying that his metaphysical thinking was grounded in the physical world, and there is plenty of evidence that it was. When I come to his treatment of the mind, in chapters 6 and 7, it will be abundantly evident that for him the body calls the tune.

Objection: 'Even if there is only one extended substance and it is thinking, that doesn't imply monism; for there might be other thinking substances which were not extended.' Well, in chapter 6 we shall see that Spinoza has a case for holding that the thesis 'The one extended substance is thinking' covers every mentalistic item which is in any way related to anything physical. So if there is a gap in his argument, it concerns thinking substances which are not related at all to the physical—e.g., minds which are disembodied and not physically manifested, and so on. I suppose that Spinoza would regard the impossibility of a disembodied mind as being too deep and too certain to be demonstrable.

2. To grasp his best reason for holding that there is only one extended substance (my aim in this chapter), we must first understand what leads to and what follows from his view that substances cannot have parts (my aim in this section).

No substance 'can be divided', Spinoza says in p12, taking this to mean that no substance 'consists of parts' (p15s at 57/25). Although p12 is not used in later demonstrations, it is mentioned three times in p15s, which is Spinoza's fullest display of his metaphysic of the extended world. In p12d he argues through a dilemma: a substance could not have parts which were substances, or parts which were not substances; and so it could not have parts. The second half of this is plain sailing. If a substance were divisible into nonsubstances, Spinoza thinks, such a division would be an annihilation, a driving right out of existence: at the start there would be an ultimate subject of predication, while at the end there would be none. And that is ruled out by 1p7 which won't let any substance be destructible.

What about a substance having parts which are substances? Spinoza reasonably does not count that as an outright annihilation, and therefore thinks that it needs additional argument. The argument in question is confusing. It takes the hypothesis that substance x is divisible into substance y and substance z, invokes p5,7,8 in some general scene-setting, and then offers three distinct reasons why the hypothesis leads to absurdity and so could not be true. The first of these is puzzling; the second relies on a version of the 'no shared attribute' thesis; the third is good. It says in effect that since x is a substance it can 'both be and be conceived' without reference to anything else, but nothing could both be and be conceived without reference to its substantial parts. That is, substances must be conceptually independent of everything else, whereas a thing depends upon its parts. As Spinoza once said: 'The parts which compose a thing are prior, in nature at least, to the thing they compose' (*Metaphysical Thoughts* at I/258/16)

This is a version of the argument reported from Leibniz in §15.3. If x has parts which are substances, then a complete account of reality need not make substantival reference to x: it can instead refer to its parts, and report the relations among them by virtue of which they make up x. It is clearer in Leibniz than in Spinoza, but probably Spinoza was the pioneer and Leibniz the follower.

3. There is more to the same effect in p13,c,s, none of which needs separate discussion. Don't be misled by a curious twist at the end of p15s, where Spinoza says that even if God—the whole extended world—were divisible, it still could not be pulled apart by outside forces, because there are no forces external to the whole of reality: 'So it cannot be said that extended substance is unworthy of the divine nature, even if it is supposed to be divisible.' Spinoza is not lowering the standards for what counts as a substance. His point is that someone who thinks it beneath God's dignity to be extended must be thinking of extended items as vulnerable to dismantling attack from the outside; and Spinoza is saying that *that* worry is groundless because nothing is outside God. It is also groundless, he thinks, because an infinite extended substance is not divisible; but he doesn't need that premiss in order to deal with this little theological trouble.

4. Now Spinoza, like all his contemporaries, thought that every ordinary physical object has parts—not merely filling a region which has subregions, but more strongly being splittable. When Spinoza speaks of 'simplest bodies', in the material inserted between 2p13 and 14, he does not mean atoms, unsplittable bodies, but merely ones which are qualitatively homogeneous throughout. I cannot cite a text where Spinoza asserts the splittability of all physical things, but Descartes does so in his *Principles* II.50, and the view was widely held in the seventeenth century, as part of the profound assumption that the micro-world differs from the macro-world only in size, never in the laws that apply. The assumption was wrong, as Broad remarked:

Until lately physical science enjoyed an extraordinary bit of luck. Experimenting with samples of matter which are enormously complex, it found certain laws governing their effects on each other in the way of starting, modifying and stopping each other's motions. It boldly assumed that these laws would apply also to the imperceptible components of these perceptible substances. To a most amazing extent this draft on the unknown was honoured by Nature. But we have now exhausted our overdraft.[1]

One of the things about which Nature has warned us is the possibility of physical items that occupy space and cannot be split (splitting them would be not merely technically impossible but downright miraculous). Although it is not agreed just what the ultimate particles are from which the physical world is made, it is widely agreed that there are such particles—'quarks'—and that the hypothesis of infinite splittability is false.

5. Does that spell trouble for Spinoza? Ought he to concede that quarks, whatever they may turn out to be, are extended substances, and that he was just wrong to think that there is only one extended substance? Of course the 'no shared attribute' thesis (1p5) won't let quarks be substances, but 1p5d has at least one serious gap in it, and it happens to be relevant to quarks (see §17.4).

---

1. C. D. Broad, 'The Nature of a Continuant', in H. Feigl and W. Sellars (eds.), *Readings in Philosophical Analysis* (New York, 1949), pp. 472–481, at p. 476, quoted with omissions.

(4) EXTENDED SUBSTANCE

Perhaps Spinoza would raise his price and say that a genuine substance must be something that cannot be created or annihilated *or acted on in any way at all*. But I can think of no reason he could give for that, once the 'no shared attribute' thesis was dropped.

Could Spinoza instead resort to the claim that a genuine substance must be not merely unsplittable but logically or conceptually indivisible? On the face of it, that would be intolerably highhanded. It is one thing for Leibniz to imply that a diamond is on a par with a herd of sheep, the difference in how tightly they are bound being of no metaphysical significance (see §15.3 above); it would be an altogether different thing for him or Spinoza to say the same about an item that was causally incapable of being split, contending that the difference between 'It is hard for x's parts to be dispersed' and 'It is not causally possible for x's parts to be dispersed' is of no importance in metaphysics. But it is hard to press that point against Spinoza, because it assumes what he rejects, namely, that something might have parts—i.e., completely fill a region of space having subregions—and yet be causally impossible to split. Such a thing would be conceptually divisible without being causally divisible, and that infringes Spinoza's causal rationalism. I think he would say: 'If your quarks are just little lumps—tiny compact quantities of matter—then there cannot be good scientific reasons for declaring them to be unsplittable. You may have failed to split them and despair of succeeding; you may even call your despair an induction to the conclusion that they cannot be split; but I refuse to found a metaphysic on something as flimsy as that.' That is not unreasonable. There is more to it, anyway, than a mere naked appeal to causal rationalism; and it would deserve our sympathy if quarks were indeed taken to be 'quantities of matter', to be thought of as like pebbles, only smaller. That *was* the view taken about chemical atoms, and they *did* turn out to be splittable.

Contemporary physics, however, depicts fundamental particles differently. They are thought of not as little lumps of matter, but rather as spheres of influence; and their unsplittability is not remotely like the end point on a line running through waterdrops, marshmallows, billiard balls, diamonds and . . . fundamental particles, quarks. This may make quarks unsplittable in a manner which satisfies the strongest demand that Spinoza could reasonably make. But it deprives them of substantial status in a different way, by making them adjectival on regions of space: the existence of a quark in a given region, according to this way of looking at things, is the region's having certain qualities. The kind of fundamental particle now contemplated by physicists, therefore, does not seriously challenge Spinoza's view that no finite extended thing is a substance. In fact, the contemporary view in physics is a *version* of Spinoza's own position, as I shall explain in §22.6.

First, something else must be attended to. If Spinoza is going to deny the title 'substance' to lumps of matter because they are all divisible, how can he defend the thesis—which I attribute to him—that the whole of space, or the entire extended realm, is a substance?

§21.   *Why space has no parts*

1. In p15s a lot is said to the effect that the extended world cannot have parts since it is a substance; but why not use p12 to run the argument contrapositively, saying that since the extended world manifestly does have parts, it is not a substance? If the scholium addresses itself to that, it is in this remark:

It is no less absurd to assert that corporeal substance is composed of bodies, or parts, than to assert that a body is composed of surfaces, the surfaces of lines, and the lines, finally, of points. (p15s at 59/6)

If Spinoza is merely comparing *degrees* of absurdity, then this is rhetoric, not argument. Perhaps he is comparing *kinds* of absurdity, saying that the first alleged absurdity is significantly like the other three. Like them in what way, though? If the claim is just that each consists in an attempt to make certain items add up to something they cannot add up to, then there is still no helpful argument here. But perhaps we are supposed to see that the first view is absurd by comparing it with the other three; that would be a definite argument, and I now show that it is a wrong one. It is absurd to suppose that a line is composed of points because:

> Each point has zero length, so every accumulation of points has zero length, so no accumulation of points can be a line.

But if we try mechanically to derive from this a reason why the extended world cannot be composed of bodies, we get:

> Each body has zero extent, so every accumulation of bodies has zero extent, so no accumulation of bodies can be the extended world.

But that is no use, because its premiss is false. The only other analogue to the point-line argument which I can find reflects Spinoza's repeated stress on the infinite extent of the world. It is this:

> Each body has finite extent, so every accumulation of bodies has finite extent, so no accumulation of bodies can be the extended world.

This has a true premiss, but now the first step is invalid: from the fact that each body is only finitely extended, it follows only that every *finite* accumulation of bodies has finite extent. Spinoza may have objections to

85

A) but he denies title 'substance' not (empirically) determinable divisibility but lack of being self-caused.

B) substance is not the whole of space or the whole extended realm the notion of an infinite accumulation; but I can't find them, and if they exist I am sure they are not well grounded.

2. In fact, Spinoza could do better than that. We should be stressing the fact that the item whose substantiality he is defending is space. Once it is clear that he is talking not about the totality of things in space, nor about space together with that totality, but just about *space*, his view that the item in question does not have parts becomes much easier to understand and even to accept. Of course he does regard space as infinitely extended, but that is not the crux of his view that it is indivisible.

If space does have parts, they must be regions of space; but regions don't relate to space in any way that would jeopardise the latter's status as a substance. We saw that in p12d Spinoza envisages a thing's having parts either (i) in such a manner that by dividing it you annihilate it (the second horn of the dilemma), or (ii) in such a manner that it depends conceptually on its parts, so that the thought of it involves the thought of them, and not vice versa (the first horn of the p12d dilemma). Now space could not be destroyed by its regions' coming apart from one another; so there is no threat from direction (i). But space is safe from (ii) as well, Spinoza can say, because the thought of a whole space is not built up out of thoughts of its subregions, whereas the thought of any finite region of space must involve the thought of a larger region—or the whole of space— within which it is embedded. Space does not relate to its regions as Leibniz's army does to its men. Whereas the story of the army could in principle be told as a complex story about a lot of men and their interrelations, the story of space could not be told as a complex narrative about regions. The difference is that each man could be identified without implying or presupposing that he belongs to an army, but the very concept of a spatial region involves the concept of the space of which it is a region.

Any division of space into regions is arbitrary, since regions can be as large or small as you like and can overlap. That could give Spinoza a further reason for saying that space could never be supplanted in our ontology by a set of its regions, but I have no evidence that that thought occurred to him.

3. Before expounding Spinoza's metaphysic, I should make explicit certain assumptions of his about space.

One is that there is such an item as Space, i.e., the one and only complete space. This is to assume that everything spatial is spatially related to *here*: Spinoza did not entertain the thought of two spaces with no spatial relations to one another. So far as I know, Kant was the first philosopher who saw a need to explain how we know that there cannot be two unrelated spaces; and Anthony Quinton was the first to argue that we do not know this because it is not true. Quinton undertakes to describe a possible sequence of experiences which would make it reasonable to conjecture that there is a real spatial world which is at no distance and in no direction from here.[2] If there were two such unrelated spaces, they would presumably be 'parts' of the whole extended world in some damaging sense—I mean damaging to the world's claim to be accounted a single substance. But there is nothing more to be said about this: if it is a possibility, it never occurred to Spinoza. From now on I shall assume that there is only a single space, i.e., that all spatial items are spatially related to one another. There is no evidence to the contrary.

Being a child of his time, Spinoza also assumed space to be Euclidean and infinite in all directions: he lived too early to get mathematical help with the notion of a finite but unbounded space. To get a handle on this notion, think of a two-dimensional creature whose space is the surface of a sphere; work out what he might discover about the properties of that space, e.g., that eventually all roads lead to home; then reapply in three dimensions. This matter, incidentally, has nothing to do with the previous one. If there were two spaces such as Quinton imagines, either or both might be finite and unbounded, but they could both be infinite and Euclidean; it must not be thought that if both were infinite there would not be room for them! In this paragraph I am using 'infinite' properly, and not in Spinoza's sense in which an infinite space must contain all the space there is.

I cannot see that it makes much difference to the roots of Spinoza's metaphysics that there are non-Euclidean geometries one of which could describe real space. Still, some of his formulations presuppose that the true geometry is Euclidean, so we should get ourselves into a Euclidean frame of mind.

4. These points help to explain Spinoza's peculiar remark about how a thing can be 'finite in its own kind':

That thing is said to be finite in its own kind which can be limited by another thing of the same nature. For example, a body is called finite because we always conceive another which is greater. Likewise, a thought is limited by another thought. But a body is not limited by a thought nor a thought by a body. (d2)

Applied to extension, this says that any finite extended item must be surrounded by a larger extended item. Taking 'finite' in our present sense, this is true on Euclidean assumptions, but not otherwise, since a non-Euclidean space could be finite without being nested in a larger space. If

2. Anthony Quinton, 'Spaces and Times', *Philosophy* vol. 37 (1962), pp. 130–147. Spinoza would probably have replied in a manner similar to P. F. Strawson, *The Bounds of Sense* (London, 1966), pp. 150–2.

by 'finite' Spinoza means 'less than all there is', then what he says is true on—but only on—the assumption that reality does not consist of two or more unrelated spaces. If Quinton's possibility were realized, our space would contain less than all the space there is but it would not be nested within a larger space.

I cannot make analogous sense of the suggestion that a thought which is finite in its own kind must be 'limited by another thought', because I cannot find a plausible mental analogue for my geometrical interpretation of 'limited'. The best I can do (suggested to me by Alston) is to guess that Spinoza is saying that thoughts with a merely finite content are somehow contained in thoughts with a richer content; on an analogy with saying that a true proposition which incompletely describes reality is a conjunct in—and is in that sense 'contained in'—a proposition which says more. That, however, does not look much like an analogue of the Euclidean treatment of spatial finiteness and limitation. I am inclined to think that this is one of the places where Spinoza says something that he has worked out for extension, then optimistically extrapolates it, hoping to cover thought as well, without working out the details.

Having failed to find a good interpretation of the mental side of 'finite in its own kind', I should confess further that I do not know why Spinoza here speaks both of what 'is' and 'is not', and also of what 'can be' and what 'we conceive' to be, limited.

It does not matter much that we have trouble with d2. It is used in demonstrating p21,22, but they amount to the proposition that what follows from a necessary proposition is itself necessary, and this is a theorem of modal logic which we do not need Spinoza's help in grasping. The only other use of d2 is in p8d which argues that 'Every substance is necessarily infinite'. The argument is simple: a finite substance must (by d2) be limited by another of the same kind, but that would involve two substances sharing an attribute, and that is impossible by p5. The reliance on the 'no shared attribute' thesis limits one's enthusiasm for this argument; but in any case no one has ever found plain sense for its conclusion except as applied to extended substance. Let us take p8 as saying that the only extended substance must be the whole of what is extended (and, if you like, must be 'infinite' in our sense as well). That is something for which Spinoza has better reasons than can be extracted from the obscure d2 and the imperfectly argued p5.

§22. *Space as substance*

1. Let us grant that the claim of space to count as a substance is not destroyed by its having 'parts' in a damaging sense, and further that there may be no other successful candidates for the title 'extended substance'.

We shall still need a lot of convincing that space itself is the one extended substance.

The central idea in this part of Spinoza's metaphysics can be approached through a story of Newton's.[3] God decides to add a mountain to the world, which he does by modifying a certain mountain-shaped and -sized region of space so that it affects everything else just as mountains do: other bodies cannot enter; if they reach the region quickly, sound is emitted and they are bent or shattered; light is reflected, and so on. If the job were done right, Newton says, we would have every reason to suppose that a mountain had been added to the furniture of our world; and he takes this to support his suggestion that actual physical things are just regions of space which have been suitably thickened, so to speak.

Never mind why Newton was interested in this idea. For Spinoza it points to a way of bringing the concept of a substance to bear on the extended world without implying that mountains are, or are made of, substances. It suggests that there is just the one substance—namely, the whole of space—regions of which get various qualities such as impenetrability, mass, and so on, so that any proposition asserting the existence of a body reduces to one saying something about a region of space.

2. That is only an approximation; it is not really right, for if we associate each object with *a* region of space, then no object can move. So we must associate each object rather with a spatio-temporally continuous set of place-times, which I call a *string* of them. If there is a string R_1–T_1, R_2–T_2, . . . such that each R_i is qualitatively unlike its spatial neighbours at T_i, and is qualitatively like the other regions on the string, then that string defines the trajectory of what we call an object in space; and the object is a logical construction out of the string which satisfies those conditions. Informally, the idea is this: to find the string associated with object x, find that string of place-times R_1–T_1, . . . such that (to put it in un-Spinozistic language) x snugly occupies R_i at T_i for each i on the string. But our account of the world does not start with objects and their locations and then move on to talk about strings of place-times. Rather, we start with facts about strings of place-times, and out of them we logically construct 'objects' and a relation of 'occupancy' between them and regions. This does not add physical objects to our basic ontology; all that that contains is the one substance, space.

When a thaw moves across a countryside, as we say, nothing really moves; there are just progressive changes in which bits of the countryside are frozen and which are melted. Analogously, Spinoza's view is that

3. For details, see J. Bennett and P. Remnant, 'How Matter Might at First be Made', *Canadian Journal of Philosophy*, supplementary vol. 4 (1978), pp. 1–11.

the movement of things or stuff is, deep down, the passing along of something qualitative—a change in which regions are F and which are not, for suitable values of F.

3. Newton, in his joke about God's way of creating a new mountain, cut a corner when he helped himself to the idea of God's making the relevant region impenetrable to light and snowflakes and human bodies, etc. If we start merely with the concepts of 'region' and 'impenetrability', we cannot answer the question 'not penetrable *by what?*' Trivially, no region is penetrable by another region, whatever God may do; and the answer 'not penetrable by bodies' is acceptable only if our ontology already contains bodies. It is essential to Newton's version of the story that it adds a body to a world already containing bodies; so it doesn't show us how we could develop this metaphysic from the ground up.

To make it work, we need some non-relational property which is possessed from time to time by some regions and not by others. Suppose that at various times some spherical regions of space are F—*red*, if you like, or *warm*—while the rest of space is not. Suppose further that whenever a spherical region is F at a certain time, that place-time belongs to a temporally lengthy string each member R_i–T_i of which satisfies the condition: R_i is F at T_i. This gives us the beginnings of a space full of spherical atoms—little globules of redness or warmth or whatever—which are our first stab at constructing physical objects. Then we can say what it is for *these* to be impenetrable to one another, namely, its being impossible for any place-time to belong to two strings.

We could then introduce some elementary mechanics, making the spheres elastic, bouncing off one another in ways determined by their direction and speed and by their relative sizes. If we let the bounces be a function of those factors and K, where K is a number which varies from sphere to sphere but is constant for any given sphere through all its collisions, then we have something approximating to a concept of *mass*. Of course a string does not itself have a velocity, because strings don't move; but we can define speed of objects out of properties of strings.

Much more must be done before the story tells the basic truth, or even what looked like the basic truth in the seventeenth century, about actual bodies in space. But my sketch shows how in principle the story could be completed, and that is all I need just now.

4. The story cannot be told without using spatial and temporal notions—topological and also metrical ones—for it would be a poor mechanical theory that had things bouncing off one another but at no particular speed. It is often thought that the very concepts of 'how far' and 'for how long' depend on the contents of space and time: spatial amount is definable only in terms of what a region contains, and temporal extent only by what happens during a period. Something like this might be right;[4] but even if it is, that does not block the development of the meta-physic I have been sketching. The physical theory and the spatio-temporal metric can be developed together and can support one another.

5. Spinoza is committed to agreeing that space is the one extended sub-stance, though he does not put it quite like that and for all I know would decline to do so. He would certainly refuse to say that space is God, or that space is a thinking substance, but we can allow that refusal. He can say that there is a single substance which is both extended and thinking, and that 'space' is a name for it when it is thought of as extended, while 'God' and 'Nature' are the names to call it by when it is not being thought of under one attribute in particular. We shall see later that Spinoza has a doctrine which implies things like this: 'There is one item—not a sub-stance—which has at least three correct names, one for it *qua* extended, one for it *qua* thinking, and one which is attribute-neutral—the names are "Ryle's body", "Ryle's mind", and "Ryle".' Analogously: 'the extended realm' (or 'space', or 'Nature *qua* extended'), and 'the thinking realm' (or 'Nature *qua* thinking'), and 'Nature' (or 'God'). Thus, Spinoza can say of 'Space thinks', as of 'Ryle's body thinks', that although not strictly false it is deeply infelicitous.

6. This metaphysic—or ideas closely related to it—can be found in many writers in the three centuries since Spinoza's time. Something like it was entertained by Kant in his *Metaphysical Foundations of Natural Science*, and he made part of the case for it in the remark: 'We are acquainted with substance in space only through forces which are active in this and that space, either bringing other objects to it . . . or preventing them from pene-trating into it.'[5] And some contemporary theorists about diachronic iden-tity—i.e., about what it is for something to last, persist, have a history—have been drawn to the idea that qualitative variety in space is the key to the concept of things in space.[6]

One of the chief figures on the scientific side was the nineteenth century physicist Michael Faraday, who held that an atom is a *point* with 'an at-mosphere of force grouped around it', and who identified matter with that 'atmosphere of force'.[7] And I am given to understand, as I remarked

4. Really, that is too simple: space and time are on different footings in this regard, for a reason Leibniz gives in *New Essays*, p. 155.

5. Kant, *Critique of Pure Reason,* B 321). For more details, see J. Bennett, *Kant's Dialectic* (Cambridge, 1974), §55.

6. See Eli Hirsch, 'Essence and Identity', in M. Munitz (ed.), *Identity and In-dividuation* (New York, 1971), pp. 31–49, at p. 36 (the 'Duration Rule').

7. I quote Faraday's phrase from Mary B. Hesse, *Forces and Fields* (London, 1961), p. 200.

(4) EXTENDED SUBSTANCE

in §20.5, that something like the metaphysic I have attributed to Spinoza is considerably in vogue among physicists today. Here is a popular statement of the position, which I am told is tolerably truthful:

According to quantum field theory, fields alone are real. *They* are the substance of the universe and not 'matter'. Matter (particles) is simply the momentary manifestations of interacting fields which . . . are the only real things in the universe. Their interactions seem particle-like because fields interact very abruptly and in very minute regions of space.[8]

On the strength of this similarity, whose importance I am not in a position to gauge, I shall use the phrase 'the field metaphysic' as my name for the doctrine of extended things which I am attributing to Spinoza.

§23. *Bodies as modes*

1. Spinoza says that finite particulars are 'modes'. The Latin is *modus*, meaning a *way* that something can be, or be done, or be the case. Many of Spinoza's uses of the word are best rendered by 'way', for example 'The human body is affected in many ways' (2p14d). It is a good idea to reserve 'way' for these untechnical contexts, and to use 'mode' only when expressing Spinoza's doctrine that finite *things*, ordinarily so-called, are modes. This is not an ambiguity in *modus*: Spinoza really is saying that ordinary particular things are ways that reality is. He is quite explicit about this in many places, including d5: 'By mode I understand the states of a substance . . . '. And then there is p25c, which can be translated thus:

Particular things are nothing but states of God's attributes, or modes [*modi*] through which God's attributes are expressed in a certain and determinate way [*modo*].

But there would be no inaccuracy, only a breach of translator's decorum, if we instead put: 'Particular things are nothing but states of God's attributes, or ways in which God's attributes are expressed, determinately and in detail.' In short, Spinozistic 'modes' belong on the property side of the line between things and properties.

2. I labour this because it has been denied by one of the best Spinoza commentators. Curley writes:

The Cartesian distinction between substance and mode . . . involved . . . a distinction between independent and dependent being, and a distinction between subject and predicate. . . . If I understand him correctly, Spinoza, in classifying particular things as modes, was intent on emphasizing the fact that the two distinctions do not coincide, that what is the subject of predication is not an independent entity.

8. Gary Zukav, *The Dancing Wu Li Masters* (New York, 1979), p. 200. Although its slant is very different from mine, I cannot forbear to mention also Mendel Sachs, 'Maimonides, Spinoza, and the Field Concept in Physics', *Journal of the History of Ideas* vol. 37 (1976), pp. 125–131.

He did not intend to say that the relation of particular things to God was in any way like the relation of a predicate to its subject.[9]

If I am right that Spinoza espoused the field metaphysic—and in §24 I shall present evidence that he did—then he could say that the relation of particular extended things to the one extended substance is enormously 'like the relation of a subject to its predicate' or (to move out of Curley's linguistic idiom) the relation of a thing to a property that it has.

Notice how radical and improbable Curley's thesis is. It credits Spinoza not only with silently depriving 'mode' of half the meaning it had in Descartes's idiolect and in the Latin language generally, but with positively implying that he has not done so. I allude to his defining 'mode' in terms of 'state'. The Latin for that is *affectio*, which Curley translates as 'affection': that is a tolerable archaism, since 'affection' used to mean 'quality or property or state'. If Curley thinks that Spinoza's *affectio* means something else, and if he also means that same thing by his 'affection', he does not say what it is. And if that is not his view, he must concede that according to his theory Spinoza has defined 'mode' just about as misleadingly as he could possibly have done.

Curley seems to think that we must endure these discomforts, since Spinoza applies the term 'mode' to items that obviously are subjects of predication—human bodies and specks of matter and planets. To that extent he is right, of course: Spinoza does classify as 'modes' all sorts of items which *are* ordinarily handled substantively. But that does not divorce 'mode' from 'predicate'. Spinoza's position is that most items that are usually treated in a thing-like manner *can*, and in a fundamental metaphysic *must*, be conceptualized differently: anachronistically expressed, some things need not be quantified over in a basic metaphysics.

Objection: 'Then why does Spinoza proclaim that particular things *are* modes, rather than remarking that they could be treated modally and that there is philosophical insight to be gained from noticing this?' Well, if he did mute his thesis in that way, it could only be in deference to the fact that particular things are, *ex hypothesi*, ordinarily treated substantively. But Spinoza cares little about that sort of fact: he regards some of the most heavily drawn lines in the plain man's conceptual structure as the misleading surface shadows of something deeper and different.

3. Curley's book contains an answer to what I have been saying. His willingness to swim against the current of traditional Spinoza interpretation comes from his not seeing how bodies could possibly be adjectival on the world. Until his book appeared, it was usual to take Spinoza's term

9. Curley, *Spinoza's Metaphysics*, p. 37. For a similar view, expressed with less clarity and control, see Gueroult, vol. 1, p. 63. What I take to be the correct view is well stated in Parkinson's 'Being and Knowledge in Spinoza', at pp. 26f.

(4) EXTENDED SUBSTANCE

'mode' at its face value, vaguely credit him with holding that finite particulars have a property-to-thing relation to the universe, and leave it at that. Curley was right to call the tradition's bluff by asking how this could be true:

> Spinoza's modes are, prima facie, of the wrong logical type to be related to substance in the same way Descartes's modes are related to substance, for they are particular things, not qualities. And it is difficult to know what it would mean to say that particular things inhere in substance. When qualities are said to inhere in substance, this may be viewed as a way of saying that they are predicated of it. What it would mean to say that one thing is predicated of another is a mystery that needs solving.[10]

To this impeccable passage I add only that I claim to have solved the mystery; which frees us to align ourselves with the traditional interpretation, in good conscience, and not be pressured into supposing that Spinoza used 'mode' with only half its usual meaning.

(Some philosophers have postulated items—which might be called 'states' or 'modes'—which are at once particular and universal. As well as this box and the property of cubicness which it shares with other things, they have thought, there is *the cubicness of this box*. It is not the box, but only an aspect of it; but it is an aspect *of this box*, and is not to be identified with the cubicness of anything else. If Spinoza meant modes and states to be items of that kind, Curley and I would both be wrong. Curley's 'mystery' would have a solution, but not the one I propose for it. I am glad there is no direct evidence that Spinoza did believe in these particularized universals, for I think they are nonsense. I cannot prove him to be innocent of them; but I am willing to suppose that he was, since I can explain all the texts through an interpretation which allows modes and states to be honest universals.)

My account applies only to extended things. As for Spinoza's thesis that all particulars—minds as well as bodies—are modes: I have to suppose that he started with a sound doctrine about the modal nature of extended particulars and then stretched it over mental ones as well on the strength of a *general* thesis that the extended world is mirrored in detail by the mental world. I shall show in §32 that he had sober reasons for that general thesis, and it is indubitable that he did do most of his metaphysical thinking in terms of extension, and was willing to reapply his results to thought without working out the details. So I am not embarrassed by my account's being given purely in terms of extension.

As well as the 'mystery that needs solving', Curley is encouraged in his radical interpretation by a couple of specific difficulties which he and others have seen in the thesis that particular things are states of a single

10. Curley, *op. cit.*, p. 18.

94

substance. After a needed preliminary, I shall show that each difficulty is eminently removable.

4. The field metaphysic does, in a fairly clear sense, make particular extended things adjectival on regions of space. A blush is adjectival on a face because the existence of the blush is the face's being red; and a pebble is adjectival upon space because the existence of the pebble is space's being thus and so. More specifically, it is space's containing a connected sequence of regions belonging to a string of place-times which satisfy certain conditions.

You might think that this makes the pebble adjectival not upon space but upon regions of it, for it looks as though 'The pebble is spherical' means something of the form 'There are regions which are G'. But I have argued on Spinoza's behalf in §21.2 that any mention of regions is, at least implicitly, a mention of space; so that the proper form of the statement is 'Space contains regions which are G'. Still, the objection can be renewed: we are now making substantival mention both of space and of regions, so that it is no longer clear why this metaphysic should be described as according a substantial status only to space.

This is not a real difficulty, I think. There can be no question of allowing regions to take over the role of substance from space as a whole, if only because there is no one right way of dividing space into discrete regions. Still, it would be more comfortable if we could see how the metaphysical story might be told without naming any regions and without quantifying over regions. It will have to be done with adverbs. We already have some adverbs of the required kind: for example, we can replace 'Some regions are F' (which quantifies over regions) by 'Space is F somewhere' (which does not); and we can replace 'Some regions are F and are interspersed with regions which are not F' by 'Space is F intermittently'. And we could enlarge our stock of locational adverbs, e.g., replacing 'There is a spherical F region surrounded by a non-F region, surrounded by...etc., to infinity' by 'Space is F onionwise'. There are obvious reasons why we don't have that locational adverb, but the mere possibility of it indicates that there could be a stock of adverbs enabling the field metaphysic to be constructed without quantifying over regions.

A complete Spinozist account of the world would have to provide replacements not only for quantifications over regions but also for mentions of individual regions. But we have adverbs for that too, for we can replace 'Region R is F' by 'Space is F there' while pointing to R, or by 'Space is F here' while occupying R. Those adverbs are indexical—i.e., they are essentially tied to *oneself* and to *the present*—but that is no drawback. There are good reasons for thinking that any reference to a particular—as distinct from a statement of the form 'There is an F' where there happens to be only one F—does involve an indexical element, something logically on a par with pointing to the particular and saying 'the thing I am now pointing at'.[11] Spinoza's hostility to the I-now viewpoint might disincline him to let indexical adverbs into his metaphysic, but then he must pay the price of not being able to cope with facts of the form Fa, as distinct from ones of the form 'For some x, Fx'. He does indeed tend to neglect facts of the former kind, making too little of the difference between a person and the person's nature, for example. Anyway, this is a general issue about indexicality and individual reference, which carries through unchanged into the context of the field metaphysic. So it is irrelevant to my present concerns.

I conclude that the field metaphysic can be made to work, with no need to name or quantify over regions. What will it quantify over? Nothing. If your ontology says that there is only one thing, then quantifiers are useless, because there is no difference between 'The thing is F' and 'Something is F' and 'Everything is F'.

5. Now for the two special difficulties which have been seen in the view that particular things are states of God. One is that if I say that the puddle in my driveway is slimy I am saying that God is slimy, and that is contrary to the divine dignity. Even if this point were right, it would not challenge the field metaphysic, but only Spinoza's calling the one substance 'God'. But in fact it is not right. If the puddle is a state of the universe, then any proposition expressible in the form 'The puddle is F' is really a proposition of the form *The universe is G*, but it does not follow that F = G. Analogously, the fight was a relation among the men, and to predicate 'protracted' of the fight is to say something about the men, but not that they were protracted. To say that the puddle is slimy is to say that a certain region of space is slimy*—i.e., has that property of regions which we conceptualize by saying that there are slimy things in them. And to say that there is a slimy* region is to say that *space is slimy* locally*—where 'locally' is just my place holder for whatever adverb would do the required job.

The second alleged difficulty is this: Since there are wet things and unwet things, if all predications are fundamentally on God then contradictory things must be said about God. This is prima facie graver than the other, but even easier to solve. If at this moment my pencil is yellow and my desk top is not yellow, the Spinozist does not have to say that space is yellow* and is not yellow*. On the contrary, he will use locational adverbs to block the contradictions. Just as temporal adverbs can turn a contradiction into a report of an alteration (yellow then, not yellow now), so spatial adverbs can turn a contradiction into a report of synchronic variety (yellow there, not yellow here).

11. See P. F. Strawson, *Individuals* (London, 1959), ch. 4 ('Monads').

§24.   *Where does Spinoza say that space is substance?* I p 15s ; Descartes' Princ.

1. If we approach Part 1 of the *Ethics* with the hypothesis that Spinoza meant it to embody the field metaphysic, things start falling into place. Above all, we are enabled to make good sense of the thesis that bodies are 'modes' of a single substance without having to deprive 'mode' of most of its seventeenth century meaning and flout Spinoza's definition of it in terms of 'state'. If I had to rest my case on that alone, I would do so. But there is more specific textual evidence, which I shall now present.

Most of it occurs in p15s. Here is one relevant passage, which I lighten a little by putting 'qua' for 'insofar as it is' on five occasions:

Matter is everywhere the same, and parts are distinguished in it only insofar as we conceive matter to be in different states, so that its parts are distinguished only modally, but not really. For example, we conceive that water can be divided and its parts separated from one another—qua water, but not qua corporeal substance. For qua substance it is neither separated nor divided. Again, water qua water is generated and destroyed, but qua substance it is neither generated nor destroyed. (59/32)

If Spinoza's metaphysic is as I have described it, this passage makes perfect sense. We can mark off bits of the extended world from one another only to the extent that various regions are qualitatively ('modally') different from one another. We can break a drop of water into smaller, separate drops, but that is merely to alter which regions are watery; it does not involve scattering that which is watery, namely, the original region of space. Again, you can perhaps drive a drop of water clean out of existence, but that could only be a matter of making one region unwatery without making any other watery; and similarly with the creation of water.

My account of Spinoza's metaphysic of extension is strongly confirmed by how well it handles that passage. I know of no rival account that does as well.

2. Notice what Spinoza says about annihilation: what we would ordinarily think of as the annihilating of something is really just an altering of space, which stays in existence throughout. Suppose we ask him: 'Could there be a real, deep-down annihilation, which was not really an alteration of an underlying something which remained all through?' Just once Spinoza addresses himself to that question, and his strange reply is perfectly explained by my account of his metaphysic of extension.

It is near the end of Letter 4, where he says: 'Men are not created, only generated, and their bodies existed before, although formed in another way.' Considered as expressing the field metaphysic, that is not very good. It sounds more like a claim about the permanence of particles of matter: my body 'existed before' in the sense that its constituent atoms existed in 1929 although they did not then make up a human body. Still, poor as the fit is, I believe Spinoza to be trying to say that bodies are not basic and that space is: my body 'existed before' in the sense that my body at this moment is a certain F region of space, and that region existed in 1929 although it was not then F. We must suppose that that is what Spinoza is getting at if we are to make sense of what follows. He has just said that your beginning was not a true origination, and has implied that your ending will not be a true annihilation either. What, for him, would count as a true annihilation of something extended? It would have to be the *annihilation of a region*. But if there is just one complete Euclidean space, that would have to involve the *annihilation of space*: it is nonsense to speak of the destruction of, say, a spherical region while leaving all the rest of space intact. With that by way of preparation, look now at the whole remark:

Men are not created, but only generated, and their bodies existed before, although formed in another way. From this something follows which I willingly accept, namely that if a single part of matter were annihilated the whole of extension would vanish with it.

Although the first sentence might be taken in different ways, the second points uniquely to the field metaphysic. On that metaphysic, the second sentence is exactly right; I can find no other basis on which it is even sane.

It is only one sentence in an early letter. But it is so striking that it does count significantly in favour of my present reading of Spinoza, given that there is also confirmation in the *Ethics*.

3. Another vivid piece of evidence occurs in a passage which commentators have neglected. It is a further part of p15s, and I must treat it at some length: as well as confirming that Spinoza had the field metaphysic, it contains things which, if not properly understood, might suggest that he didn't. Here is the passage:

If corporeal substance could be so divided that its parts were really distinct, why, then, could one part not be annihilated, the rest remaining connected with one another as before? And why must they all be so fitted together that there is no vacuum? Surely, of things which are really distinct from one another, one can be, and remain in its condition, without the other. Since therefore there is no vacuum in Nature (this is discussed elsewhere), but all of its parts must so concur that there is no vacuum, it follows that they cannot be really distinguished, i.e. that corporeal substance, insofar as it is substance, cannot be divided. (59/11)

There are two ways of taking this argument. One stays close to the text, and uses 'vacuum' as you and I use it; the other requires more filling in, and uses 'vacuum' in an utterly strange way. I adopt the latter interpretation. I am not deterred by its requiring us to give Spinoza a lot of help, for we know that his minimalism often leads him to underexpress his thought. I am positively encouraged by the strange meaning of the term 'vacuum' it involves, because there is independent evidence that that is Spinoza's meaning for the term. And I am further encouraged by the fact that the argument which stays closer to the apparent meaning of the text proceeds cloudily from a premiss which Spinoza probably didn't accept to a conclusion which is barely intelligible; whereas the argument I shall extract goes cleanly from a premiss he accepted to a clear and possibly true conclusion.

The bad argument involves taking 'vacuum' to mean 'region of space which does not have mass'—using 'mass' to stand for whatever you think makes the difference between vacuum and occupied space.

On that reading, Spinoza's statement 'There is no vacuum' means that all of space has mass: it is all thick, none of it thin. And the whole passage must mean something like this:

> If you could hold all bodies still while annihilating one of them and leaving the rest intact, that would have to create a vacuum, i.e., something extended and massless. So from the premiss that there is no vacuum we can infer that *such a vacuum-producing event cannot happen.* But what is to prevent it? Why cannot one body be annihilated while the others remain intact and immobile? It must be because what happens to one body is logically tied to what happens to others. How could that be? It must be because bodies are not really distinct parts of the extended world. Q.e.d.

That argument was run in the contrapositive direction by Locke: assuming that the annihilation of one body implies nothing for any other, Locke used the possibility of such an annihilation to prove that there could be 'vacuum' in the sense of something extended and massless.[12] That is a good argument. But taken the other way, from the denial of vacuum to the denial that bodies are distinct from one another, it is worthless.

For one thing it requires the premiss that there could not be a vacuum. I can think of no reason why Spinoza should deny that there are massless regions of space, let alone denying that there could be any. Also, the conclusion is confusing and obscure: it says that bodies must fail to be 'really distinct from one another', so that the annihilation of one would result in . . . what? The others' closing in to fill the gap? I can't see what else emerges from the argument. But that conclusion is just silly. It does not say that bodies are not really distinct, but rather that they are somehow joined, as though by metaphysical rubber bands.

4. To get the argument right, we must get 'vacuum' right. The key to this is Spinoza's 'this is discussed elsewhere' (*de quo aliàs*) which I think refers to the one place in his published writings where vacuum is mentioned. It is in a part of *Descartes's Principles* (I/187/10 to 188/26, quoted below with omissions) where Spinoza is obviously speaking for himself as well as for Descartes:

12. *Essay* II.xiii.21.

The nature of body or matter consists in extension alone. Space and body do not really differ [because] body and extension do not really differ, and space and extension do not really differ. It involves a contradiction that there should be a vacuum, [i.e.] extension without bodily substance. For a fuller explanation, and to correct the prejudice about vacuum, [Descartes's] *Principles* II.17–18 should be read. The main point there is that bodies between which nothing lies must touch one another, and also that nothing has no properties.

To see what he is getting at, consider the question: If we pump all the air out of a jar, what is left in it? There cannot be literally *nothing* left, for if there were nothing between the two sides they would be contiguous. We might try to get out of allowing that there is *something* in the jar by saying that there is *a distance* between its sides. But Descartes has a good reply to this. Distance, he says, is a mode—a property or quality or measure—and there must be something it is *of*: you can have a mile of road, or a yard of fabric, but you cannot have a sheer mile or a naked yard. The moral is that the jar must still contain something extended: it may lack mass, solidity, impenetrability, etc., but it must be something with size and shape—not a nothing with size and shape, a case of size and shape which aren't of anything.

(Descartes and Spinoza do not remark that the relational fact that the sides of the jar are *apart* from one another might be basic, and not a consequence of there being something between them. It might be held, I suppose, that concepts of spatial relations admit of no further analysis of any sort; or it could be maintained that they are further analysable in nonspatial terms, perhaps along the lines of Leibniz's sketchy suggestion that spatial relations are constructs out of causal ones.[13] The general idea has been popular enough in the history of philosophy; but because it has never been worked out in detail, we do not know whether it is viable. Anyway, it marks a possible gap in the thinking of Descartes and Spinoza about space. Having acknowledged it, I shall pass on.)

Having made a reasonable point about what it is for there to be nothing between two things, Descartes ties it to two bad terminological decisions, in each of which he is followed by Spinoza. First, he takes 'vacuum' to mean something like 'extended nothing', i.e., to be a nonsense term. Second, he uses 'body' and 'matter' to mean nothing more than 'that which is extended', so that for him the adjective 'bodily' (or 'corporeal') means merely 'extended'. Where it would seem better to say that extended items divide into matter or body (which has mass) and vacuum (which lacks mass), Descartes allows the terms 'matter' and 'body' to sprawl over the

13. 'Space . . . is nothing at all without bodies, but the possibility of placing them.' In G. H. Alexander (ed.), *The Leibniz-Clarke Correspondence* (Manchester, 1956), Leibniz's third letter, §5.

100

whole realm of what is extended, and lets 'vacuum' stand only for a non-realm—viz., for the nonsense concept of 'extended nothing'.

Thus, when he says that the pumped out jar contains bodily substance rather than vacuum, Descartes means *only* that it contains something extended rather than a cylindrical nothing. What he is consideredly saying allows that the 'something extended' may be what you and I would call vacuum, that is, something extended but lacking mass (or density or hardness or etc.). Descartes distinguishes what he means by 'vacuum' or 'empty space' from what is ordinarily meant by such terms:

Having examined this pebble, we shall find that our true idea of it consists only in our clearly perceiving that it is a substance which is extended in length, breadth and depth; but just that is included in our idea of space, not only space that is full of body but also space which is called empty.[14]

However, occasional reminders in the form of phrases about what is 'called empty' are not enough. Given that Descartes's whole point is that where there is extension there is something extended, it is a pity that he words this possible philosophical truth so that it sounds like a scientific falsehood.

As one might expect, Descartes sometimes forgot that he was using 'vacuum' and 'matter' in these peculiar ways, and took himself to have implied that wherever there is extension there is mass, which he then thought had implications for physics. For example, he tried to explain away the phenomenon of the vacuum pump, by supposing that as air leaves the jar some 'subtle matter' filters in through tiny pores in the glass. Also, thinking he had implied that the extended world is jammed full of 'matter' (in some normal sense), and that no two quantities of 'matter' (in this same normal sense) can fill the same space at the same time, he concluded that all motion must be circular and that causal propagation by impact must be instantaneous. These are excessively grand results to infer from the mere rejection of the nonsense concept of extended nothing!

My present concern is not with Descartes's strayings, but with what he primarily did mean by 'matter' and 'vacuum', for it is those primary meanings which Spinoza takes over, consistently and without muddle in our present context.[15] That explains his saying that 'space and body do not really differ'. It also justifies us in taking his uses of 'matter' and 'corporeal substance' to refer to space. So when he says that there is no vacuum, he is not predicting what you will find if you ransack the physical universe. His point is a conceptual one: if two extended items do not touch, there must

14. *Principles* II. 11; see also, especially, 16–17.

15. In Letter 13, unfortunately, he does slip into assuming that 'There is no vacuum' has predictive value.

be something between them. With that weapon in our hands, let us return to the vacuum argument in p15s.

5. Suppose there are three contiguous bodies, A, B, and C, with B standing between the other two. Suppose further that during a time when A and C remain in existence, and nothing moves, an event occurs which comes as close as possible to fitting the description 'B is annihilated'. Spinoza will try to convince us that that event cannot have been an annihilation.

If before the event A and C do not touch, and during it they remain in existence and motionless, *it follows logically that after it they do not touch.* What does their not touching consist in? What is the positive fact from which flows the negative fact that they are not contiguous? I contend that Spinoza, in his compressed remark about vacuum in p15s, means to argue that only his metaphysic can acceptably answer this question. Setting aside the relational view that the apartness of A and C is the fundamental spatial fact, not resting on any fact about what is between them, there are four prima facie possible answers, one of which is Spinoza's. It is a sign of the extreme abstractness of the argument that the differences between the answers can be stated purely in terms of differences between something and nothing, same and different, one and two.

'A and C do not touch because there is sheer distance between them, an extended nothing, a rectangular expanse which is not something extended. That explains the logical consequence emphasized above: there was a something in there; it was annihilated; so what remains is a nothing.' That is the nonsense answer which Spinoza is rejecting when he says 'There is no vacuum'.

'What lies between A and C after the event got there during the event, without moving: it came into existence, just there, when B was annihilated.' This is not nonsense, but it does seem silly and cannot be right. It implies that if a thing goes out of existence while nothing moves, a new thing of exactly the same size and shape *must* come into existence there and then. How could it be absolutely necessary that every annihilation is either accompanied by movement or followed by a creation?

The third answer is Spinoza's own. 'The event was not really an annihilation, but rather an alteration—a qualitative change in something which stayed in existence throughout. It was not the replacement of a massy thing by an extended nothing, or by a new un-massy thing, but rather a region's altering, becoming un-massy. Something lay between A and C before the event and is still between them after it.'

Unlike the first answer, this one makes sense. And unlike the second answer, it can explain why the emphasized logical consequence is valid. The annihilation of one thing could not necessitate the origination of another, but that supposed pair of events now turns out to be two descriptions of a single event, namely, the altering of a region. There is no more mystery here than in the fact that if you annihilate the heat of a cup of coffee you create its coolness.

This third answer is generated by the field metaphysic which I have attributed to Spinoza. He is arguing that that metaphysic is strongly confirmed by the fact (as he takes it to be) that it yields the best and perhaps only tenable account of the A-B-C situation I have been considering. And my attribution of the field metaphysic to him is confirmed by the fact that it yields this reading of the vacuum argument.

The fourth possible answer to our question says that before the event there were two things between A and C and after it there remained only one: before, there was B and the region occupied by it; after, there was only the empty region; and the event was a real annihilation. That seems intelligible, and it does justice to the logical consequence which the second answer could not explain: if of two things just one is annihilated, it unmysteriously follows that the other remains. Spinoza does not discuss this alternative—i.e., the view that space is a substantial container, a something which contains other somethings. I shall return to it in §25.3, arguing that it is inferior to the field metaphysic.

§25.   *What good is the field metaphysic?*

1. Let us have a final run at the question of what Spinoza is entitled to say about extended substance(s). He can say that there are none, and that the extended world is an appearance to us of an unextended reality. That was Leibniz's option, and it is one of Spinoza's glories that he did not take it.

He might say that there are many extended substances, each being a physical particle which cannot be divided, where 'cannot' means something strong enough to ensure that a substance does not have parts on which it even conceptually depends. He would not and should not settle for mere little lumps of matter which we have found no way of splitting; he reasonably wants the things in his basic metaphysic to be indivisible in a stronger way than that. That demand probably cannot be met by particles which are tiny quantities of matter. Contemporary physics postulates constituents of matter which may be indivisible in a very strong way, not being 'aggregates' in any sense, however generous. But they achieve that by not being things at all, but rather properties of regions or sets of regions; and that disqualifies them as substances. As I remarked in §20.5, contemporary 'atomism' is not a rival to Spinoza's field metaphysic, but a version of it.

How many extended substances are there? Failing the answers 'None' and 'Many', there remains 'One'. This answer is doomed if it picks out some extended item from among the multitude: it must somehow pick out the totality of them. But there appears to be no way of doing that, while still maintaining that the one substance does not have 'parts' in some damaging sense, except by supposing that that substance is not the whole assemblage of physical things but rather the one space which they occupy. And that seems to be Spinoza's view of the matter.

2. Perhaps, though, we can see him not as giving the answer 'One' but rather as rejecting the question. That is, perhaps his metaphysic takes 'substance' not to be a count noun like 'pebble' but rather a mass noun like 'water'.

The Latin text does not settle this question, because Latin has no articles and so their absence from a given phrase is not informative. Early in the *Ethics* 'substance' is often used as a count noun, with an actual or implied plural (for instance p2,4,5,6), but from p15s to the end of the work it is kept resolutely in the singular. In p14c1 Spinoza says that 'there is only one substance', and he repeats this in p30d and something like it in 2p4d. Strictly speaking, that is using 'substance' as a count noun; but perhaps it is a mistake to be strict about it. Someone who thinks there is only *substance*, confronted with other people who think there are substances, might say 'There is only one substance' meaning only that the plural is inappropriate.

There is, anyway, reason to believe that throughout most of the *Ethics* Spinoza thinks of 'substance' mainly as a mass term. When he implies that there is an 'infinite quantity' of substance (15s at 58/23) he virtually enforces a mass reading; in expounding him I often find it natural to adopt the mass usage; and I have the impression that English translations of the *Ethics* omit articles before 'substance' more often than not, thus treating it more often as a mass than as a count noun. I do not know how best to square that with the fact—as I presume it to be—that for Spinoza 'God' cannot be a mass noun.

That is enough about that. I have not been able to find any real problem whose solution turns on whether Spinoza thinks that there is one substance or rather that there is substance. There is philosophical significance in the difference between those,[16] but none of it seems to have worked its way into the *Ethics*.

3. There is one remaining approach to the problem of applying the concept of substance, or a substance, to the extended world: it was mentioned briefly at the end of §24 and must now be confronted. It is the view that the extended world consists of *space* and *what is in space*. The field metaphysic allows us to introduce the notion of occupancy of space, one level up: we state conditions on strings of space-times, and announce that whenever they are satisfied we shall describe the situation as 'an object moving through space'; but the ground-floor metaphysical story does not include space and also its contents. So we have here a real rival to the field meta-

16. For various explorations of the difference, see F. J. Pelletier (ed.), *Mass Terms: Some Philosophical Problems* (Dordrecht, 1979).

physic, as was evident in the fact that the two gave different answers to the 'vacuum' problem in §24. Whereas the field metaphysic says that the event is not a real annihilation, and that the thing between A and C before the event is the same as the thing between them after it, this 'container space' view says that before the event there were two things between A and C and that then one of them was annihilated, leaving the other.

Our concern is with the idea of 'space plus what it contains'. I shall not take this in the form 'space plus extended substances in it' because I don't want to revive the questions about whether sticks and stones, or for that matter quarks, can be Spinozist substances. In order to filter out that range of problems, I shall take our topic to be the idea that the extended world basically consists of space plus the *matter* (mass term) which it contains, taking it that matter is substance (mass term). Whether on this theory space is also substance, or a substance, is something I shall not discuss.

Spinoza does not mention the 'space plus contents' metaphysic. But the strongest objection to it is one he would have liked, namely, that it is ontologically extravagant. Where Spinoza sees a region R which has property F^*, the 'space plus contents' metaphysic sees a region R with only geometrical properties and, snugly fitting into it, a portion of matter having property F. The matter is inserted between the region and the property, like an infinitely fine silk lining between a hand and a leather glove. This lining makes no difference: it is a purely verbal insertion, and so we should cut it out.

4. All in all, the field metaphysic fares extremely well against its rivals when it comes to trying to apply a seventeenth century concept of substance to the extended world. And there is more to be said in its favour. Nobody would suggest that we should actually confine ourselves to the ground-floor concepts of this metaphysic; but by grasping that it is theoretically possible to tell the whole truth about the extended world in that manner we can do ourselves good, increasing our conceptual control and philosophical open-mindedness. I have two examples of this.

The field metaphysic puts us, at last, in control of the old, vexed question of whether it is in any way possible for two things to occupy the same place at the same time. Some philosophers have thought this to be absolutely impossible, others have held that although conceivable it never happens, and Leibniz among others was not sure.[17] The proper Spinozistic answer is that there are logically possible events in space that could reasonably be characterized as instances of co-occupancy, just so long as our occupancy concept is based on some quality admitting of differences of degree. Think of two one-pound spheres, each with a two-inch radius, merging to form

---

17. His discussion in *New Essays*, pp. 122–4, indicates something of the heat and dust surrounding the question.

a two-pound sphere with that same radius; and then coming apart again; with no independent evidence that either of them is less than perfectly solid. Looked at one way, it seems obvious that that is conceptually possible. The sense that perhaps it is impossible, after all, comes from the thought: What can it mean to say that something *occupies* the whole of a region of space if not that it keeps everything else out of that region? The answer is that although occupancy must involve some tendency to exclusivity, it need not be absolute; and the proper cure for the belief that it must be absolute is to think the issue through in terms of the field metaphysic.

This metaphysic also brings freedom by helping us to see that space might contain items other than portions of matter and constructs out of them. There could be qualitative variety amongst regions which was not well handled by the concept of a physical *thing* but which did invite the use of some concept of 'occupant of space'. It might be the concept of a *force* which is not just a body's tendency to move, or the concept of a *wave* which is not merely an undulating movement of bodies.

Of these two doors that are opened by Spinoza's metaphysic, the former seems not to lead to anything actual; but the latter—the door to the possibility of occupants of space which are not bodies or properties of bodies—seems to be precisely what has drawn contemporary physics in the direction of field theory.

§26. *Motion and rest*

1. Spinoza attributes to the extended world something he calls 'motion and rest'. If this is asserted at his most basic metaphysical level, as it seems to be, he cannot mean by 'motion' and 'rest' what we mean by them. Only things in space can move; and at Spinoza's basic level there are no occupants but only space, its different regions altering in orderly ways. One could speak of a *quality* as 'moving' through space, as one speaks of a thaw as 'moving' across a countryside; but that is not movement literally so-called. This was understood by Hallett:

A genuinely indivisible whole, which does not itself move, cannot 'contain' (and certainly not 'produce') movement in the sense of change of place in time. These facts were perfectly clear to Spinoza, and I thus infer that if Extended Substance expresses itself as infinite and eternal motion and rest, it follows that these must be given another significance than that of motion and rest as [we ordinarily understand them].[18]

Whether or not these facts were clear to Spinoza, let us make them clear to ourselves.

Spinoza ought to use 'motion and rest' to mean something like 'those

18. Hallett, *Aeternitas*, p. 85.

alterations in space which can be conceptualized, one level up, as movements of things in space'. He would accept that, I believe, though he would add that the phrase 'motion and rest' refers also to the laws governing the alterations—laws which, one level up, become the laws of physics.

Spinoza, incidentally, sees these laws as not merely regulating what happens but as keeping it happening. He does not picture the world as inherently inert and kept moving by an interfering God; and he would never entertain the thought—later embodied in the second law of thermodynamics—that the universe is running down. So he thinks of the world as somehow self-moving, perhaps like an animal. Although he attached importance to this, I can't make it yield interesting philosophy, because I can't find any clear content in it beyond the two denials I have mentioned—of an extramundane God and of increasing entropy. I shall say no more about it.

2. In some 'lemmas' and other material inserted between 2p13 and 14, Spinoza uses the phrase 'motion and rest' in a different, unbasic manner. Here, as indeed through most of the *Ethics*, he has moved up to a level where there are bodies, things *in* space, and now he is talking about *their* motion and rest—thus using 'motion' and 'rest' in their ordinary senses. Commentators who are unaware of this difference of level, but who are otherwise thinking hard, make heavy weather of the lemmas.

The concept of motion and rest plays two different roles in the lemmas. One of them is in Spinoza's theory of organisms. The lemmas present a sketchy physics and biology, culminating in an account of what a complex, structured, enduring *individual* is. Spinoza uses 'individual' as a technical term, without defining it, but it is clear that the paradigmatic individuals are organisms. Now, he offers an account of what happens when a single organism stays in existence while changing—e.g., digesting and excreting (lemma 4), growing or shrinking (5), changing posture (6) or changing location (7). In lemma 5 he says that the organism's persisting depends on its retaining the same 'nature' or 'form'; but later on he says, a little more specifically, that the same individual persists so long as its parts 'preserve towards one another the same proportion of motion and rest', and similar phrases. The phrase 'the same proportion of motion and rest' is still highly abstract. I see it as a placeholder for a detailed biological theory that still lay in the future, and I think Spinoza did too. It does, however, express his confidence that the true biological theory will handle everything in terms of movements of parts.

In this Spinoza shows himself to be a child of his times. His metaphysic reveals glorious vistas of worlds whose physics is not exclusively the science of how matter moves in space; but it seems not to have occurred to him that the actual world might be other than a 'movement of matter' one. The depth of that assumption shows in the choice of the label 'motion and rest', on the ground floor, as Spinoza's name for an 'immediate infinite mode of

(4) EXTENDED SUBSTANCE

God', i.e., for an aspect of reality which follows immediately, in one step, from reality's being extended. Although at the ground floor 'motion and rest' means something special, Spinoza would not have chosen that phrase if he had not assumed that 'motion' and 'rest', in the ordinary senses of these terms, will be the key concepts when we move up to the level where space has things in it.

3. But I have not yet brought out how much work motion and rest are expected to do in Spinoza's account of the extended world. I may have seemed to make him say this: Given the facts about space which we conceptualize as facts about things in space, the remaining story about the extended world can be told in terms of the movements of those things. But Spinoza's real view is more radical. He holds that the concepts of motion and rest generate all the variety in the extended world.

On one interpretation this may be right; on another, it cannot be. (a) If it means that all the world's variety can be explained in terms of Spinoza's ground-floor concept of motion and rest, it could be true. Because we have been told almost nothing about that concept—except the clue we get from Spinoza's name for it—we cannot deny that it is rich enough to generate all the world's qualitative variety. That seems to be what he is claiming when, in answer to a friend's request for examples, first, of some feature which follows immediately from the world's being extended, and second, of a feature which follows from the first one, Spinoza replies: 'The examples for which you ask are, of the first kind, . . . motion and rest; of the second kind, the make of the whole universe.' (Letter 64 at IV/278/24) (b) Spinoza is in trouble, though, if he means that all qualitative variety can be explained in terms of facts about 'motion' and 'rest' as ordinarily understood, i.e., as found one level up from the ground floor. If the field metaphysic is right, this is wrong; for the ordinary concepts of motion and rest are applicable only if we already have things in space, and that requires that there already be variety. For there to be a moving body, according to the field metaphysic, there must a suitable string of spacetimes each member of which is F^* while its immediate surroundings are not F^*, and that will give us an F body moving through a non-F medium. This means that there is qualitative variety that underlies the movement and therefore does not result from it.

Even without digging so deep, we can still attack the thesis that all qualitative variety results from motion and rest as ordinarily understood. According to that thesis, the extended world at any instant is homogeneous, and qualitative variety comes in only along the temporal dimension. But that is impossible: if at each instant there is synchronic sameness, then no stringing of instants along a temporal dimension can produce synchronic variety. The most we could get is diachronic variety, with the whole extended universe altering from totally blue to totally green, say, or from warm to cold.

However, a very small input of qualitative variety might suffice to generate the rest. In particular, if the extended world consists of homogeneous quantities of matter and homogeneous regions of empty space, that may be enough to let us explain all the rest of the world's variety in terms of differences in structure and movement. But there must *first* be that difference between body and vacuum, ordinarily so called.

At least once Spinoza indicates that he thinks there is no vacuum, in your and my sense of the term, and I am afraid that he infers this from his thesis that there is no vacuum in the peculiar Cartesian sense of 'extended non-substance' or 'bulky nothing' (Letter 13, IV/65/25). There is also a hint going the other way, suggesting that at the proper level he does distinguish space from the bodies occupying it (Letter 32, the phrase 'no space and no other bodies' at IV/172/2). I am not sure about this. I am sure that Spinoza does not see his need to distinguish space from bodies, or bodies from bodies, as a preliminary to applying the ordinary concepts of motion and rest. This is clear in the Part 2 lemmas. In the scholium to the lemmas he says that a complex individual may have parts which are complex individuals whose parts are . . . etc.; but he implies that a limit is always reachable. At the limit, the individual is decomposed into 'simplest bodies' which 'are distinguished from one another solely by motion and rest'. See also lemma 1: 'Bodies are distinguished from one another by reason of motion and rest, speed and slowness, and not by reason of their substance.'

4. Probably Spinoza did not become perfectly clear about the difference between the ground floor and the next level up, and thus about the difference between the technical and the ordinary notions of motion and rest. That might explain his offering one level up an indefensible thesis which would be all right if offered at the ground-floor level.

Perhaps the influence of Descartes is relevant. Here is what he said about qualitative variety:

There is only one matter in the whole universe. All the properties which we clearly perceive in it may be reduced to the one, viz. that it can be divided and moved according to its parts, and that it is capable of all the various dispositions which we observe can arise from the motion of its parts. All the diversity which is found in the forms of matter depends on movement.[19]

That is indefensible, for reasons I have given; but it may have influenced Spinoza.

While the Descartes passage is before us, notice how it relates to Spinoza's metaphysic of the extended world. Descartes was well on his way to

---

19. *Principles* II. 23, quoted with omissions.

having the field metaphysic himself: he had the idea of one extended substance, or of extended substance (mass term); but in allowing that it has 'parts' which can be 'moved' he shows that he has not thought the position through as deeply as Spinoza has. Descartes seems to picture an extended world consisting of an infinite quantity of matter occupying an infinite space, and to assume that the matter is movable. In contrast, the field metaphysic tells us to start not with matter in space but with space; we do not get to anything which literally *moves* except through qualitative variety, which is why movement cannot be the source of all such variety.

5. Just once that I know of, Spinoza pulls back from the Cartesian doctrine of qualitative variety: 'The mind cannot determine the body to motion, to rest, or to anything else (if there is anything else).' (3p2) If he had reconstructed the *Ethics* in conformity with this, allowing that 'motion and rest' may not be the whole story, he would have needed many rephrasings, a significant change of tone, and a running admission of a still unsolved problem about what the basic qualitative differences in the extended world are. But those changes would not have eaten into the main structure of his philosophy.

5

Necessity

In certain ways Spinoza commits himself to the remarkable conclusion that there are no contingent truths, i.e., that this is the only possible world. In other ways he commits himself to the opposite. This chapter will explore those commitments, and will also canvass the question of what Spinoza actually thought—as distinct from what his doctrines entail—about contingent truths. The texts on this are difficult and inconclusive; but they bear on other aspects of the *Ethics* as well, so we have good reason for attending to them.

§27. *The commitment to allowing contingent truths*

1. That the universe has A, for each attribute A, is something that Spinoza regards as straightforwardly necessary; he even thinks its truth can be discovered *a priori*. This necessity of 'The universe has A' is inherited by 'The universe has M' where M is one of the modes which are entailed by the attribute of extension, for example 'motion and rest', which is a mode of extension because it entails extension, and is infinite and eternal because extension entails it.

It is in p21 that Spinoza says that whatever follows from an attribute is itself 'infinite and eternal', to which he adds in p22 that whatever follows from an infinite and eternal mode must itself be infinite and eternal. Now, we know from d8 that 'eternal' is supposed to entail 'absolutely necessary', so that p21,22 are saying in part that what follows from something necessary is itself necessary, which is the most fundamental theorem of any modal logic. The remaining content of 'infinite and eternal' is roughly that of 'instantiated everywhere always', which adds to p21,22 the content: Whatever follows from what is universally instantiated is itself universally instantiated. This too seems obvious. It is puzzling that Spinoza should offer such a horribly convoluted demonstration for this pair of propositions.

2. The attributes and the modes that are deductively reachable from them have a great deal of content, Spinoza thinks, because they are repositories of all causal laws. For example, 'motion and rest' is not just a system of description and classification but somehow embodies the whole of physics. The laws of physics are supposed to be part of the 'extension' package— an extended world must obey them—and since every possible world is extended it follows that our physics is true at every possible world. This is Spinoza's causal rationalism, as applied to physics.

It is false, of course, and when Spinoza is challenged on it he does not respond convincingly (Letters 80–83). He is asked how it can be necessary that whatever is extended must involve motion and rest. His questioner reminds him that Descartes said that the definition of 'matter' in terms of extension does not entail the laws of physics, which must therefore result from God's interference. Spinoza replies that Descartes has to say so because his definition of matter is too thin: 'Matter is badly defined by Descartes as extension, [and] must necessarily be explained by an attribute which expresses infinite and eternal essence.' (Letter 83 at IV/334/24) I don't think he means to retract his own thesis that extension is the essence of the physical world. His point is that a proper metaphysic needs a richer concept of extension than Descartes's—one which includes not merely geometry but also physics, and a dynamic principle ensuring that any extended world bowls along for ever without outside help (see §26.1). That enriched concept lets him say that necessarily any extended world involves motion and obeys the actual laws of physics, but by the same token it makes it harder to argue that necessarily any world is extended.

I should remark that Spinoza holds the system of causal laws to be comprehensive as well as necessary. Because they are necessary, there cannot be a miracle (falling under the antecedent of a law but not its consequent), and because they are comprehensive, there cannot be a random event (not falling under antecedent or consequent of any law). These two doctrines are strikingly conjoined in the *Theological-Political Treatise* (at III/86/27), where Spinoza writes: 'I do not recognize any difference between an event against the laws of Nature and an event beyond the laws of Nature (that is . . . an event which does not contravene Nature though Nature is inadequate to produce or effect it).'

They are also run in harness in the *Ethics*: 'From a given determinate cause, the effect follows necessarily; and conversely, if there is no determinate cause, it is impossible for the effect to follow.' (a3) The first half says that the laws cannot be broken, while the second half rather clumsily says that the laws are never silent. The first half also rules out something Spinoza never thought of, namely, basic causal laws which are probabilistic. For him, the thesis that every event conforms to a system of causal laws is the thesis of strict determinism, according to which states of the universe fix later states in every detail.

3. So far, we have found Spinoza according an absolutely necessary status to a system of propositions embodying the logic, the geometry and the physics of every possible extended world. These propositions attribute to the world its 'infinite and eternal' features: they are instantiated everywhere and always, so they do not include features the world has locally or temporarily. These are treated in p28, which concerns 'particular things, or things which are finite and have a determinate existence'. Despite the use of the word 'thing', Spinoza's topic here is every sort of item that is local or temporary or both, including states and events and situations, at any metaphysical level. I shall call them all 'particulars', but this does not correspond to any noun of Spinoza's. What follows will be easier if 'particulars' are thought of as particular events.

Spinoza says in p28 that the causal ancestry of each particular includes another particular, whose causal ancestry includes yet another, 'and so on, to infinity'. Here is his argument. Every item must be caused by something; particulars cannot be caused by anything infinite and eternal; and the only remaining option is that they be caused by other particulars. The first premiss is explanatory rationalism. Let us look at Spinoza's argument for the second.

He derives it from p21.[1] According to p21, whatever follows necessarily from something that obtains always and everywhere must itself obtain always and everywhere; and so particulars, being local or temporary, do not follow necessarily from any such infinite and eternal items. The argument is sound. If a particular clap of thunder were necessitated *by* the laws of physics, there would be thunder everywhere and always. What we can say, according to Spinoza, is that every clap of thunder is caused by an antecedent particular, this causation proceeding *through* the laws of physics.

4. This persuasive picture of the causation of particulars makes no difficulty for Spinoza's thesis that everything is caused by God. We have here two different kinds of causal input: an infinite chain of finite items (the causally prior particular events), and a finite chain of infinite items (the sequence of ever more general physical laws, ending soon in the attribute of extension).[2] Each of these inputs belongs to God: the former is a series of God's finite modes, while the latter is an unfolding of one of God's attributes in its infinite modes.

Nor is there any trouble for the thesis that 'God is the indwelling [*immanens*] cause, not the crossing over [*transiens*] cause, of all things' (p18). Obviously, Spinoza's God cannot send causal influence over to anything else, because there is nothing else; so God's causality must be exerted upon God. But that is all right. When a particular comes into being, causal influence does cross over to it from an antecendent particular, but its causation by God—whether as embodying the laws, or as ultimate subject of both particulars—is indwelling.

---

1. This is the only important use of p21. There are four other uses, two dispensable and two downright idle.

2. This elegant formulation comes from Curley's *Spinoza's Metaphysics*, p. 68.

5. I shall use the phrase 'particular proposition' to mean 'proposition reporting the existence of some particular', e.g., reporting the occurrence of some event.

Now, there is a certain class of propositions all of whose members are absolutely necessary; they predicate attributes and infinite and eternal modes on God. Spinoza says that no particular proposition follows from any of them. Does that entail that every particular proposition is contingent?

It does, according to most systems of entailment logic, in which it is a theorem that a necessary proposition is entailed by every proposition. I hold the majority opinion that this theorem is true;[3] but it is controversial, it has not been well known throughout the history of logic, and I have no reason to think Spinoza was aware of it. Let us set it aside and ask whether Spinoza has in any other way committed himself to there being contingent truths.

There is nothing else in p28 that entails that particular propositions are contingent. It is true that p21,28 incite us to ask *how* such propositions could be necessary—where their necessity could *come from*, so to speak— but that does not positively imply that they are contingent.

6. The strongest pressure on Spinoza to allow that at least some propositions are contingent comes simply from its being hard to do good philosophy while staying faithful to the thesis that this is the only possible world. Many of Spinoza's philosophical moves are invalid if there is no contingency: for example, his uses of the concept of a thing's *essence*, meaning those of its properties which it could not possibly lack, are flattened into either falsehood or vacuous truth if there are no contingent truths; because then every property of every thing is essential to it. See for example the argument attributed to Spinoza in §17.3, which depends on the idea that some of a substance's properties are accidental to it. See also 3p6d, which purports to show that nothing can, unaided, cause its own destruction: if all a thing's properties are essential to it, then this argument ought to conclude that nothing can, unaided, cause any change in itself. See also 2a1.

§**28.**   *The commitment to ruling out contingent truths*

1. I have described Spinoza as an 'explanatory rationalist', meaning that he thinks there is a satisfactory answer to every why question, and have pointed out that this requires him to be a causal rationalist (§8.4). The reason is that if causal laws are not absolutely necessary then the

---

3. I defend it in J. Bennett, 'Entailment', *The Philosophical Review* vol. 78 (1969), pp. 197–236.

question 'Why did the law hold on this occasion?' is a good one which can have no answer.

However, even when Spinoza does take causal necessity to be all one with absolute necessity, he is still threatened with an unanswerable why question. Let P be the great proposition stating the whole contingent truth about the actual world, down to its finest detail, in respect of all times. Then the question 'Why is it the case that P?' cannot be answered in a satisfying way. Any purported answer must have the form 'P is the case because Q is the case'; but if Q is only contingently the case then it is a conjunct in P, and the offered explanation doesn't explain; and if Q is necessarily the case then the explanation, if it is cogent, implies that P is necessary also. But if P is necessary then the universe had to be exactly as it is, down to the tiniest detail—i.e., this is the only possible world.

In short, an explanatory rationalist is under intense pressure to suppose that there are no contingent truths—that this is the only possible world.

2. Leibniz, writing soon after Spinoza's death, reports that he had earlier 'found myself very close to the opinions of those who hold everything to be absolutely necessary', and that he was 'pulled back from this precipice by considering those possible things which neither are nor will be nor have been'.[4] In his mature philosophy, he deliberately makes room for contingent truths. Yet his much prized 'principle of sufficient reason' is a strong version of explanatory rationalism: it says that there is a reason for everything, and thus forbids him to countenance any brute facts.

Leibniz tries to accommodate contingent truths, while not letting in brute facts, by invoking the will of God. The answer to 'Why is this world actual, rather than some other?' is that God so chose.

But why did God so choose? Leibniz holds that this is the best possible world, so that the right question to ask about God's choice is: 'Why did God choose to actualize the best possible world rather than some inferior one?' Here is his answer:

It is reasonable and assured that God will always do what is best, even though what is less perfect implies no contradiction. [Contingent truths rest on] the sequence of things which God has freely chosen and which is founded on the first free decree of God, which leads him always to do what is most perfect . . . Although God assuredly always chooses the best, this does not prevent something less perfect from being . . . possible in itself, even though it will never happen, for it is not its impossibility but its imperfection which causes God to reject it.[5]

It is 'assured' that God always chooses the best because God is good, and that *is* absolutely necessary—anyone who doubts God's goodness hasn't

4. Loemker, p. 263.
5. Loemker, p. 311.

grasped the concept of God. So contingency squeezes into Leibniz's metaphysic through the narrow slit between God's character and his actions: it is absolutely necessary that God is good, but not that God always acts in character, for if that were necessary too then God would lose his radical freedom and the world its contingency.[6] For God to have acted otherwise, says Leibniz, would involve no 'logical absurdity' but only a 'moral absurdity'.[7]

At best, this is a preliminary skirmish. Leibniz will not have shown how to reconcile contingency with the principle of sufficient reason until he has explained how God's character relates to his actions; it is not enough merely to say that the relation is dependable but not necessary. In fact he does not complete the account. He says that God's motives 'incline without necessitating', without explaining what that means. When he says the same thing about human motives,[8] he means a jumble of things, none of them applicable to God.

Leibniz's project of reconciliation could not be completed, I think, because if there are contingent facts then there must be brute facts. Confronting Leibniz's position, we can ask: 'Why, in the chronicle of God's actions, are there no moral absurdities?' The answer cannot be that such absurdities are impossible, for Leibniz says they are not. Nor are we helped to answer the question by pointing to the necessary goodness of God's character: that tells us which actions would be morally absurd, but does not explain why God never performs any of them.

3. Still, the appeal to the free acts of a personal God provides at least a semblance of reconciling explanatory rationalism with contingency. Spinoza was well aware of that move: 'Ordinary people understand God [to have] free will and [a] right over all things which are, things which on that account are commonly thought to be contingent' (2p3s, 87/15). He could not adopt this view of contingency, since he denied that God is personal or acts in any manner which is 'free' as opposed to necessary. He says as much in a passage about 'the eternal and infinite being we call God or Nature'—each time the item is referred to, Spinoza uses both its names—saying that he/it 'acts from the same necessity from which he/it exists', and does not 'act for the sake of an end' (4 Preface, 206/22). Not that Spinoza's rejection of a personal, choosing God is his whole line of attack against the Leibnizian kind of position. In p33s2 at 75/4 he says that even if he did admit a personal God who decides how to act, this

6. See H. T. Mason (ed.), *The Leibniz-Arnauld Correspondence* (Manchester, 1967), pp. 62f.

7. Loemker, p. 488.

8. *New Essays*, p. 175.

could be rendered intelligible only on the basis that God's choices were determined by his will, and that in turn by his character; so that necessity is reintroduced after all.

Nor is that all. Even if he were wrong about that too—Spinoza says, in effect—he would not admit contingent *explicable* facts. At the end of p33s2 he contrasts two views which conflict with his own: (i) that some of God's actions are arbitrary, and so create brute facts, and (ii) that God's actions, although not necessary, are not arbitrary because they are guided by good reasons. Of these, (ii) is the Leibnizian attempt to have contingency with nothing left unexplained. Spinoza says that although they are both wrong, (i) is 'less far from the truth' than (ii), thus implying that if he had to admit contingent facts he would go the whole hog and admit brute ones. His point is that if God contingently acts so as to produce the best result, that means that there are standards of worse and better which are independent of God—standards 'to which God attends as a model' in acting. Spinoza finds that absurd. It amounts, he says, to subjecting God to something imposed from the outside (*fatum*, what is ordained).

4. So Spinoza is under pressure to deny that there are any contingent truths; and the most plausible way of resisting that pressure is one he will have no truck with. There is, I believe, only one other prima facie possible way of escape. Even if Spinoza says that all particular propositions are contingent, he can still claim that each of them can be explained: the journey back up the causal chain is infinitely long; it does not 'end'; and so the explanatory sequence of particulars need contain no member which is not explicable in terms of another member further back in the chain. The only challenge to explanatory rationalism comes from the question that addresses itself not to any part of the sequence but to the sequence as a whole: 'Why is there this infinite sequence of particulars rather than some other?' Now, this challenge might be met by denying the legitimacy of the question. That seems to be Kant's position, in the *Critique of Pure Reason* (B 525–35), where he seems to hold that we make needless troubles for ourselves by pretending that we have the impossible thought of a whole infinite series. But if that is Kant's view, he is wrong: there is nothing unintelligible about the idea that things might always have been different from how they actually have been; so the question why they have always been as they have is a good one.

Spinoza does not state the Kantian opinion about the great question 'Why was this rather than some other possible world actualized?', and I don't think he held it. His use of the names 'God' and 'Nature' suggests that he thinks we can have the thought of the whole of an infinite sequence. Still, he apparently tends to *overlook* the hard question about the entire series, writing as though our ability to answer the why question about any particular proposition is enough to meet the demands of explanatory rationalism. In Letter 40 he writes:

> If someone asked by what cause such a finite body is set in motion, I could reply that it is done by another body, and this body again by another, and so on to infinity. This answer . . . is available because the question is only about the motion, and by positing each time another body, we assign a sufficient and eternal cause of such motion. (IV/198/8)

Spinoza goes on to say that this regressing series of answers leaves one question standing, but it is not the question 'Why is there the whole series?' He has been discussing a book copied from a book copied from . . . etc. *ad infinitum*, and he says that the infinite regress explains 'the form and arrangement of the letters' but not 'the thought and meaning which their arrangement expresses'. That is not the explanandum I have been discussing.

If Spinoza were forced to address the question about the entire series, he would doubtless say that it is explained by the nature of God. But that could refer either to God's attributes and infinite and eternal modes (God seen from above, so to speak), or to all the particular facts about God, i.e., the local or temporary modes (God seen from below). To explain the whole sequence of particulars by reference to God from below would be to say that P is true because P is true; and to explain it in terms of God from above would be to give to P—and thus to every conjunct in P— the status of absolute necessity. And it would also be to deny p21 which says that particular propositions are not entailed by ones concerning infinite and eternal properties of God.

5. Spinoza's failure to abide consistently by the implications of his explanatory rationalism is connected, I think, with his not always sharply distinguishing between God from above and God from below. In Letter 64 he says that if extended reality is described from the top downwards, the first item is extension, followed immediately by motion and rest, followed at some distance by 'the make of the whole universe' (see §26.3). These all belong to that 'infinite and eternal' material from which particular facts cannot be extracted by logic alone; and so the third of them— the make of the universe—cannot be what its name suggests, namely, the totality of particular facts about the extended world. Never mind what it *is*. My point is just that Spinoza's terminology is dangerous: an item which is said to be entailed by an attribute is given a name which suggests that every particular fact is entailed by it. Well might Samuel Alexander speak of 'infinite modes which as it were break the fall from Heaven to earth'![9]

6. In passing I should mention some technical terminology which has

9. Samuel Alexander, 'Spinoza and Time', in Kashap, pp. 68–85, at p. 71.

grabbed the attention of some readers of the *Ethics* and has been accorded an importance which it does not have. I refer to Spinoza's phrases 'naturing Nature' and 'natured Nature' (p29s). These partition the features of reality not along the line between God from above and God from below but along the line with the attributes on one side and the modes on the other.

Thus, natured Nature includes *all* the modes, finite and infinite. What they have in common, justifying the passive implication of 'natured', is that they can all be explained through something else, since even infinite and eternal modes are derivable from attributes. The attributes, on the other hand, get the active label 'naturing' because they are self-explanatory —explanations flow from them, but none flow into them.

The terminology had a long history before Spinoza, and he introduces it into the *Ethics* because he likes capturing in his own terms as much as he can of rival philosophies. It is quite without significance in the *Ethics*, and we need not linger on it. Its only use is in p31, which has no deductive progeny, and that use of it is dispensable. The point that p31 is making is just that *intellect* is not to be equated with *thought* and is only a mode of it. Whether it is instantiated only locally and temporarily, or rather is infinite and eternal, intellect does not belong at the very top because it is not itself an attribute. Or, as Spinoza puts it in the vexatious terminology which I am now using for the last time, intellect 'must be referred to natured Nature, not to naturing Nature'.

§29.   *What does Spinoza think about contingency?*

1. I have argued that Spinoza has good reasons for affirming that there are contingent truths, and that he has a fundamental assumption which commits him to there being no contingent truths. Where does he in fact come out?

2. He says: 'Things could not have been produced by God in any other way or in any other order than they have been produced.' (p33) I used to think this said that there are no contingent truths.[10] But I now think that that was wrong, and that a careful reading of p33d shows that what is being asserted is just causal rationalism: the causal laws which govern the universe—determining the 'way' and the 'order' in which things are produced—could not possibly have been different.

Again, one might see necessitarianism in the p34 equation of God's power with God's essence, especially in the light of p35d where it is taken

10. It is thus understood by Matson in his 'Steps Towards Spinozism' (a paper from which I have learned much, though disagreeing with it on this point). Friedman in his 'Spinoza's Denial of Free Will in Man and God', at pp. 60–62, gives reasons different from mine for saying that 1p33 does not deny that there are any contingent truths.

to equate 'can' with 'must', saying that the seemingly weak 'in God's power' is equivalent to the strong 'follows necessarily from God's essence'. There are two readings for this, corresponding to two understandings of 'in God's power' (they also correspond to different understandings of 'God's essence', but we can safely leave that out of the discussion). (i) It could mean that if it is possible that P then it is necessary that P, i.e., that what is true at some world is true at all; and this is indeed the denial of contingency. (ii) There is another reading, arising from Spinoza's determinism, which implies that every true particular proposition is causally necessitated by antecedent states of the universe. Spinoza thinks it morally important to grasp that whatever happens had to happen, was locked into place by prior events, was as unstoppable as if it were itself absolutely necessary. We cannot think our way back—he holds—to a point in the world's history at which it really was an open question whether that event would some day occur; there is no place for any 'might have been' or 'nearly didn't'. Now, he could be talking about this inevitability in p34 and also in the associated p35: 'Whatever [is] in God's power, necessarily is', which on this reading would mean only that if P is not causally ruled out by how the world is up to a certain time then it is inevitable. Whereas in reading (i) 'God's power' covers whatever is the case at any possible world, in reading (ii) it covers only what is consistent with causal laws and with all the facts about some initial segment of the actual world.

Which reading should we choose? If we look to deductive ancestries we find that p35d relies on p34, and that the demonstration of that is too loose to help us with our present question. So we must look at progenies, and here we do better. Our two propositions are used only three times in the *Ethics*. Of these, the invocation of p34 in 3p6d is too weak to throw any light on our question; but the other two (1p36d and 2p3d) seem to me decisively to favour reading (ii), that is, to imply that 1p34,35 were seen by Spinoza as expressing determinism rather than meaning that this is the only possible world.

3. Where I call an event 'inevitable', Spinoza sometimes calls it 'necessary by reason of its cause'. Here, for example: 'A thing is called necessary either from its essence and definition or from a given efficient cause.' (p33s1 at 74/5)

At other times, he more boldly calls the inevitable item 'necessary'. For example:

The reason why a circle or triangle exists, or why it does not exist, does not follow from the nature of these things, but from the order of the whole of corporeal Nature. For from this [order] it must follow either that the triangle necessarily exists now or that it is impossible for it to exist now. (p11d2 at 53/6)

Perhaps this is all right. Perhaps Spinoza means something of the form

Necessarily (Nature → Particular),

which is innocent. But what his words actually mean is rather

Nature → Necessarily (Particular).

This implies that every particular proposition is itself necessary, that being the dangerously false thesis towards which his explanatory rationalism is pushing him. (Compare the passage quoted in §28.4, where Spinoza says that by explaining particular movements in terms of earlier ones, and so on backwards, 'we assign a sufficient *and eternal* cause of such motion'.)

Spinoza might plead that in p11d2 he is speaking of the triangle's being necessary or impossible 'by reason of its cause', and that this is harmless. While we have him making that plea, we had better cram into his mouth an explanation of what looks like an inconsistency in his text. In p11d2 we have seen him say that 'from the order of Nature it must follow either that the triangle necessarily exists now or that it is impossible for it to exist now', yet in 2a1 he says that 'from the order of Nature it can happen equally that this or that man does exist, or that he does not exist'. The two cannot be reconciled by any supposed difference between triangles and men. The only escape for Spinoza that I can see is to say that in the former passage he is speaking about the triangle's being necessary or impossible by reason of its cause, while in the latter his point is that no man's existence is necessary by reason of the man's own inherent nature.

But the need for such an apologetic explanation is ominous, and we shall see shortly that the notion of 'necessary by reason of its cause' is mischievous.

4. First, though, I remark that there should be no difficulties from Spinoza's saying that 'In Nature there is nothing contingent' (p29), for by 'contingent' he means 'neither necessary nor inevitable'. To deny contingency in this strong sense is not to say that this is the only possible world, but only to affirm determinism.

Even in this strong sense of 'contingent', we are ordinarily inclined to think that there are contingent truths. Spinoza sets that down to ignorance:

A thing is called contingent only because of a defect of our knowledge. For if we do not know that the thing's essence involves a contradiction, or if we do know very well that its essence does not involve a contradiction and nevertheless cannot certainly affirm anything about its existence because the order of causes is hidden from us, it can never seem to us either necessary or impossible. So we call it contingent or possible. (p33s1 at 74/11)

This epistemic sense of 'contingent' is put to work in, for instance, 2p31c and 2p44c1. Later on, Spinoza enforces a distinction between 'contingent' and 'possible', giving the former the meaning of 'not necessary (in the proper sense of that term)' (4d3) and the latter the meaning of 'not inevitable' (4d4). This terminological distinction is put to work only once and is not important. From now on I shall use 'contingent' in our contemporary fashion, i.e., in the narrow sense of 4d3 rather than the broader sense of 1p33s1.

5. Although many things Spinoza says which seem to imply that this is the only possible world really express his doctrine of inevitability, or some relative of that, other passages are harder to explain away.

Here is one of them: 'From the necessity of the divine nature there must follow infinite things in infinite ways (i.e., everything that can fall under an infinite intellect).' (p16) There are two ways of making this imply that ours is the only possible world. The proposition has the form 'From x there necessarily follows y', and we have to decide what x and y are.

(i) It is natural to take x, 'the necessity of the divine nature', as embodying only necessary truths about the universe. If that is right, and if y, 'everything which can fall under an infinite intellect', is the totality of truths, then p16 entails that every truth follows from a certain body of necessary truths. But what follows from what is necessary is itself necessary. So now p16 implies that *everything true is necessary*, i.e., this is the only possible world.

(ii) Even if we construe x more generously, as embodying the whole truth about the universe and not just some necessary truths about it, we can still get p16 to imply that this is the only possible world. Spinoza sometimes uses the notion of an 'infinite' or unlimited intellect to express the notion of what is possible; and on that reading, p16 says that a certain body of truths (x) entails everything that is possible (y). But what is entailed by truths is itself true, so now p16 implies that *everything possible is true*, which is again to say that this is the only possible world.

(iii) If we combine the two readings we get the result that *everything possible is necessary*. This is only apparently stronger, since really the three results are equivalent. They say: (i) what holds here holds at all worlds, (ii) what holds at any world holds here, and (iii) what holds at any world holds at every world. Each of these is equivalent to the proposition that there is only one possible world.

It is not easy to avoid all of those readings of p16. But I do not say that Spinoza was using p16, explicitly and deliberately and in full consciousness of what is involved, to say that this is the only possible world. Indeed, when he purports to repeat the content of p16 in p17s he makes it much weaker than either (i) or (ii), with a beefed up x and a toned down y, so that it falls well short of ruling out all contingency (62/15).

6. Although I have cleared p33 from the charge of saying that this is the only possible world, I do not see how to avoid such a reading of the main thrust of p33s2. This is the marvellous scholium in which Spinoza says that even if he attributed a will to God, he would not use it as a basis for loosening anything which is tight in his actual metaphysic. The climax of the argument is this:

If it is permitted to attribute to God another intellect and another will, without any change of his essence and of his perfection, why can he not now change his decrees about created things, and nevertheless remain equally perfect? (75/23)

In short: If God's character does not determine God's actions, we are left with unanswerable why questions. This is absolutely right. Whether it is evidence of Spinoza's thinking that there are no contingent truths depends on what facts 'about created things' are in question.

Well, I took the reference in p33 to the 'way' and the 'order' in which 'things are produced' to refer merely to the causal laws that govern the sequence of particulars. On that reading, Spinoza is there asserting the absolute necessity not of all truths but only of causal laws. In p33s2 we again find 'way' and 'order'; but we find other things implying that what is at issue is the necessity 'that each thing is what it is', that there is this and not 'another nature of things', that it could not have happened that 'something else concerning nature' obtained, that things could not 'be different' from how they actually are. It is hard not to conclude that in this scholium Spinoza is defending the absolute necessity of all truths. The same is true of a passage in Letter 54, starting at IV/251/21.

7. In summary: Spinoza is under pressure to say that there are no contingent truths, and sometimes he writes as though that were his opinion. If I had to choose between (i) 'Spinoza consciously, explicitly held that this is the only possible world' and (ii) 'Spinoza consciously, explicitly held that this is not the only possible world', I would opt for (i), though it is not really right. But (ii) is not right either: it seems that Spinoza did not think his situation through. In particular, he did not properly face up to the questions: If each particular proposition is derivable only from other particular propositions, how can any of them be, in itself, necessary? And if none are necessary, then isn't there at least one great fact which has no explanation?

This failure of intellectual thoroughness was probably helped by a certain philosophical mistake, embodied in the phrase 'necessary by reason of its cause'. I suggest that Spinoza tended to think that something whose necessity is not inherent but only conferred by something else is still as strongly, completely, absolutely necessary as something inherently necessary. That assumption surely underlies his statement in the *Metaphysical Thoughts* that 'If men clearly understood the whole order of Nature, they would find everything to be just as necessary as the things treated in mathematics', although earlier in the same work he has said that 'Created things have no necessity of themselves' (I/266/25 and 241/20). And I think the assumption is still at work in the *Ethics*.

In thinking he can distinguish 'What necessity does P have?' from 'Where does P get its necessity from?', Spinoza is adopting a concept of acquired necessity. Compare this with acquired authority. Your inherent excellence makes people conform to your wishes, whereas they conform to mine because authority was conferred on me by a political appointment. I may have as much authority as you, but its source is different.

That would explain Spinoza's use of phrases like 'necessary by reason of its cause'. It would also provide a way for him to hold (i) that this is the only possible world, while still acknowledging (ii) that particular propositions are not necessary *in the way* that truths of logic and mathematics are, thus doing justice (i) to the demands of explanatory rationalism and (ii) to the prima facie evidence that there are contingent truths—and especially to p28.

To get what he needs out of this, Spinoza must hold that there is a single concept of necessity according to which *both* what is necessary is true at all possible worlds, *and* that something not inherently necessary can have necessity conferred on it by something else.

The assumption is wrong, of course. We can define various concepts of 'acquired necessity' by adopting the schema

P has acquired necessity $=_{df}$ P is entailed by some Q which . . .

and filling in the blank in various ways. We might, for instance, put ' . . . by some Q which describes an earlier stage in the world's history than any referred to by P'; this would define 'acquired necessity' as 'inevitability' or 'necessity by reason of its cause'. But Spinoza needs acquired necessity to be absolute: a proposition which has it must be true at all possible worlds, for otherwise the demands of explanatory rationalism cannot be met. The only constraint on Q which yields that result, however, is the one given here:

P has acquired necessity $=_{df}$ P is entailed by some Q which
is absolutely necessary.

Nothing less will suffice. But that definition makes acquired necessity identical with necessity: any P satisfying it is as inherently necessary as any other. Spinoza was no logician; his modal thinking seems to have been neither skilful nor knowledgeable; and it would not be surprising if he flirted with the notion of acquired necessity and failed to grasp that it could not meet his needs.

6

Thinking Substance

§30. *The structure of Part 2*

1. Part 2 of the *Ethics* is about 'the mind'. In Spinoza's use of it, 'mind' (*mens*) is a specialized though vague term which applies only to certain highly complex modes of thought. Human minds are the only examples Spinoza gives, and may be the only ones he has: every Part 2 proposition that uses 'mind' indicates that its topic is humanity by also using 'human' or 'us' or 'someone'. I shall follow Spinoza in using 'mind' in this narrow way, but I shall continue to use 'mental' rather than 'thinking' as my preferred adjective for the attribute of thought as a whole.

Spinoza says at the start of Part 2 that its topic is 'the human mind'. Four of its axioms are explicitly about 'man' or 'us', and one can hardly doubt that the remaining one, 2a3, is also so intended.

The first nine propositions make no specific reference to human beings. They present Spinoza's general metaphysic of thought in relation to extension and do not draw on any of the Part 2 axioms. Then come p10–31 which are specifically about people, and mainly about how their minds relate to their bodies.

A cluster of theories about belief, knowledge, truth and error are the topic of p32–47. A couple of these, p39,47 are explicitly confined to human minds. Some others—namely p34,36,38,40,43—are stated or demonstrated so as to imply a restriction to the human case, but these restrictions are not needed for the arguments. They narrow the focus because it's people that Spinoza wants to talk about, not because what he is saying is false of chimpanzees and elephants. In four of the five cases this narrowing is achieved on the strength of p11c which says that human minds are modes of thought—so that whatever holds for modes of thought generally must hold for human minds.

Finally, p48,49 concern human will or volition. The former of them vigorously rejects free will in favour of a strong mental determinism. Since that doctrine pervades the moral psychology of Parts 3, 4 and 5, it is odd that 2p48 has no deductive progeny there. Its only demonstrative use is a rather weak one in demonstrating 2p49. The latter belongs to Spinoza's theory of belief and of error: it and its scholium are largely an attack on Descartes's view that because we believe things voluntarily it is our fault if we have false beliefs.

2. The axioms that explicitly mention humanity are used in demonstrating 2p10,11,13 which then generate many of the remaining propositions. But they are not the chief source of input about humans. More important is some material contained in seven lemmas and some other items sandwiched between 2p13 and 14. These give Spinoza's general theory about complex physical 'individuals', with special reference to organisms and the human body above all, though he admits that the human part is speculative (see the opening sentences of 2p17cs). Spinoza has not *strayed* into physics and biology: he knows what he is doing. As he explains when introducing his theory of organisms, a grasp of people's minds requires an understanding of their bodies:

> To determine what is the difference between the human mind and others, and how it surpasses them, we have to know the nature of the human body. In proportion as a body is more capable than others of doing or undergoing many things at once, so its mind is more capable than others of perceiving many things at once. And in proportion as the actions of a body depend more on itself alone, so its mind is more capable of understanding distinctly. (2p13s at 97/3, quoted with omissions)

This is not mere parallelism, a *matching* of facts about the body with facts about the mind. What Spinoza says here is asymmetrical, with the body having primacy. In the penultimate sentence of Part 3 the asymmetry is even plainer: 'the value of ideas', Spinoza says there, 'is measured by the value of' the corresponding bodies. In allowing that some descriptions of mental items depend on how the corresponding physical items are described, is Spinoza allowing an explanatory flow from physical to mental and thus deserting his dualism? I shall argue in due course that he is not.

3. The move from 'God' in Part 1 to 'Mind' in Part 2 is a double contraction—from all the attributes to just one, and from the whole universe to the higher mammals. We could even question whether the break between the Parts should come where Spinoza puts it. The alternative is to attach 2p1–9 to the end of Part 1, and then in Part 2 to move straight from the axioms to 2p10—the first proposition using any Part 2 axiom, and the first in which the concept of humanity occurs.

On the whole, however, Spinoza's division is satisfactory. Although Part 1 is about all the attributes, its scholia contain a lot of doctrine about extension; and although Part 2 is supposed to be about the human or mammalian mind, it sets that topic within the broad framework of the attribute of thought generally. So the important line between the Parts is perhaps the line between extension and thought.

Anyway, this chapter will explore the general mental metaphysics of Part 2, not what it says specifically about people.

§31. *Parallelism*

1. As Spinoza's thought unfolds in Parts 2 and 3, it becomes increasingly clear that he accepts and advocates a doctrine of parallelism between the mental and physical realms. This seems to be the doctrine that there is a one-one relation correlating mental items with physical ones, mapping similarities onto similarities and causal chains onto causal chains. If x is a physical item, then the correlated mental item is what Spinoza calls 'the idea of x', which I shall symbolize by $I(x)$. Using that symbolism, then, the parallelism thesis says that if x resembles y then $I(x)$ resembles $I(y)$, and if x causes y then $I(x)$ causes $I(y)$.

Spinoza sometimes calls x the 'object' of $I(x)$. This is not doctrine, I think, but merely terminology: 'is the object of' is by definition the converse of 'is the idea of'. I shall sometimes use the operator $O(\ )$ for forming names of items out of names of the ideas of them, so that $O(y)$ is the object of the idea y. It is thus a theorem that $O(I(x)) = x$, and that $I(O(y)) = y$.

2. In §32 I shall offer respectable reasons, which Spinoza could have had and I think did have, for accepting this drastically strong thesis that a mental realm runs parallel in the finest detail to the physical realm. But it will be seen that these reasons, which depend heavily on empirical fact and on certain broad assumptions about science, could not easily have been shaped up into the sort of demonstration Spinoza liked to give in the *Ethics*. I conjecture that that is why he instead offered the weak, cryptic argument that we find in the text. Here is the whole of his most famous statement about parallelism, together with the whole of his demonstration of it:

The order and connection of ideas is the same as the order and connection of things. *Demonstration:* This is evident from 1a4. For the idea of each caused thing depends on the cognition of the cause of which it is the effect. (2p7,d)

This offhand 'demonstration' refers us to 1a4, which says: 'Cognition of an effect depends on and involves cognition of the cause.' The Latin word is *cognitio*. It is often translated as 'knowledge', but we shall later find abundant evidence that Spinoza means it more broadly than that.

Most of Spinoza's uses of 1a4 make it out to be fairly tame, by his standards. Although 'cognition' can be a term in psychology, Spinoza is also willing to use it to mean 'concept', taking the latter to belong to logic. (For evidence of this, see how 1a4 and 1a5 are combined in 1p3d.) If 1a4 is read in a logical way, it says that if x causes y then there is a conceptual link between them, this being a version or a part of causal rationalism. And that is how Spinoza construes the axiom in his seven other uses of it.[1] In 2p7d, however, the axiom must be taking 'cognition' to stand for something mental: if x causes y then a mental item related in a certain way to y must involve a mental item related in the same way to x. Otherwise the axiom cannot even seem to imply a parallelism between the physical and the mental.

3. The alternative is to read both the axiom and the parallelism doctrine as logical. That is what Balz and Curley do (see §14.4). Curley's thesis that Spinoza's attribute of so-called thought is logical and not psychological (except in the doctrine of 'ideas of ideas', when it switches to psychology) provides him with a neat account of the parallelism.[2]

It takes ideas to be propositions. That is right: Spinoza makes it clear that ideas are propositionally structured, so that if psychological they are beliefs and the like, and if logical they are propositions. Curley must confine them to true propositions, but that is all right too, since it is uncontroversially true that Spinoza has to discriminate against false ideas, even if these are psychological items such as beliefs.

On the other side, Curley says that modes of extension are facts about the physical world. I cannot square this with his treatment of modes discussed in §23.2 above. Nor can I see how to fuse it in with a general statement of Spinoza's ontology. If the fact that my watch is made of gold is a mode of the attribute of extension, what is the watch itself? Is it a mode too? Either answer brings trouble.

Given those accounts of what there is under the two attributes, the parallelism is secure: it is a correlation between *facts* and *true propositions*. This gets Spinoza out of any conceivable trouble with his parallelism, but only by making it so empty as to lack all metaphysical significance. Curley quotes someone who said that 'one is tempted' to think that for Spinoza an idea is just 'the truth about each particular event', for this reason: 'Since there are ideas of inanimate as well as animate objects and processes, ideas can scarcely be regarded as individual psychical entities.'[3] That implies that Spinoza cannot have embraced comprehensive psycho-physical parallelism, presumably because he was too sensible for that. I am not sure how sensible he was, but I know him to have been original, profound, and intellectually courageous. These traits show in his embracing psycho-physical parallelism to solve a real problem which I shall expound shortly, but not in the tame parallelism doctrine to which Curley confines him.

1. Six of them are 1p3,6c, 2p5,6,16 and 5p22. In 1p25d the axiom is still construed as logical, but is illegitimately converted, a common mistake in Spinoza's writings.

2. Curley, *Spinoza's Metaphysics*, pp. 119–126.

3. *Ibid.*, p. 118.

My main objection to the logicising of the attribute of thought, however, is that I cannot believe it as a reading of the text. Admittedly, the logical interpretation must always be borne in mind, and sometimes helps to explain things Spinoza says; but I see no case for making it paramount and saying that the *Ethics* is silent about mentality. Curley implies that Spinoza is willing to give the title 'Paul's mind' to the set of propositions which truly describes Paul's body.[4] I just don't believe that Spinoza would be willing to use 'mind' in that eccentric fashion.

4. So, as I said, I think we must take 1a4 psychologically, so as to make it support a psycho-physical parallelism. How is that support to be given? Well, the axiom implies: 'If x causes y, and Cog(y) exists, then Cog(x) exists.' From that, conjoined with determinism, it follows that if Cog(y) exists for some given y, then there is an infinite sequence of items of the form Cog( ), corresponding to the infinite causal chain leading up to y. And assuming, as it is surely right to do, that cognitions are ideas, we get an infinite chain of ideas running up to I(y), matching the infinite chain of physical items running up to y. Furthermore, each cognition 'depends upon' its predecessor; if this dependence is causal, it follows that the physical causal chain is matched by a mental causal chain.

I have just done my best to stretch 1a4 so that it will touch 2p7. But I have done nothing to make 1a4 believable on a psychological reading, and that task is too much for me. It is hard even to suggest reasons for Spinoza's finding it plausible. He may have been influenced by its plausibility when read logically. Perhaps he was also encouraged by the fact that the axiom is reasonable if it is taken to mean that if x causes y then a *full* understanding of y requires *some* understanding of x; though on that reading of the axiom it no longer supports the argument I have given, for if we do not have the very same Cog( ) twice in the axiom, we cannot reapply it to generate an infinite series of cognitions. Or perhaps Spinoza is thinking of some stratospherically high standard of cognitive perfection —some sort of utterly comprehensive knowledge—which we cannot have of a thing unless we have just as good knowledge of its cause. We shall see in §43 that he has a theory about one kind of cognitive process— he calls it 'reason'—which is like that. One of the difficulties about it is that it seems to imply that any instance of 'reason' must include an infinite mental embrace—a cognition of something, and of its cause, and of *its* cause, and so on. That is a lot to swallow; but it is just what Spinoza needs for the argument I have suggested from 1a4 to 2p7, and it may be that in advancing 1a4 Spinoza partly has in mind his own theory of 'reason'.

5. If so, then he may have a case for the axiom; but now we are forced

4. *Ibid.*, p. 126. Cf. Balz, *Idea and Essence in the Philosophies of Hobbes and Spinoza*, p. 44.

to notice a gap between it and 2p7—the gap was there anyway, but now it has dramatically widened. Remember that to generate an infinite series of cognitions we needed an initial Cog(y) to get things going. But if we are to understanding Cog(y) to be an instance of superhumanly perfect and comprehensive knowledge, then perhaps Cog(y) does not exist for any y, and the axiom is only vacuously true, not yielding the least fragment of a mental realm.

This problem exists even if the standards for Cog(y) are set less high. Let us now forget about making 1a4 plausible; let us give it its best chance of supporting 2p7, by taking it to say simply: 'If x causes y, and I(y) exists, then I(x) exists.' Heaven knows why we should believe this. But it does come closer to 2p7: it starts only with the existence of the modest I(y) rather than a Cog(y) which might mean something intolerably strong; and it does entail that there is a chain of ideas matching the infinite chain of physical causes, just so long as I(y) exists.

But it still falls short, for it remains the case that I(y) may not exist. There may be a physical causal chain with no mental counterpart anywhere along its length, or a chain which has such a counterpart for some distance and then loses it. The axiom won't let mentality *start up* after the physical causal chain has begun, but it does allow it to *drop out*.

And there is another gap between 1a4 (on this or any other version) and psycho-physical parallelism, namely that 1a4 does not rule out mental items which do not match any physical items.

6. These troubles result from assuming that 2p7 bears the whole burden of the parallelism doctrine. That is what commentators usually assume, and so did I for many years; but it is wrong. Really, it is 2p3 that asserts the existence of a mental item corresponding to every physical item; but it tells us nothing about the correspondence relation except that it justifies speaking of ideas 'of' things. Then 2p7 adds the further claim that this correspondence maps causal chains onto causal chains (and thus maps causally important similarities onto causally important similarities). So really, if 2p7 is to assert the entire parallelism doctrine, it must be inferred from 2p3 which says that I(y) always exists, and from 1a4 which says that in that case an infinite causal chain leading up to I(y) also exists and matches the causal chain leading up to y.

Here is 2p3: 'In God there is necessarily an idea both of his essence and of everything which necessarily follows from his essence.' Three of Spinoza's uses of this are strange and problematic (2p5, 5p22,35), but the other three are plain sailing (2p9c,20,24), and they all make it clear that 'God's essence and everything which necessarily flows from it' covers everything that is the case about God, not just those infinite and eternal aspects which I call God as seen from above. So p3 says that there exists an idea—a mental counterpart—of everything that exists or is the case.

Spinoza's demonstration of this bold hypothesis boils down to this: (i) God can have an idea of every reality (because by p1 thought is an attribute of God), and (ii) whatever God can do, God does (by 1p35); therefore, etc. This argument is unacceptable, because premiss (ii) is not entitled to mean more than *Whatever is not causally ruled out by how the universe is is true* (see §29.2); but then (i) ought to mean that the nature of the universe does not causally rule out there being a mental counterpart of everything; but we cannot extract that from the mere assertion that thought is an attribute of the universe! Perhaps we can say (i)′ that it is logically possible that there is a mental counterpart of everything; but then the second premiss must say (ii)′ that *whatever is logically possible is true,* i.e., that this is the only possible world. If that is what the argument is relying on, then I reject it for that reason. Nothing can save it.

Perhaps Spinoza would also defend 2p3 on the grounds that thought, being an attribute, is 'infinite', all-encompassing, subject to no negations such as would be involved in the proposition 'There is an extended item which does *not* have a counterpart in thought'. That should not sway us much either.

Still, bad as the arguments for it are, 2p3 is there. If it carries part of the burden of parallelism, the inference from 1a4 to 2p7 is less bewildering. And, indeed, 2p3d suggests how Spinoza might have closed the other gap in the argument—the one about mental items with no physical counterparts. He says nothing about them, and I suspect that he assumed, at a very deep level of his mind, that the mental realm could not outrun the physical. But, as Jesse Bohl has pointed out to me, there is an argument Spinoza could have used, similar to p3d and no worse than it. If it follows from p1 (thought is an attribute) that there can be an idea of every object, then it ought to follow from p2 (extension is an attribute) that there can be an object for every idea; add that whatever can exist does exist (by 1p35), and out rolls the conclusion.

Summing up: Given 1a4 and 2p3, we can argue pretty well for a strong doctrine of psycho-physical parallelism. But Spinoza gives no reason for 1a4, and I cannot think of any, except by taking Cog(y) so strongly that even with the aid of 2p3 there is no route to parallelism. And the official argument for 2p3 seems to be unrescuable. The situation is about as bad as it was over the argument for substance monism. Let us, here as there, turn aside from the official arguments and see if we can do better, still using lines of thought to which Spinoza would be sympathetic.

§32.   *A better case for parallelism*

1. I say to you 'There's a spider on your sleeve', you then think there's a spider on your sleeve, and you look at your sleeve. Physical input, mental event, physical output; and there is enough of this in our experience, with enough pattern to it, to make it certain that it is not coincidental. It seems natural to suppose that in that transaction there are two causal connections: my impact on your eardrums causes a belief to be acquired, and that causes a movement of your eyes.

Spinoza cannot accept either half of that account, however, since he will not allow causal flow between the attributes, and that gives him a reason for conjecturing that there is a psycho-physical parallelism in the universe. Take a very simple example: I stab you, you feel pain, you cry out. Spinoza cannot allow the causal chain from stabbing to feeling to crying, but he must grant that some deep, reliable connection is involved. His parallelism thesis lets him explain the data without admitting interaction, because it says that there are two causal chains:

$$\text{Stab} \rightarrow \text{O(Feeling)} \rightarrow \text{Cry}$$
$$\text{I(Stab)} \rightarrow \text{Feeling} \rightarrow \text{I(Cry)}$$

I am still using 'I(x)' to name the idea of x, and 'O(x)' to name the object of x. The proposal, then, is that there is a physical transaction whose middle item is a complex brain event about which we don't know much, and a mental transaction about whose first and third elements we don't know much; we focus on the bits of each that we are acquainted with and so conclude, wrongly, that there is causal flow both ways between the attributes. This hypothesis about matched causal chains criticises our belief that stabs cause pains which cause cries, while also explaining why the belief is so plausible, namely, because the ingredients of the mixture are always there.

Here is an example of how the same data can be handled in terms either of interaction or of parallelism. Descartes wrote against Gassendi:

I do not agree with you when you say—confidently but without any good reasons—that the mind waxes and wanes with the body; for from the fact that it does not work equally well in the body of a child and in that of a grown man, and that its actions are often impeded by wine and other bodily things, it follows merely that while it is united to the body it uses the body as an instrument in its normal operations, but not that the body makes it more or less perfect than it is in itself.[5]

Spinoza could have had that passage in mind when he wrote:

But they will say that they know by experience that unless the human mind were capable of thinking, the body would be inactive. But does not experience also teach that if on the other hand the body is inactive, the mind is at the same time incapable of thinking? I believe everyone has found by experience that as the body is more susceptible to having this or that image aroused in it, so the mind is more capable of regarding this or that object. (3p2s at 142/20, quoted with omissions)

5. Reply to Fifth Objections, in Alquié, vol. 2, pp. 794f.

This is a pretty contrast. Descartes says 'They don't rise and fall together—the mind uses the body', while Spinoza says 'The mind doesn't use the body—they rise and fall together'.

2. Objection: 'Granted, there are many seeming interactions between the attributes—too many to be a coincidence—and the best explanation of the facts, other than through interaction, is Spinoza's hypothesis of parallelism. But that is so extravagant that this line of thought surely makes an overwhelming case for causal flow between the attributes. We don't have to remove any ponderous obstacles to the acceptance of interaction: all we need is to reject dualism or causal rationalism; and surely the conjunction of those two is not so unassailable that we must preserve it at the cost of accepting parallelism?'

I shall not discuss the merits of dualism in this work. I am content to adopt it as a premiss for the serious consideration of Spinoza. If you regard it as so patently false that you cannot keep your mind focussed on any philosophical work that assumes it, then you must dismiss this chapter and the stretch of the *Ethics* which it discusses; but you need not be put off from the rest of Spinoza's book or of mine. Dualism permeates both, but most of what matters would survive a careful excision of the dualist underpinnings. I should add that I have little sympathy with those who are *sure* that dualism is false. Their attitude is not well supported by how the debate over physicalism has gone during the past two decades.

If we suspend dualism, my topic in this chapter is annihilated. The same does not hold for causal rationalism, however; so let us set that aside, and declare that mental-physical interaction is not downright impossible. Are there still reasons for thinking it does not happen? And, if so, would their force have been felt by Spinoza? If we can answer Yes to both questions, we shall have found new strength in the case that was available to him in support of his parallelism of causal chains.

3. If there is flow from mental to physical, that implies something extremely uncomfortable for physical science. For then some questions of the form

> If at T there is a state of affairs answering to the following complete physical description, . . . , what will its state be at T+d?

can be answered when, but only when, we know how if at all that physical system relates to a mind. It is not impossible that some events in my brain cannot be predicted or assigned a precise probability from a full description of the antecedent state of my brain, but can be if some fact about how I am thinking is taken into account. Most of us find this implausible, however. Science has done very well by assuming that all the causes of physical phenomena are physical.

(6) THINKING SUBSTANCE

It would have been reasonable for Spinoza, who knew some physics and who as a professional lens-grinder must have been acutely conscious of the scientific promise held out by the recently invented microscope, to object on scientific grounds to allowing that the mental intrudes causally into the physical realm. And he explicitly denies there is any known need to allow this, in a sharp comment on those who say that human behaviour could not be explained through purely physical laws:

Experience has not yet taught anyone what the body can do from the laws of Nature alone, insofar as Nature is only considered to be corporeal. . . . For no one yet knows the structure of the body so accurately that he could explain all its functions—not to mention that many things are observed in the lower animals which far surpass human ingenuity, and that sleepwalkers do a great many things in their sleep which they would not dare to do when awake. This shows well enough that the body itself, simply from the laws of its own nature, can do many things which its mind wonders at. (3p2s at 142/5)

4. There is no comparable basis for saying that the physical cannot act on the mental. We cannot speak admiringly of how well science has done, over the centuries, by assuming that mental effects always have mental causes! But there are other objections to allowing causal flow in that direction.

It is often said these days that if we deny causal flow from mental to physical but allow it the other way, we commit ourselves to something intolerable, namely 'danglers'. Those are laws according to which causal influence runs along a certain channel and then stops, rather than producing effects which in their turn have a causal bearing on the rest of the world. If the situation were that physical items could cause mental items which were not themselves causes of anything, that would conflict with Spinoza's 1p36 which says that everything has some effects. His argument for this is notably bad, however, as it was bound to be: there are no powerful reasons why every effect must be a cause. Even if there were, we might suppose that physical items cause mental items which then have further effects, but only mental ones. The opponents of 'danglers' will still object: the very idea of a causal route into territory from which there is no way back, they will say, is offensive to the established picture of total basic science as a unified structure in which pressures can be transmitted from any part to any other.

I cannot see that we are committed to all of that picture, and I think that the recent philosophical literature has made too much of this worry about 'danglers'. No deep assumption that has been hard at work in Western science conflicts with the view that causation runs into the mental realm but not out of it. This view does not threaten harm as does the idea that physical items have nonphysical causes.

5. I conclude that Spinoza cannot make a case against physical-to-mental causal influence except by objecting to all causal flow between attributes.

This is disappointing, but it matters less than it might seem to, for the following reason. It looks as though mentality is associated with at most a large part of the animal kingdom, not with plants and certainly not with inanimate nature. Even within such physical structures as human bodies, there seem to be many events—e.g., salt transfers in the kidneys—which send no messages to the mind. If someone holds that physical systems have mental effects, therefore, it will be natural for him to hold that some do and some do not. And there are two serious objections to this form of the thesis that body acts on mind, both of which still have dualism as a premiss but not causal rationalism or any general ban on causal flow between the attributes. I give them in my next section.

§33.   *Panpsychism*

1. Someone who thinks there is a line through the physical world, with the mental-causing items on one side of it and the rest on the other side, must think that mentality is an effect of certain kinds and degrees of physical complexity. This raises a question.

We understand how a complex can have effects which nothing simpler has, if it does so in an *analysable* manner. Suppose that in a universe containing no clockwork, some genius builds a pendulum clock. All of a sudden the universe contains a complex object exhibiting 'horological behaviour', meaning that one of its wheels rotates uniformly twice a day and another once an hour. A complex system has achieved this feat, and much simpler ones could not do it; but we understand *how* the complexity made the difference, because the case is 'analysable', in the following sense. Someone who understood elementary mechanics, and studied a detailed blueprint for the clock, could infer how it would behave. He could reasonably predict, on the strength of his knowledge of the physics of simpler systems, that if those elements were assembled like that, the resulting system would behave horologically. The structural description of the clock, in conjunction with physical laws governing simpler portions of matter, logically entails a conclusion about how the clock will behave when it is constructed.

The causation of life by chemical structures is probably analysable too. It looks as though a superhuman genius who grasped a complete chemical blueprint for some organism, and who knew the laws governing the molecules, could infer 'That would be alive'. The chemical facts about your body's structure, conjoined with the laws of chemistry, *entail* that you are alive.

In neither case is there anything special about the causal laws. One physical complex causes horological behaviour, the other causes vital behaviour, and in each case the causation is exhaustively covered by laws which are also instantiated by simpler systems which neither live nor keep time.

2. The 'life' example is less certain than the other, of course. It used to be thought by many that it was not an analysable example, i.e., that the facts about vitality were not logically reducible to facts about chemistry. This led some to suppose that vitality is an emergent property of some physical systems, meaning that it is caused by them but not analysably—i.e., not so that one could in principle 'see it coming' by attending to structure and to laws governing simpler systems.

Emergence is unpopular amongst scientists and philosophers. Far more than the concept of a 'dangler', it offends against the spirit of Western science, which has for centuries assumed that the properties of any complex can finally be understood through its structure and the laws governing its constituents. Perhaps emergence just *is* a feature of our universe, but we ought to resist this conclusion if we reasonably can.

3. However, if some physical systems produce mentality and others do not, and if concept dualism (see §12) is true, then mentality must be emergent. The only escape from emergence would be to suppose that a full enough understanding of the chemistry and biology of my body would entitle a supergenius to conclude 'That would have to have thought'. This is not to say that mentality entails any particular chemistry and biology, but rather that some characterizations in terms of chemistry and biology entail mentality; and that is part of what dualism denies. I am here arguing only from concept dualism, which denies any logical flow between the mental and the physical. The denial of a causal flow is derived from that by argument: If there is no logical flow, then complex biology cannot relate to mentality as complex chemistry does to life, or as clockwork to time-keeping; so if it is causal it must involve emergence, and that is unacceptable because defeatist and unscientific.

4. I do not attribute that argument to Spinoza. But another objection to emergence is clearly implied by some passages in the *Ethics*.

If there is a level of complexity below which mentality does not occur and above which it does, there cannot be a good explanation of why the line should fall just there on the complexity scale. Dualism won't let there be an explanation of this, as there is for the fact that clocks keep time while matchboxes do not, and that bacteria are alive whereas pebbles are not. This unexplainability must be deeply offensive to Spinoza.

This gives him reason to postulate that the mental realm is as extensive as the physical. Explanatory rationalism will not let him suppose that the mental runs a certain distance with the physical and then inexplicably stops, and dualism will not let him suppose that it runs and then explicably stops; so he has to conclude that it never stops. This reasoning does not require drastic standards for what counts as an explanation. If dualism is correct, then there cannot be *any* reason why the line should fall where it does. When Spinoza says that there cannot be action of mind on body (or, he could have added, of body on mind) because 'there is no common measure' and 'no comparison between the forces of the mind and those of the body' (5 Preface at 280/13), he is making the above point. The lack of 'comparison' means that there is not enough conceptual overlap between the two attributes for even a weak explanation for any given placing of a line between physical events which do and ones which do not have mental associates.

Although Leibniz had nothing extended at his fundamental metaphysical level, he did hold that there is no logical overlap between mental and physical concepts. And he inferred from this that there cannot be a line through the physical world with mind-associated items on one side of it and mindless ones on the other:

I think that there is always perfect correspondence between the body and the soul. . . . I even maintain that something happens in the soul corresponding to the circulation of the blood and to every internal movement of the viscera. . . . If during sleep or waking there were impressions in the body which did not touch or affect the soul in any way at all, there would have to be limits to the union of body and soul, as though bodily impressions needed a certain shape or size if the soul was to be able to feel them. And that is indefensible if the soul is incorporeal, for there is no relation of proportion between an incorporeal substance and this or that modification of matter.[6]

This implies that if God wanted to assign mental counterparts to some events in my body and not to others, there is nothing which could make his drawing of the line other than wholly arbitrary. The plausibility of that is a measure of how strong the pressure is on Spinoza, who had even fewer resources for resisting it, to say that there is no line to be drawn.

5. What are the alternatives? One is to drop concept dualism, accept philosophical behaviourism or functionalism, and thus allow that physical statements could be logically sufficient for the truth of mental ones. Another is to agree that the logical barrier is there, and to conclude that nothing falls under the attribute of thought, i.e., that our mental statements are insulated from purely physical concepts but are all false. Neither of these options—reductive and eliminative materialism—was entertained by Spinoza, and I shall not discuss them.

All that remains is panpsychism—the thesis that no mental/nonmental line cuts across the physical realm because everything would lie on the mental side of it. That is Spinoza's conclusion: there is a mental counterpart to every physical item, however simple and dead; the mental complex which is my mind results from putting together an enormous number of simpler mental items which relate to parts of my body—especially my brain—just as my entire mind relates to my entire body.

6. *New Essays*, p. 116.

(6) THINKING SUBSTANCE

This is not to say that every physical thing has a mind properly so-called, or indeed that it has anything we would recognize as mental. All Spinoza needs to claim is that the phenomena we would recognize as mental are complexes of, and are thus causally continuous with, phenomena associated with very simple physical things. This position has been helpfully put by Thomas Nagel:

New properties are counted as physical if they are discovered by explanatory inference from those already in the class. A similar chain of explanatory inference beginning from familiar mental phenomena would lead to general properties of matter that would not be reached along the path of explanatory inference by which physics is extended. If such properties exist, they are not physical in the sense explained . . . [7]

. . . and could be regarded as 'mental' in a serious sense, even though they are not in the least like anything commonly regarded as mental; just as a lot of what falls within physics is utterly unlike anything *commonly* regarded as physical.

What are these mental properties like? Spinoza must admit that he does not know, and this ought to embarrass him. For reasons that will emerge, he should be troubled by the fact that—to put it in a nutshell—we do know elementary physics but do not know elementary psychology, i.e., the concepts and laws governing the mental counterparts of simple physical particles. I shall partly defend him on this score in §51, but shan't get him right out of trouble. Still, the problem is not fatal; it leaves Spinoza's panpsychism deserving of attention.

6. As for the extent of mentality as ordinarily understood: for Spinoza that is a matter of degree, depending on the kind and amount of physical complexity. He writes:

The things we have shown so far are completely general and do not pertain more to man than to other individuals, all of which, though in different degrees, are nevertheless *animata*. For of each thing there is necessarily an idea in God, of which God is the cause in the same way as he is of the idea of the human body. (p13s)

The Latin adjective *animatus* is cognate with our 'animate' and with the French *âme* (soul). It might be rendered as 'alive' or as 'be-souled', and I agree with the common opinion that Spinoza means both. He is crediting all individuals not merely with life but with souls, something on a continuum with minds.

But that is said about individuals, not about all particular things. Spinoza may confine the term 'individual' to organisms; certainly he does not extend it to physical items that do not have a fair degree of organic complexity.

---

7. Thomas Nagel, 'Panpsychism', in his *Mortal Questions* (Cambridge, 1979), p. 183, quoted with omissions. Nagel is describing the thesis, not advocating it.

He does say that besouledness is a matter of degree, and I am pretty sure he thinks that how much of it a thing has depends upon the degree to which it is an individual or organism. But matters of degree never appear in Spinoza's basic metaphysics, and what he is saying here must be regarded as relatively superficial. Underlying it, as he says, is the fact that every *thing* (not a matter of degree) has a corresponding *idea* (not a matter of degree either) in the mental realm. We shouldn't mix the stern underlying panpsychism with these surface remarks about organisms and normally recognizable mentality.[8]

7. Spinoza primarily links mental complexity with complexity of physical structure; but since that is causally linked to perceptual capacity and behavioural versatility, he could also tie the complexity of a person's mind to those. And so he does: 'In proportion as a body is more capable than others of doing many things or undergoing many things at once, so its mind is more capable than the others of perceiving many things at once' (p13s at 97/8). Even more strikingly in 5p39s he connects mental excellence with having 'a body capable of a great many things', but that is mixed up with some other doctrines of his which I don't want to get into. The general point is clear enough. It is a commonplace in our day, though less so in Spinoza's, that how elevated a mind we can attribute to a given creature depends on the complexity of its behavioural repertoire (doing many things) and the sensitivity of its responses to its environment (undergoing many things). That is what Spinoza is saying, pointing towards the insights of the behaviourists and functionalists.

But he would not agree that this is a start towards a complete analysis of our mental concepts. That would be to relinquish concept dualism. It would also imply that the concept of the mental fades off into inapplicability when you get low enough on the scale of behavioural complexity; and that is to relinquish panpsychism. Spinoza agrees with the behaviourist that no sharp mental/nonmental line divides the physical realm; but where the behaviourist says that the mental/nonmental line is not sharp, Spinoza says that it does not divide the physical realm but instead encloses it. He will concede to the behaviourist that there are unsharp lines through the physical—e.g., the fuzzy circumference of the circle of things with minds (see §30.1), and of the larger circle of things which are in moderate degree besouled—but those lines have no metaphysical significance.

§34. *Spinoza's explanation of the parallelism*

1. Spinoza thinks (i) that there is a mapping between the physical and mental realms, and (ii) that there is no causal relation between them.

8. If we do, we will get into the kind of muddle found in Gueroult, vol. 2, p. 165.

Might it be that (i) is right and (ii) is wrong? The arguments of §33 were all in favour of (i), the panpsychism, but they had no bearing on whether panpsychism should take Spinoza's form or rather consist in the theory that the mental realm contains counterparts of every physical item because it is caused to do so by the physical realm.

Spinoza cannot rule that out decisively except by rejecting, on principle, all causal flow between attributes. However, is he under real pressure to accept a form of panpsychism in which body acts on mind? Yes, for one simple reason, namely, that the parallelism version of panpsychism seems to generate a mystery which its rival does not: if there is no causal flow between the two attributes, then what keeps them in step?

Because Spinoza cannot answer by appealing to divine intervention, this is an acute problem for him. My arguments in §§32–3 give reasons for believing *that* parallelism obtains, but they do not explain *why*. In that respect p3d and p7d aim higher: they offer reasons for believing *and* reasons why, by deriving parallelism from the essential nature of reality. But they are bad arguments.

And they do not even pretend to explain why there is *this* parallelism. Showing why there must be some correlation between physical properties and mental ones is not showing why P_1 is paired with M_1 in particular, and P_2 with M_2, and so on. Why is my sort of brain correlated with my sort of thoughts rather than with yours? Spinoza's demonstrations do not try to answer that.

How *could* he explain why there is this parallelism rather than some other? The explanation of why P_1 is instantiated when and only when M_1 is instantiated cannot lie in those two properties themselves, i.e., some overlap between them; nor can it lie outside them, in something deeper with which both are connected. Each of these is ruled out by the fact that the properties belong to different attributes.

The concept of representation might look helpful. Spinoza does speak of $I(x)$ as the idea *of* x, and seems to think of it as somehow about x, or as representing x: he takes it to point to x in a way in which x doesn't point to $I(x)$. Using that notion, he might say that if you have P_1 and are wondering which mental property is paired with it, you look among mental properties for the one which represents it in the right way. But although this is theoretically available as an answer, Spinoza gives no content to the notion that $I(x)$ represents x, and I do not think he could equip it to explain the details of the parallelism. I shall return to representation in §37, though not to this suggestion.

2. Spinoza is, then, in a deep hole. But he has a further body of theory which constitutes a bold and ingenious attempt to get out of it. It is a metaphysical speculation which I suppose is not true, and it is not even philosophically useful as an object lesson. But I care whether I am right in attributing it to Spinoza, since it displays his basic metaphysic as more coherent and better thought out than any previous commentator has found it to be.

The core of it is a thesis which I have not so far mentioned. We know that according to Spinoza the thinking substance is (identical with) the extended substance, physical and mental particulars are modes of that one substance under its different attributes, and there is a mapping relation which pairs off physical modes with mental ones. But he also says, astonishingly, that between a physical particular and its mental correlate there is not only a correlation but an identity—that is, $x = I(x)$—and that is why parallelism holds. The crucial statement of this will be quoted shortly, but here is one to be going on with:

The mind and the body are one and the same thing, which is conceived now under the attribute of thought, now under the attribute of extension. The result is that the order or interlinking of things is one, whether Nature is conceived under this attribute or that. (3p2s at 141/24)

How is this explanation supposed to work? And what does Spinoza mean when he says, for instance, that my mind is my body?

The clue to that is his thesis that these particulars are modes, ways that reality is, properties of the universe (see §23). If my mind is a mode and my body is a mode, and my mind is my body, it follows that my mind is the same mode as my body. I submit that that is Spinoza's doctrine: his thesis about the identity of physical and mental particulars is really about the identity of properties. He cannot be saying that physical $P_1 =$ mental M_1; that is impossible because they belong to different attributes. His thesis is rather that if P_1 is systematically linked with M_1, then P_1 is extension-and-F for some differentia F such that M_1 is thought-and-F. What it takes for an extended world to contain my body is exactly what it takes for a thinking world to contain my mind; just as what it takes for a two-dimensional figure to be a circle is exactly what it takes for a three-dimensional figure to be a sphere—namely being bounded by a set of points equidistant from one point.

There are two escapes from this 'mode identity' interpretation of Spinoza's mind-body identity thesis. One is to suppose that when he said that my mind and my body are one and the same thing he had forgotten that my mind and my body are modes. The other is to suppose that he held the 'relative identity' thesis (see §16.6), and thought that even if x is a mode and y is a mode, x could be the same thing as y without being the same mode as y. Neither of these should be entertained unless we run into disaster by interpreting the texts, as I am doing, in a less intrusive and more accepting manner. I shall argue that my rather literal reading encounters no disasters and, on the contrary, solves some of the hardest problems in Spinoza exegesis.

It does bend the text slightly. Spinoza usually takes it that a mode 'involves the concept of' an attribute (2p6d), so that entailments run upwards from mode to attribute; but in our present context I must suppose him to be thinking of modes—or 'things', as he calls them—as having their attributes peeled off, i.e., as consisting in the F which must be *added* to extension to get my body or to thought to get my mind. I do not apologize much for having to credit Spinoza with this change of tune: this is the price for letting him mean that a certain mental mode is a certain physical mode, rather than dismissing those texts as lapses or rescuing them through the 'relative identity' manoeuvre.

3. Mind-body identity is not entailed by the thesis that thought and extension are attributes of a single substance. Why should not a thinking and extended substance have details under one attribute which are not also details under the other? So we must see Spinoza as asserting separately (A) that the extended substance is the thinking substance, and (B) that each extended mode is a thinking mode and conversely. There is no obstacle to that in the wording of p7s. Here is the relevant passage:

[A] The thinking substance and the extended substance are one and the same substance, which is comprehended now under this attribute, now under that. Likewise, [B] a mode of extension and the idea of that mode are one and the same thing, but expressed in two ways. (90/6)

I have rendered the Latin *sic* as 'likewise', which is one of its meanings. Another meaning is 'therefore'; but I think its sense here is comparative rather than inferential. Two identity propositions, each involving a straddle of the attributes, are being laid side by side and rightly implied to be similar.

Now we have to bring into our story (C) the thesis of mental-physical parallelism. Shortly after the passage quoted above, Spinoza writes:

For example, [B] a circle existing in Nature and the idea of that circle . . . are one and the same thing, which is explained through different attributes. And that is why, [C] whether we conceive Nature under the attribute of extension or under the attribute of thought, . . . we shall find one and the same order or one and the same connection of causes. (90/12)

The crucial fact here is that Spinoza asserts (B) the mode identity thesis and takes it to explain (C) parallelism. The two are linked by the connective *ideò*, which means 'for that reason' or 'on that account'. Spinoza says, in effect, 'B is true, and that explains why C is true.'

Strictly speaking, however, the explanation of C requires (A) the one-substance doctrine as well as (B) the mind-body identity thesis. Given B alone, we could infer a mapping of physical *propositions* onto mental ones; but parallelism asserts a mapping of physical *facts* onto mental *facts*—it says that for every true physical proposition there is a corresponding true mental one, and vice versa. That is secured by adding to B the thesis (A)

that when any of these modes are instantiated it is always by the same substance: given that reality is (Extended and F) and is Thinking it follows
that it is (Thinking and F). And so, for example, if it contains my body it
contains my mind.

When Spinoza says 'B is true, and that is why C is true', I take him to
be operating against the assumed background of A. And, indeed, he has
asserted A a little earlier in the scholium, and can reasonably be understood
as meaning 'A is true and B is true, and that is why C is true.' (If modes
were not properties but rather the particularised universals that I described
in parentheses in §23.3, then A could be left out of the picture, and C
would follow from B alone.)

Notice that A and B together can explain not merely there being some
panpsychist parallelism, but there being precisely this one. If we ask why
P_1 is always co-instantiated with M_1 rather than with M_2, Spinoza has an
answer: it is because there is some differentia F such that P_1 is (Extension
and F) and M_1 is (Thought and F). That is the explanation I promised
in .2 above.

§35. *A threat to dualism?*

1. When I set up dualism in §12, I allowed very few concepts to be
combinable with both attributes—possibly only ones pertaining to logic,
cause, and time. But now I am interpreting Spinoza's mind-body identity
thesis as implying that almost all properties are transcategorial: instead of
saying that hardly anything escapes the dualist split, I am now saying that
only extension and thought themselves fall within its range. How am I to
reconcile these?

Well, it is not just my 'mode identity' interpretation that has trouble in
this area. It is generally agreed that there is a tremendous strain between
Spinoza's dualism, according to which the attributes cut so deeply into the
substance that there can be no contentful bridge between them, and his
thesis in p7s that the bridge is thick enough to support not merely a contentful substance-identity but a complete parallelism of details. The substance monism is clearly offered as somehow explaining the parallelism;
but how can it do that if the notion of substance—the substance which *has*
the attributes—is without content? This problem exists for everyone who
wants to make sense of this part of Spinoza's thought: it is not a product
of my interpretation, which is special not in creating the problem but in
showing the way to a solution. Until now, nobody seems to have got further
than Donagan:

Why not think of the essence of [the one] substance as standing in a unique relation
to each of its attributes: a relation neither of definitional identity nor of causality;
a relation, moreover, which might reasonably be signified by speaking of each
attribute as 'constituting' or 'expressing' that essence? A fundamental formal prop-

erty of this relation would be that two attributes might on the one hand be really distinct, and on the other constitute or express the same essence.[9]

Why not indeed? But Donagan's proposal tells us nothing about the actual content of Spinoza's doctrines. It says only that his substance monism means *something* consistent with his property dualism: we are not given a glimmering of *what* doctrine the monism might be, let alone an explicit statement of it such as my interpretation supplies.

2. But the problem remains. If I am right in supposing that Spinoza thinks that physical things involve the very same differentiating properties as do mental ones, does not that conflict with his concept dualism by allowing a logical flow between the attributes? For example, it seems to imply that the whole truth about my mind is derivable from the whole truth about my body in conjunction with the mere further premiss that there is a mental realm. For, according to me, that inference has the form

> Reality is (Extended and F);
> Reality is Thinking;
> ∴ Reality is (Thinking and F),

which is strictly valid. It does not derive a mental conclusion from purely physical premisses, admittedly; but its mental premiss is enormously weak, and the argument seems to allow more of a flow between attributes than Spinoza would countenance. I repeat that this is my special form of a problem which confronts us all.

I can solve it if I am allowed to conjecture that Spinoza held a certain opinion which he did not explicitly state. That will get me out of this difficulty, and will also let me explain two parts of the text which have never before been explained: one has baffled everybody, the other seems not to have been noticed. I count it as a point in favour of my reading of p7s that it leads to this conjecture which then does so much good work.

I attribute to Spinoza the opinion that, although the truth about my body has the form

> Reality is (Extended and F)

for a value of F such that the truth about my mind has the form

> Reality is (Thinking and F),

it is absolutely impossible for any mind, however powerful, to have the thought of F in abstraction from both thought and extension.

There are in fact unabstractable differentiae, or so it seems. If we ask 'What is the value of F such that redness is colouredness-and-F?' there

9. Donagan, 'Essence and the Distinction of Attributes in Spinoza's Metaphysics', p. 180. See also Friedman's 'An Overview of Spinoza's *Ethics*', at p. 72.

seems to be no answer (except the trivialising one 'It is the property of being either not coloured or else red'). I am suggesting that Spinoza saw all of the finite modes as relating to extension and to thought as that red-making F relates to colouredness.

But how does that rescue concept dualism? Spinoza seems still to be committed, on my account of him, to allowing that there is a rich logical current flowing between the physical and mental realms. Even if it is carried by differentiae or modes which cannot be grasped in abstraction from any attribute, that is a fact only about what logical currents can be followed, not about what currents there are.

That is wrong, though, for Spinoza does not distinguish what follows and what can be understood to follow. On the contrary, he regularly states theses about logical connections in terms of understanding, explaining, conceiving. And in p7s, immediately after saying that (A) substance monism is true, and likewise (B) the mind-body identity thesis is true, from which it follows (C) that there is the parallelism, he goes on to reconcile this with his dualism by stressing that for him causal or logical connections depend on what is intellectually graspable. Here is the passage, expressed with some of my shorthand, and with the crucial phrases italicised by me, but otherwise following the text faithfully:

When I said before that God is the cause of I(x) only insofar as he is a thinking thing, and the cause of x only insofar as he is an extended thing, this was simply because the inherent nature of I(x) *can be perceived* only through another mode of thinking as its immediate cause, and that mode again through another, and so on to infinity. Hence, so long as things *are considered* as modes of thinking, *we must explain* the order of the whole of Nature . . . through the attribute of thought alone. And insofar as they *are considered* as modes of extension, the order of the whole of Nature *must be explained* through the attribute of extension alone. (90/18)

Applying this to the question of how to reconcile dualism with my 'mode identity' interpretation of Spinoza: the *concept* dualism is not threatened, but we must drop the idea that there is a concept corresponding to every property. On the contrary, the trans-attribute differentiae cannot be intellectually grasped or conceived, i.e., there are no concepts of them, and so we do not get a *property* dualism. The apparent conflict vanishes.

The content and placing of the passage quoted above are extremely significant. The entire scholium boils down to this: 'A is true and so is B, which is why C is true. When I asserted logico-causal dualism, what I meant was . . .', followed by a restatement of the dualism in terms that do not use 'cause', 'follows' or 'reason', but only 'perceive', 'explain' and 'consider'. On my account of Spinoza's thought, including the conjecture about unabstractable differentiae, this is *exactly* what he ought to be doing at this point in his exposition.

3. That is some support for the 'mode identity' interpretation. And there is more. In §16.5 I left dangling the question of why Spinoza defines 'attribute' in terms of what is 'perceived as'—or it could be 'perceived as if'—an essence of a substance. If an attribute is an essence of a substance, why not say so? If it is not, then what is Spinoza trying to say? This is one of the oldest, hardest problems in the interpretation of the *Ethics*; I now claim to have a complete solution of it. Instead of having to treat Spinoza's definition of 'attribute' as something to apologise for, explain away, re-interpret, or wonder about, I can show it to be exactly right, just as it stands.

In that definition the term 'essence' is being used in the Cartesian sense of a fundamental property of a thing, not a special case of something deeper and more general. Now, according to my 'mode identity' interpretation, there is a good sense in which the most basic properties of the one substance are not the attributes but the modes, since they lie deep enough to combine with both attributes. Of course extension is more basic than squareness; but to be square is to be extended and F, for an F which does not entail extension because it is also combinable with thought. Given that there are such Fs, Spinoza rightly won't say that an attribute is an essence = most fundamental property, but only that it must be conceived or perceived[10] as basic, since to get deeper we would have to think of finite modes in abstraction from either attribute, which is impossible. In short, 1d4 is perfect.

In referring to 1d4 at the start of 2p7s, Spinoza takes it to have said that an attribute is perceived by 'an infinite intellect' as an essence of a substance. I take that to mean 'an unlimited intellect'. Spinoza is telling us that his thesis is not about human limitations: the impossibility of abstracting the trans-attribute properties lies deeper than that.

So 1d4 implies that there is something in the nature of an illusion or error or lack of intellectual depth or thoroughness in taking an attribute to be a basic property. But that is hardly surprising. Someone who says that an F is 'what intellect perceives as' a G must be invoking a distinction between appearance and reality, unless his use of 'what intellect perceives' is mere idle prolixity. The only previous commentator to face up to this plain fact was Wolfson, who took Spinoza to be implying that the attributes are not really distinct from one another although we perceive them as being so. Refuting Wolfson is now standard practice among commentators,[11]

10. Conception is weakly distinguished from perception in the explanation following 2d3, but usually they are equated. For instance, ' . . . perceptions, or the faculty of conceiving' (2p49s at 133/26).

11. All the needed ammunition can be found in Haserot, 'Spinoza's Definition of Attribute'.

and I have no doubt that he was wrong. Spinoza certainly thought that there are at least two attributes, each of which really is instantiated. But the gunfire aimed at Wolfson's interpretation goes wide of mine. I say that Nature really has extension and thought, which really are distinct from one another, but that they are not really fundamental properties, although they must be perceived as such by any intellect.

4. In the passage quoted in .1 above, Donagan implies that Spinoza says that each attribute 'constitutes' or 'expresses' the essence of substance. That is not correct. Spinoza brings together the trio 'attribute', 'constitute' and 'essence' only in 1d4 and in two later allusions to it (1p10d, 2p7s), and in each of these he says that an attribute is *perceived as* constituting an essence. When he uses the form 'x constitutes the essence of y' without help from 'perceive', x is never an attribute and y is never a substance.[12] Furthermore, in none of those passages is 'essence' being used in its 1d4 sense of 'basic property'.

What are the other senses of 'essence'? Well there is the 2d2 sense of 'necessary and sufficient condition for existence'. And there is a sense in which God's essence is either the whole truth about God or some part of it which is logico-causally sufficient for the rest: 'All things that happen . . . follow from the necessity of God's essence' (1p15s at 60/10). There is no question of an attribute's being (perceived as) an 'essence' in this sense of the term. And when this sense is being used, Spinoza says that each attribute *expresses* God's essence.[13] My interpretation makes good sense of this. God's essence, in this 'source of the whole truth' sense, is all or part of the system of trans-attribute differentiae; this system is 'expressed' through a given attribute in that the attribute combines with it and makes it accessible to intellect. The attributes let the essence 'come through', so to speak.

I do not say that all of this was explicitly present in Spinoza's mind. Clearly it was not, as can be seen from his not acknowledging the ambiguity of 'essence' and occasionally using it in two senses at once (1p19d). But the structure I have been describing is there in the text, and presumably it operated at some level of Spinoza's mind.

5. It has been argued against my interpretation of 2p7s etc. that in 1p1 Spinoza says that a substance is prior in nature to its states, and derives this from the definitions of 'substance' and 'mode', the latter definition saying that modes are states. So he is saying in effect that substances are prior in nature to their modes, and he never says this about substances in relation

---

12. For example, 'constitutes the essence of the idea' (1p49s at 135/11), ' . . . of the mind' (3p3d), ' . . . of a man' (2p10c).

13. See 1d6,p16d,19d. When in 1p25c Spinoza says that the modes express the attributes, I suppose this is a slip for the converse.

to attributes.[14] I am not much perturbed by this. The only use of 1p1 in the *Ethics* is in 1p5d; and in §17 I have shown that that argument requires 1p1 to be taken as applying not to all modes but only to the accidental ones, the ones which a substance could have lacked while still being the same substance. It is probably to take our minds off the essential modes, i.e., the infinite and eternal ones, that in 1p1,5d Spinoza does not use the term 'mode' but always the term 'state'. So it looks as though 1p1 is seriously present in the *Ethics* as a proposition not about all modes but only about some of them, and that what it says about them is just that they are accidental rather than essential to the substances that have them. There is nothing in this that challenges my account of 2p7s. The opening stages of Part 1 do offer a genuine contrast between attributes and all modes, implied by the statement (1d5) that any mode is 'conceived through something else'; no such thing is said about attributes. But that contrast, far from clashing with my account of 2p7s, is explained by it. Nothing more basic than an attribute can be conceived, and so an attribute cannot be conceived through anything else; whereas a mode can be conceived only as a complex containing some attribute as a constituent, and so we can conceive of something more basic than such a mode, namely, the attribute that it involves.

Another bit of text that might seem to make trouble for my interpretation is 1p2: 'Two substances which have different attributes have nothing in common with one another.' If this means that whatever properties are combined with one attribute are uncombinable with any other, then it conflicts with my 'mode identity' interpretation. But is that what 1p2 means? It is not what it *says*, for it speaks of the attributes of *two* substances, whereas the doctrine I attribute to Spinoza concerns only one substance. His position might be that although there is an F such that the truth about my body has the form 'The world is (Extended and F)' and the truth about my mind has the form 'The world is (Thinking and F)', no F can combine with distinct attributes unless they belong to a single substance.

I don't know how Spinoza could justify that, but at least it is a possible position. Even without it, however, the threat from 1p2 can be neutralized. The only serious work it does for Spinoza is in an argument that runs like this:

> x has no attribute in common with y
> ∴ x has nothing in common with y (by 1p2)
> ∴ x cannot cause y (by 1p3),

with 1p3 being based on 1a5 which says that there cannot be logico-causal relations between things which have nothing in common. Spinoza could

14. This is argued by Margaret D. Wilson, 'Notes on Modes and Attributes', *The Journal of Philosophy* vol. 78 (1981), pp. 584–6.

have made it axiomatic that there cannot be logico-causal relations between different attributes; that would take him directly from the premiss of the above argument to its conclusion, thus letting 1p2,3 disappear from the argument and thus from the *Ethics*. But even if the presence of 1p2 is insisted upon, we should note that it is used only to impose a logico-causal barrier between the attributes; so that we can reasonably bring it within the scope of Spinoza's re-explanation of that barrier in 2p7s. When he says, in effect: 'When I said that I(x) does not cause x, I meant that x cannot be explained through I(x)', he may mean this to apply *mutatis mutandis* to every notion that he has used in the service of the logico-causal barrier. If so, he also meant: 'When I said that if there is no attribute in common there is nothing in common, I meant that there is nothing which can be perceived or understood as being in common.'

Or perhaps he wrote 1p2,3 before thinking hard about how one substance can have several attributes and so on, and thus before developing his 'mode identity' thesis. It is not flattering to him to suggest that he failed to go back and look hard at the opening propositions of the *Ethics* in the light of those later thoughts, but we already have evidence that that is right— namely, his apparently assuming in 1p5d that there cannot be a substance with more than one attribute (see §17.5).

6. My candour about textual problems confronting my 'mode identity' interpretation may encourage some to think they can dismiss it out of hand. I think it should not be rejected except in favour of a superior rival, and so far there are none in the field. Any rival must tackle these questions: (1) What does Spinoza mean by (B) his mind-body identity thesis? (2) How does B relate to (A) substance monism and (C) parallelism? (3) Why does Spinoza immediately follow his A–B–C presentation with a severely intellect-related restatement of his doctrine about flow between the attributes? (4) Why is 'attribute' defined in terms of 'what an intellect perceives'? (5) What does Spinoza mean when he says that God's essence is 'expressed' by this or that attribute? (6) What content can he give to the thesis that thought and extension are instantiated by a single substance?

I have not found in the literature a clear, unevasive, tenable answer to even one of these important questions. My account of this part of Spinoza's thought, centred on the 'mode identity' interpretation, offers clear and forthright answers to all of them.

§36.   *The order of explanations*

1. We have seen Spinoza saying something of the form: 'A is true, and likewise B, which is why (C) the parallelism thesis is true.' He cannot be trying to convince us of C on the grounds that it follows from A and B, because he has not defended B, which has just made its first (and almost its only) appearance in the *Ethics*. I think C is meant to stand on its own feet as something we are obliged to believe; we then ask why it should be true, and can find no tolerable answer except 'If B were true, that would entail and explain C's truth'; and that gives us reason to accept B as well. In short, (B) the mind-body identity thesis is a metaphysical hypothesis whose best recommendation is that it saves us from having to admit an intolerably large and improbable brute fact.

That presupposes that we have reasons for accepting (A) that there is only one substance. So far, Spinoza has offered only his fragile argument from the definition of 'God' as 'substance with infinite attributes'. I have been unable to improve on that as I improved on 2p3d,7d by finding decent reasons for (C) the parallelism thesis. If I am to bolster (A) substance monism with an argument that is at once Spinozist and deserving of respect, it must resemble the case for (B) the mind-body identity thesis. The two arguments together will go as follows. We have good grounds for believing (C) the parallelism thesis; the best explanation for its truth is the double hypothesis that A and B are true; and that gives us reason to believe both A and B.

That may not have been Spinoza's view of the case for A. For all I know, he thought 1p14d to be cogent, and based A on it. Still, my suggested argumentative strategy is more persuasive, yet not out of touch with what actually goes on in the *Ethics*. What work does substance monism do in the pages of the *Ethics*? So far as I can see, its only function is to make the parallelism believable.

2. If I have understood (B) the mind-body identity thesis correctly, then Spinoza had better not argue for it independently. No such argument could succeed. The claim is that each instance of the parallelism is explained by there being some one property F which is instantiated by reality in combination with both thought and extension, thus:

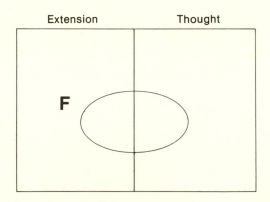

A rough analogy might be this: 'Successful politicians are always neglectful parents, because there is a single character trait F which constitutes success in politics and neglectfulness in parenting.' Something like that might be true, but it could not be known unless we could know what the F was. If someone claimed that a single trans-activity character trait explained the concomitance of political success and parental failure, but added that the concept of this character trait could not be grasped except in combination with the concept of some activity through which it is manifested—e.g., politics or parenting—we would have no reason to believe him. Similarly with the theory I am attributing to Spinoza: why should we believe that the facts about my body and my mind are explained by there being an F which is instantiated in (Extended and F) and also in (Thinking and F), if we cannot abstract it from the former combination and track it across to the latter one?

In the face of this, Spinoza could reasonably say: 'You are right that I could not adduce a single instance of the phenomenon I am talking about. To single out an instance would be to abstract, so it wouldn't be an instance. But I do have a general reason for thinking that there are these unabstractable trans-attribute differentiae. If there are, the parallelism is deeply and beautifully explained; if there are not, it is a strange, universal, brute fact.'

3. The ensuing chapters will not assume the truth of my thesis in §§34–6. If I were wholly wrong about B, and what is going on in p7s, and the definition of 'attribute', and so on, I could still stand by my independent arguments for the parallelism thesis, and could suppose them to have influenced Spinoza also. I would then have no decent Spinozist argument for substance monism, and no answer to the question 'How could Spinoza avoid seeing the parallelism as anything but an ugly, universal, brute fact?'—no answer, that is, except to suppose that he claims extravagant amounts of success for p3d and p7d. But these would be lacks which I shared with all previous Spinoza commentators.

The remainder of Spinoza's book, and of mine, would not be much affected. What counts elsewhere is the parallelism—the mapping of causal chains onto causal chains—and that would be untouched by a failure of my conjecture that Spinoza had a theory about trans-attribute properties and used it to explain parallelism.

7   *Cognitive Psychology*

In this chapter, assuming the doctrine of parallelism but not assuming that I am right about how Spinoza would explain the truth of that doctrine, I shall examine his views about the cognitive aspects of the mind, especially belief and perception. Desires are examined in chapter 9, emotions in chapter 11.

§37. 'Idea of'

1. We must start by looking into what Spinoza means when he speaks of ideas as being 'of' their objects. Under the parallelism scheme, each idea is paired with a physical item which is its object; Spinoza speaks of the idea *of* the object, and also of the object *of* the idea. He seems to think there is an important asymmetry, however: I(x) is somehow about x, it points to it or represents it, whereas x is not similarly about or representative of I(x).

First, a warning. Spinoza's actual parallelism thesis says not merely that if x is *physical* then I(x) exists, but that if x is *real* then I(x) exists. That is, he has not a thought-extension parallelism but a thought-everything parallelism, and eventually he infers from this that there are 'ideas of ideas': if I(x) exists then so does I(I(x)). Thus, 2p3 says there is an idea of everything—not just everything physical—that follows from God's essence; and 2p7 matches the order and connection of ideas with the order and connection of things—not only physical things. However, until I discuss 'ideas of ideas' in §44 I shall stay with the milder parallelism thesis that there is a mapping of the physical realm onto the mental realm. Thus, sometimes there will be an overhang as you descend from a quoted passage to my narrower gloss on it; I shall not comment on such discrepancies.

2. Some occurrences of the concept of representation in the *Ethics* involve a pair of technical terms, *formaliter* and *objectivè*. These are still sometimes rendered by 'formally' and 'objectively', respectively, but in the twentieth century that produces unintelligible results. What a thing has *formaliter* are its inherent features; whereas it has *objectivè* the features which it represents or depicts—those which are possessed not by it as a psychological episode but rather by its meaning or content. Thus, my present thought of Spinoza's death is characterised *formaliter* by the date 1982 and *objectivè* by the date 1677. This is unlike how 'objectively' is used these days; indeed, that word has almost reversed its meaning over the centuries, going from 'considered in respect of its object' to 'considered as an object'.

The most important occurrence of these terms is in 2p7c, where Spinoza infers from 2p7 that:

God's actual power of thinking is equal to his actual power of acting. That is, whatever follows *formaliter* from God's infinite nature follows *objectivè* in God from his idea in the same order and with the same connection.

I take that to amount to something like this:

The universe's mental resources are equal to its physical resources. That is, if the physical nature of the universe makes it actually the case that P, then the nature of the mental side of the universe generates, in a corresponding way, a mental item which is the thought or idea that P, i.e., which represents the fact that P.

Having given that one example of the use of the Latin, I shall henceforth use 'inherently' for *formaliter* and 'representatively' for *objectivè*.[1] Thus, I render Spinoza's trial run for 2p7c in Letter 32 as: 'There exists in nature an infinite power of thought which . . . contains within itself, representatively, the whole of Nature.' (IV/173/18)

In inferring 2p7c from 2p7, Spinoza glides smoothly from 'Every physical item is matched by a mental one' to 'Every physical item is represented by a mental one'. He makes this move repeatedly, as in moving from 'idea of' to 'cognition of' in 2p9cd, and from 'is the object of' to 'is perceived by' in 2p12d. He never says what makes the move valid.

Of course, if the members of one set are correlated with those of another, one lot might be used to represent the others; hence, the mere thesis of parallelism as such yields a representation relation of a sort. But it will be symmetrical: if certain correspondences enable me to use the marks on a piece of paper to represent the roads in Sussex, then I could use the Sussex road system to represent the marks on the paper. When Leibniz squeezed a theory of representation ('perception') out of a matching relation, he got symmetry; but that was what he wanted, because he held that the states of every monad represent (are perceptions of) those of every other. Spinoza, however, has no use for a symmetrical relation: he assumes that I(x) represents x, and that the converse does not hold. It is true that he says that human bodies contain physical 'images of' other bodies, but *that* 'of' is apparently not a representing one. When he says: 'The images of things are states of the human body, *the ideas of which* represent external bodies' (3p27d), he takes pains to assign the representative role to the mental side, giving none to the physical image.

---

1. Following G. E. M. Anscombe and P. T. Geach (eds.), *Descartes: Philosophical Writings* (London, 1954), p. 185. For more on this terminology, see A. Kenny, *Descartes* (New York, 1968), pp. 131f.

3. I suspect that Spinoza's glide from 2p7 to 7c was mediated by a deep assumption that it is of the essence of the mental, as such, that mental items are representative, about something, pointed outwards. That may well be true, and a lot of contemporary philosophy of mind is sympathetic to it, but I am sorry that Spinoza does not discuss it. Had he done so, he would surely have discovered that it cannot be true in the form in which he holds it. According to him (2p11,13), my mind is the 'idea of' my body: if x is my body then I(x) is my mind, and if I(y) is just one of my thoughts then y is the corresponding cerebral event. Now, when I think sadly about today's weather, there is a corresponding event in my body—mostly in my brain—and Spinoza will say that my weather thought is the idea of that cerebral event. We are under no conceptual pressure to suppose that the 'weather' thought represents the cerebral event, except in the trivial and symmetrical sense of being systematically matched by it; yet Spinoza thinks otherwise, saying that whatever happens in my body 'must be perceived by' my mind (2p12). There are no good reasons for that. If there are reasons for thinking that mental items are essentially representative, that is because mentality must be rooted in what an organism represents to itself about its situation. As I shall explain in §39.4, it is plausibly arguable that what launches the concept of mind is the notion of how an animal's achievement of its goals is helped by its *beliefs*; and since beliefs are representative, that plausible view puts representation right into the heart of the concept of mentality. But it is not a representation by mental events of their cerebral counterparts! The latter may be important in many ways, but not in the part of the story which requires a concept of representation. *That* is all concerned with the representation of states of affairs having to do with risks of predators, prospects of food, and the like.

Spinoza does not go on at length about the representative aspect of the I( ) concept: this view of his flits past in 2p7c and is not directly alluded to again. But I needed to attend to it for the following reason. Later in Part 2, Spinoza provides for a second 'of' relation between an idea and something physical. That is, taking I(x)—here and always—to name the mental counterpart of x under the parallelism, he provides a sense in which I(x) can be 'of' something other than x. I shall say that I(x) is *directly of* x, and *indirectly of* this other item. Now, the 'indirectly of' relation is clearly a representative one, and one might be tempted to suppose that to be the primary distinction between the two: the parallelism yields a matching 'of' relation, while Spinoza's extra bit of theory (to be expounded shortly) yields a representative 'of' relation.[2] But that conflicts with 2p7c where the matching relation is taken to be representative; and, more im-

2. That is the position taken, in effect, in Radner's perceptive 'Spinoza's Theory of Ideas'.

portantly, it does violence to much of what happens in Part 2. We shall see that of Spinoza's discussions in which representation is involved, some clearly do involve the 'directly of' relation, and some hover between the two 'of' relations without clearly choosing between them.

That is not to say that Spinoza had no distinction between them. He did. It is important to grasp that he provides for two ways in which a feature of my body can be represented in my mind: directly, by its systematic mental counterpart; or indirectly, as when I learn things about my body by observing it—e.g., when I *see* my right arm. When Spinoza says that my mind contains ideas of every aspect of my body, he does not liken me to an omniscient anatomist and physiologist, for that would be to have a large amount of knowledge indirectly of my body.[3]

Now let us get down to some details about ideas indirectly of 'external bodies'.

4. Spinoza introduces the 'indirectly of' relation in 2p16,c1,c2. On the strength of an 'axiom' saying that when two physical things interact the outcome depends on what each is like, he contends in p16 that if x is a state of my body caused by some other item y, then I(x) must 'involve the nature of' y as well as of x. The 'axiom' is surely true, Spinoza's inference from it is sound, and so his conclusion is true: the states of my mind can reflect what my environment is like because they can be caused by my environment.

Except that he cannot say exactly that, since he denies that a physical environment can cause a state of mind. When I see a splash on the surface of a lake, he postulates two causal chains—from Splash to Cerebral Event, and from I(Splash) to I(Cerebral Event). This last is my mental awareness of the splash; and I(Splash) is a hypothetical entity required by the parallelism thesis, and asserted on theoretical grounds to relate to Splash as my mental state does to Cerebral Event, and to be the cause of my awareness. In p5,6,9 Spinoza hammers away at this theme of parallel causal chains with no crossovers.

5. He says that if y causes state x of my body, then I(x)—which is my idea directly of x and indirectly of y—'involves the nature of' x and of y, from which he infers that in having I(x) I 'perceive' both x and y (see p16c1). He does not explain 'involves the nature of' nor justify the move from it to 'perceives'.

Much later in the *Ethics*, nature-involvement will be nature-sharing: one thing will be said to 'involve the nature' of another because they are alike. But that cannot be what is meant in our present context, where the

---

3. This point is made explosively and at length in Hallett's 'On a Reputed Equivoque in the Philosophy of Spinoza', and with quiet brevity in Caird's *Spinoza*, pp. 198f.

involvement holds across the boundary between attributes. Because causality requires conceptual overlap, in Spinoza's opinion, he can say that if y causes x then there is a similarity between *them*, but that cannot generate a similarity between y and I(x). He would do best to say (and I suppose that if pressed he would say) that I(x) 'involves the nature of' y in the sense that it partly depends on y: it is because of what y is like that my mental state is as it is. From that starting point, he might launch a general theory of perception, direct and indirect, contending that to perceive something is to be in a mental state which causally depends on it in certain ways. More would have to be said, of course, if the theory were not to imply that my sudden mental blaze of light is a perception of the hammer which has just hit me on the head, that my auditory state is a perception of the humidity of the air in the concert hall, and so on. But Spinoza might be uninterested in such further refinements. His view that I directly perceive everything that happens in my body suggests that he might be willing to equate perception with qualitative dependence, unrestrictedly.

This is all a theoretical vacuum, then. We do not know what load Spinoza wanted 'perception' to carry, or how he thought the carrying should be done. Even in this vacuum, however, we can note that the 'indirectly of' relation is more like perception as we ordinarily understand it than is the 'directly of' relation. For one thing, 'indirectly of' permits there to be different perceptions—even in different minds—of the very same item, whereas 'directly of' is one-one. Also, and more prosaically, we are obviously closer to home when we speak of perceiving shoes and ships and sealing wax than when we speak of perceiving events in our own brains.

6. One's perception of an external thing involves qualitative dependence on that thing, mediated by the states of one's own body: 'A human mind does not perceive any external body as actually existing except through the ideas of the states of its body.' (p26) This is probably the real basis for p16c2: 'The ideas which we have of external bodies indicate the condition of our own body more than the nature of the external bodies.' Spinoza is right about this, just so long as 'indicating' here, like 'involving' earlier, conforms to something like the following: The fact that Fx indicates the fact that Gy if and only if there is some general principle from which, in conjunction with Fx, it follows that Gy. This will be true if, for instance, Fx is caused to be the case by Gy's being the case and could not have been caused in any other way. Now, by this standard every fact about my body is indicated by some fact about my mind; the parallelism sees to that. But many facts about external bodies will not be thus indicated in my mind, because they will concern aspects of the external bodies which made no difference to—had no effect on—my body, and therefore did not 'show up' in my mind.

In p18s Spinoza says that if I(x) is an idea indirectly of y then it *involves* the natures of both x and y but that it *exhibits, unfolds, spreads out*, the nature only of x. The crucial verb is *explicare*, which can usually be translated by 'explain'; but its root meaning is that of unfolding something so as to reveal all its detail, and that is its meaning here. So this is p16c2 all over again: I(x) has a feature matching each feature of x, but not one for each feature of y.

7. A striking example of how an idea can part company with its indirect object is provided by the case in which the object goes away, or even goes out of existence, without this affecting the body of the person who had formed an idea indirectly of it. Here is how Spinoza puts it, lightly edited:

If someone's body is in a state which involves the nature of an external body, his mind will regard the external body as actually existing, or as present to it, until his body comes to be in a state which excludes the existence or presence of that external body. (p17)

Two elements in this are worth comment. (i) Although it allows me to have an idea indirectly of y at a time when y is absent, it still conforms to the requirement that the physical counterpart of the idea be caused by y: the gap between idea and reality comes about purely through my body's not having kept up to date on what is happening in its environment. Thus, no provision has been made for my having an idea indirectly of something which has not acted on my body at all. (ii) In p17 we suddenly encounter the notion of 'regarding as'. Spinoza has been making the point that even after y has departed I may still be in the same sensory state as when seeing y; but now he seems to have turned that into a different point—or to have added a further one to it—namely, that even after y has gone I may still think that y is present to me. This is not a mere slip: Spinoza holds as a matter of doctrine that all mental states approximate to the nature of beliefs, so that he cannot deeply distinguish depicting something as F from believing it to be F.

He uses 'imagination' to cover the whole range of the sensory and quasi-sensory: I 'imagine' something when I see it for real, and when I see it in my mind's eye. Thus, to have an idea indirectly of something is to 'imagine' it, in Spinoza's terminology. Now, in subsequent demonstrations he usually treats p17 as a proposition about what we 'imagine' (for example, 3p13, 19,56), but some of them equate imagining y as present with regarding it as present (see 2p44c1s, 3p28, 5p7). Spinoza is open about this equation:

The states of the human body whose ideas represent external bodies as present to us we shall call images of things, even if they do not reproduce the things' shapes. And when the mind regards bodies in this way, we shall say that it imagines. (2p17cs at 106/7)

This is a mere warning shot. Spinoza's views about belief will be explored in §39.

§38. *Deciding what to believe*

1. The treatment of belief in Part 2 is rather tangled, in the exposition if not in Spinoza's thought. In this section I shall draw a single thread out of the tangle, which will make it easier then to unravel the rest.

The thread is Spinoza's treatment of Descartes's view about how belief fits in with the other doings of the mind. Here is what Descartes says:

> We have only two kinds of thought, namely the perception of the understanding and the action of the will. . . . Thus sensing, imagining, and even conceiving purely intelligible things are just different ways of perceiving; but desiring, holding in aversion, affirming, denying, doubting are different ways of willing. . . The will has a greater extent than the understanding, and that is why we commit errors.[4]

That introduces Descartes's account of why God is not to blame for our errors of judgment: although whatever is in our understandings is put there by God, our assents and dissents proceed from a will which is 'free' in a radical sense which clears God of any responsibility for how it is exercised.

Spinoza is not interested in defending the good name of a personal God. Nor would he use a concept of freedom which is radical enough to conflict with strict determinism. Since he discusses these matters in p49 and its long scholium, right after p48's assertion that 'In the mind there is no absolute or free will', it is easy to see the discussion wholly in the light of his rejection of radical, anti-deterministic freedom. That would be a mistake. There is another line of thought as well, having to do with belief and not with freedom, which I now expound.

2. Descartes puts sensing, imagining and abstract thought into one grand mental category, while putting (dis)liking, affirming and denying in the other. It is an odd grouping. Philosophers have traditionally distinguished a person's 'cognitive' aspects—comprising knowledge, belief and understanding—from his 'conative' aspects, which are supposed to include (dis)liking, wanting, intending and trying. Descartes's division seems to cut across that, by lumping the conative 'desiring and holding in aversion' in with the cognitive 'affirming and denying'. He classifies mental activities in that way because he thinks that affirming, denying, accepting or rejecting propositions, require 'will' as well as 'understanding', and thus depend on the conative as well as the cognitive side of the person. My understanding puts the proposition before my mind, and then I voluntarily affirm or deny or suspend judgment on it.

I take it that something falls within the province of the will only if it

---

4. *Principles* I.32, 35. See also the middle third of the Fourth Meditation.

could be directly influenced by inducements such as threats and bribes. (It might be thought that that excludes likes and dislikes, but really it doesn't. You cannot bribe me into not enjoying apples, but you can, by bribes or threats, make the eating of apples something I want not to do, something I 'hold in aversion'.) So Descartes is implying that we can be induced, by bribes or threats, to believe things. If he isn't, then I do not know what his thesis is.

If I have understood the thesis correctly, then I agree with Spinoza that it is wrong. Of course I may voluntarily undertake to be conditioned into changing my beliefs: for example, I may be convinced by Pascal's wager argument, and try to acquire Christian beliefs by living a Christian life. But this is not a case of acquiring beliefs at will. It involves only what Leibniz called the will's 'action at a distance' upon the judgment. Descartes's purposes are not served unless he means that when I believe something wrongly, the fault can be mine just as immediately as it is when I deliberately spill ink on the carpet; and that is what Spinoza, like most philosophers, rejects.

Why is it false? Is it a contingent fact that we cannot switch beliefs on and off at will? I suspect that it is rather a conceptual necessity, stemming from the structure of the concept of belief; but I have no proof of that, and not for want of looking for one.

3. Spinoza, however, does not put this point by saying that what we believe is determined by cognitive factors—what evidence we have, and how we evaluate it—and that the will is irrelevant to this. Rather, he says that in this context 'The will and the intellect are one and the same' (p49c). This reflects his decision to use the term 'will' to stand for 'the faculty by which the mind affirms or denies something true or something false, and not the desire by which the mind wants a thing or avoids it' (p48s at 129/31). It is only in this final segment of Part 2 that 'will' is used in this way: in 1p17s at 62/33 it is clearly implied that will and intellect are distinct; and in 3p9s and elsewhere 'will' is linked in the usual way with wanting etc. My own uses of the word follow that normal usage.

His odd terminology aside, Spinoza is making a perfectly accessible claim, namely, that it is not the case that in judging or acquiring beliefs there is an intellectual process in which material comes before the mind and then a voluntary action of making a judgment about it. We can voluntarily decide whether what we *say* shall accord with 'what we are aware of' —i.e., with our cognitive possessions, the evidence we have and the weight we give it—but there is no such decision to be made about what we shall *believe*. Spinoza suggests that Descartes may have thought that to believe something is in a fashion to assert it: 'Those who confuse words with . . . the affirmation itself . . . think that they can will something contrary to what they are aware of, when they only affirm or deny with words something contrary to what they are aware of.'[5] In his next sentence, Spinoza remarks that this error will be avoided by anyone who remembers that words are physical items whereas 'thought does not at all involve the concept of extension'; but that is not true. A Cartesian might say: 'I am quite clear about how uttering the sentence "God is good" differs from mentally judging that God is good. But both are voluntary, because they differ only in that one is physical and the other mental, and that cannot alter their relation to the will.' So Spinoza ought to be attacking the idea that believing is saying in one's heart, and is therefore as voluntary as saying out loud is; and that attack is not helped by the reminder that believing is mental and not physical. Still, most of his discussion shows a firm control of the issue.

4. All Descartes needs for his immediate purposes is that the will should govern the suspension of belief: he wants us to avoid error by having fewer beliefs, like avoiding inebriety by drinking fewer martinis. He might give in about believing and disbelieving, yet stand his ground on the difference between having an opinion and suspending judgment. Spinoza anticipates that move:

It can be objected to us that experience seems to teach nothing more clearly than that we can suspend our judgment so as not to assent to things we perceive, and thus to teach that the will, or faculty of assenting, is different from the understanding. (132/32 and 133/2, lightly edited)

Spinoza denies that we can choose whether or not to have an opinion on a matter:

I reply by denying that we have a free power of suspending judgment. For when we say that someone suspends judgment, we are saying nothing but that he sees that he does not perceive the thing adequately. Suspension of judgment, therefore, is really perception, not free will. (134/11)

We should not lean hard on the word 'perception'. The basic point is clear enough: someone suspends judgment if his cognitive situation will not let him commit himself, i.e., if he sees that it would be inappropriate to have an opinion. Thus, a suspension of judgment arises from a judgment, a seeing or perceiving or realizing that something is the case, and is thus no more directly under the command of the will than any judgment is. The suspension of judgment or belief belongs, Spinoza is rightly saying, to the province of intellect and not to that of a separate will; it is not to be compared with deciding to leave the apple on the tree.

5. p49s at 132/12. There is more to the same effect in *Short Treatise* at I/83/18.

(7) COGNITIVE PSYCHOLOGY

§39. *Ideas as beliefs*

1. In agreeing with Spinoza against Descartes that believing is not a voluntary intellectual act which we choose to perform on a given proposition, most of us would be willing to say something like this: 'When I am entertaining a proposition, it is not my will—not what I decide or what I want—that determines whether I believe it, disbelieve it, or suspend judgment on it.' That agrees with Descartes that (i) belief or judgment consists in entertaining a proposition plus having a further attitude to it, and disagrees with his view that (ii) the further attitude is voluntarily chosen. Spinoza, however, denies (i) as well, maintaining that propositions come before the mind *as* beliefs. That is the real reason why 'will and intellect are one and the same'. I have pretended that this means only that we don't have a cognitive process and then a further voluntary act; but really it means something more radical, namely, that we don't have a cognitive process of bringing propositions into the mind and a further process—even an involuntary one—in which they come under propositional attitudes.

This thesis is presented in the middle part of p49s, where Spinoza musters and successively answers four objections to his view about how belief fits into the story of the mind. (i) The first concerns Descartes's view that the will is 'infinite' and the intellect 'finite', the idea being that there are limits to the amount of cognitive material we can get into our minds but there is never any impediment to our simply refusing to assent to some presented proposition. Spinoza rightly thinks this to be false, though his handling of the 'infinite'/'finite' version of the point is peculiar. (ii) The second objection will be my topic shortly. (iii) The third objection says that we have a power of affirming which works equally well on propositions of all kinds and levels, dignified and squalid, true and false; and this shows that the affirming of a proposition is distinct from what is affirmed. The first part of Spinoza's response to this is obscure. The second part denies the premiss: 'I deny absolutely that we require an equal power of thinking to affirm [a truth] as to affirm [a falsehood].' I am sure that this is wrong. If Spinoza has a reason for it, it lies in his theory of error, which I shall present in §40. (iv) The fourth objection concerns determinism and radical freedom, and is not relevant to my present theme.

2. The second objection has two parts, as does Spinoza's reply. First there is the argument and counterargument reported at the end of §38: the Cartesian claim that suspension of judgment is purely voluntary, countered by Spinoza's reply that, on the contrary, when someone suspends judgment that is purely because of facts about his cognitive situation.

The rest of the exchange drives deeper. Even someone who disagrees with Descartes may still think that belief is just one propositional attitude

162

among others, and that suspending judgment is having the proposition in your mind without having enough else there to produce either a Yes or a No. He may defend this on the ground that a person is not necessarily guilty of error just because his mind contains the thought that P, for some false P, since he may be merely pretending or fancying that P. In the words Spinoza gives to his objector:

No one is said to be deceived insofar as he perceives something, but only insofar as he assents or dissents. For instance, someone who mentally constructs a winged horse does not on that account grant that there is a winged horse, i.e. he is not on that account deceived unless at the same time he grants that there is a winged horse. (132/35)

Spinoza's reply includes this:

I grant that the imaginings of the mind, considered in themselves, involve no error. But I deny that a man affirms nothing insofar as he perceives. For what is perceiving a winged horse other than affirming wings of a horse? For if the mind perceived nothing else except the winged horse, it would regard it as present to itself, and would not have any cause of doubting its existence, or any faculty of dissenting, unless the imagination of the winged horse was joined to an idea which excluded the existence of that horse. (134/27)

He is maintaining that the thought (or idea or imagining) of an F will be present in my mind as the belief that there is an F, unless something blocks me from believing that. Just before this passage, he has spoken of an inexperienced child who somehow acquires a mental picture of a winged horse and, being defenceless against it, 'necessarily regards the horse as present'. A merely entertained proposition, then, rather than being undisturbed by assent or dissent, is a proposition that is subject to roughly equal pulls in both directions.

3. Spinoza has no argument for this, so far as I can see. In the passage about the child he says: 'Since this imagining involves the existence of the horse (by p17c), and the child does not perceive anything else which excludes the existence of the horse, he will necessarily regard the horse as present.' The mention of p17c is significant. In §37.7 I called attention to the way p17 suddenly moves from 'imagining x as present' to 'regarding x as present', of which the latter obviously involves the concept of belief while the former does not obviously do so. Well, here it is again, bearing a lot of weight but still undefended.

I can think of evolutionary reasons why higher organisms might strongly tend, when 'imagining' an F, to believe they are confronted by an F: since such beliefs will usually be true, a disposition to form them will be advantageous and genes for them will tend to be selected. Spinoza could not have argued like that, of course, though he might have offered a social variant on the argument, stressing the effect on a child of finding that certain belief-forming strategies are successful. But he needs something much stronger than that: he contends not merely that when my mind contains a propositional thought I will believe it unless prevented from doing so, but more strongly that such thoughts come into the mind *as* beliefs. The thesis seems to be that if you doubt Spinoza's 'It's a belief unless prevented', that shows not that you are ignorant of human psychology but rather that you don't understand what an idea is. Recall that he speaks of judgment and belief acquisition in terms of volition and of 'affirmation', and then consider this: 'In the mind there is no volition, or affirmation and negation, except that which an idea *qua* idea involves' (p49). This seems to imply not merely that I shall make my idea the content of a belief unless I am prevented from doing so, but that the idea actually is a belief.

Also, Spinoza warns us against thinking that 'an idea is something mute, like a picture on a panel', because really it is 'a mode of thinking, viz. the act of understanding itself' (p43s at 124/10). And later on: 'They look on ideas as mute pictures on a panel, and, seized by this prejudice, they do not see that an idea *qua* idea involves an affirmation or negation.' (p49s, at 132/9) These passages seem to imply that every idea is intrinsically belief-like.

(This is not in conflict with Spinoza's statement that 'The imaginings of the mind, considered in themselves, contain no error.' He does not mean that they are mere sensory states which could not have truth-values. His claim is not about belief, but about error. I shall explain it in §40.)

Many recent philosophers have thought that a good account of the mind should be founded on a concept of something like belief. That is a thumbprint of the attempt to analyse mental concepts through their role in explaining behaviour. But that approach, though putting the spotlight on the notion of belief, does not exclude mental contents which are not incipient beliefs—it merely says that their status must be explained through their relation to beliefs.[6] Others have defended a thesis that may be as strong as Spinoza's, namely, that what we immediately take from objects in sense-perception—the intake which used to be called 'sense-data'—consists in dispositions to believe things about our environment.[7] According to this view, when it seems to me that I see something red my environment is disposing me to believe that I am seeing something red—that's *what it is* to seem to see something red. This theory may have no room for mental contents which are not belief-like, and so it may be like Spinoza's. I do not know how close it is to what he had in mind, however; and the motivations for it would certainly not be his. The plan has been to analyse 'sensory

6. See *Linguistic Behaviour*, pp. 49f.

7. For example: D. M. Armstrong, *Perception and the Physical World* (London, 1961), and George Pitcher, *A Theory of Perception* (Princeton, 1971).

state' in terms of 'belief', and then to analyse 'belief' in a behaviourist manner, thus making a case for out-and-out physicalism. Spinoza would have no interest in such a programme as that.

4. Because he thought that ideas are *ex officio* beliefs, Spinoza saw no need for a theory of belief that would explain what marks it off from the other propositional attitudes. This is a serious gap in his philosophy, and it would still be a gap even if he were right in his weaker thesis that any thought will be believed unless something prevents that. Geach says:

Possibly a thought is assertoric in character unless it loses this character by occurring only as an element in a more complicated thought. In Spinoza's example, the boy whose mind is wholly occupied with the thought of a winged horse, and who lacks the adult background knowledge that rules out there being such a thing, cannot but assent to the thought of there being a winged horse. This would be a neat solution to the problem of how thought is related to judgment.[8]

If that last phrase alludes to the problem of explaining how entertaining differs from believing, then Geach is being too charitable. An explanation is needed, and it would not be provided merely by the doctrine that thoughts strongly tend to be beliefs.

Many philosophers, including Leibniz and Berkeley, have ducked the problem of explaining what belief is, or what 'judgment' or belief-acquisition is. Locke tried to explain judgment, but in the course of his attempt he said that 'the mind takes its ideas to agree or disagree', as though he had no need to explain what it is to *take* something to be the case. Hume had a disastrous theory according to which believing that P is just vividly imagining that P. Descartes spoke of belief as a voluntary act, but he did not venture to say *what* act. The philosophy of belief seems to have been a series of evasions and disasters until, during the past half-century, philosophers have tackled belief as one of a trio, the other two members of which are desire and behaviour. This approach was heavily foreshadowed by F. P. Ramsey, and—so far as I know—first developed into an explicit analysis of belief by R. B. Braithwaite:

Braithwaite identifies belief in a proposition with its entertainment together with a dispositional readiness to act as if it were true. 'Being ready to act as if P were true' has at first sight a suggestion of circularity. . . . But . . . I act as if P were true if I act in a way which would satisfy my desires if P were in fact true.[9]

That was just a start, which has been developed by later writers. The basic

---

8. P. T. Geach, 'Assertion', *The Philosophical Review* vol. 74 (1965), p. 457.

9. A. M. Quinton, 'Knowledge and Belief', in Edwards, vol. 4 at p. 351. R. B. Braithwaite's 'The Nature of Believing', which first appeared in 1932, is in A. P. Griffiths (ed.), *Knowledge and Belief* (Oxford, 1967). For Ramsey's adumbration, see 'Truth and Probability' in his *Foundations* (London, 1978).

fact is that observations of how a creature behaves will tell you what it believes if you know what it wants, and will tell you what it wants if you know what it believes. If we seek to learn about a creature's mind from its behaviour, then, we must advance on both fronts at once, progressively correcting conjectures about belief and about desire or intention in the light of growing data about behaviour. The project might seem to be threatened with circularity or vacuity, but it is not.[10] The thesis that belief is a function from desires to behaviours, and that desire is a function from beliefs to behaviours, is not the whole story but it is a better start on it than anyone had in the seventeenth century.

The improvement was helped by a shift of emphasis from the notion of (episodic) judgment to that of (durable and largely dispositional) belief. For many years you have believed that we are further from the sun than from the moon, but you have not been busily judging that this is so. I do not deny that there are episodic judgments. In fact, there are two sorts of mental episode that might be so-called—ones in which you bring a belief explicitly and consciously before your mind, and ones in which you acquire a certain belief. The latter is relevant to our present purposes: what I have treated as a history of failure to understand belief has largely been a history of focussing on the acquisition of beliefs and neglecting them as durable possessions. It has been a help to recent theorists of belief that they have started at the other end, first tackling durable belief and then understanding belief-acquisition in terms of that, rather than starting with acquisition—under the label 'act of judgment'—and then casually treating durable beliefs as merely the results of such 'acts'. Spinoza is more attentive to episodic judgments than to durable beliefs—a fact which I have neglected since it seems not to affect the main outlines of his doctrines about cognition. It may affect details, however. In the Part 3 account of the emotions, for instance, phrases like 'the idea of an external cause [of my pleasure]' occur frequently, and it may make some difference whether 'idea' there refers to a belief or to the acquisition of one. I have not done the work needed to discover whether it really does make a difference.

More important than the judgment/belief matter is the following. Even if Spinoza had seen the need for some theory of belief, properly so-called, he could not have had the currently popular Braithwaitean kind of theory. Its behavioural emphasis need not have inhibited him: he is always ready to get at mental distinctions through physical ones. But he positively cut himself off from using a satisfactory concept of desire. His reasons for doing this will appear in chapter 9. They arose from a profound insight, but the results were calamitous, and the worst of them was the loss of any chance of having a good account of belief.

10. This is shown in *Linguistic Behaviour*, pp. 50–52.

5. The thesis that all ideas are beliefs contains the thesis that all ideas are propositionally structured. Geach has shown that these two are often conflated by philosophers, to the detriment of their work;[11] and I am not certain that Spinoza is innocent of this mistake. He sometimes announces the big doctrine as though it were obviously right, and this may be because he is conflating the big doctrine with the smaller one nested inside it.

For example, when he says: 'What is perceiving a winged horse other than affirming wings of a horse?' the question is rhetorical, inviting us to reply 'What indeed?' There is no reason why we should be swept into agreeing that a winged-horse sensory state is a belief; but we might be easier to budge if Spinoza were only arguing that a winged-horse sensory state has propositional structure, i.e., that to imagine an F thing as G is to have a thought of the form 'The F thing is G'.

Again, we have looked at p49 which seems to say that ideas are beliefs. In p49d Spinoza argues at length for the tame thesis that a certain 'affirmation' about triangles 'involves the concept or idea of a triangle', and then asserts without argument that conversely 'this idea of a triangle must involve this same affirmation'. It is puzzling that we should be expected to swallow this whole, if 'affirmation' means 'belief'. It is less puzzling if Spinoza has slid into arguing for the more modest thesis that the apparently subpropositional thought *triangle* really has the form *thing with three sides* which should be understood as unfolding into the propositional form *The thing has three sides*.

Anyway, although I do not accept the big doctrine, the smaller one has much to be said for it, and I applaud Spinoza's letting himself off from the 'problem', which has defeated many philosophers, of explaining what goes on in the mind when its subpropositional elements are assembled to form propositionally structured thoughts.[12]

§40. *Error*

1. Spinoza's epistemology famously leaves no proper room for false beliefs. There is a reason for this in the official doctrine and a more interesting one in the strong, subtle undercurrents of the work.

Doctrinally the trouble starts in 1a6: 'A true idea must agree with its object.' Spinoza's use of this shows it to be meant as a biconditional—an idea's agreeing with its object is sufficient as well as necessary for its being true. He does not say what 'agree' means, but he assumes that $I(x)$ agrees

11. Geach, *op. cit.*

12. See *Essay* IV.v.5 (nicely criticised in *New Essays*, p. 396), and Bertrand Russell, *The Analysis of Mind* (London, 1921), pp. 250–52. See *Treatise*, p. 96 for a neglect of the problem by a philosopher who ought to be addressing it.

with x, i.e., that every mental item agrees with its systematic physical counterpart, its direct object. This is natural enough, given that the parallelism of 2p7 is assumed in p7c to involve a representing relation (see §37.2)

So parallelism guarantees that every idea agrees with its object, and 1a6, suitably interpreted, says that an idea which agrees with its object is true. From these premisses Spinoza concludes that 'All ideas, insofar as they are related to God, are true' (2p32).

The fierce impact of 'All ideas . . . are true' is softened a little, but not much, by the clause 'insofar as they are related to God'. What Spinoza means is that all ideas are true so far as their relation to God is concerned, that is, true so far as agreement-with-object is concerned. In p33 he adds that ideas contain nothing positive which makes them false: he doesn't mean that an idea may contain something negative which makes it false, but he does allow that error occurs, and he will argue that it consists not in the having of certain kinds of ideas but rather in the lack of certain kinds of ideas. He thinks that if an idea is not accompanied in my mind by certain others, then it will be erroneous; and p32 lets us say that an idea can be false in that way, or false by that standard. But I shall reserve 'false' for the property that Spinoza thinks no idea can have—namely, the property of not fitting 1a6—and shall always use 'error' as a neutral term for the admitted phenomenon which has to be explained.

2. Given p32, it is reasonable for Spinoza to infer that there is nothing positive about ideas which could make them false (p33), and thus that error must consist in a lack of something (p35). It must surely be some kind of lack of knowledge;[13] but Spinoza points out that it cannot be just any kind, because pebbles lack knowledge but are not ordinarily said to err (p35d). We might, then, equate error with lack of knowledge by an item capable of knowledge. But that would be to equate error with ignorance, and Spinoza objects that 'To be ignorant and to err are different', so that error cannot be ignorance as such (*absoluta ignorantia*); from which he infers that it must be some special kind of ignorance. In §42 I shall discuss his view about *what* kind, but first we must consider the general view that error is *some* kind of ignorance. Let us start with what he says, principally in p17cs,35s, to convince us informally that this surprising theory of his is right. (In p47s at 128/24 he says that 'most errors' are mere verbal slips in speaking or writing, with nothing wrong in the mind of the person concerned. This attempted shrinkage of the domain of error is not plausible, but it doesn't matter: so long as there are some errors in the mind, Spinoza has to explain what they consist in.)

---

13. I here render *cognitio* by 'knowledge' rather than the broader 'cognition'. This makes for naturalness, and does no harm in negative contexts, as it does in positive ones.

3. In p17cs he offers to 'begin to indicate what error is' by discussing the relation between error and an 'imagining of the mind' on which an error is somehow based. One naturally takes him to be thinking of these 'imaginings' as sensory states, possible bases for beliefs but not themselves beliefs. Here is what he says:

> The imaginings of the mind, considered in themselves, contain no error. The mind does not err from the fact that it imagines, but only insofar as it is considered to lack an idea which excludes the existence of those things which it imagines to be present to it. For if the mind, while it imagined non-existent things as present to it, at the same time knew that those things really did not exist, it would of course attribute this power of imagining to a virtue of its nature, not to a vice. (106/12)

What Spinoza is getting at, I suggest, could be put like this:

> Suppose I hallucinated a tiger, and for a while thought I was seeing an actual tiger. When the error occurred, my mind *contained* a tigerish bit of imagining, and *lacked* intellectual support for the belief that there were no tigers nearby. But we take error to be something bad, whereas that bit of 'imagining' is perfectly good in itself, an agreeable addition to the rich pattern of my inner life. So the error—the bad part of the initial situation—must consist in my lack of certain beliefs about the local fauna.

That is the best I can do for Spinoza, but it is not good enough. It implies that my lack of knowledge *was* my error about the tiger, but really that lack *caused* the false belief. The original situation contained not merely a positive tigerish imagining but also a false belief based on it, and that false belief, having been caused partly by ignorance, was dislodged by new information. The same criticism applies to an example Spinoza gives in p35s:

> When we look at the sun, we imagine it as about 200 feet away from us, an error which consists not simply in this imagining but in the fact that while we imagine it in this way we are ignorant of its true distance and of the cause of this imagining. For even if we later come to know that it is more than 600 diameters of the earth away from us, we nevertheless imagine it as near. (117/21)

Here again, he treats an error as *consisting in* a lack of knowledge rather than as *arising from* it, and it seems clear that he is wrong in this.

In discussing these passages, I have assumed that 'imaginings of the mind' are mere sensory states, items with no truth values. Spinoza should protest at this, and claim that my imagining of a tiger is not a 'picture' but rather a judgment or belief. I am sceptical about this. When he writes that 'The mind does not err from the fact that it imagines . . .', isn't he inviting us to equate imagining with the having of sensory states which are not beliefs? When he revives the 'sun' example in 4p1s he sharply distinguishes 'we imagine y as F' from 'we think y to be F', thus implying that an 'imagining' is or includes an element of sheer sensory state, not a belief.

Anyway, if imaginings are belief-like items, how does that help Spinoza's attempts to convince us that error is a lack? He will have to say: 'Because imaginings are beliefs, you were wrong to describe those situations as involving a sensory state and a belief based on it. Once it is understood that the so-called sensory state, the imagining, *is* a belief, your analysis of the case collapses.' But then so does Spinoza's. If my imagining of a tiger is a sort of belief, what belief is it? The only candidate I can find is: *the belief that I am in the presence of a tiger*. But that puts something false into the essential nature of a positive imagining, and blows Spinoza's theory out of the water.

4. That theory is not confined to errors linked with imagination. Here is a favourite example of Spinoza's: 'Men are deceived in thinking themselves free, an opinion which consists only in this, that they are conscious of their actions and ignorant of the causes by which they are determined' (p35s at 117/12). The mistake is obvious. Spinoza was, and knew that he was, ignorant of the causes which determined his actions, yet he did not think himself radically free. The belief in freedom is perhaps caused in some people by the ignorance of causes, but in nobody is it identical with that ignorance. If Spinoza replaced 'ignorant of the causes etc.' by 'ignorant of the fact that their actions have determining causes', he would still be in trouble. *He* would no longer be a counterexample to his own theory, but other people would—namely, ones who are agnostic both about determinism and about radical freedom.

5. Why did Spinoza let himself in for these difficulties? It is not credible that he saddled himself with the theory that error is a species of ignorance just because he saw himself as forced into it by 1a6's tying of truth to agreement with an object and 2p7c's saying that every idea does agree with an object. We need to know why Spinoza accepted 1a6, in its biconditional meaning, if it was going to generate such an implausible result. I don't think he can have regarded himself as bound to the axiom because it expresses the fundamental assumption that truth is a matter of correspondence with reality. Of his four other uses of the axiom, one is indescribable and the remaining three take it merely as letting him equate 'consider x truly' with 'consider x as it is in itself'.[14] Whatever that means, it is surely not a tight metaphysical straightjacket! Anyway, even if he did take 1a6 to express a deep commitment to a correspondence theory of truth, why did Spinoza link it with 2p7c? Why, that is, did he invoke that rigidly correlating relation rather than the more flexible and versatile 'indirectly of' relation which may obtain between an idea of mine and your body? Give the latter the starring role in a theory about truth as correspondence and you have a theory according to which my idea of your body is true if it relates suitably to your body, rather than having to be true because it relates suitably to mine.

14. See the demonstrations of 1p5 and 2p29,44,c2.

6. Well, I can't answer for Spinoza's reasons, but I can show that even if he had defined truth in terms of the 'indirectly of' relation he would still have left far too little room for error. When he introduces the 'indirectly of' relation in p16 and its corollaries, he says that I(x) is an idea indirectly of y only if y is a cause of x, and only if the nature of I(x) 'involves the nature of' y. It follows that I cannot have an idea indirectly of y unless y does exist and has qualities which are somehow represented in my idea of it (see §37). That excludes most kinds of error, allowing only for the time-lag kind: I have an idea which *was* truthful about y but *is* now false because y has changed and my body has not been affected by the change. But this is only a tiny proportion of the territory of error as we ordinarily conceive it; so Spinoza would have been left with most of his problem, even if he had tied truth to the 'indirectly of' relation.

Perhaps he was subliminally aware of this. That would explain the odd fact that although the error problem is launched by the 'directly of' relation Spinoza repeatedly discusses it through examples involving the 'indirectly of' relation, as though that were equally troublesome for him. I think he thought it was. I conjecture that he was guided by an inexplicit realization that in his scheme of things any concept of positive false belief must be either excluded or constricted: positive error 'directly about' something is excluded by the universal scope of the 'directly of' relation; positive error 'indirectly about' something is constricted because Spinoza's account of that relation is too perfunctory—the relation has not been given enough structure to support a rich concept of error.

Reasonable as that explanation is, I don't think it gets us to the bottom of Spinoza's view about error. If it did, that would mean that Spinoza's stance arose from his having one problem about 'direct' error and, by sheer coincidence, a completely different one about 'indirect' error. That is not probable. I shall now present something deep and unitary which I think does explain Spinoza's holding that error is a lack—not merely thinking he is committed to this view, but thinking it to be right.

§41.   *Error, ignorance, and truth-values*

1. In 4p1s where Spinoza again produces the 'distance of the sun' example, he throws in a phrase on which I want to build a great deal. I have noted this passage as one where 'imaginings' really do seem to be sensory states and nothing like beliefs; and this of course greatly helps Spinoza to maintain that 'the imaginings by which the mind is deceived' are intrinsically innocent, as is shown by the fact that when the deceptions are set right the imaginings 'do not disappear'. My present concern is with something else Spinoza says about those deceiving imaginings, namely, that 'they are not contrary to the true' (211/33). There is a similar though less potent use of 'contrary to the true' in 5p37d. There are no others in the *Ethics*.

(7) COGNITIVE PSYCHOLOGY

I contend, however, that that phrase reflects a strong, deep current in Spinoza's thinking. It is evidence that in trying to show that error is not a positive addition to the world's contents, Spinoza is led by the thought that *nothing real can be contrary to the true*. This thought is also reflected when Spinoza says that true relates to false as being does to nonbeing (2p43s at 124/28). And when in p33d he says that 'a positive mode of thinking which constitutes the form of falsity . . . cannot be in God', I think he would confidently assert this even if he could not back it up with his definition of truth as agreement-with-object. In short, I submit that Spinoza wants to ensure that 'not P' does not occur in his description of a universe in which P is the case. Underlying his trouble about error, like so many of his troubles, there is a profound insight. This time it can be put as a wonderful question: How could a false proposition be entitled to a place in a true description of the world?

2. We know that 'not P' can occur in a consistent story which also includes P as a conjunct, because 'not P' can be embedded in larger propositions which do not entail 'not P'. But most ways of doing this are obviously irrelevant to our present problem: truth-functional embeddings, as in 'Q or not P'; modal ones, as in 'It is possible that not P'; evaluative ones, as in 'It ought to be the case that not P'. Only two kinds of embedding look relevant, and neither would be acceptable to Spinoza as solving the problem.

One is epistemic embedding, as in 'John believes that not P'. With that staring him in the face, shouldn't Spinoza have availed himself of it, contentedly accepting that actual beliefs can be 'contrary to the true'? No. It is part of his greatness as a philosopher that he will not help himself to a concept or an assumption just because it is common currency, if he cannot justify it in his own terms. His naturalism about the human condition, which I described in §10, forbids him to say anything like this: 'Although in general "not P" cannot occur in a true description of a world in which P is the case, this can happen within the scope of a belief operator—it is just a fact about the concept of belief that a true proposition can assert the occurrence of a false belief.' It would be clean contrary to the spirit of Spinoza's enterprise to say this without earning the right to it, and he cannot see how to entitle himself to all of it. He finds a way of allowing that error occurs, he thinks, but not by including errors among the real furniture of the universe.

3. Of course the proper way to earn the right to it is to produce an analysis of the concept of belief which explains how an actual belief can be false. Spinoza is not well placed to do this, since he offers no theory of belief. The sort of theory I like best—the sort presented in §39.4—says that I believe that P if I am disposed to 'act in a way which *would* satisfy my desires if P *were* true'. Notice that this uses a counterfactual conditional:

172

that is the other kind of embedding to which I referred, namely, of false propositions in true counterfactuals. I contend that that is the source of the possibility of embedding false propositions in true reports of actual beliefs. Counterfactuals could also help other parts of Spinoza's philosophy of mind, e.g., enabling him to have a richer and more flexible 'indirectly of' concept.

In the course of the *Ethics* he makes a gingerly use of counterfactual conditionals on a few occasions, but I think that he did not like them, regarding them as dangerous because they imply or suggest that things could have been other than how they are. Even today a few philosophers hold that if determinism is true then no counterfactuals are true; I am sure they are wrong, but their view is not absurd, and I find it plausible to attribute it to Spinoza. One fragment of supporting evidence occurs in one of the letters. Spinoza has been asked 'whether by our precaution we can prevent what would otherwise happen to us'. This is a counterfactual question, rating the answer: 'Yes; for it can happen that I put on a coat and stay dry, where otherwise I would have got wet.' Here is Spinoza's reply: 'Since one could ask a hundred such questions in an hour without arriving at any conclusion about anything, and since you yourself do not press for an answer, I shall leave your question unanswered.' (Letter 23 at IV/152/12). Even when we remember that Spinoza was never at his best in letters, we must regard this surly rebuff as needing explanation. I suggest that it reflects discomposure in the presence of a counterfactual conditional.

4. I should say a little about ignorance. The abstract relation between it and error is simple. There is error when

$$(x \text{ believes that } P) \text{ and not-}P$$

and there is ignorance when

$$\text{not-}(x \text{ believes that } P) \text{ and } P.$$

Notice that if x were free of error and ignorance, it would be true for every P that

$$x \text{ believes that } P \text{ if and only if } P.$$

In that case, the concept of *x's belief* would be idle: it could be deleted from every statement containing it, without affecting the truth-value. So a working concept of belief must involve ignorance or error or both.

To the extent that Spinoza's theory of belief is tied to the 'indirectly of' relation, he has room for ignorance: I have no idea indirectly of any aspect of the outer world that does not affect my body. Thus, the 'indirectly of' relation potentially ranges over the entire universe, but selects only a few facts about it. In contrast, the 'directly of' relation lets my ideas range only over the states of my body, but within that range it is not selective: every

173

fact about my body is registered in my mind. 'Whatever happens in the object of the idea constituting a human mind must be perceived by the human mind, i.e., there will necessarily be an idea of that thing in the mind.' (p12) If this is not to collapse in the face of obvious facts of introspection, Spinoza must say that many events in my body are reflected in my mind but not so that I am aware of them.

That was Leibniz's way out. His philosophy implies that my mind reflects every state of every thing in the universe—his 'perception' is unrestricted in range *and* unselective in operation—which forced him to say we are not aware of all we perceive. But although he had things to say about which perceptions reach our awareness and which do not, Leibniz simply helped himself to the concept of awareness, apparently seeing no need to explain or justify it. Since Spinoza's naturalistic programme will not permit *him* to behave in that manner, he has a problem about how to defend his philosophy from a charge of epistemic overload: he must explain how our minds contain so many details of which we are unaware. I am afraid that he did not squarely face this problem and probably did not see its gravity. The only doctrine of his which might be meant to solve it is singularly unsuccessful; I shall present it in §44.7.

5. As well as finding error and ignorance recalcitrant, Spinoza tends to forget their existence. Because they do exist, there is the phenomenon of *opacity*: this occurs when a proposition (. . . P . . .) can have a different truth-value from P itself; the label comes from the idea that in such a case the context in which P is embedded is 'opaque' to P's truth-value, preventing it from getting through and irradiating the entire proposition. Spinoza often writes as though opacity did not exist. For example, he uses the following argument:

People are pleased when they think their enemies are headed for destruction (3p20); and to be in an unpleasant state is to be headed for destruction (3p11s); therefore people are pleased when they think their enemies are in an unpleasant state. (3p23d, my wording)

That is patently invalid. The premisses could be true and the conclusion false, e.g., if people are ignorant or in error about how unpleasantness relates to destruction. Remove 'they think' from the first premiss and from the conclusion, and the result is sound. This is one of several places where Spinoza allows arguments to run into psychological contexts and then out again, as though those contexts had no effect on validity. That manifests his general neglect of the fact of opacity.

An even more striking example occurs when in 3p27 he says something of the form

If x resembles y, and x believes that Fy, then Fx,

and then in 4p68s he purports to refer back to that but really adduces something of the form

If x believes that x resembles y, and Fy, then Fx.

In this transition, a 'believes that' operator is dropped from one clause and added to another: the truth-conditions of the two are utterly different, but Spinoza is apparently blind to the difference. Of course they would be equivalent if all and only the truths were believed, i.e., if there were no ignorance and no error.

Some examples involve not the context 'x believes . . .' but the context 'x wants . . .'. This is also opaque, for we cannot validly argue from 'She wants Germany to be Stalinist, and if Germany is Stalinist it will be miserable' to 'She wants Germany to be miserable'. There is a double example of Spinoza's neglect of this kind of opacity in 5p19d, which purports to show that someone who loves God cannot want God to love him back. Simplifying the argument a little, it amounts to this: If God loved me back, God would be destroyed; if God were destroyed, that would be unpleasant for me; therefore if I wanted God to love me back I would be wanting to be in an unpleasant state—and Spinoza thinks that to be impossible. It is clear that the argument fails because even if the conditional premises are true I might be ignorant or in error with respect to them.

6. Sometimes Spinoza does better, and in one place he virtually calls attention to opacity as such. But that seed does not germinate, because he misunderstands the force of what he is saying. The passage is 4p1s, where he makes the point that when an ungrounded fear is dispelled by true information the mental mechanism is the same as if it were a justified fear being dispelled by false information. This is a big step towards a grasp of opacity; but Spinoza thinks that it supports 4p1: 'Nothing positive which an idea has is removed by the presence of the true insofar as it is true', and thus to support the thesis that error is not something positive but just a sort of ignorance. Crushed under this load of spurious significance, Spinoza's fear-dispelling example cannot help him to a proper grasp of the opacity of psychological concepts.

§42.   *Inadequate ideas*

1. Having argued (cogently enough, given his premises) that error is some kind of ignorance, Spinoza tells us what kind of ignorance it is. Error, he says, 'consists in the lack of knowledge which inadequate and confused ideas involve'. This has a 'So' in front and a 'Q.E.D' behind, but of course it does not *follow*: we have not been shown that there are not other candidates for the title of 'differentia which marks off error from other kinds of ignorance'. Still, Spinoza has if not reasons then at least motivations for his choice of candidate, as I shall explain in due course.

To understand this part of the *Ethics*, and especially to grasp how it fits with Parts 4 and 5, one must understand Spinoza's technical term 'inadequate'. His official definition of it has almost nothing to do with how the word is used in the *Ethics*. Let us get that definition out of the way first:

By adequate idea I understand an idea which, insofar as it is considered in itself, without relation to an object, has all the properties or intrinsic marks of a true idea. *Explanation*: I say intrinsic so as to exclude what is extrinsic, viz. the agreement of the idea with its object. (2d4)

Broadly speaking, an adequate idea is a belief that you can know to be true *a priori,* either by seeing it to be self-evident or by deriving it from others which are self-evident. Spinoza does not argue that there are such beliefs, let alone explain how they are possible; he merely coins a name for them.

Anyway, what are the 'intrinsic marks of a true idea'? Why isn't an idea's *being an idea* a sufficient mark of its being true? This question leads into a tangle which I shall not present and unravel; it includes the remark in Letter 60 (at IV/270/18) that 'true idea' and 'adequate idea' are co-extensive.

The 2d4 sense of 'adequate idea' is left over from the *Emendation*, where it figures in Spinoza's struggle with Cartesian scepticism.[15] Spinoza sees scepticism as arising from a demand that whatever is believed be justified, and he replies that some truths occur in the mind with their own warrant: they need no further justification because they have the 'intrinsic marks' of truth, i.e., because they are 'adequate'. It is not a good discussion. Fortunately, the interest in scepticism which prevails in the *Emendation* is almost absent from the *Ethics*. All we find there is the proposition: 'He who has a true idea at the same time knows that he has a true idea, and cannot doubt the thing's truth.' (2p43) This is supposed to concern scepticism, as can be seen from the supplementary remark: 'What can there be which is clearer and more certain than a true idea, to serve as a standard of truth? As the light makes both itself and the darkness plain, so truth is the standard both of itself and of the false.' (p43s at 124/14) I think that Spinoza is muddled about scepticism. Suppose that, in Cartesian fashion, I am wondering whether I am entitled to be sure that P, or whether I know that P, or whether my idea that P is clear and distinct or 'true' in some special sense. Then Spinoza tells me that if I have a true idea then I know that I do. That is no help at all, for it merely implies that I should wonder not only whether P meets my standards but also whether I know that it does. The other part of p43—'He who has a true idea cannot doubt the thing's truth' —implies that all actual scepticism is justified, which strikes me as foolish and unfounded. This muddle about scepticism is inherited from the *Emen-*

15. *Emendation* §§33ff, especially §35.

dation. Mercifully, the *Ethics* contains very little of it: of the four deductive uses of p43, two are weak and none have to do with scepticism.[16] It is interesting that even p43 is demonstrated without help from the official definition of 'adequate idea' in 2d4.

As for 2d4 itself: it is explicitly invoked only twice in the entire work; neither demonstration rests much weight on it; and neither conclusion carries much further weight in the *Ethics*.[17] I now turn my back on it and approach the serious uses of 'adequate idea' in the *Ethics*.

2. To start with, Spinoza speaks not of inadequate *ideas* but rather of inadequate cognition, or of cognizing or perceiving things inadequately. But I shall not attend to that difference, since Spinoza does not (see 2p43d).

Spinoza starts to introduce '(in)adequate idea' in p11c, as follows:

When we say that God has this or that idea, not only insofar as he constitutes the nature of a human mind, but insofar as he also has the idea of another thing together with the human mind, then we say that the human mind perceives the thing only partially or inadequately.

This seems to imply that you perceive x inadequately if x is a physical item some of which lies outside your body. If you are standing close to a hot stove, p11c implies that you perceive only inadequately the total radiant effects of the stove, because some of these lie outside your body. However, when Spinoza purports to employ this in p24d it changes. Indeed, it has to change, because p24 says: 'A human mind does not involve adequate knowledge of the parts composing the human body', and yet it seems that in the p11c sense that would be a perfect paradigm of adequate knowledge, namely, knowledge of something none of which lies outside the confines of the knower's body. What we find in p24d is that an idea of mine is inadequate if it is *caused from* outside my mind: thus, for instance, my idea directly of the heat of my own body is inadequate simply because that heat is caused from outside my body and so, by the parallelism of causal chains, the idea is caused from outside my mind.

The two senses have in common the use of 'adequate' to express something about completeness: to have a p11c adequate perception of x is to have an idea directly of the whole of x; to have an idea which is p24d adequate is to have an idea which is wholly caused from within one's own mind. This completeness notion also turns up in 'express adequately' and 'agree adequately' (both p29d) and also in 'adequate cause' (3d1,p1d).

16. For a useful discussion of Spinoza on scepticism, see Doney's 'Spinoza on Philosophical Skepticism'.

17. 2d4 is used in demonstrating 4p62 (which supports 4p66 and nothing else), and in demonstrating 5p17 (which through its corollary supports 5p19 and nothing else).

But although the two notions of (in)adequacy share that much, they are structurally quite different from one another. Take any idea I(x) in someone's mind and ask whether it is adequate in the p11c sense. The question has to be amplified: we have to ask 'Is it adequate with respect to such and such an object?' And then the answer is that it is adequate in respect to x, but inadequate in respect to anything of which x is only a proper part. Now let us ask whether I(x) is adequate in the p24d sense. This time the question must be amplified differently: we must now ask 'Is it adequate with respect to such and such a mind?'. And the answer is that I(x) is adequate with respect to a mind which contains both it and its cause. The p24d question and answer do not involve any relation to any object of the idea.

Relations between the two concepts of (in)adequacy are not worth discussing any further, since it is clear that what Spinoza employs throughout the rest of the work—even in places where he invokes p11c—is the p24d notion, according to which an idea of mine is adequate if and only if it is wholly caused from within my mind. The p11c notion does not pick out anything worth focussing on, whereas the p24d one is of vital importance, since it is one of Spinoza's principal handles on sense-experience. All my perceptions of outer things are caused from outside my mind, and so they are all 'inadequate' in the sense of p24d. Spinoza makes that connection in p26c.

From now on, therefore, I shall stick resolutely to the notion of an 'adequate idea' as one which is wholly caused from within the mind in which it occurs. If anyone's ideas are to be 'adequate' in this sense, that must involve only their whole *proximate* causes lying inside the person's mind; it could not be the whole infinite causal chain leading to the idea. I cannot find that Spinoza ever properly confronts that issue.

3. Adequacy is a relation, not a property. What we need to deal with it is not the monadic '. . . is (in)adequate' but rather the dyadic '. . . is (in)adequate in . . .', relating an idea to a mind. An idea of mine which is inadequate with respect to my mind could be adequate with respect to some larger mental item containing my mind; and no idea is inadequate with respect to the entire mental realm.

But the relational language is tedious. I shall write as though 'is (in)adequate' were a monadic predicate, but please understand: When I speak of an idea as (in)adequate, I am referring to an idea in the mind of a human being and saying that it is (in)adequate with respect to that mind.

4. I have understated Spinoza's doctrine about error. What he actually says in p35 is that error is the lack of knowledge involved in ideas which are 'inadequate, or mutilated and confused'. He clearly means '. . . i.e. mutilated and confused'. I think he is trying through that phrase to equate error with a lack which has positive defects associated with it, hoping to make Spinozistic error look more like error as you and I understand it. But never mind that. I shan't give a second hearing to the theory that error is nothing positive. I am interested, for its own sake, in the view that all inadequate ideas are mutilated and confused. Let us start with mutilation.

If an idea of yours is inadequate, then the boundary of your mind slices across the causal flow into it; but why call it 'mutilated'? Being caused from outside, it is the mental equivalent of imported goods; but Spinoza invites us to think of it also as *damaged* goods—a bleeding chunk of the mental realm, hacked out in a manner which leaves its edges tattered. Why? He would have an answer if he could show that when the boundary of your mind lies between one of your ideas and its cause you are more prone to error in respect of it. But that needs an acceptable theory of error and a defended link between error and inadequacy; and Spinoza has neither.

It may be that inadequacy is supposed to involve mutilation because 'Cognition of an effect involves cognition of the cause' (1a4). Taking this to mean that one's intellectual grasp on any item is weakened by one's ignorance of its cause (see §31.4), Spinoza might infer that there must always be something unsatisfactory about an inadequate idea—something which could rather fancifully be described as the idea's being 'mutilated'.

But why should we accept 1a4 on that interpretation of it? Such plausibility as it has comes from its being taken to imply, for instance, that I would have a better grasp of the French Revolution if I knew more about what led up to it. It is true that ideas of external items would usually be better cognitive possessions if they were accompanied by ideas of suitably related other external items. Spinoza was much impressed by this truth; he eloquently expresses it in a famous passage in Letter 32, where he imagines a sentient 'worm in the blood' which perfectly understands how particles in the blood affect one another, but has no knowledge of 'the relation of the blood on one hand and external causes on the other'. But this says only that ideas indirectly of things ought to be accompanied by other ideas indirectly of things; it gives no reason to think that all such ideas, just because they are caused from outside, are damaged goods.

5. So much for mutilation. What about confusion? Spinoza's view is that if I(x) is inadequate then it is a confused idea *of* x even though it is x's systematic counterpart under the parallelism. That is made clear when he writes: 'An imagining is an idea which indicates the present constitution of the human body, . . . , not distinctly, though, but confusedly.[18] That

---

18. Spinoza opposes 'confused' to 'distinct' and sometimes to 'clear and distinct' (2p28,s and 3p9). The latter phrase echoes Descartes on scepticism, but that echo is not developed in the *Ethics*.

is how it comes about that the mind is said to err.' (4p1s) There is the whole package: inadequacy involves confusion, which turns ignorance into what is called error.

Why does inadequacy involve confusion? At the end of 2p28d Spinoza says that my inadequate ideas of the states of my body are 'like conclusions without premises', from which he immediately infers that they are confused. I don't see that it follows. Worse, I don't see why Spinoza thinks it obvious that it follows.

6. I am not convinced that Spinoza is entitled to use the concept of confusion at all. His sternly naturalistic account of mankind, which gives him the problem of how anything real can be false, seems also to make it problematic whether anything real can be confused. He tackles this in 1 Appendix, where he says that 'x is confused' is, like 'x is good', really a statement about how x relates to the speaker's condition. When things are such that 'we can easily imagine them' then 'we say that they are well-ordered'; and when we cannot easily take them in through our imaginations 'we say that they are confused' (82/2).

That is nicely in tune with Spinoza's scheme of things. But it cannot be applied to his thesis that inadequate ideas are 'confused', for that would imply that I call an idea of yours 'confused' because I have difficulty taking it in; and that is wildly off the mark. We might shift to the suggestion that an idea of yours is confused if *you* 'cannot easily imagine' it, but that is patently wrong too.

If there is a way into understanding Spinoza's notion of confusion of ideas, I think it must lie through what he says about confusion of (physical) images:

A human body, being limited, is capable of forming distinctly only a certain number of images at the same time. If that number is exceeded, the images begin to be confused, and if the number is greatly exceeded, they will all be completely confused with one another. (p40s1 at 120/30, quoted with omissions)

That seems to be poised to explain mental confusion as a counterpart, under the parallelism, of physical confusion, as though a confused thought could be explained as a thought of something which is confused. (Leibniz: 'When there are many confused and indistinct motions in the brain . . . it naturally follows that the thoughts of the soul cannot be distinct either.'[19])

But Spinoza had better not mean that some bodily states are inherently, monadically confused; any attempt to make that good would surely fall under the axe of his discussion in 1 Appendix. I think he can and would avoid that difficulty by saying that when he calls an image 'confused' he means only that it confusedly represents the item which caused it, i.e., the

19. *New Essays*, p. 117.

item it is an image of. Or, to respect his assumption that only mental items can represent, let us take him to say that the image confusedly *indicates* the nature of the item which caused it. This use of the concept of confusion as adverbial on verbs like 'represent' and 'indicate' looks promising, and it fits what Spinoza says just after the passage last quoted: 'When the images in the body are completely confused, the mind also will imagine all the bodies confusedly, without any distinction.'

Still, we should press harder. What does it mean—moving now to a simpler example—to say that the state of a waxen surface confusedly indicates the nature of a coin which has been pressed against it? I think it can only mean that the wax *incompletely* indicates what the surface of the coin is like. By that interpretation, Spinoza's account of how confusion results from piling up images means that as the images accumulate within a single brain each one destroys some of the detail in the others, so that eventually each has a nature which indicates only a few features of the item which caused it.

This however, defends 'confused image of y' by turning it into 'image which confusedly indicates y's nature', and then turning that into 'image which only partially indicates the nature of y'. If 'confused idea' is explained on the model of this account of what a confused image is, the confusion of ideas is no longer suggestive of error: the proposal that error is the lack of knowledge which confused ideas involve is no longer persuasive.

Objection: 'But we do distinguish between a representation which loses detail and one which is confused. If we can draw that line, why can't Spinoza? Why do you insist that for him a confused representation is simply an incomplete one?' Because when we say (for instance) that the surface of a piece of wax gives a 'confused' indication of the natures of the objects that have been pressed against it, we are thinking of a person who looks at the wax, wonders what the things were like, and *becomes confused*. I suggest that Spinoza applies 'confused' to images basically because he thinks of them as apt to produce confusion in people, and that he has no independent analysis of mental confusion. To make good sense of 'confused idea', I think, he would need the notion of error: a confused state of mind is one in which the person is apt to follow unsound arguments, to miss some similarities and invent others, to mistake one thing for another, and so on. Spinoza does informally treat the concept of confusion like that: 'Those who do not know the true causes of things confuse everything, and, without any awareness of self-contradiction, feign that both trees and men speak . . . [etc.]. So also those who confuse the divine nature with the human easily ascribe human affects to God.' (1p8s2, at 49/31). If that is the best he can do, he is lost. For it involves explaining confusion partly through error, which is fatal to his endeavour to explain error partly through confusion. There are legitimate 'bootstrap' procedures in which two concepts help one another up, but I see no prospect of that in the present case. Spinoza is stuck unless he makes room for a notion of error as something positive.

And even if all those difficulties could be met, Spinoza has only described images which are confused because many of them have accumulated on top of one another, so to speak. He has not argued that every image—every physical state caused from outside—is confused, or, therefore, that every inadequate idea is confused.

§43. *Reason, the senses, and error*

1. Spinoza's concept of 'inadequate idea' stands at the centre of a bold, sweeping strategy which I shall now expound.

In 2p40s2 he describes three kinds of cognitive process. The first kind is sense experience, the having of inadequate ideas; the second is reason, the having of adequate ideas; the third is called 'intuitive knowledge', and I shall say nothing about it until chapter 15 because Spinoza drops it until he comes to Part 5.

Even 'reason' is not much heard from until 4p26: the scholium introducing it is followed by four propositions about it, but nothing is deduced from them until Part 4 is reached. It is as though Spinoza were more interested in reason for its moral role than for its place in cognition. Still, it is introduced first as a cognitive faculty, and the little that Spinoza says about it in that regard is interesting and important.

Since reasoning is a process which does not use input from one's environment, Spinoza is entitled to suppose that it involves only ideas of the kind he calls 'adequate', i.e., ones caused from within. I do not think he could plausibly defend his converse view that any having of adequate ideas is reasoning; but we can forget that until chapters 12 and 13.

Now, it is commonly thought that in reasoning we are not prone to error as we are in using our senses. No professional philosopher or mathematician would accept that, just as it stands; but there is an approximate truth in it, and for present purposes—i.e., for getting closer to Spinoza's thought—the approximation doesn't matter. Let us pretend to accept the simple formula that the senses can deceive us and reason cannot.

Philosophers who hold that opinion ought to explain why it should be true, and no one has yet succeeded in this. Indeed, we haven't even explained how we can achieve even fallible results by reasoning, i.e., how we can be entitled to any opinions about what is necessary or possible or impossible. I think the commonest seventeenth century explanation for the supposed fact that reasoning is infallible was the kind implicitly given by Locke: reasoning is a process of attending to one's ideas, construed as immediately apprehendable states of mind; so the certainty of reason comes from the certainty we can supposedly have about first-person present-tense psychological statements. It is not a good explanation, and it would be surprising to find Spinoza using it. Although he is not perfectly thorough about separating psychology from logic, he does not conflate them as firmly as this explanation requires. Also, he does not have infallibility about present states of mind as one of his principal themes.

2. Actually, his explanation is totally different. Having argued that error is a kind of ignorance, he conjectures that what marks off this kind from other ignorance is that inadequate ideas are involved. He is no doubt encouraged in this by the thought that inadequacy induces mutilation and confusion, which sound right as elements in a theory of error. But he is also encouraged by the fact that his conjecture lets him explain why error is not possible in the use of reason. The explanation is that ignorance counts as error only if inadequate ideas *are* involved, and cognition counts as reasoning only if inadequate ideas *are not* involved, and so . . . etc. That explanation is presented in 2p41d.

I cannot accept it, if only because I do not agree that error is any species of ignorance. But it is bold and ingenious: to understand why reason cannot err we are not to look for special features of reason; rather, we take the most obvious feature of reason—namely, that it does not involve causal input from one's environment—and combine that with a special feature of error.

3. On the account of reason given so far, it might seem that Spinoza makes it a faculty of self-knowledge after all. If I reason only when having ideas caused by myself, how can reason tell me anything about what is outside myself? It may be with this difficulty in mind that he says in p38 that an idea in my mind is adequate if it is of a property which is 'common to all, and is equally in the part and in the whole'. This allows us to have adequate ideas of geometry and physics, I take it, and thus frees reason from the prison of the body of the reasoner.

That assigns a motivation for adding p38 to the doctrinal structure, but it does not give a defence. Nor can I do so: the enormously obscure p38d has defeated me. But although I do not understand it, I have the following reason for thinking that it must be invalid. Its conclusion is of the form 'If . . . then x is conceived adequately', and the only premisses which involve the concept of adequacy have the form 'If . . . , then x is perceived inadequately'. That makes it probable—to put it mildly—that the demonstration is defective.

Still, we can guess informally at Spinoza's real line of thought here. I think he was impressed by the notion that inadequate ideas are caused from the outside in a manner which usually 'mutilates' them—i.e., that most causal flow from an environment into a human body involves a 'bump', a qualitative discontinuity of which the mental counterpart is mutilation. I now suggest that he further thought that in a causal flow involving only features which the body shares with its environment the 'bump' does not occur, there is no mutilation, and so the idea in question is adequate. This puts a dangerous amount of weight on the frail concept of mutilation, but I think it is probably right all the same. For one thing, it lets us explain p39 as well. If the essential thought underlying p38 concerns a 'bump' at the boundary of someone's body, then it should apply not only to features of his body which it shares with everything, but also features which it shares with its immediate environment; it ought not to matter whether they also characterize more remote parts of the universe. And that is in effect what p39 says: an idea is adequate in my mind if it is caused by aspects of other bodies which they share with my body. I doubt if Spinoza has anything specific in mind here—as he surely has geometry and physics in mind in p38—but he is *committed* to allowing that if my body shares features with contiguous bodies, even if not with the whole extended realm, my ideas of those will be adequate.

4. In later parts of the *Ethics* the concept of reason does dramatic other work for Spinoza, allegedly on the basis laid down in Part 2. The essential fact about reason, as initially introduced, is that it involves adequate ideas, i.e., causal self-sufficiency; and we shall find that in Part 4 Spinoza cashes in on that by opposing reason to the passions. The very word 'passion' is supposed to suggest a passive state, one caused from the outside; and sense-experience also involves being acted on from the outside. They look very different, but Spinoza thinks that they have enough in common for each to stand in opposition to 'reason', with this understood in a single unambiguous manner. Details will be presented in later chapters.

§44. *Ideas of ideas*

1. Spinoza says in p3 that there is an idea not just of every extended mode, but of every mode; and so, he concludes in p20d, there is an idea of every idea, and of every idea of an idea, and so on *ad infinitum*. If an extended thing x is compared with a thin circular disc, then its mental counterpart could be compared with an infinitely high column made up of a disc $I(x)$ surmounted by a disc $I(I(x))$ surmounted by a disc $I(I(I(x)))$ and so on. This confirms what p3 seems to imply, namely, that Spinoza should be credited with a thought-*everything* parallelism: every item, whether physical or mental, is represented in the mental realm; and it is from p3 that Spinoza derives the doctrine of ideas of ideas.

The key propositions are p20–22. The doctrine is that Nature contains an idea of the mind (p20) which relates to the mind as that does to the body (p21), and by virtue of which the mind perceives not only the states of the body but also its own perceptions of those (p22). It is crucial that $I(I(x))$ relates to $I(x)$ 'in the same way as' $I(x)$ relates to x: Spinoza says this because he must. If in addition to the $I(\ )$ operator on the names of physical items he laid claim to a distinct operator $I^*(\ )$ on names of mental ones, that would introduce into his system a radically new element for which no provision had been made.

What *is* the relation between $I(x)$ and x? I have given one answer in terms of mental-physical parallelism; but in the strange world of mental-everything parallelism we can no longer avail ourselves of that material, and must rely exclusively on Spinoza's official doctrines. Well, in p7s he says that the relation between $I(x)$ and (x) is identity: each mental mode *is* a physical mode, and conversely. Let us now hold him to that (though not necessarily to my handling of it in §34). So we start with the thesis that $I(x)$ is x, though they are somehow conceptually different. But then Spinoza should say that $I(I(x))$ is $I(x)$, though they are . . . conceptually the same! Because 'idea of' is univocal, the identity claim of p7s re-applies between $I(I(x))$ and $I(x)$, without even a saving touch of difference because the items belong to different attributes. Strangely, Spinoza accepts this consequence:

The mind and the body are one and the same individual, which is conceived now under the attribute of thought, now under the attribute of extension. So the idea of the mind and the mind itself are one and the same thing, which is conceived under one and the same attribute, viz. thought. (p21s)

There seems to be nothing left to stop $I(I(x))$ from collapsing into $I(x)$ —i.e., to stop the identity from being so total and unqualified that the 'ideas of ideas' terminology becomes idle.

2. Spinoza's ideas of ideas are under pressure from other parts of his system too. I don't mean pressure from the demand, taken seriously by some, that there be as much reality in the physical realm as in the mental; for I don't know what that means. If I did want to solve that 'problem' on Spinoza's behalf, I would suggest that $I(x)$ has half as much reality as x, thus giving each mental column exactly as much reality as the corresponding physical disc. This nonsense is better than Robinson's nonsense—he proposed to make the mental column finitely high by making each mental disc infinitely thin![20] The real pressure on the columns to collapse into mere discs is as follows.

The doctrine of ideas of ideas will ruin Spinoza's system unless it squares with the parallelism of causal chains. Ideas of ideas must exhibit the same 'order and connection' as ideas which are not of ideas, or Spinoza is quite lost. And he says as much, giving p7 as the reason why $I(I(x))$ 'follows in God and is related to God in the same way as' $I(x)$ (p20d). So each column must behave as a unit in any causal explanation, e.g., there must be no causally potent fact at the seventh floor which is not matched by one

20. Lewis Robinson, *Kommentar zu Spinozas Ethik*, vol. 1 (Leipzig, 1928), pp. 273f.

at street level. The one explanatory network connecting the extended discs must be matched by *one* network connecting the mental columns, or connecting their bottom discs which then carry their columns with them. It further follows that the properties or states at any level in a column match those at every other level. The only alternative is to have qualitative differences which are causally idle, and Spinoza rejects that (1p36).

As we move up a column, then, we must go on telling the same story—qualitatively and causally—at each level. But then why is this a column, and not merely a sequence of useless redescriptions of the bottom disc? This threat of collapsing the columns into discs comes not from the p7s identity thesis but from the very heart of Spinoza's metaphysics, the parallelism of causal chains.

3. However, there is a conceivable way out of this tight spot, and I think Spinoza meant to take it. If each level in the column represents only its immediate lower neighbour, then the levels are distinct from one another because what they represent is different. At the ground floor $I(x)$ represents something physical, namely x; $I(I(x))$ differs from it because it represents something mental; $I(I(I(x)))$ is different again, because it represents something which represents something mental; and so on up the column to infinity. This could be consistent with parallelism of similarities and causal chains, just so long as we can allow that $I(I(x))$ and $I(x)$ are exactly alike intrinsically although unalike in what they represent.

There's the rub. How can two items be intrinsically exactly alike and yet have different representative features? Two intrinsically alike ideas might be *indirectly of* different items; but we are here concerned with representation through the 'directly of' relation, for which Spinoza has offered no theory whatsoever. He is therefore not in a position to explain how as we climb a column we meet ever different representative stories yet always the same intrinsic story.

What is needed to make this account work is something with the structure of this: I take a photograph of you, then a photograph of that photograph, then a photograph of *that* photograph, and so on. I contrive that each photograph is exactly like the one it is of; and yet only one of the series is of you, only one is of a photograph of you, only one is of a photograph of a photograph of you, and so on upwards. This is a coherent story, but when we say of two indiscernible photographs that one is of you and not of a photograph, while the other is of a photograph and not of you, this is true only because of a difference in how the two came into being. That is no use to Spinoza, since one level of a column cannot have a different causal history from any other level.

4. What is the evidence that Spinoza does seek to differentiate the levels in a column by what they represent? There is only one tiny fragment, and even that has to be amended. Spinoza says: 'The idea of the idea is nothing but the form of the idea insofar as the latter is considered as a mode of thinking without relation to the object.' (p21s) The words 'form' and 'object' are cognate with 'intrinsic' (*formalis*) and 'representative' (*objectivus*), respectively. I take Spinoza to be saying here that $I(I(x))$ picks out the intrinsic properties of $I(x)$ but not its representative ones; it sees down into $I(x)$ as a psychological particular, but does not take in what it represents or is about, i.e., does not see through it to x.[21]

There would be no question about that interpretation, I think, if Spinoza had said 'The idea of the idea *represents* the form of the idea etc.', rather than it *is* the form of the idea etc. I am supposing that he did not quite say what he meant. If I am wrong, and he really does mean that $I(I(x))$ is the form of $I(x)$, meaning that it is the intrinsic properties of $I(x)$, then two unwelcome results follow. (i) Because $I(I(x))$ relates to $I(x)$ as the latter does to x, Spinoza would have to say that ideas in general are the forms of their objects, i.e., that if x is physical then $I(x)$ is just the form or nature or properties of x; we need not specify 'intrinsic' properties, since x has no others. I cannot make sense of Part 2 on the basis of any such interpretation as that.[22] (ii) If $I(I(x))$ is the form or intrinsic nature of $I(x)$, then Spinoza is committed to holding that $I(I(I(x)))$ is the form or intrinsic nature of $I(I(x))$. But what is the form of a form? I see no chance of Spinoza's giving an answer which will enable him, even prima facie, to construct a column which does not collapse into a mere disc or two.

If I am wrong about how Spinoza proposed to stop his theory of ideas of ideas from collapsing, then he presumably had no way of trying to do this. Either way, the theory is doomed.

5. Why did Spinoza introduce ideas of ideas in this profligate fashion? It is entailed by his thought-everything parallelism; to avoid that he would need to weaken 2p3 to the statement that God has an idea of everything *physical*; and I do not see how he could plausibly alter p3d to yield the weaker conclusion but not the stronger one. But then p3d is already implausible. It is one of Spinoza's opportunistic bits of freehand logic, and I cannot believe that he saddled himself with ideas of ideas simply because he was forced to it by p3.

He must, then, have expected this doctrine to do something for him. Joachim suggests that Spinoza intended ideas of ideas 'to restore that unity and continuity in all our thinking which Spinoza's conception of the mind as a complex of ideas seems to have destroyed',[23] but rightly says that the

21. I got this good idea from Gueroult, vol. 2, pp. 249–53.

22. It is, however, treated with respect by one of the deepest and most challenging Spinoza papers in recent years, Benardete's 'Spinozistic Anomalies', at pp. 64f.

23. Joachim, *A Study of the Ethics of Spinoza*, p. 140, slightly modified.

doctrine cannot do that work: if a number of street-level mental discs are not unified, then neither are the columns resting on them. Yet if that is not what the doctrine is for, Joachim concludes forlornly, 'what place has it in the system?'[24]

6. Spinoza gives the answer: his doctrine of ideas of ideas is to serve as a theory of self-knowledge; that I have ideas of my own ideas is his way of saying that I have knowledge not only of the physical world but also of my own mind. It is characteristic of him to handle the matter in one grand sweep: no complexities, no 'If this then thus, if that then so', but simply an idea of every idea. This provides a vertical pile-up of knowledge which Spinoza takes in his stride, announcing as though it were obvious: 'As soon as someone knows something, he thereby knows that he knows it, and at the same time knows that he knows that he knows, and so on to infinity.' (p21s) It also provides a grand horizontal sweep: not only is every aspect of my body registered in my mind, but my mind contains knowledge of each of those registerings.

If this were a theory of consciousness or awareness (I do not distinguish between those two), it would be absurdly excessive. Someone who wants to hold that I am consciously aware of every fact about my mind had better thin out the facts about my mind more than Spinoza does—e.g., saying (with Descartes) that only a few happenings in my body cause changes in my mind, rather than saying (with Spinoza) that every happening in my body is reflected in my mind. Given his mind-body parallelism, Spinoza could not follow Descartes's view about conscious awareness without flying in the face of the evident facts of introspection.

But I am not suggesting that 'ideas of ideas' are meant as a theory of conscious awareness. I distinguish the question 'Does that mental item occur consciously in his mind?' from the question 'Does he know that that mental item is present in his mind?', because in a given case we might answer No to the former question and Yes to the latter. If I can unconsciously believe that my grandmother was a tyrant, why can I not unconsciously believe that I think that my grandfather was a hero?

In Part 5 Spinoza will present some kinds of mental discipline which involve becoming consciously aware of certain facts about one's own mind. There could be no question of bringing things up to the conscious level unless they were already in the mind at an unconscious level. I see the 'ideas of ideas' doctrine as providing the basic store of self-knowledge—of items which are there to be brought into consciousness.[25]

Of course Spinoza needs some account of self-knowledge, not only to help

24. *Ibid.*, p. 142n.

25. Here I agree with Neu, *Emotion, Thought and Therapy*, p. 76.

his views about the therapeutic value of conscious awareness of one's mental processes, but also for the more humdrum reason that there is such a thing as self-knowledge and he ought to be able to fit it into his scheme of things. If he had nothing to say about how a person can know that he is in pain, say, that ought to be an embarrassment.

7. Perhaps it is all right for Spinoza to have such a sweeping theory of self-knowledge, given that he can insulate it against introspective evidence by pleading that most mental content does not reach conscious awareness. But then he urgently needs a theory of awareness, and unfortunately the *Ethics* does not contain one. Whereas Leibniz theorizes at length about 'perceptions' whose subject is not aware of them, sharply distinguishing himself from Descartes and Locke on this point, Spinoza does not even mention the matter. I am not complaining that he does not defend his thesis that my mind can have content of which I am not aware, for I agree with Leibniz that the onus is on the other side, and that Descartes and Locke owe us an argument to 'show that it is of the essence of thought in particular that one be aware of it'.[26] But Spinoza should provide some account of what makes the difference between conscious and unconscious mental content. It is characteristic of him to provide the all-in theory of self-knowledge, but to shirk the development of a selective theory of conscious awareness.

But perhaps he is obliquely addressing himself to the latter in the following quartet of propositions: 'A human mind does not involve adequate cognition of the parts composing the human body' (p24); 'The ideas of the states of a human body . . . are not clear and distinct, but confused' (p28); 'The idea of the idea of any state of a human body does not involve adequate cognition of the human mind' (p29); 'A human mind . . . does not have an adequate but only a confused and mutilated cognition of itself, of its body, and of external bodies' (p29c). These involve the concepts of mutilation and confusion through which the concept of inadequacy is supposed to explain what error is (see §42); but taken as a group they seem also to be meant to explain why in our conscious knowledge we fall so far short of omniscience even about our own bodies, the suggestion being that many of the relevant ideas somehow get lost in the confusion and fail to cross the threshold of conscious awareness.

If that is not what those four propositions are for, then why are they included in the *Ethics*? They are almost entirely idle in the rest of the work.[27] I think they are primarily meant as a treatment of the omniscience difficulty,

---

26. *New Essays*, p. 113. For Descartes's two conflicting attempts to answer this, see his *Passions of the Soul* I, 19 and 26.

27. Two are pointlessly mentioned in 2p36d, one is feebly used in 3p3d, and one is irrelevantly mentioned in 4p64d.

protecting Spinoza's parallelism doctrine from the charge of clashing with the data of introspection.

That is not to say that they succeed. For a real success, Spinoza needs a good concept of confusion, an independent concept of consciousness, and arguments to show that confusion can stop things from coming to consciousness. In fact he has none of these. In Part 5 of the *Ethics*, where he presents therapeutic techniques for becoming calmer, stronger, happier and more free, much is said about the advantages of adequate over inadequate ideas; and one might think that Spinoza's proposals for making our ideas more adequate and less confused is intended as a way of bringing more of them within reach of our consciousness. There is no direct textual support for this, but it is an idea which might be worth working out in a 'go it alone' manner, as has been done by some writers who want to liken Spinoza's doctrines to those of the psychoanalytic movement.[28] But even the best of those writers has not developed the idea much, offering comparisons rather than connections: 'The operation of confused and inadequate ideas is very like the operation of unconscious ones', he says, and also remarks that the Spinozist move towards having more adequate ideas 'is very much like the movement towards freedom and self-determination through making the unconscious conscious'.[29]

8. I have to admit that the only two doctrines of Spinoza which use the notion of consciousness are derived from 'ideas of ideas' in a manner implying that the latter is after all a theory about conscious self-knowledge.[30] This is a blemish in Spinoza's handling of 'ideas of ideas', but it is less grave than it might at first appear, as I shall explain shortly. Here are the facts. (i) Spinoza defines 'desire' as 'appetite together with consciousness of it' (3p9s), resting this on the claim in 3p9d that 'the mind is necessarily conscious of itself'. This is said to follow from 2p23, which it doesn't; but Spinoza presumably means it to follow from 2p20—the ideas of ideas doctrine —just as 2p23 does.[31] (ii) In 4p8 Spinoza says something which I interpret as meaning that what underlies the ordinary person's value judgments is his 'consciousness' of his emotional ups and downs. In demonstrating this, Spinoza says that a person must have an 'idea of' his emotional state, citing

---

28. For example, Bickel, 'On the Relationships between Psychoanalysis and a Dynamic Psychology', especially pp. 86f.

29. Neu, *Emotion, Thought and Therapy*, pp. 149, 148.

30. The uses of 'ideas of ideas' that do not involve consciousness are 2p43d,47d and 5p3d.

31. I was helped to track from 2p20 to 3p9 through the smokescreen of 2p23 by Margaret Wilson's very helpful 'Objects, Ideas, and "Minds"'.

2p22 in support of this; and then he silently assumes that this is tantamount to saying that a person must be 'conscious' of his emotional state.

These are mistreatments of the 'ideas of ideas' doctrine, which has not a hope of being true unless it is regarded as a theory about one's not necessarily conscious thoughts about oneself. But the trouble is not fatal. In these two strands in Spinoza's thought there is no insistence that we are conscious of all our appetites and pleasures and unpleasures. All he needs, and all he actually avails himself of, is the thesis that we are conscious of some of them. When in 3p9d and 4p8d he says things of the form: 'When someone is F, he is necessarily conscious of being F (by 2p20–22)', his purposes would have been just as well met by saying instead: 'When someone is F, he may be conscious of being F; the cognition of his Fness is present in his mind (by 2p20–22), and so it is to that extent available for consciousness.' That formulation, though, would have provided an uncomfortable reminder that the *Ethics* badly needs a theory of selective consciousness, of which it contains not a trace.

8   *Time*

Spinoza's views about time and eternity are interesting and, in part, well developed if not always well expressed. In this chapter I shall expound and discuss them, and some related matters. Although much of this material belongs to general metaphysics, it involves some epistemological issues which had to come after chapter 7.

§45.   *Three clusters of temporal concepts*

1. We have three distinct clusters of temporal concepts which should be looked at before we turn to Spinoza.

The topological group contains the concepts we use in temporally relating events and processes to one another without relating them to the time of speaking—for example in saying that an E event occurs before an F event occurs, that an E occurs simultaneously with an F, that an E occurs during an F which overlaps a G, and so on. In those formulae I intend the verbs tenselessly. I say 'An E occurs before an F occurs' only as a way of temporally relating the E to the F—not relating either to the present, which is what tenses are for.

The topological cluster can be combined with names of particular events and, standing on their shoulders, names of particular times: if only one E event ever occurs, there is a time that we can name 'the time of the E event'. Such names of times can be called 'dates', for short. Like ordinary dates they imply nothing about how the named time relates to the time at which one is naming it.

Next comes the *tense* group, whose members relate events and processes to the time of the relating: if I say that an E has occurred, I relate the time of its occurrence to the time when I speak. Tenses are tied to the concepts of past, present and future: to say that an E *has occurred* is to say that an E *occurs* (tenseless) *in the past*, and analogously for 'is occurring' and 'will occur'. The whole content of the system of tenses can be arrived at, therefore, from the topological concepts with the addition of just the concept of the present, by defining 'the past' as the time before now and 'the future' as the time after now.

Third, there are the *metrical* concepts, i.e., ones having to do with amounts of time. Obviously these can be combined with members of either of the other groups.

2. If tensed statements can be reduced to ones that are purely topological except for containing the concept of the present, it might seem that we can carry the reduction still further. Suppose that whenever a tensed statement is being made some unique event is occurring. Then a speaker can use an expression of the form 'the time of the E event' as a *date* which picks out his present, i.e., does what is more ordinarily done explicitly by 'now' or implicitly by tenses. So he doesn't need the concept of the present, since he can get by with topological concepts and *ad hoc* dates. Thus, instead of saying 'My tooth cavity has been filled' he could say 'A filling of my tooth cavity occurs (tenseless) before the time of my first mention in this room of a filling of my tooth cavity'.

So the argument goes. Nobody would recommend that we actually replace tenses and 'now' by topology and dates, but it is interesting to consider whether that replacement is possible without loss of content. I think it is not possible. The trouble with treating 'now' as a shifting date, equivalent in each uttering to an expression of the form 'the time at which an E event occurs', is that our concept of the present is separable from all the content of the present, and thus from any E event which we might use to construct a date. In wishing that it were now Christmas Day, I need not be wishing for any change in the temporal relations among any events, but merely wishing I were now further along the world's history than I actually am. It is as though I were surveying a tenseless history of the universe, complete with all its events and processes and their temporal relations, and saying 'We are now here [pointing], but I wish we were there [pointing again] instead'. It is an intelligible wish; and therefore the concept of the present is not reducible to the topological cluster.

Of course, since each moment could be named by a date, any tensed descriptive statement is matched by an untensed one—using only topology and a date—which has the same truth-value. The inadequacy of topology and dates appears in counterfactual conditionals, and in optatives and expressions of pleasure and regret and the like. I learned this point about the concept of the present from A. N. Prior, who illustrated it with an expression of relief.[1] The dentist finishes his work and I arise from his chair saying 'Thank goodness that's over!' With topology and a date this comes out as something like 'Thank goodness the end of the drilling occurs (tenseless) before the time of my leaving this chair!' But that is equivalent to 'Thank goodness my leaving this chair occurs (tenseless) after the end of the drilling!'—and, Prior demands, where is the cause for gratitude in that?

3. It is sometimes said that tenses or past-present-future are needed because an account of the world given purely in terms of topology and dates

---

1. A. N. Prior, 'Thank Goodness That's Over!', *Philosophy* vol. 34 (1959), pp. 12–17.

must omit the phenomenon of *becoming*. I am puzzled by this.[2] From the topological story we can learn that something is not F at one time and is F later. Why is that not to learn of the thing's becoming F? It is objected that this is a static account of becoming: the topological propositions about how the world is at various times are eternally laid side by side, quite immobile. This is puzzling too. Of course the topological history of the world is static. But if a three-dimensional world can be encompassed in a one-dimensional history, and an analogue world within a digital history, why not a changing world within a static history?

Reply: 'Although at any time one can truthfully say "An E event occurs (tenseless) at T", the truth of that sentence depends wholly upon a reality which exists at T and at no other time. So the most fundamental and metaphysically satisfactory way of expressing it is to say, at T, "An E event is occurring now". That sets a standard which can be met only by a world history which occupies all the time the world occupies—a running commentary, with no forecasts and no replays, but just a contemporaneous flow: 'Now it is F, now it is G, now it is H . . .".'

I sympathize with that, but I cannot decide what weight finally to give it, because I cannot transmute it from a mere attitude into a discussable theory. What about the theory 'Only the present is real'? That is no good. When someone affirms it at a given moment, does he mean that only what exists then is *ever* real? Or that only what exists then is real *then*? The former is too obviously false, and the latter too boringly true, to be worth discussing.

4. Still, I have agreed with Prior that if tenses and past-present-future are omitted from an account of the world, something is lost. What is lost is the viewpoint of an individual inhabitant of the world. This is an essentially first-person singular matter. Suppose we have a complete topological and dated history of a world which has no temporal relation to our own, and that this history tells us that while an E event is occurring an inhabitant of the world in question says 'I am glad the E has occurred at last!' How are we to understand him? There is no feature of his world—as given in our topological and dated account of it—which we can point to as the object of his pleasure. We can understand what he says only by imagining ourselves as being in his position and saying what he said. (As well as this connection between tense concepts and the first-person singular, they are also similar. Just as 'now' can be floated off the whole content of the present, so 'I' can be floated off most of the facts of one's own nature; or so it is maintained, plausibly, by those who believe in the 'transcendental I'.)

Spinoza resolutely resists doing philosophy in a first-person way. He is as far as possible from Descartes's stance in the *Meditations*: 'Here I am,

2. So is J. J. C. Smart. See his 'Time', in Edwards, vol. 8 at p. 128.

with my own inner states; where, intellectually, do I go from here?' Where Descartes and Leibniz are both sure that the mind or soul is absolutely simple and indivisible, Spinoza insists, as he ought to, that 'a human mind is not simple, but composed of a great many ideas' (2p15). He rightly accords to a person's mind only such unity as mirrors the functional unity of that cloud of particles which is his body. As for the question that probably influenced Descartes, certainly influenced Leibniz, and was at the centre of Kant's great discussion of the simplicity of the soul—the question, namely, 'Since I can think of something as a composite only if *I* bring its parts together into some kind of relationship, how can I possibly think of myself as a composite?'—Spinoza never mentions it. I think that is because the emphasis on *I* was so foreign to his way of thinking.

It is therefore not surprising that in the *Ethics* there is no hint of the special aspects of tenses, and of past-present-future, which engage the first-person singular attitude of mind.

§46. *Number and measure*

1. When Spinoza uses the noun *tempus* he never means 'time' in the broad sense that we give that word, but always time considered as conceptualized in certain ways. One of these is by bringing it under a metric, and in translating passages where that is Spinoza's topic I shall translate *tempus* by '(measured) time'. When I use 'time', unadorned, I use it as my broadest noun corresponding to the adjective 'temporal'.

In some of his early writings Spinoza brackets measured time with measure generally and with number: 'Of these, (measured) time serves for explaining duration, number for discrete quantity, and measure for continuous quantity.' (*Metaphysical Thoughts* at I/234/14) Also: 'Measure, (measured) time and number are nothing but modes of thought, or rather imagination.' (Letter 12 at IV/57/6) I shall look at these separately, starting with number.

2. I can find no good or Spinozistic reason for holding that 'number is nothing but a mode of imagination', by which Spinoza ought to mean that number concepts are usable only in shallow, impressionistic sorts of talk and not in basic metaphysics or science. Frege in his *Foundations of Arithmetic* credits Spinoza with an important insight about the concept of number, namely, that in applying a number term to the contents of some region of space-time we must do it under a concept. What the region contains is heavy, is metallic, is expensive, is gleaming; but we cannot say that it is one, or is twenty, or is millions—rather, we must say that it is one chain, twenty links, millions of molecules. (See Letter 50.) Although Frege is right that we cannot count without knowing what items we are counting, I am not convinced that they must be brought under a single concept. Consider 'The man on the rock and the woman in the water and the boy on the shore are three': Frege has given no adequate arguments for insisting that if that makes sense it *must* be taken to mean '. . . are three people'. Why should it not simply say of those three items—those three numerabilia—that they are three?[3] For present purposes, however, let us just hand Spinoza his Fregean point, and then try to understand how it leads him to think that 'number is nothing but a mode of the imagination'.

Hypothesis: Spinoza thinks that a statement about how many Fs there are must contain an F which gets its meaning from a hazy piling up of images in the body (see §11.2), and may not contain a firm, deep F that carves up nature at the joints. Thus, for instance, 'two horses' is well formed but 'two attributes' is not. That would explain his banishing number concepts from basic metaphysics.

It would also explain something else. Having made his Fregean point in Letter 50, Spinoza continues: 'Hence it seems clear that nothing can be called one or single unless some other thing has first been conceived which agrees with it.' That seems quite indefensible. It implies that no proposition of the form 'Necessarily there are no Fs' or of the form 'Necessarily there is exactly one F' can be true, and that is absurd. But when Spinoza continues that since 'we can form no general idea of God's essence' we ought not to 'call God one or single', there is a gleam of what may be light. Why doesn't 1d6 count as expressing a general idea of God's essence? Perhaps because Spinoza is talking about general ideas formed in the imagination, and is assuming that number concepts must be teamed up with them. From that assumption it does follow that 'There is one God' and 'There is one substance' are both unacceptable (though *not* because of our lack of the concept of 'some other thing which' etc.). But I have no direct evidence that my hypothesis is true. And if it is, I do not know why Spinoza should hold the view it attributes to him.

There is a different though related position for which he does have a reason. He might hold that serious, objective counting must be of basic irreducible things, items that (as we might say) would be quantified over in a fundamental metaphysic. That implies that we should be interested only in counting substances, and not in the vaporous activities of 'counting' such 'things' as men and stars and pebbles and triangles. And it follows for Spinoza that the only cardinality that has real work to do is *one*, since there is only one substance.

That is not what he says in the passages under discussion, but it may have been in his mind and have influenced them. And it surely bears on the passage in the *Ethics* where he apparently removes the cramps from numerical concepts sufficiently to allow the number *one* a place in the doctrinal struc-

3. See W. P. Alston and J. Bennett, 'Cardinality and Identity: Frege and Geach', *Philosophical Review* 93 (1984).

ture: 'God is unique, i.e. in Nature there is only one substance.'[4] An attempt that has been made to reconcile this with Letter 50, by supposing that 'unique' and 'one' are not now being used in a numerical sense,[5] was presumably based on the view that Spinoza was right first time. If we think that the treatment of number in Letter 50 was wrong, we are spared these desperate shifts and are free to suppose that Spinoza came to see the error of his ways sufficiently to put number concepts on a longer leash. Since they are not explicitly discussed in the *Ethics*, we cannot be sure.

3. When Spinoza speaks of 'measure', he seems always to have in mind kinds of metric that are fundamentally spatial. The crucial passage is 1p15s, where he says that 'infinite quantity is not measurable, and is not composed of parts'. His point is that to measure something you must divide it, so that spatial metrics must operate one level up from the metaphysical foundation, applying only to qualitatively demarcated regions of space, or to bodies or other occupants of space (see §23). Spatial measurement involves, in words Spinoza uses later in the same scholium, thinking about quantity 'abstractly, i.e. superficially, as we commonly imagine it'. He goes on: 'If we attend to quantity as it is in the imagination, which we do often and more easily, it will be found to be finite, divisible, and composed of parts', and, he would have been willing to add, measurable.

Granted that a spatial metric must rest on facts about some kind of occupant of space, and thus belongs a level up from the ground floor, this hardly justifies Spinoza's dismissive remark that 'measure is nothing but a mode of imagination'. If it did, then Spinoza ought to say the same about all concepts that enter at that level; but he would never give the back of his hand to the concept of a *body*, calling it 'nothing but a mode of imagination'.

4. Although Spinoza's attitude to measured time is like his attitude to measure generally, some different issues are raised which require separate treatment.

It is generally agreed that there is no metric inherent in the structure of time itself. If there were temporal atoms, i.e., shortest periods of time, that would provide a metric because longer periods could be measured by counting their constituent atoms. But since we think that time is continuous, or at least 'dense' in the mathematical sense, we seem to have no basis for an inherent temporal metric. I am sure that Spinoza would have agreed.

Where do we look for a temporal metric? To physical processes. Our thoughts about amounts of time depend on our taking some kinds of process as definitive of certain temporal lengths. Standards are chosen not because

4. 1p14c1; see also, among its progeny, 1p17c2, 1p24c, 2p4.

5. Gueroult, vol. 1, pp. 156–58, including this: 'That which excludes all multiplicity is in the metaphysical sense a One, a Unique, above all number, even the number one.'

of how well they match up to the rate of flow of time itself, but because of how well they serve us in our pursuit of unified and intelligible physics. The rotation of the earth was a good standard for a long time; but as measuring techniques were refined it transpired that if the earth always rotates at the same speed then countless other kinds of process are speeding up. We could not explain those accelerations, whereas we can explain the earth's slowing down; so that standard was relinquished in favour of one based on other processes.

5. A temporal metric, then, requires us to look at the empirical world, and so it belongs to the province of what Spinoza calls 'imagination'. But he seems to mean more than this by his dismissive phrase 'nothing but a mode of imagination' (Letter 12), which suggests that facts about amounts of time are not facts about fundamental reality. That suggestion is even more strongly conveyed by the statement: '(Measured) time is not a state of things but rather a mere way of thinking.' (*Metaphysical Thoughts* at I/244/26) Perhaps he meant to be less dismissive than this in the *Ethics*, but I doubt it.

Well, what account of the temporal metric do we find in the *Ethics*? There is nothing much. In a comment appended to 4d6, Spinoza talks freely about imagining things as more or less distant in time, speaks of temporal intervals which we can 'imagine distinctly', and says that intervals which are too long to be imagined distinctly tend to be imagined as equal. He badly needs a supporting account of what it is to imagine—i.e., perceive —an interval of time. Perhaps that is supposed to be provided by a remark in 2p44c1s: 'We imagine (measured) time from the fact that we imagine some bodies to move more slowly, or more quickly, or with the same speed.' This is puzzling. On the face of it, my perceiving that the yacht is going faster than the dinghy is my observing that the yacht covers a given distance in less time than the dinghy does. That is, it seems to involve judgments about measured time, and thus not to be a possible basis for them. The only way I can find for Spinoza to escape this objection is to explain that by 'I imagine x to move slowly' he does not mean 'I observe that x moves slowly' but rather 'I have a subjective sense of long-drawn-out-ness as x moves'. That would make his puzzling remark a statement of the view that our temporal metric rests ultimately on an unanalysable experience of time passing; rather in the manner of Bergson, who thought that the concept of 'amount of time' is tied less directly to the behaviour of an egg-timer than to the impatience of the person awaiting breakfast. If that were Spinoza's view, that would explain his thinking that our temporal metric has an insecure hold on reality. But he would be wrong: we may be confirmed in our choice of metrical standard by its roughly aligning with our intuitive impression of how much time has passed, but those impressions are not the whole story nor even its chief part.

I am indebted to C. L. Hardin for the following suggestion. Even if Spinoza had a good grasp of the real basis for temporal measurement, he could say that our standards, however well grounded, are still ultimately conventional: we could have retained the earth's rotation as our final standard and inferred that atomic oscillations are speeding up; that we chose otherwise does not show that we recognized a truth but only that we prefer simple theories to complicated ones. And so, Spinoza might say, no facts about how long anything lasts are fully objective facts about how the universe really is.

That presupposes that some of our theory of the world is entirely unconventional, is accepted through our recognition of sheer truth untouched by considerations of theoretic convenience. That is a mistake, I think, but Spinoza would be just the man to make it, and to think that it marks off real truth about reality from such devices as our system for measuring time.

6. The most interesting thing Spinoza says about measured time in the *Ethics* involves 'imagination', but only in its role as his all-purpose term for empirical knowledge; it throws no light on why he regards temporal distance as less than fully real.

It starts at 4p9d, where Spinoza speaks of imagining something without imagining it as present. As I have explained in §39.2, he holds that a person who imagines x will imagine it as present—i.e., will believe it to be present—unless he is prevented from doing so by something else which he imagines. And so in 4p9d we find him saying that to imagine x without imagining it as present is to imagine x while imagining 'something which excludes the present existence of' x. (He is thinking about temporal nonpresence, but his line of thought cannot be stopped from applying equally to spatial nonpresence.) This offers a basis for 'I imagine x as past or future', but not for the metrical 'I imagine x as far off in the past or future', nor even for the comparative 'I imagine x as further off than y in the past or future'.

The comparative notion, out of which a metric could be developed, is introduced in 4p10d where Spinoza takes the difference between

(a) imagining x as temporally far away and (b) imagining x as temporally closer

to be equivalent to, or based upon, the difference between

(a′) imagining something which greatly excludes x's presence and (b′) imagining something which excludes x's presence less.

The notion of degree or amount of exclusion is not explained: the equivalence of the above two contrasts is said to be 'known through itself', i.e., to be something we can discover by thinking hard. The deductive ancestry is no help either: Spinoza mentions 4p9, but in fact nowhere in 4p9,d,s,c is there any concept of a difference of degree which could generate the notion of *how much* x is excluded by y. Spinoza's 'excludes less' (*minus secludit*) remains unexplained.

The 'exclusion' in question is logico-causal, and not itself a matter of degree: Spinoza cannot mean to speak of something which slightly excludes or greatly excludes x's presence. His 'less' must qualify not the exclusion but the excluder, so that he is speaking of there being more or less of whatever it is that keeps x from being present. If the excluding items are countable events of a recurring kind which we take as a metrical standard, e.g., the revolutions of a clock-hand, then he can use 'more' and 'less' in the sense of 'more (or less) numerous'. On this reading, he is saying that to imagine x as far from the present is to imagine it as excluded by a large number of events of some kind which we use for measuring time.

7. That might sound all right, but it is ambiguous. On one reading it is plain sailing, tame, and true; on a different reading it is dark, difficult, controversial . . . and possibly still true. On the tame reading, it says that when I judge something to be temporally distant, I include some thought of clock-revolutions (say) to fill the temporal gap which I judge to exist. This does not use clocks to explain or analyse or ground my judgments about temporal distance: it credits me with making them, and then uses clocks to add one detail. On this reading, it is misleading to say that clock-revolutions 'exclude' the item from being temporally present, for they enter the story only on the basis of an independent judgment that the item is not temporally present.

The other reading points to the following. My mind contains two propositions Fx and Gx, or, as Spinoza would say, I imagine x as F and as G. Since logic and physics imply that x cannot be at once F and G, I cannot imagine it as F now and as G now; and for some reason the imagining as G wins out over the imagining as F. (That will require that imaginings differ in epistemic weight, but I think Spinoza is entitled to that and could explain it.) Thus, in Spinoza's terminology, the presence of x's being F is excluded by x's now being G. Let us take my imagining of x as G to include my whole system of beliefs about the present condition of the world. That is legitimate, for if I cannot believe that Fx now, that must be because x's being F is inconsistent with beliefs I do have about how the world is now. Here I am, then, with my believed account of the world now, and the excluded proposition that Fx. If I believe that the world's present condition will cause it to be the case that Fx, then I can believe that x will be F; and my judgment about how far in the future x's being F lies will depend purely on the size of the causal chain which I think must run from the world now to x's being F. In this account, what excludes the presence of x's being F is the causal chain which will cause x to be F; and my belief in this causal chain is not a mere detail added to my judgment that x's being F lies in the future; rather, it *is* my belief that x's being F lies in the future.

That squeezes a lot out of a tiny fragment of text; but what could Spinoza mean if not that?

And it may even be right. Objection: 'We can think that x will be F five hours from now without thinking that the present state of the world will take five hours to cause x to be F.' But can we reasonably do so? How could we be entitled to the former judgment if not on the basis of the latter?

On the other hand. this account cannot be right for judgments about distance into the past. We cannot defend it in a manner analogous to the defence just given, saying that if we are entitled to think that x was F five hours ago, this must be because we think that it would take a five-hour causal chain to lead from that to the present state of the world. What spoils that analogy is the fact that although only causal reasoning can tell us about the future, memory as well as causal reasoning lets us reach back into the past. In short: Spinoza may here be onto an important aspect of our concept of temporal measure, but it cannot be the whole story.

In expounding this matter, I have helped myself to the difference between two ways of not being temporally present—being past and being future. I shall pick that theme up again in §49.5. Before getting on with the philosophy, however, we must sort out some terminology.

§47. Tempus *and duration*

1. Spinoza's basic temporal noun is *duratio*, always rendered by 'duration'. He uses *tempus* only under special conditions, of which I have mentioned one, namely, the topic's being measured time. He also uses *tempus* when he is speaking of time from a tensed or past-present-future standpoint. The Concordance of Michel Gueret and his colleagues has enabled me to run down every occurrence of *tempus* in the *Ethics*, and I can report that in some of its uses it refers to measured time, in others to tensed time, and in yet others to both.[6]

Are these two supposed to be connected? Spinoza does not comment on them, either separately or conjointly, so we must work it out for ourselves. Fortunately, we can. The answer is Yes, Spinoza does think that the tense cluster of concepts shares an important feature with the metrical cluster.

6. It is probably used metrically in 3p8, and is so in 4 Preface at 209/8, in 4p62s where the *tempus* of a thing's existing is how long it lasts, and in 5p23s and 5p29d. It is used in connection with tenses and not measure in 3p18d, in Part 3 at 198/15, 4p9c, 4p13d, 4p62s. It involves both tense and measure in 2p44c1s, the paragraph following 4d6, 4p10, and 4p12cd. A few other significant occurrences will be discussed in the text.

2. What connects them with one another, and also links them with spatial measure, is the concept of a cut, a borderline, a demarcation. We saw Spinoza emphasizing that when we measure amounts of stuff we are treating the extended world as divisible into parts. That obviously holds for temporal measure also: to say that something lasted for an hour is to divide time into a discontinuous part when the item did not exist and a continuous part when it did. It also holds for past-present-future: you cannot use the tense cluster of concepts without distinguishing some part of time from all the rest.

The link between *tempus* and the concept of a particular moment or period is especially visible in Spinoza's phrase 'particular things insofar as they are considered in relation to a certain time and place' (5p37s). Here 'time' translates *tempus*; there is nothing here about measure or explicitly about past-present-future, but *tempus* is used because the thought concerns a particular moment or period—a cut into time, or a part of time. *Tempus* is also the word for *a time*, or for *times*, because any temporal count-noun must refer to parts of time. Spinoza does sometimes use *tempus* in the plural or in the singular in a manner which invites the use of an indefinite article. He also uses it as a mass noun, e.g., saying that eternity has no relation to *tempus*, but he is now referring to the one continuous time considered as divided into parts.

So really *tempus* is associated not only with measure and tense, but also with the topological concepts. To say that an E event occurs (tenseless) before an F process ends—or merely to say that an F process ends (tenseless)—is to distinguish some parts of time from others, by implying that something happens during some parts of time and not others. No part of time is measured, and none is related to the present, and yet the statement makes cuts within time; it marks out distinct times; it involves *tempus*.

3. Thus, *tempus* is Spinoza's word when any of our three concept clusters is at work. And 'duration' is his word for time considered as a perfectly uncut, undifferentiated continuum. He defines it as 'an indefinite continuation of existing' (2d5). This does not mean that something with duration lasts for ever, but only that to attribute duration to something is to say nothing about how long it lasts. Spinoza offers to explain why he puts 'indefinite' into the definiens, but I cannot see that the explanation works. Anyway, my explanation suffices: 'indefinite' is there because 'duration' just is Spinoza's *non-cutting* temporal word, and to say something definite about a thing's enduring is to *cut*.

Duration, Spinoza says, 'can be made definite [*definiri*] by *tempus*' (5p23d). He means that propositions of the form 'x has (tenseless) duration . . .' can intelligibly be supplemented by the metrical '. . . for exactly a year', or the topological '. . . which ends before some F event begins', or

203

the tensed '. . . at some time in the past'. Each of these adds something to the unspecific proposition that the thing has duration.

Spinoza clearly thinks of duration as basic, with *tempus* being reached by 'determining' or 'limiting' duration. He would therefore not be willing to explain 'duration' in terms of *tempus*. That does not forbid him to explain 'duration' by equating 'has duration' with 'lasts through some period of time', because the latter phrase does not involve *tempus*, since it does not name any moment or period, and does not entail that anything is the case at some parts of time and not at others.

Anyway, the fundamental position seems clear. To attribute duration to x is to say that it lasts, and to say nothing about how long it lasts or when if ever it starts or stops exising. Such information can be added. If what is added implies that x is not sempiternal, then its duration is being 'determined' and the concept of *tempus* is at work. If what is added is that x lasts throughout all time, then Spinoza does not count this as a use of the concept of *tempus*, or as determining x's duration. That is why we find him in 1p21d equating 'x has a determinate existence or duration' (66/1) with 'x at some time did not or will not exist' (66/4). Two sorts of temporal concept have duration as an ingredient, then. One is the concept of sempiternity, the other is the great mass of conceptual material which goes under the label *tempus*.

§48. *Eternity*

1. Spinoza distinguishes sempiternity, or existence at all times, from 'eternity' which he defines thus:

By eternity I understand existence itself, insofar as it is conceived to follow necessarily from the definition alone of the eternal thing. *Explanation*: For such existence, like the essence of the thing, is conceived as an eternal truth, and on that account cannot be explained by duration or *tempus*, even if the duration is conceived to be without beginning or end. (1d8)

This says that a thing might exist throughout all time—have 'duration without beginning or end'—without being eternal, i.e., having a nature which absolutely must be instantiated. Spinoza is tying 'eternal' to 'logically necessarily existing', which latter he thinks is equivalent to 'having a definition (or essence) which includes existence'.

Some commentators have attributed to Spinoza the view that eternal things are not sempiternal because no temporal concepts get any grip on them. But this comes from misreading certain passages and flouting others. What Spinoza says in 1d8 is that eternity cannot be *explained* by duration, i.e., that you can't define eternity as unlimited duration, for eternity involves an extra ingredient—namely, absolute necessity of existence. Spinoza says it again in 5p23s, where he takes a thing's being 'eternal' to imply that 'the existence it has cannot be . . . explained through duration'.

In the same sentence he also says that a thing's being eternal implies that its existence cannot be limited or made definite (*definiri*) by *tempus*. The meaning is perfectly plain: to the statement that x has duration we can add 'for an hour only', or 'until quite recently', or 'not yet but soon', or 'almost but not quite always', etc., but nothing like that can be added to the statement that x is eternal. As Spinoza says in 1p33s2 at 75/12, 'In eternity there is neither *when* nor *before* nor *after*'. That is, if something is eternally the case then it is always the case: *eternity entails sempiternity*.

The two-part remark I have been discussing is this: 'We feel that [x] is eternal, and that this existence it has cannot be *limited by tempus* or *explained through duration.*' That is precise and correct. Eternity is like sempiternity in resisting limitation by any temporal cut, and unlike it in not being analysable in terms of duration.

2. In 5p23s Spinoza says that eternity 'cannot have any relation to *tempus*'. On my account of his position, that is wrong. Eternity is a species of duration, marked off by the differentia 'necessary' (or its equivalent 'necessarily sempiternal'), and *tempus* is also a species of duration. Between them, therefore, there obtains a clean, crisp relation, namely '. . . is a species of a genus of which . . . is also a species'. I don't mind, though, since no interpretation could make the quoted remark come out true: there could not conceivably be two items with *no* relation between them. Presumably, Spinoza was using 'have any relation' to mean something narrower than we mean by it, but he did not explain what. There is no evidence that if he had explained, his remark would have turned out to be one with which my account of his position would conflict.

3. In taking Spinoza's view to be that eternity entails sempiternity, I am taking one side in a controversy, agreeing with Martha Kneale[7] against the majority of Spinoza commentators down the years. Much of the debate has focussed on Spinoza's peculiar doctrine that part of the human mind is eternal, his handling of which suggests that he takes eternity to entail sempiternity. That morass will be the sad topic of chapter 15, and I shan't venture into it here. Nor do I need to. Spinoza often speaks in temporal terms of eternal items, in accordance with his view that eternity entails sempiternity and thus duration. For example, he combines tenses with eternity when he speaks of what 'has been actual from eternity and will remain [so] to eternity' (1p17s at 62/19), and when he says that infinite and eternal modes 'have always had to exist' (1p21); and he says that 'an infinite thing must always exist necessarily' (2p11d). And then there is what he says early in Letter 35 about what a necessarily existing being must be like: 'It must be eternal: for if a determinate duration were attributed to

---

7. Martha Kneale, 'Eternity and Sempiternity'. Donagan's 'Spinoza's Proof of Immortality' is also relevant.

it, then that being would be conceived as not existing, or as not involving necessary existence, beyond that determinate duration. This is inconsistent with its definition.' Here a thing's being eternal is opposed to its having determinate or limited duration, which goes with Spinoza's thinking that it does have unlimited duration (though that is not what its eternity consists in).

4. If Spinoza did hold that eternity entails sempiternity, he should have thought that God is sempiternal and thus has duration. Did he in fact think this?

In the *Metaphysical Thoughts* he explicitly rejects it, giving two bad arguments. One is that what has duration has temporal parts, whereas God cannot have parts of any kind (I/250/31). This is open to the reply that if spatial extent does not make God divisible in a manner inconsistent with being a substance, then the same should hold of temporal extent. The point about space is that its regions depend conceptually on their surroundings: the notion of a region of space involves the concept of a larger region in which it is embedded, so that regions do not relate to space as men do to an army. It seems equally plausible to say that the notion of a period of time essentially involves the concept of a longer period containing it. (I don't say that either line of thought is certainly right; only that one is as good as the other.) Hallett has denied this, arguing that duration is more dangerously divisible than extension; but his argument rests the indivisibility of space on the fact that divisions within it are arbitrary, whereas at any moment there is a highly unarbitrary division of time.[8] As I remarked in §21.2, the 'arbitrariness' point is not the chief reason Spinoza can give for saying that the extended world does not have parts which deprive it of its substantiality.

The other bad argument (I/250/29) depends on two theses. (i) Anything that has duration has lasted longer by now than it had by this time yesterday, and (ii) it is absurd to say such a thing about God. Martha Kneale rightly denies that it is obviously absurd to credit God with having a longer history up to today than up to yesterday. But (i) is wrong too, for reasons in the mathematics of infinity which Spinoza could not know. To explain them to him we would have to use the concept of infinite past time, and I am afraid he would reject that, too, because of a pair of bad arguments (I/270/26).

5. That all relates to the *Metaphysical Thoughts*. Although in the following years Spinoza did not get clear of his troubles about infinity, he seems to have dropped the view that God cannot have duration. The overall position I have credibly attributed to him implies that God can have duration, and I can find no evidence in the *Ethics* of his rejecting that im-

8. Hallett, *Aeternitas*, p. 9.

plication. On this whole matter, his performance is more consistent and controlled than the secondary literature might lead one to believe.

If a stray denial of duration to God does turn up, that will be because Spinoza has momentarily slipped, moving from (a) his official definition of 'duration' in terms which merely leave necessity out, to (b) a definition of it which includes contingency. But (b) is not his considered position. And even if it were, we could coin the term 'duration*' with a meaning derived from that of 'duration' by peeling off contingency. Duration* would still be a thoroughly temporal concept: the interesting question would be whether God has duration*, and the answer would be Yes. But we don't need 'duration*', since the work it would do is in fact done for Spinoza by 'duration'.

§49.   *The reality of change*

1. Given that Spinoza attributes duration to God or Nature—a point which should never have been controversial—there is a real question about how he thinks the concept of *tempus* relates to Nature as a whole.

I have dealt with the metrical aspect in §46. Spinoza seems to think that facts involving amounts of time are not fully objective, either because they lie in the domain of 'imagination', i.e., of empirical fact, or because their basis is conventional. I don't agree but don't regard his mistake as fatal. I used to think that any viable concept of time must include a temporal metric,[9] but I am now less sure about that. Consider a possible world W containing events and processes in definite temporal relations to one another, but not obeying our physics. There can be no basis in W for applying any of our measures of time: the four-colour problem is formulated in W and later solved, but we can have no basis for saying that between formulation and solution there elapsed fewer than a trillion of our years, or more than one of our microseconds. W might have its own internal metric, so that between the formulation and the solution of the four-colour problem in W there elapsed thirty-seven zeons, where 'zeon' is defined in terms of certain kinds of process in W. But must that be possible? Does every possible world which is genuinely temporal have a basis for some sort of temporal metric? I do not see why.

Still, that is not to endorse Spinoza's dismissive attitude to measured time. And it is not an attitude he can afford to take, since it commits him to describing as shallow and imaginative his own physics and biology. These are a level up from his basic metaphysics, but they are supposed to lie pretty deep; and they use 'motion and rest' in a manner which surely involves a temporal metric.

2. Of course Spinoza does not think that his basic metaphysics—his ac-

9. J. Bennett, *Kant's Analytic* (Cambridge, 1966), p. 175.

count of God—has any place for tenses or for past-present-future. He seems to have seen how these are linked to the viewpoint of the individual inhabitant of the universe; and that alone would, in his eyes, disqualify them for deep theoretical purposes. That does not mean that he should not use them at all, and I have noted that he does make some use of the concept of the present. But only in a safe manner: everything he says could be expressed in terms of topology and dates; he does not address—and presumably was not aware of—the special feature of the concept of the present, namely, its being able to survive the removal of all the empirical content associated with it (see §45.2).

There are just two main uses of the concept of the present. One is in Spinoza's doctrine that if I imagine Paul I will imagine him as (spatio-temporally) present to me unless I also imagine something else which rules that out. This could perfectly well be put in the language of temporal topology: if at a given time someone imagines a certain thing, he imagines it as existing in his vicinity at that time, unless . . . etc.

Similar remarks apply to Spinoza's use of 'present' in his doctrine that in our practical deliberations a state of affairs weighs more or less heavily with us depending on how far removed it is from the present (4p62s). This could be put in the language of topology and dates: at any time T a person gives more weight to possible goods and bads which are temporally close to T than to more remote ones.

3. That brings us to the big question: How do the concepts of temporal topology and dates fit into Spinoza's basic metaphysic? When he says that *tempus* is a mere 'mode of the imagination', is he banishing from his metaphysical scheme not only measured and tensed time but every sort of cut into the continuous durational flow? If so, then he is presumably denying the reality of change.

Some things in his work tend that way, especially the tendency to regard God as a subject only of necessary truths and never of contingent ones, i.e., to identify God with what I call 'God as seen from above'. I think that explains the statement that 'God, or all of God's attributes, are immutable' (1p20c2), and the implication that God is 'immutable and eternal' in 5p20s at 294/12.

If there were no truths about God except eternal ones, then it would indeed follow that no predicate of the form '. . . is F at T_1 and is not F at T_2' is true of God. But although Spinoza may have been pulled that way, he did not go the whole distance. There are the two quoted immutability remarks, but he does not weave into the fabric of his work the thesis that the one substance does not change. A bit before 2p14, at 102/13, he speaks of Nature as an (organic) 'individual' which undergoes no 'change' although bodies within it 'vary'. But his topic has been the way an individual can alter without undergoing a change of 'form', this being a radical change

—a kind of death or going out of existence. There is no need to read this passage as implying the entire immutability of God. The same is true of uses of 'change' in 4p20s at 224/32, and 4p39s at 240/21,23.

4. Still, if Spinoza does not explicitly deny that there is change at the deepest metaphysical level, neither does he clearly admit it at that level. He is indeed strangely silent about time in the initial stages of his metaphysic: whereas spatiality is loudly heralded as an attribute, temporality is not announced and paraded as a trans-attribute aspect of Nature. But if it is not there at all, what can Spinoza say about such facts as that the lightning preceded the thunder? There are two prima facie possibilities.

One is to deny that there are any such facts, claiming that all diachronic variety in the universe is 'fictitious and illusory'.[10] This strikes me as intensely un-Spinozistic, as well as being philosophically unattractive. We ought not to take it seriously unless we are given some account of how the illusion of temporality arises, and it seems impossible that this should be done. Any attempt at it must avoid saying that although nothing of the form

(i)   At T_1 the universe is F, and at T_2 it is not F

is true, we have the illusion that some such propositions are true because some of the form

(ii)   At T_1 the universe seems to be F, and at T_2
it does not seem to be F

are true. The trouble with that is that (ii) is itself of the form of (i). But then how could one possibly explain an illusion of temporality *without* saying something like (ii)?

The alternative is to introduce temporality, by conceptual construction, at some unbasic level of the metaphysic. Here is a sketch of how Spinoza might try to do this; it follows his usual practice of focussing on extension, and letting thought tag along. Specifically, the focus is on 'motion and rest'. I said in §26.1 that we must construe this phrase, in its ground floor occurrences, as referring not to ordinary motion but to patterns of qualitative *change* in space which can be conceptualized one level up as movements of things in space. But that admits *time* on the ground floor. If it too is to be a construct, Spinoza had better dig deeper, taking motion and rest to be something which does not basically involve change, but only atemporal patterns of causal dependence which can be conceptualized, one level up, as changes.[11]

10. Caird, *Spinoza*, p. 21. He says the same about synchronic variety.

11. This line of thought was suggested to me in conversation by C. L. Hardin, to whose 'Spinoza on Immortality and Time' I am indebted for my awareness of the problem.

That is surely his best bet if he wants temporal concepts to be unbasic. Here is why I don't think it could work, however. The fundamental fact about time is that it transmutes contradictions into changes, e.g., turning the impossible 'Fa and not Fa' into the eventful 'Fa at T_1 and not Fa at T_2'. So any basis for our temporal account of the world must contain contradiction-blocking adverbs, saying things of the form 'a is F *thus*' and 'a is not F *so*', where 'thus' and 'so' stand for adverbs which have the same logic as 'here' and 'elsewhere', or 'at one time' and 'at another time'. But then what stops those adverbs from counting as temporal? Instead of saying that the temporal 'Fa at T_1 and not Fa at T_2' is *based on* an atemporal 'a is F thus and a is not F so', why can we not say that 'thus' means 'at T_1' and 'so' means 'at T_2'?

Did Spinoza in fact envisage such a constructing of temporal concepts out of metaphysically deeper materials? Yes or No—take your pick. There is no direct evidence that he did; but indirect evidence is provided by his making no provision for temporality at the bottom level, yet giving an account of the world which in so many ways requires the reality of time and change at some level.

5. One might hope for help from his treatment of our knowledge and experience of time, but the hope is disappointed. I need not reraise his handling of our experience of amounts of time (see §46.5–7); that confirms his making measured time unbasic, but it does not help with my present question about the place in his metaphysical scheme of temporality as such, with or without a metric. We need a discussion by Spinoza of what in our experience leads us to say that one event occurs (tenseless) before another, or that a certain event is past, or is future.

Well, he says nothing about before-after as such; and his remarks about past-present-future are not helpful. At the start of 3p18s1 and in 4d6 he ties 'past' and 'future' to tenses; but that is trivial. For the rest, we have only 4p9,10,13, concerning such facts as that a present rattlesnake is more frightening than a past or future one. Here the notion of what is *present* is taken as basic, and the concept of the *nonpresent* comes in through the presence of something which 'excludes the presence' of something else. So far, so good, perhaps; but this cannot generate a theory of temporality as such unless it shows how to split the nonpresent into past and future, and how to determine which is which. That distinction, however, is expressed here only through unexplained uses of tenses, and through the term 'memory'; and if we go back to 2p18,s for Spinoza's account of what memory is we find that the temporal direction of memory is fixed through tenses and the word 'subsequently', i.e., in a manner which presupposes that we already have a full range of temporal concepts at our command.

He could try to get a concept of temporal direction out of the notion of causal direction, as follows. Developing the line of thought I tentatively gave to Spinoza in §46.6, let us take it that the judgment

> The world is (tenseless) F at some time, but not now,

must be based on three judgments:

> The world is now G;
> No world can be F and G at once;
> No world can be G without being F at some time.

Now, there may be two different bases for that third judgment. There might be a distinction between 'A world's being F is necessary as a means to its being G' and 'A world's being G is sufficient for its being F', the difference being a difference in causal direction. Equipped with that distinction, we could then construct temporal direction on the basis of it, thus splitting the nonpresent into the past and the future.

I am not optimistic for the chances of this account of judgments about temporal direction. For one thing, it needs a robust concept of causal direction which owes nothing at all to time's arrow, and that looks impossible. Also, the account assumes that our judgments about nonpresent times all rest on inferences from the present to other times, and that is wrong because memory provides a different basis for some of them.

In any case, I have no reason to think that anything like the proposed account ever occurred to Spinoza. Nor have I meant to imply that in any of the passages discussed in this subsection Spinoza is trying to give definitions or analyses of temporal concepts and to get them into the epistemic story in that way; my point is merely that if that is what he is trying do, he fails. I would rather not see him as trying. Still, I suspect that at some level of his mind he did think he was constructing, explaining or introducing, because he was partly aware that he was using temporal concepts without having provided for them in the foundations of his system.

9

Goals

It is a famous fact about Spinoza that he rejected 'final causes', teleological explanations, anything in the nature of a pull rather than a push. In this chapter I shall explain in literal terms what his position is about this, what philosophical insight it rests on, and why I think it is wrong.

§50. *The denial of divine purpose*

1. Most of what Spinoza says against 'final causes' is aimed at the belief in cosmic goals or divine purposes—'The rain fell so that the crops might grow'. Some commentators have been led to overlook the more sweeping attack on the concept of purpose as such—'He raised his hand so as to shade his eyes'. Even Schopenhauer, usually a shrewd reader of his predecessors, goes wrong here. He includes Spinoza among the 'three great men' who 'have entirely rejected teleology', and says that 'in the case of all three . . . the source of this aversion [is] that they regarded teleology as inseparable from speculative theology'.[1] That is not true, though it is an understandable mistake, given the brevity of Spinoza's attack on teleology generally, as distinct from cosmic teleology in particular. The latter is nothing like as important and instructive as the former, either in itself or in relation to other parts of the text. Still, the assault on divine purpose is worth a section.

The material is nearly all in 1 Appendix. In presenting it I shall rearrange it a little.

2. Spinoza offers two undermining explanations of why people attribute purpose to God or to the gods. One is that if we explain things purely through their efficient causes, the answer to every why question throws up a new why, whereas these vexatious series can be painlessly brought to a halt by a pseudo-answer in terms of final causes. As Spinoza memorably says:

. . . They will press on, for there is no end to the questions that can be asked: but why was the sea tossing? why was the man invited at just that time? And so they will not stop asking for the causes of causes until you take refuge in the will of God, i.e. the sanctuary of ignorance. (81/8)

1. Arthur Schopenhauer, *The World as Will and Representation*, trans. E. F. J. Payne (New York, 1969), vol. 2, p. 337.

On the face of it, this is implausible. Why should anyone be embarrassed by having to say, a short distance along the backwards explanatory chain, that he doesn't know what the earlier items in the chain are?

Perhaps Spinoza was confusing that explanation with the following more plausible one. People are discomfited by the thought that you cannot explain a particular item without saying something which calls for explanation in turn; so they are drawn to suppose that something terminates the explanatory regress; and they take this terminal item to be an uncaused purposive act on God's part. Since this has nothing to do with a 'sanctuary of ignorance', I cannot offer it as an interpretation of the quoted passage; but I think it is lurking in 1 Appendix all the same.

Why must it be an uncaused purposive act? Well, if it is caused then it does not terminate the explanatory regress, for the question as to why *it* occurred will invoke its cause, about which a new question will arise, and we shall be off and running again. On the other hand, we are dealing with people who, like Spinoza, think that every why question has some answer; and so they will not be satisfied with a sheerly arbitrary divine act, for which there is no answer to 'Why did He do it?' So they have to suppose that the act in question was purposive, i.e., that there is an explanation of why God performed it, namely, one of the form 'He performed it so as to bring it about that P'. To put all of this in technical terminology which Spinoza sometimes uses: an act that terminates the regress cannot have an efficient cause, but there must be an explanation of its occurrence, and so it must have a final cause. (This is all a repeat of §28.2.)

3. Spinoza seems to think that the belief in divine purpose is nourished also by the observation that many things are advantageous to us, which seduces people into the assumption that 'there was someone else who had prepared those means for their use' (78/37). After a clever, funny treatment of the route people follow in reaching their conclusions about 'the temperament of these [divine] rulers', Spinoza modulates into a positive attack on the belief in benevolent divine purpose. Even if we suppose that God is personal, and that purposes are all right, the traditional view of benevolence is absurd, says Spinoza. (This is his usual technique in attacking the tradition.) He adduces the problem of evil; why would a benevolent deity allow so much that is adverse to our interests? Believers try to explain this by attributing bad things to the gods' anger at human misconduct, Spinoza says; but the distribution of misfortune among humans is quite out of line with any sane assessment of moral desert, and so: 'While they sought to show that Nature does nothing in vain (i.e. nothing which is not of use to men), they seem to have shown only that Nature and the gods are as mad as men are.' (79/15) Spinoza's beautiful treatment of the problem of evil as it presents itself for his own 'theology' is given on the last page of the Appendix.

He has earlier given a different argument against the view that God acts so as to bring about the best possible results, if this means that there are independent standards of good and that God acts in the light of them. It is a shrewd argument, but I need not elaborate on my report of it in §28.3. Less good is the argument in 1 Appendix that it is impious to attribute purposes to God because 'If God acts for the sake of an end, he must want something which he lacks' (80/22). That reflects the widespread assumption that purposive activity is unintelligible unless directed to a future which is preferred to the present: as Locke said, in effect, 'Why should I act unless I am discontented with the *status quo?*' There are many answers to that. The crucial point is this: if someone acts, he prefers a certain possible future—not to the present but to other possible futures.[2]

§51.   *The denial of all purpose*

1. Mixed in with the attack on divine purpose there are two arguments which, if they are any good at all, count against any kind of teleology— against 'He raised his hand so as to shade his eyes' as well as against 'Elbows are formed like that so that men can raise their hands'. This more drastic attack is easy to overlook in 1 Appendix, because it is well buried in a discussion of God's purposes and also because Spinoza there seems at times to concede that men do have purposes which explain their behaviour. We shall see in §52 that he offers a partial rescue of that sort of talk: his concept of 'appetite', which is free of the supposedly noxious elements in teleological concepts, might have seemed to him to underpin such remarks as 'Men always act on account of an end, namely on account of their advantage, which they want' (1 Appendix at 78/21). Or perhaps the seeming concessions of human teleology in 1 Appendix may be due to Spinoza's having written most of his polemic against divine teleology before his case against all teleology occurred to him, and neglecting to revise the text when that discovery was at last made.

Anyway, the radical attack on teleology should be taken seriously. For one thing, it is needed for the attack on divine teleology: if human beings were allowed to act purposively, Spinoza would have as much reason to say that God has purposes as he does to say that God thinks. Furthermore, brief as it is the radical attack on teleology is *there*, and many aspects of Part 3 cannot be understood unless one grasps that Spinoza is trying to develop a nonteleological theory of human motivation. Miss that and you miss most of what is interesting in Part 3.

2. Spinoza argues that nothing has a final cause because everything has an efficient cause:

2. For more on this, see J. Bennett, 'Leibniz's *New Essays*', *Philosophic Exchange* vol. 3 (1982), pp. 25–38.

Nature has no end set before it, and all final causes are nothing but human fictions. I believe I have already sufficiently established this, . . . from 1p16,32c, and from all those [arguments] by which I have shown that all things proceed by a certain eternal necessity of Nature. (80/3)

The phrase about 'a certain eternal necessity of Nature' is a reference to Spinoza's efficient-cause determinism. He is implying that something which is caused mechanistically, i.e., by a 'push' from behind, cannot properly be explained also in terms of goals or purposes or desires, i.e., in terms of a 'pull' towards a resultant state of affairs.

If final causes are rivals of efficient ones, then teleology involves radical freedom, i.e., the falsity of (efficient-cause) determinism. Spinoza links these two in some of his discussions of common beliefs, contending in 1 Appendix that the belief in divine purpose is connected somehow with men's belief in their own freedom (78/18); I don't fully understand that passage, and suspect it of muddle. Things are clearer in Spinoza's famous jibe in Letter 58 that if a stone in flight could think it 'would believe itself to be completely free, and would think that it continued in motion solely because of its own wish' (IV/266/16), which neatly gives one clause to freedom and one to teleology, taking them to stand together.

This link between teleology and radical freedom is a mistake: there is no reason why something which is done with a purpose or end in view should not be fully efficiently caused. It may be easier to see this now that we have stopped using the phrase 'final *cause*' in our talk about teleology. That does not mean that we have dropped the real content of the word 'cause' in that phrase, namely, the implication that the role of the concepts of purpose, goal, desire etc. is to help *explain* behaviour. I shall return to this shortly.

3. Spinoza also objects against teleological explanations that they purport to explain events by reference to their effects. A stone is thrown at me, and I raise my hand in time to deflect it: the event Raise causes the event Deflect. But if we purport to explain Raise by saying that it was performed 'so as to deflect the stone', we are using Deflect to explain Raise. Spinoza protests: 'This doctrine concerning the end turns Nature completely upside down. For what is really a cause, it considers as an effect, and conversely. What by nature comes before it puts after.' (1 Appendix at 80/10). He thinks that one cannot explain an event by reference to a later event, because one cannot explain an item by reference to something which it causes.[3]

Let us suppose that Raise was caused by an antecedent event Brain. Then

---

3. In an earlier writing on this topic, I made temporal order the whole point rather than just an important special case. For a correction of this, and other good things, see Parkinson, 'Spinoza's Conception of the Rational Act'.

Spinoza's two objections, side by side, run as follows. It is wrong to explain Raise by reference to Deflect because (i) Brain caused Raise, and (ii) Raise caused Deflect. Because of (i), the role of 'Raise-explaining event' is already filled, and because of (ii) it couldn't be filled by Deflect, anyway, because between that and Raise the causal flow runs the other way.

Together, these objections amount to a challenge to show how an event can be legitimately explained by reference to something which is temporally later or causally subsequent to it. That is the challenge I shall offer to meet in §53.

4. The point about 'turning Nature upside down' contains a trap. It focusses on cases where there are two events, such as Raise and Deflect, and it says that a teleological explanation puts them wrong way around. But often there is only one event: 'He raised his hand so as to deflect the stone, but he was too slow and the stone got through.' Furthermore, as those remind us, in a teleological explanation the event is usually explained by reference not directly to an effect of it but rather to an antecedent thought about an effect of it. In saying 'He raised his hand so as to deflect the stone' we are saying that Raise happened because he thought it would cause the stone's being deflected. What is there in that for Spinoza to object to? Why can he not just accept it, saying that the subsequent event enters the story only as something represented in an antecedent thought, so that 'the [thought] of the "final cause" functions as "efficient cause" '?[4]

Spinoza does himself explain actions by reference to the agent's thought about the future, as we shall see; which suggests that he has no case against such explanations. I shall maintain, on the contrary, that he objects to them strenuously, and that he is caught in an inconsistency—explaining actions in a manner which he ought to condemn. If his attack on teleology were intended only to condemn explaining Raise with help from Deflect, and to allow the explanation of Raise in terms of a thought about a deflection, then it is a noisy assault on a minuscule target. Spinoza is hunting bigger game than that. Much of Part 3, and especially his concept of 'appetite', is explicable only if he is trying to avoid letting even the concept of—or a representation of—something subsequent to x help to explain x.

5. Of course Spinoza's dualism forbids any thought to cause a physical action. And he uses his dualism in that way, inferring from it that what physical things are like 'does not follow from the divine nature because [God] has first known the things' (2p6c). But that is not my whole present point. Although Spinoza's dualism rules out the causal chain

$$\text{Thought of deflection} \rightarrow \text{Raise}$$

it does not rule out the chain

4. R. B. Braithwaite, *Scientific Explanation* (Cambridge, 1953), p. 325.

(1)   O(Thought of deflection) → Raise,

where O(Thought of deflection) is the physical counterpart, under the parallelism, of a thought about a deflection of the stone—presumably consisting mostly of an event in the brain. Nor does it rule out the chain

(2)   Thought of deflection → I(Raise),

where I(Raise) is the mental counterpart, whatever it might be, of the raising of the hand. If (1) and (2) were all right, an event would be explainable by reference to something which conceptually involves something subsequent to it,[5] and that would be unacceptable to Spinoza. He cannot now appeal to the prohibition of causal flow between the attributes, since neither (1) nor (2) sins against that. Then what objection can he bring?

The answer might be: 'None—he simply failed to notice that he had no decent case against this kind of teleological explanation.' That answer, if I had to give it, would not shake my confidence that Spinoza did set himself against teleological explanations such as (1) and (2) would generate. Still, we can do better, finding a solid Spinozistic objection to using (1) to explain Raise or (2) to explain I(Raise).

It turns on the fact that a cause of x has features which do not contribute to its causing x, including some which do not contribute to its causing anything. The fall of a vase may be caused by a push which occurs across the middle of the table in a northerly direction, is accompanied by a snapping of fingers, and is just like a certain movement that Olivier makes in his film version of *Hamlet*. The first of these features is relevant to the push's causing the fall, the second is relevant to some of its causal powers though not to that one, and the third is probably irrelevant to all its causal powers.

In making that point I implicitly distinguish events from facts. That is, I assume that a single *concrete* event x which caused the vase's fall is the subject of a multitude of distinct facts, *abstract* objects—that x was a movement, that it was a fast movement, that it was a movement northwards, that it resembled a movement of Olivier's, and so on. Spinoza makes little of that distinction, probably for two reasons: his whole cast of mind makes him insensitive to the difference between concrete and abstract objects, and his causal rationalism is especially hostile to events and friendly to facts. I shall explain the latter point. Causal rationalism is hard to make plausible when applied to statements of the form 'x caused y', where x and y are concrete particular events, but is more plausible when applied to statements of the form 'The fact that an F event occurred explains the fact that a G

---

5. I would say 'which represents something subsequent to it', but apparently that would be wrong for chain (1), since Spinoza does not allow physical items to represent anything. See the end of §37.2.

event occurred', where F and G are kinds of event. In the latter kind of statement the relata are abstract items, facts, with no hidden or unstated properties; and to the extent that Spinoza's causal thinking is conducted in these terms, so far he will be unlikely to have thoughts like mine about the event which caused the vase's fall. But this is a tendency, not a doctrine: Spinoza does not ever explicitly favour explanatory relations between facts over causal relations between events, or abstract items over concrete ones; nor does he say outright that the world is everything that is the case, or anything like that. So, although his thought tended in that direction, it may also sometimes have made room for ideas going the other way, and I conjecture that it did: at some level of his mind, I think, Spinoza was influenced by certain views which imply that a cause may have causally irrelevant features such as the 'like Olivier's gesture' feature of the event which caused the vase's fall. I shall explain.

Consider the causal chain (1), running from O(Thought of deflection) to Raise. I conjecturally attribute to Spinoza the following view: Raise is caused by a certain physical event x, and x is indeed O(Thought of deflection), but that fact about it is not causally potent—none of x's causal powers depend on its being the counterpart of a thought with such and such a content, i.e., the counterpart of something which is an idea indirectly of a so-and-so. The physical theory inserted between 2p13 and 14 firmly assumes that physical events are to be explained purely in terms of the shapes, sizes, positions, velocities etc. of particles of matter. There is no work to be done by representative features. (Except, trivially, for I(x)'s feature of being a supposed representation of x. That is irrelevant to our present topic, which concerns thoughts of possible future states of affairs, not of brain events; representations indirectly of things, not directly of our own bodies.) The point is not just that in describing x as 'O(Thought of deflection)' we are bringing in the attribute of thought, which is causally insulated from that of extension. Even if we had a Spinozistic way of making x represent the deflection of the stone other than by corresponding to an idea which represents it, that representative feature of x would still have no part in the physical causal theory. So Spinoza would say, I conjecture, and he would be right. Analogously, the causal powers of a page with ink marks on it may depend on size, shape, chemical composition etc., but will never depend upon whether it is a map of Sussex. Even if we take the map's powers to include not only its effects but also their mental correlates, thus giving it a power to alter beliefs, still its powers do not depend on its representative features. Its power to bring into your head the thought 'This is a map of Sussex' depends on what it and you are intrinsically like at that moment; and as long as those intrinsic features were the same the transaction between the map and you would have been the same, even if Sussex had never existed.

If that is Spinoza's line on the physical chain (1) from O(Thought of deflection) to Raise, then he ought also to apply it to the mental chain (2) from Thought of deflection to I(Raise). That is, he ought to hold that when I have the thought that P, this thought is a psychological particular with various features contributing to its causal powers, but its representative feature—its having the content *that P*—must be causally inert. The parallelism of causal chains forces this onto Spinoza. If a physical item's causal powers depend solely on facts about positions, velocities etc. of particles, then the causal powers of mental items must depend upon features of them which are systematically correlated with *those* physical features. And that implies that the causal powers of mental items do not depend on their representative features, what they are indirectly 'of' or 'about' or 'that'. Spinoza's parallelism doctrine is a lot to swallow, but it would be even harder to choke down the thesis that features having to do with positions and velocities etc. can be systematically mapped onto such mental features as *being about Vienna* or *having the content 'This will deflect the stone'*. It seems reasonable to suppose—and these days it is widely supposed[6]—that different kinds of cerebral event might serve in different brains, or even at different times in one brain, as the physical correlate of a thought about Vienna; and if that is right, then a psychological theory which was isomorphic with some physical theory such as cerebral neurology could not have *being about Vienna* as a causally significant feature of a thought.

Spinoza was obliged to take this position, and I conjecture that the obligation subliminally affected his thinking. Is this just charitable anachronism? Is it absurd to connect Spinoza with something which appeared explicitly in the philosophical literature only about a decade ago? I think not. Any philosopher who thought seriously about how the representative content of thoughts relates to intrinsic brain states would be almost certain to conclude that there is no simple mapping between them: once the question is raised, the answer is pretty obvious. And what Spinoza has in common with his materialist and functionalist successors is, precisely, a reason for caring a lot about how mental states relate to associated states of the brain.

6. As well as being pushed into denying the causal efficacy of the representative features of thoughts, Spinoza may have been pulled that way by a certain advantage which that denial can bring him.[7] The parallelism thesis implies that there is a science of the mental which is isomorphic with physics, and Spinoza must admit that although we know a lot of physics we

6. See for example Jaegwon Kim, 'Causality, Identity, and Supervenience in the Mind-Body Problem', *Midwest Studies in Philosophy* IV (1979), pp. 31–49.

7. In what follows, I develop an idea which was given to me by C. L. Hardin.

know almost nothing of the corresponding mental science. He ought to see this as a problem. It is understandable that the thick detail of human psychology defeats us by its complexity, matching the complexity of the still unknown fine structure of the human brain; but Spinoza should be troubled by our knowing no general psychology, corresponding to elementary physics.

There are two things he can do to reduce this embarrassment, making our ignorance of basic psychology look less brutally contingent than it threatens to be. (i) He can suppose that we don't yet know how to classify mental items in a manner suitable for psychological theory: we have no glimmerings of psychology, for about the same reason that someone could have no glimmerings of chemistry if he tried to found his chemical theory on the categories 'dirt', 'rock', liquid' and 'greenery'. (ii) And he can explain our lack of a good taxonomy by supposing that we know almost nothing about thoughts except their representative features, which are irrelevant to the causal powers of thought and thus to scientific psychology.

That leaves unexplained our ignorance of the intrinsic natures of thoughts; but it is better than no explanation—better than saying 'It's just a fact that we know some physics and no psychology'.

Do we know so little about the intrinsic qualities of thoughts? Spinoza is entitled to say Yes, given his emphasis on 'ideas' as items with propositional content. Our awareness of differences in the subjective feels of sensory states—e.g., the intensity of sensations—would not interest him much. He is interested in ideas such as my present thought that I shall be in New York City on Friday; and about them he is right in the position I am conjecturally attributing to him. My New York thought is a particular episode in the history of my mind, but if I were asked to describe it, what could I say? I could say when and in what mind it happened, and what else I was thinking and experiencing at the time; but that would be all I could report, except for the episode's representative feature—its being a that-I-shall-be-in-NYC-on-Friday thought. And so it is in general with mental items which have content: we know virtually nothing about them except their content.[8]

§52. *Spinoza's substitute for purpose*

1. That Spinoza really is rejecting teleological explanations, right across the board, can be seen from his offering a nonteleological concept of 'appetite' to replace the notions he is condemning. He says: 'Desire can be defined as appetite together with consciousness of the appetite' (3p9s), and:

8. Ronald Messerich has pointed out to me that this is a good place for the physicalist to intervene: 'There is nothing else to know about them under the attribute of thought. Intrinsic natures are all physical, and the concept of mentality comes in only because of the representational features of physical states of organisms.' I will say only that the question of dualism's truth is off-limits in my book, as in Spinoza's.

'The decisions of the mind are nothing but appetites' (3p2s at 143/33), and: 'By the end for the sake of which we do anything I understand appetite' (4d7), which announces flatly that he will have no truck with the language of final causes unless it is construed in terms of his harmless notion of appetite.

What is appetite? Spinoza says in 3p9s that a man's appetite for staying in existence 'is nothing but the very essence of the man, from whose nature there necessarily follow those things which promote his preservation'. That concerns *appetite for survival.* Abstracting from it a general account of *appetite* we get this: to have an appetite for x is just to be so constituted that you will behave in ways which increase the probability of your getting x; or, in shorthand which I find convenient, to be so constituted that you will 'move towards' x. Spinoza does not explain appetite in probabilistic terms, but it strengthens his position to put it like that, and has no effect on the main points I want to make. The general account of appetite emerges from Spinoza's dizzyingly abstract definition of desire (which he has already identified with appetite), in the first of the Affect Definitions at the end of Part 3: 'A desire is a man's very essence, insofar as it is conceived to be determined, by some specific state it is in, to act in some way.' (190/2) It is odd for Spinoza to refer to states of the man's essence rather than of the man, but it comes to the same thing. The thesis, pretty clearly, is that 'appetite for x' is to be analysed in terms of 'intrinsic state which causes one to move towards x'.

Incidentally, when Spinoza first launches this idea, in 3p7 ('The trying in which each thing tries to stay in existence is nothing but the thing's actual essence'), he demonstrates it with help from 1p29,36. He apparently takes these Part 1 propositions to be saying that a thing's behaviour is explicable only through its intrinsic nature. This is by far the most significant invocation of Part 1 in Parts 3–4–5; I mentioned it in §3.2.

2. In this account, a desire or appetite is identified with some aspects of the essence or nature of the person, something which could be fully described without mentioning any subsequent state of affairs. If my being F is my having an appetite for warmth, that is because my being F is impelling me towards being warm; but that fact does not explain why I move as I do. To explain my movement we must say 'He moved because he was F'; and that explanation, since it does not mention any subsequent state of affairs such as my becoming warm, is not teleological, does not introduce a final cause.

In summary: The plain man thinks that an action can be caused or explained by a desire which essentially involves the future—meaning by 'the future' 'something *causally* subsequent to the action'. Spinoza replaces that concept of desire by one which he thinks covers roughly the same territory without implying that anything involving the future helps to explain the present. In Spinozist appetite there is the person's intrinsic state, which is explanatory but not about the future; and there is where he is being driven by his state, which is about the future but does not explain his behaviour.

3. Thus, the difference between what Spinoza will allow in this area and what he won't is more sharp and definite than commentators have realized. Of previous accounts of Spinoza's position on teleology, the one I like best is Roth's:

Human beings . . . , like everything else and in spite of the fact of self-consciousness, work out *from* conditions which are already set, not *towards* ideals which are to be realised. In the words of the decisive 4d7: 'By the end for the sake of which we do anything I understand appetite.' What is appetite? Blind impulse. We follow ends and ideals, but these ends and ideals are projected from behind us.[9]

That feels right, but what is it saying? The contrast between 'from' and 'towards' is metaphorical, like mine between pushes and pulls at the start of this chapter; and Roth does not cash it out in literal terms. Again, when Roth says that we don't 'work towards ideals which are to be realized' although we do 'follow ideals', it is not clear what is being denied and what asserted. Further, he calls Spinozist appetite 'blind impulse', but 'blind' is wrong: Spinoza says that we are often conscious of our appetites—not just of their existence but of where they are driving us. (He does speak of 'blind' desires, but only to characterize some desires, not to theorize about all of them.) Deleting 'blind', we are left only with the unhelpful remark that appetites are impulses. As for 'projected from behind': that is unclear even by the standards of metaphors.

However, we can slide literal theory under Roth's metaphors, taking them to express Spinoza's view that what explains my present behaviour lies (causally and temporally) behind me, and neither involves nor represents the future. We can also explain why 'blind impulse' is a tempting phrase to use: although I am not always blind in respect of my appetites, since I can often see where they are taking me, what *explains* the taking is 'blind' in the sense that it does not essentially involve any representation of where I am being taken.

We can also explain a haunting, puzzling statement of Spinoza's which Roth quotes just after that passage. Having defined 'appetite' as the causal basis of a given kind of behaviour, and defined 'desire' as appetite of which one is conscious, Spinoza continues: 'From all this, then, it is clear that we do not try for, will, want, or desire anything because we judge it to be good; on the contrary, we judge something to be good because we try to get it, will it, want it, and desire it.' (3p9s) Ignoring the first three words of

9. Roth, *Spinoza*, p. 114.

this, it might express the familiar view that value terms such as 'good' are used only to report or express attitudes and desires, rather than reporting value facts which somehow engender our attitudes: it is a mistake about *good* to think that desires result from beliefs about what is good. That was indeed Spinoza's view, and at the start of p39s he attaches that view to the passage I have quoted from p9s. But that cannot be the whole story, for Spinoza's puzzling thesis about desiring and judging to be good is said to be clear 'from all this'; and what immediately precedes it is not about value but about desire and its kin. 'Desires result from beliefs about what is good' —Spinoza may think that this is an error about *good*, but he certainly thinks it is an error about *desire*. What error?

My account of his position answers this. If I desire x, I am in an intrinsic state which will cause me to move towards x, and that state—which *is* my desire for x—explains the other features of the situation. In particular, my thought about possibly obtaining x is explained by my desire, my intrinsic state, because the representational features of thoughts are supervenient on their intrinsic features. The basic story is always intrinsic, not representational; so a derivative place is given to every thought about a possible outcome, including the thought 'It would be good to obtain x'. Thus, desires explain value judgments on outcomes, and are not explained by them.

On this account, a state's being a desire is not an intrinsic feature of it. A given complex condition of your body and mind counts as a desire only if it causes you to 'move towards' something in my sense of that phrase (see .1), and whether that is the case will usually—and perhaps always—depend in part on how you relate to your environment. No scrutiny of your mind and body, however thorough, can tell an observer that you are going to take an apple from a tree rather than a pear, or rather than nothing. The facts about what lies under your mental and physical skin do not determine what you have a desire for or, by parity of reasoning, whether your state is a desire at all.

At least once Spinoza says something which embarrasses my interpretation: he speaks of a man as having, 'from his imagining the conveniences of domestic life', an appetite to build a house (4 Preface at 207/7). If the 'from' is causal and the imagining points forward, this passage belies my account. But perhaps the 'from' is not causal, or the imagining does not point forward; or perhaps the forward pointing aspects of the imagining are not supposed to cause the appetite. Or perhaps Spinoza is saying something he ought not to have said; that happens often enough, as we shall see in due course. I don't therefore retract my account of his basic position, because it explains so much that is otherwise mysterious.

4. The best way to criticize Spinoza's concept of appetite is to show that there is no need for it, i.e., to show how the concept of what might result from an action can play a part in explaining the action. I shall do that in my next section. Independently of that, I now argue that in any case Spinoza's 'appetite' is further than he thinks from being a salvage of our ordinary statements about desire and purpose. No doubt he means to criticise those statements; but he needs to show that they contain a grain of something defensible, for otherwise his attack on ordinary teleology would be too radical to be credible. It is important, then, that his attempted salvage fails.

The proposal is that we find in such statements as 'He raised his hand because he wanted to deflect the stone' the grain of truth that he was in an intrinsic state F such that: he raised his hand because he was in F, and his being in F disposed him to move in stone-deflecting ways. In one way, that is too strong, because it does not cover the case where a person's desire for x leads him, through clumsiness or ignorance, to act in ways which prevent his obtaining x. In another way it is too weak, because our intrinsic states often cause us to move towards outcomes which we would not ordinarily be said to desire.

We might illustrate the weakness by accusing Spinoza of implying that when I plug in the defective heater I have an appetite not only for warmth but also for electrocution. Spinoza has a reply to this, however, at least so far as his concept of desire is concerned. He says that desire is appetite of which one is conscious, so that my plugging in the heater does not manifest a desire for electrocution unless I am conscious that my conduct is apt to get me electrocuted. But even if he had laid a proper foundation for this by providing for thoughts about the future, and for some but not all of them to be conscious, this reply would still be inadequate: it excludes from the scope of a desire the unexpected consequences of the action, but not the expected though regretted ones. It looks as though he must say that one part of the ordinary concept of desire which he cannot salvage is the distinction between 'what I expected to ensue from what I did' and 'what I wanted to ensue from what I did'. He would be encouraged in this by encountering the now common view that what makes it true that I wanted or intended to achieve x by my action is the fact that (i) I expected the action to lead to x, and (ii) that expectation *explains why* I performed the action. Still, however strongly motivated, his rejection of that distinction is uncomfortably radical.

5. Hobbes also had a replacement theory for the rejected teleological concepts, and Spinoza may have been influenced by it as by other parts of Hobbes's thought. Hobbes's version contains a detail which Spinoza's lacks, which may remedy the latter's defect of unwanted weakness. Hobbes writes:

These small beginnings of motion are commonly called endeavour. This endeavour, when it is toward something which causes it, is called appetite, or desire. When the endeavour is fromward something, it is generally called aversion. The words, appe-

tite and aversion, both signify the motions, one of approaching, the other of re-
tiring.[10]

It is not important that for Hobbes an appetite is a movement whereas for
Spinoza it is the intrinsic state causing the movement. What does matter
is Hobbes's saying that an appetite or desire for x must be caused by x.
That lets him say that some of the consequences of one's actions are not
desired, even if they are expected: my movement towards the apple was
also towards the slug, but it was caused only by the apple and so it was a
desire only for the apple.

For this advantage, Hobbes's theory pays a steep price: it won't count
me as having an appetite for x unless x has acted on me, and so it has nothing to say about my watering the tree because I want apples from it next
autumn.

Hobbes and Spinoza were bound to fail in their salvage efforts, because
they sought to develop a concept which would be significantly like teleological concepts without allowing anything like teleological explanations.
In our century, too, some theorists have tried to introduce the concept of
a *goal* in a purely descriptive way, as though we could identify an animal's
goals and then inquire whether they help to explain its behaviour. I have
argued elsewhere that they were bound to fail:[11] if you remove the explana-
toriness from teleological concepts you remove almost everything. Spinoza,
then, committed himself to being more radical than he realized, and, as we
shall see, more radical than he had the nerve to be in practice.

§53. *A theory of teleology*

1. In this section I shall outline a theory of teleology which answers
Spinoza's implied challenge to show how an event can be explained in
terms of a possible result of it. I can offer only a sketch—the details are
given elsewhere.[12]

The crucial notion is that of an instrumental property, that is, a property
attributed to x by a proposition of the form:

x is so situated and constructed that *if Fx soon then Gx thereafter.*

In shorthand, I put this by saying that F/Gx, or that x has the instrumental
property F/G: the animal is kills/eats, the pane of glass is dropped/shat-
ters, and so on. Instrumental properties are not in themselves teleological.

10. Hobbes, *Leviathan*, ch. 6, quoted with omissions.

11. *Linguistic Behaviour* §13.

12. *Ibid.*, ch. 2. The central idea in this theory comes from Charles Taylor, *The
Explanation of Behaviour* (London, 1964).

But now suppose that there is an organism x and a property G such that for *any* property f and time t,

If f/Gx at t then fx at t+d

—that is, whenever x is does-something/becomes-G, it does the 'something'. Let Gx be 'x eats' so that x is an organism which does whatever leads to its eating: when it is kills/eats, it kills; when it is climbs/eats, it climbs; and so on. This animal has becoming-G as a goal, and its G-seeking conduct can be explained in those terms. Why did it do F at time T? Because then it was F/G—which is to say that at T the animal was so constructed and situated that if it did F shortly thereafter it would become G *a little later still*. That is how a later time enters into the explanation of what happens earlier, and how a possible result of an event can enter into an explanation of the event's occurrence.

2. There are no interesting cases of organisms conforming to a teleological law of the kind I have given. Any nontrivial teleological law must be restricted to values of f which in some sense belong to the repertoire of the given organism; and we must allow for multiple goals, for the animal's being prevented from doing F, and so on. I shall pretend that provisions for all that are silently built into the account.[13]

One complication must be treated explicitly, however. We don't expect any actual organism to do whatever *will* make it become G but only what *it thinks will* do so. We can always fix things so that an animal's doing F is the route to its becoming G (for example: walking clockwise in a circle for nine minutes is a way to get food, because we have arbitrarily chosen that reward for that performance), but we don't expect that to affect its behaviour unless the relevant instrumental fact is registered upon the animal. I use 'registration' to name a genus of which belief is a vaguely demarcated species. And I am saying that a true teleological generalization would almost certainly have to be not of the form

If f/Gx at t then fx at t+d,

but rather of the form

If at t x registers that f/Gx at t then fx at t+d.

Without that change in our teleological theory, our account of x will be too strong in one way: having no provision for ignorance, it will be refuted by every missed opportunity. And it will be too weak in another way: having no provision for error, it will not apply to things x does in pursuit of G when there is really no chance of success.

A complete theory of teleology will include a theory of belief or regis-

13. They are discussed in detail in *Linguistic Behaviour* §§18–20.

tration; and I maintain that this is the right way to start explaining what desire is. That is why I said in §39.4 that Spinoza's views about desire prevent him from developing a good theory of belief: the famous interplay between these two concepts has a deep source in the fact that they have to be analysed conjointly.

3. When a teleological law of the above kind is true of an animal, it is not—so far as we know—ever a basic truth about it. When the animal runs so as to escape from a predator, its movements are most fundamentally explained by its intrinsic state at that time, states of its brain etc. which bear traces of the recent impact on its sense-organs of sights and smells and sounds of a predator.

I am agreeing with Spinoza: the causal story will concern efficient causes only, and will bring in only their intrinsic and not their representative features. And I concede that the most basic explanatory story is the causal one. But that does not imply that teleological explanations are improper. Granted that each behavioural episode that can be explained through the f/G law can also be explained mechanistically, i.e., in terms of intrinsic states, it doesn't follow that the teleological law could be replaced by a single mechanistic law. There might be dozens of different intrinsic states the animal could be in, any one of which would constitute its registering that it is f/G for some f—seeings of different sorts of predator, hearings of different sorts of noise, smelling a characteristic odor while seeing a movement in the undergrowth, and so on. If this array of different intrinsic states, each of which causes flight behaviour, can be generalized over in teleological language and not in any other, that gives us a reason for using that language and explaining individual bits of behaviour as having occurred because, for the relevant value of f, the animal then had registered on it that it was f/G. The situation is even more dramatic if we think of teleological generalizations which apply to animals of different species: their physiological arrangements may be profoundly different, and yet they may fall under useful 'laws' about the pursuit of food or the evasion of predators.[14]

On the other hand, if everything covered by a teleological generalization were also covered by a single mechanistic one, the latter should be preferred. Even if it is true of a shellfish that

> Whenever it registers that there is something it can do
> which will save it from being eaten, it does it,

that ought not to be used to explain its behaviour if the facts it covers are equally covered by

14. For a development of this line of thought, see D. C. Dennett, 'Intentional Systems', in his *Brainstorms* (Montgomery, 1978); and J. Bennett, *op. cit.*, §21.

Whenever the amount of light impinging on it is suddenly reduced, it contracts into its shell which then closes.

In such a case it would be misleading to employ the teleological generalization, because it does no work that cannot be done by the more basic mechanistic account.

4. So teleology is a system of legitimate explanations. That lets me agree with Spinoza and with many contemporary philosophers of mind that no mental item has *causal* powers by virtue of its representative features,[15] while still holding that a thought can *explain* an action by virtue of representing a possible result of it.

If this were put to Spinoza, he would deny that there are noncausal explanations of events and would be scornful of my attempt to legitimize teleological explanations. To defend them on the grounds that they group behavioural phenomena in interesting ways which are not otherwise available is, Spinoza would say fiercely, to confuse convenience with truth. He would add that nothing can be intellectually justified by how it bears on our parochial interests and attitudes, and he would point out that a pragmatically justified theory is apt to reflect viewpoints which are limited and confused and interpersonally variable. To this I reply that there is no way of avoiding all the risk of such defects; and even if there were, we need not share Spinoza's haughty disrespect for all but the deepest and most impersonally objective levels of theory.

I do not mean to imply that he thought of the approach to teleology which I have sketched, and rejected it for those reasons. Had he come anywhere near to thinking of it, he would surely have seen how inadequate was his 'appetite' replacement for the concepts of desire and goal. There is other evidence too. In my next chapter I shall explore his doctrine about our supposed tendency towards self-preservation. We shall see that it starts out as a case of Spinozist appetite, but is transmuted into something different, supposedly explanatory of behaviour, and genuinely teleological. Although the difference is produced by a tiny logical switch—a barely audible *click* in Spinoza's formulations—the difference itself is enormous. Stripped down to its bare essentials, a Spinozist appetite for self-preservation involves the truth of something of the form

If he does it, it helps him,

and Spinoza replaces this by its converse:

If it would help him, he does it,

15. See for example Jerry A. Fodor, 'Methodological Solipsism Considered as a Research Strategy in Cognitive Psychology', *The Behavioral and Brain Sciences* vol. 3 (1980), pp. 63–73.

which is genuinely teleological. He could not have remained unaware of this if he had ever explicitly formulated anything much like the theory of teleology presented in this section.

10 *Self-preservation*

Spinoza's substantive morality will be based on a strong individual egoism: 'Each thing . . . tries to stay in existence.' (3p6) My task in this chapter will be to explain Spinoza's argument for this, and the transformations it undergoes in his hands—especially ones which allow the doctrine to start off with a Spinozist 'appetite' (a push) and end up with genuine teleology (a pull).

§54. *Essence and destruction*

1. Spinoza's thesis about self-preservation is defended by a line of argument, running through 3p4,5,6, which deserves to be tracked patiently. We must start with 3p4d, purporting to prove that 'No thing can be destroyed except by an external cause'.

2. When Spinoza thinks about the going out of existence of physical things, he never envisages an annihilation of the constituent particles, a reduction in the universe's sum of mass-energy. He could allow such an event, since for him it would be merely a qualitative alteration in a spatial region (see §24.2); but apparently he thinks that such things do not happen, for he never mentions them when destruction and survival are being discussed. Those discussions are always addressed to physical things (mental ones must presumably be dragged along by the parallelism), and indeed only to the specialised physical things which Spinoza calls 'individuals', a term he usually reserves for things having organic unity—organisms or parts of organisms such as organs and cells.

Spinoza treats these in Lemmas 4–7 between 2p13 and 14. An individual, we learn from these, is an item which at any given moment is composed of a number of particles which are so interrelated that the whole has a certain 'form'. If that form is lost, the individual is destroyed; while the form is retained the individual stays in existence. Many changes in it are consistent with its retaining its form: Spinoza mentions metabolic changes (Lemma 4), shrinking and enlargement (5), change of posture (6) and travel (7).

This, clearly, is an abstract theory of the identity of an organism through change, reminiscent of Aristotle's theory about what he called 'substances' in the *Metaphysics* (see §15.1); and Spinoza's Aristotelian term 'form' is surely meant to invite that comparison.

3. Which subset of an individual's features constitutes its 'form'? Spinoza's answer is that the form is the 'proportion of motion and rest' or 'relation of motion and rest' of the constituent particles. Thus, for example: 'Things which bring it about that a human body's parts acquire a different proportion of motion and rest to one another, bring it about . . . that the human body takes on another form, i.e. . . . is destroyed.' (4p39d) Despite one remark implying that the 'proportion of motion and rest' could be expressed in a fraction, we should not take that literally. If Spinoza did say something like this:

> If n grams of matter in the system are in motion with a mean velocity of m cms per second, and if k grams are at rest, then the proportion of motion and rest is given by the fraction $\frac{(n.m)}{k}$,

there would not be the faintest reason to think that the survival of an individual depends on the stability of *that* ratio.

But we need not hold Spinoza to anything like that. In the material between 2p13 and 14, having used motion and rest to mark off his fundamental particles (see §26.2,3), he proceeds to define 'one individual':

When a number of bodies move so that they communicate their motions to each other in a certain fixed manner, we shall say that those bodies all together compose one individual, which is distinguished from others by this union of bodies. (Between lemmas 3 and 4, at 99/27; quoted with omissions)

Spinoza is onto something good here: we do have the notion of physical individuals whose unity is constituted not by sheer pebble-like compactness but rather by coherence of organization; and such an individual can stay in existence only for as long as its parts are suitably related to one another. Furthermore, the relations in question could be described as the parts' 'communicating their motions in a certain fixed manner', so that the individual's survival does indeed *have something to do with* motion and rest.

I prefer to suppose that Spinoza did not seriously intend to go further than that. His phrase 'proportion of motion and rest', I suggest, is just a placeholder for a detailed analysis which he had not worked out, perhaps because it might involve a detailed anatomical and physiological theory of organisms which he knew was not yet available.[1] This implies that Spinoza

---

1. There is admittedly no strong textual evidence for this charitable reading, which I share with Matson, 'Death and Destruction in Spinoza's *Ethics*', p. 404. For more on Spinoza's biology—which I am skimping in a way it does not deserve— see Jonas, 'Spinoza and the Theory of Organism', and Duchesneau, 'Du modèle cartésien au modèle spinoziste de l'être vivant'.

has almost nothing to say about the identity of any given individual, i.e., about what would have to happen for this man to go out of existence. And sometimes he seems to realize this:

> I understand a body to die when its parts are so disposed that they acquire a different proportion of motion and rest to one another. For I dare not deny that a human body—even though the circulation of the blood is maintained, and the other signs which lead to its being thought to be alive—may nevertheless be changed into another nature entirely different from its own. For no reason compels me to maintain that the body does not die unless it is changed into a corpse. (4p39s)

He is right in saying that his theory does not tie identity—or, therefore, survival—to the ordinary concept of life. If 'dying' means 'being destroyed', Spinoza is saying, then dying may be different from becoming a lifeless corpse. Without affirming that one can be destroyed without becoming a corpse, he won't risk denying it either, because 'no reason compels' him to say that it cannot happen. The agnosticism of this fits my noncommittal reading of the phrase 'same proportion of motion and rest'.

Less good is Spinoza's outright assertion in 4 Preface that 'a horse is destroyed if it is changed into a man [or] into an insect'. This purports to know details about what the essences of individuals are; and, worse still, it hints that they correspond to such shallow, fuzzy, biological kinds as *man* and *horse*. But perhaps the remark about the destruction of a horse is meant to be taken seriously only as illustrating the general point that for some values of F and G an F thing's 'becoming a G' is really its being destroyed and a G's coming into existence.[2]

4. For present purposes, however, what matters is that there is *some* line between the properties of a thing which can, and those which cannot, be lost without the thing's going out of existence. In 3p4d the unlosable properties are called the thing's 'essence', not its 'form', but the meaning is the same. They are clearly equated late in 4 Preface at 208/26, and each is related to the concept of destruction in the same way.

Sometimes Spinoza uses the word 'essence' to stand for a thing's entire nature, all the nonrelational facts about it. For example, when he defines 'appetite' in terms of part of my 'essence', he just means part of my nature, part of what I am intrinsically like. But in our present context the word 'essence' is being used in the sense laid down for it in 2d2, which defines the essence of a particular thing as that set of its properties which are jointly sufficient and severally necessary for its identity: if E is the whole essence of x then x cannot exist without having E, and conversely nothing can have E without being x. The first half of this is what matters now—the statement

---

2. Notice that Spinoza does not say that after the metamorphosis there is the same body but not the same horse. This is some evidence of his not holding the relative identity thesis. (See §16.6 and §34.2.)

that in any possible world where x exists it has E. It is because of that that depriving x of E is driving it out of existence.

To say that x was deprived of its form or essence suggests that after the event x was left without its erstwhile form or essence; and that is clearly wrong. I have already quoted Spinoza falling into this trap: '. . . the human body takes on another form, i.e. is destroyed' (4p39d). If a body is destroyed, it does not exist any longer; *it* cannot have taken on another form. I shall nervously follow Spinoza in this dangerous talk about 'loss of form' or 'loss of essence', but when I say that x has lost its essence I shall always mean that at some time an aggregate of particles which constituted x came to be so interrelated that they no longer did so, and not by a metabolic process through which some different aggregate took over the job of constituting x.

§55. *The impossibility of self-destruction*

1. The proposition that 'No thing can be destroyed except through an external cause' is the only one in the *Ethics* that is demonstrated without help from previously declared doctrines. Here is the argument:

The definition of any thing affirms, and does not deny, the thing's essence, i.e. it posits the thing's essence and does not take it away. So while we attend only to the thing itself, and not to external causes, we shall not be able to find anything in it which can destroy it. (3p4d)

Why can a thing not be destroyed, i.e., caused to lose its essence, without outside interference? Well, necessarily x's essence is part of x's nature; if x were also capable unaided of destroying itself, its nature must also contain something implying the denial to x of its essence. Thus a thing capable of unaided self-destruction would have a nature which both entailed or included a certain essence and was also inconsistent with it; such a nature would be self-contradictory, and therefore could not be had by anything; so nothing can be capable of destroying itself without outside help.[3]

Since the conclusion is false, the argument is faulty. Locating the fault is a nontrivial exercise, however, and the argument is a real achievement. For a long time I thought that one root of its error lies in the assumed causal rationalism—the assumption that if x unaided brings it about that P, then facts about x's intrinsic nature logically entail P. Spinoza needs that to conclude that a self-destroyer would have an inconsistent nature, and thus to infer that it is logically impossible for anything to destroy itself unaided.

---

3. See Letter 32 at IV/171/18 for the basis of a different argument for saying that a thing cannot go out of existence as long as there is no causal flow *either way* between it and its environment.

But Carl Matheson has shown me that that does not get to the bottom of the trouble. If we leave the argument standing, except taking it to involve a causal necessity which is weaker than absolute necessity, its conclusion is still too much to swallow. For it would then conclude that a self-destroyer's nature must contain, along with logically sufficient conditions for the thing's existence, causally sufficient conditions for its nonexistence, which implies that it is causally impossible for anything to destroy itself unaided.[4]

2. The real source of the trouble is something which may be encouraged by causal rationalism, but is distinct from it, namely, the argument's neglect of the fact that causal laws cover stretches of time. From (Fx and Gx at T_1) it can follow causally that (Fx and not Gx at T_2)—which is to say that a G thing can cause itself to be non-G later. There is no logical or causal impossibility in this because, as I have remarked before, time differences turn lethal contradictions into harmless changes. And this harmlessness remains even in the special case where (Fx at T_1) leads causally to a state of affairs at T_2 which precludes x's existing at all.

3. Spinoza himself brings time into the discussion, but gets it wrong. After inferring from 3p4 that everything is trying to stay in existence, he says that this trying 'involves no finite time' (p8) because p4d is valid without restriction as to time: it could not be used to show merely that things cannot self-destruct until they are five minutes old or ten years old, or whatever. It is true that p4d won't sustain any reference to a limited period of time, but that is because it doesn't validly stretch across time at all. To conclude from it that nothing can self-destruct for the next ten years, say, would be to name a time-span which is not infinitely too short but ten years too long.

Perhaps Spinoza is here influenced by his doctrine that there is something atemporal about 'essences', taking this word now to stand for natures or properties of all kinds, not just ones which are essential to the existence of the thing that has them. He says: 'The duration of things cannot be determined from their essence, since the essence of things involves no certain and determinate time of existing.' (4 Preface at 209/6; see also 1p24,c) Spinoza says this because he rightly distinguishes essence from existence. If we want to know whether anything has nature N, it is no use our looking just at N; and so, *a fortiori*, N alone will not tell us whether anything has N for five minutes or for ten years. It is typical of Spinoza to use the concept of duration in making a point about instantiation, equating 'existing'

---

4. Matson's mostly helpful 'Death and Destruction in Spinoza's *Ethics*' calls 3p4d a warning of the unreliability of reasoning based on the distinction between 'positive' and 'negative' (p. 408). I submit that the demonstration does not rely on that shaky distinction, but only on the sound concept of a contradictory pair of propositions.

with 'existing for a while'. This link is mildly expressed in the definition of 'duration' as 'an indefinite continuation of existing' (2d5), and is powerfully at work in the inferential move from 'A man's essence does not involve necessary existence' (2a1) to 'Our body's duration does not depend on its essence' (2p30d).

It is true that no nature N could guarantee that something has N for at least ten years, say. But N might necessitate that nothing could have N for less than ten years, or for more than ten years. The distinction between essence and existence—between natures and their instantiations—does not rule out truths of the form 'If anything has N, it has N for such and such a duration'; and so it cannot help Spinoza to establish 3p4.

4. He might reply that my temporal criticism rests on a misunderstanding of his argument and of its conclusion. He says that x cannot destroy x without help from a cause which is 'external'. External to what? I have taken it that it must be external to x, because it must have properties x does not have. And so I have taken the argument to require something which is in fact false, namely, that x's entire nature at a given time—its total temporary state—cannot suffice for its destruction later. But 3p4d says that x's *definition* affirms its *essence*, as though the topic were not x's whole nature but only the subset of its properties which are absolutely necessary and sufficient for it to be x. Spinoza might hold that each thing has such an essence which never alters: x may change in respect of its accidental properties, but its essence remains constant. And then x's going out of existence at T could not be due solely to its essence, any more than the occurrence of thunder now could be due solely to the unchanging laws of physics.

This reading of the argument rescues it from another trouble which I have not yet mentioned, namely, that on the previous reading it threatens to conclude that a thing cannot unaided cause *any change at all* in itself. For the argument went like this: 'If Fx, then if x had a property which was sufficient for not Fx, then x would have an impossible nature.' I stressed the case where F is essential to x, but that restriction plays no part in the argument, which thus threatens to be drastically too strong. We may be able to avoid this only by going from

> The nature of x cannot contain sufficient conditions for x's losing any part of its nature (i.e., for x's altering)

to the isomorphic but weaker

> The essence of x cannot contain sufficient conditions for x's losing any part of its essence (i.e., for x's going out of existence).

That account of the argument, though, involves a strange reading of the phrase 'external cause', which naturally means 'external to x' rather than 'external to x's essence'. It also conflicts with 'we shall be able to find nothing in [x] which can destroy it'. Worst of all, it generates only the conclusion that if I destroy myself that must be partly because of accidental features of me—e.g., character traits which are not of my essence because I have had them for only about thirty years. We shall see that Spinoza needs a much stronger thesis than that.

There seems to be no way of deciding which reading is correct. Probably Spinoza did not properly distinguish them in his mind, and found the argument acceptable for that reason. I conjecture that the 'essence' reading underlies the first sentence of the argument, while the 'whole nature' reading underlies its second sentence and conclusion.

§56. *Suicide*

1. It is interesting to watch Spinoza trying to reconcile 3p4 with the fact of suicide. He writes:

No one, unless he is defeated by causes external and contrary to his nature, neglects to . . . preserve his being. No one . . . kills himself from the necessity of his own nature. Those who do such things are compelled by external causes, which can happen in many ways. (4p20s)

He then proceeds to sketch three ways in which someone may die by his own hand. Here is the second: 'Someone may kill himself . . . because he is forced by the command of a tyrant (as Seneca was) to open his veins, i.e. he desires to avoid a greater evil by a lesser.' Let us consider what it can mean to say that Nero 'forced' Seneca to kill himself.

Suppose that you are so built that you prefer an apple to an orange, and an orange to anything else. If I eat our only apple, have I forced you to select an orange?

No. Then Nero hasn't forced Seneca to kill himself, either. Don't say that the apple influence is weak while the Nero one is strong. Each influence is decisive, and Spinoza cannot divide decisive influences into weak and strong. Anyway, that would protect 3p4 only if the latter meant that no thing can destroy itself unless it has first been subjected to strong pressure; and it cannot mean that.

It is intuitively right to use 'forced' in the Seneca case but not in the other, but Spinoza is not interested in common intuitions unless they are explained through sound theory. This intuition rests on the weak-strong line among decisive influences, and also on thoughts about blameworthiness, and Spinoza has no room for either of those. It also seems intuitively right to say that Seneca did not want to kill himself; but Spinoza would surely dismiss that intuition and say that all things considered Seneca *did* want to kill himself.

Since he cannot drive a wedge between the Seneca case and that of the orange, Spinoza must answer my question affirmatively: *Yes*, I did force you to select an orange, by making it causally inevitable that you would do that. By that standard, however, no individual ever acts without being forced, for there is always a causal ancestry running back to the outside. That yields a vacuously true reading of 3p4: nothing unforcedly destroys itself because nothing unforcedly does anything.

2. One gets a better purchase on the Seneca case by comparing it with the first of Spinoza's three examples: 'Someone may kill himself because he is forced by someone else who twists his right hand (which happens to hold a sword) and forces him to direct the sword against his heart.' No one would call that suicide, and it doesn't feel like a problem for Spinoza. But why not? He cannot say 'Because this case involves physical compulsion': for Spinoza, all compulsion is at once physical and mental.

What he can say is that in the twisted hand case the sword's movement is caused by movements of the victim's hand, which are *at that very moment* being caused by the other person's hand. The causal energy is coming from outside the victim's body, and in that sense his death is not produced by him.

Nothing like that holds in the Seneca case. When the knife did its work, Seneca's body was not transmitting forces from the outside. The causally sufficient conditions for his act were stored within him;[5] the action flowed from his nature as it then was, including his various strengths and frailties, his attitudes to pain and shame, his capacities to think things through, *and his belief that if he didn't die that night he would suffer a worse death in the morning.* That last deadly item was caused by a message from Nero; but still it was an aspect of his nature at the moment when he slashed his wrists. Seneca's death proceeded from his nature as it then was, including his wish for dignity and good reputation, and his having the deadly conditional belief.

I conclude that Seneca falsifies 3p4. I suppose that Spinoza would deny this, saying that I have misunderstood the notion of Seneca's 'nature'. What, then, does he mean by 'nature'?

3. I have already quoted him as saying that nobody kills himself unless he is 'defeated by causes contrary to his nature'. Where I argued that Seneca's wrist-slashing flowed from his nature, Spinoza says it was contrary to it. If Seneca's nature comprises all the intrinsic facts about him at the time, then I am right; so Spinoza must be using 'nature' to stand merely for some proper subset of the facts about Seneca. But he does not say what

---

5. We must assume that background conditions—the earth's rotation etc.— have been identified and placed in the margin. Otherwise, no one could be the sole cause of anything.

subset. I can only guess that he means Seneca's 'essence', in the sense of essential properties—not broadening 'essence' but narrowing 'nature'. That goes with the reading of p4 which makes it say merely that if someone kills himself it must be partly because of his accidental properties. As I said in §55.4, that makes p4 too weak for Spinoza's needs; and I would add that it rescues p4 from obvious falsehood only by making it something we don't know how to apply in any one instance. To apply it to x we would have to know which of x's features belong to its essence; but we never know that, and Spinoza does not try to tell us, wisely offering only the abstract phrase 'proportion of motion and rest' as a placeholder (see §54.3).

4. Spinoza seems to imply that some suicides are consistent with p4 because they involve change of identity. Here is his third example: 'Someone may kill himself . . . because hidden external causes so dispose his imagination and so affect his body that it takes on another nature, contrary to the previous one, a nature of which (by 3p10) there cannot be an idea in his mind.' I suppose this points to extreme depression or psychopathology, and does not fit Seneca for that reason. But what exactly does it mean?

Well, it shows that 'nature' does not refer to all the facts about the person at the time. If it did, 'takes on another nature' would mean 'alters in some way', and Spinoza would be saying something trivial.

But if we narrow 'nature' to mean 'essence' in the strict sense, Spinoza must be claiming that there is no real suicide here because before killing himself the person became someone else: before his suicide Hemingway became a different individual Hemingway*, and *he* did the killing! This story collapses when we ask who the victim was. If Hemingway* killed himself, then we are back with a self-killing and no identity changes to help us. And Hemingway* can't have killed Hemingway, since they were never in existence at the same time.

Well, then, we must narrow 'nature' less severely: we must interpret 3p4 as saying that x can be destroyed only through causes which lie outside x's nature—meaning more than just outside his strict essence but not meaning that they must lie outside the totality of intrinsic facts about him. The trouble is that Spinoza has not introduced any such middle-strength concept of 'the nature of x'. We do sometimes use something of the kind: 'What Cressida did was not in her nature as we have known it'; but our bases for such statements are ones that Spinoza should dismiss as shallow and hazily impressionistic—not the sort of thing he wants to build theories on. I suppose that some such everyday concept was at work in his mind when he set down the third of his three examples: that would explain the performance, but nothing could justify it.

5. The third example ends puzzlingly: '. . . it takes on another nature, of which (by 3p10) there cannot be an idea in his mind.' 3p10 says: 'An idea which excludes the existence of our body cannot be in our mind, but is contrary to it.' Apparently Spinoza is making the point that someone contemplating suicide cannot mentally represent to himself the state of affairs his suicide will bring about, namely his own nonexistence.

Spinoza's reason for this is a dangerous one for him to use. It is that I cannot have an idea directly of a state of affairs not involving my own body. That is true, but then I cannot have an idea directly of a state of affairs which does not actually obtain in my body: while I am sitting down, I can't have an idea directly of my standing up, let alone of my being dead. So Spinoza should drop 3p10,d and make his point in terms of the 'indirectly of' relation: I can have ideas (indirectly) of some states of affairs that don't obtain, but not of my death. He is still in trouble, however, because the 'indirectly of' relation lets me have ideas only of items which have acted on my body: Spinoza's assumption that we can have ideas of possible future states of affairs is sheer optimism, for which no foundation has been laid.

Still, let us grant that I can have thoughts of possible states of affairs but not of ones where I don't exist. Why would Spinoza regard that as an important fact? He must answer along the following lines. 'Most deliberate conduct is, though not caused by mental representations of the expected outcome, accompanied by them. The fact that deliberate suicide cannot conform to that normal pattern is evidence that it is somehow abnormal, odd, perhaps crazy.' And he should then adjust 3p4 so that it is not refuted by such abnormal behaviour.

This may be wrong as an account of the third suicide example, but it attributes to Spinoza an error of which he is sometimes guilty—namely, implying that there cannot be a sane suicide because that would involve thinking about how good it will be to be dead. He apparently had a blind spot about this, and just could not see that a person wanting to kill himself may be thinking about how bad it will be for him if he lives. His 4p21 is relevant to this. There is also a grotesque example in Letter 23 at IV/ 152/3, where he equates 'It accords better with his nature that he should hang himself' with 'He sees that he can live better on the gallows than at his own table'. He is assuming that because no one could expect to live well at the end of the rope it is impossible that someone should actively, voluntarily, rationally, calmly seek to have himself hanged.

§57. *Deriving the self-preservation doctrine*

1. From the premiss that nothing can destroy itself without outside help (p4), Spinoza infers that each thing tries as hard as it can to stay in existence (p6). Let us track this remarkable inference through, no longer questioning its premiss.

The first move is achieved by p5d, which argues that x cannot be destroyed without causal input from something which is unlike it in some way. That follows all right. The argument for the 'no self-destruction' thesis was that x's *nature* cannot suffice for x's nonexistence, and that implies that x's destruction must come from a partly different nature—i.e., it requires something not merely distinct but qualitatively different from x. As p5 puts it, if y can destroy x then they are 'of a contrary nature', meaning that they are unalike in some respect falling under a single attribute. This use of 'contrary nature(s)' is explained in 4p29,31c, where Spinoza distinguishes it from 'different' natures which do not even share an attribute.

But 3p5 adds, as though to elucidate the rest, a drastically ambiguous clause—if y can destroy x then they 'are of a contrary nature, i.e. they cannot be in the same subject'. What cannot be in the same subject—the natures of x and y? or x and y themselves? On the former reading, the clause does just elucidate what went before, but on the latter it adds something.

This one sentence on its own could go either way. On the one hand, if the final clause refers to the natures, then we know what being 'in the same subject' means, namely, being instantiated by a single thing; whereas if the clause refers to x and y themselves, we must invent a meaning for 'be in the same subject', e.g., 'be parts of some larger thing' such as organs of a single animal. On the other hand, the sentence seems to make two predications on a single grammatical subject, namely, the pair x and y: *they* are of a contrary nature, and *they* cannot be in the same subject.

If we look at the demonstrative uses of p5—apart from its use in p6d which I shall come to shortly—we find an even split. In 3p10d and 4p30d it is assumed that 3p5 has said that x and y cannot be in the same subject, in something like the invented sense I have provided; while in 3p37d and 4p7d it is taken to have said only that the natures of x and y cannot be co-instantiated.

If we look at how 3p5 itself is demonstrated, we get a strong reason for taking it to say that the final clause means only that the natures cannot be instantiated by one thing. Taken that way, the proposition follows, as I showed in the second paragraph of this section. Taken the other way, it does not. From the fact that y could destroy x, it does not follow that they cannot be parts of a larger thing z. If they were, it would follow that z could, without outside help, destroy a part of itself; but that does not offend against p4, since destroying a part of yourself is not destroying yourself: z's health might sometimes require that some of its parts be destroyed by others. Yet p5d could be read as a statement of that invalid argument.

2. And the use of p5 in p6d leaves little doubt that this is the reading Spinoza has in mind. What p6 says is: 'Each thing, to the extent that it is in itself, tries to stay in existence.' The subordinate clause presumably means 'to the extent that it is not acted on from outside', or, in terminology

Spinoza introduces in d2, to the extent that it is active. The demonstration first sets the Spinozistic scene, and then proceeds to the real argument, namely:

> No thing has anything in it by which it can be destroyed, or which takes away its existence (by p4). On the contrary, it is opposed to everything which can take its existence away (by p5). Therefore, to the extent that it . . . is in itself, it tries to stay in existence.

The mention of p4 is otiose. The real argument uses only p5: since any thing must be of a contrary nature to whatever can destroy it, it must be opposed to any such thing; and for something to be opposed to whatever could destroy it is for it to try to stay in existence.

Put like that, the argument is glaringly fallacious. The conclusion should mean that x *exerts itself against*, while the premise should mean only that x *is unlike*, anything that could destroy it. It looks like a mere drift from '. . . is contrary in nature to . . .' in one sense to '. . . is opposed to . . .' in a quite different sense.

But Spinoza has been encouraged by that extra, ambiguous clause tacked onto p5—'i.e. they cannot be in the same subject'—taking it in the sense to which he is not entitled. That is, the reading of p5 which he needs to pull it towards p6 is the one that pulls it away from p4. On that reading, p5 says something to the effect that if x and y are both 'individuals'—something like organisms—and y can destroy x, then they cannot both be parts of a single individual unless it is much bigger than either of them. The stipulation about relative size is needed: the universe is supposed to be an 'individual' in Spinoza's sense, and p5 must not imply that if x can destroy y then they cannot coexist in the same universe. Similar considerations apply at smaller sizes. For example, if y is a person who can destroy person x, they could still belong to the same nation; but Spinoza might say that their belonging to the same village or same family would tend towards creating the impossible situation of an individual (a village or a family) which could destroy itself without outside aid.

From that strengthened version of p5, he could reasonably infer that if y could destroy x then they must always be at a distance from one another, since if they came too close they would threaten to unite within a single individual which would then risk being self-destructible. From that he might infer that x could be depended upon, if necessary, *to keep y at a safe distance*; and from that he might drift into thinking, in p6d, that x would always *do whatever would reduce the threat from y*—perhaps keeping it at arm's length but perhaps instead launching a preemptive strike against it.

3. That argument is disgracefully bad; but I can find no kinder or more plausible account of the surface of the move from p5 to p6. However, not everything is on the surface. Although I cannot rescue the inference, I shall contend that something deeper and more interesting is going on in it than I have so far displayed.

The verb 'try', in its ordinary meaning, is teleological: to try to climb a mountain is to do things because you think that they will get you up the mountain. Spinoza ought, in using this term, to see a need to detoxify it by showing that it does not really involve explaining items in terms of their possible effects. He thinks he can do this with 'desire' and 'appetite', which he analyses nonteleologically, saying that my appetite for x is just those aspects of my nature which cause me to move towards x (see §52.1). And now we find him offering the very same analysis for 'trying': 'The trying by which each thing tries to stay in existence is nothing but the actual essence of the thing.' (p7) This claims that Spinoza's 'trying' (*conatus*) belongs to his general concept of 'appetite', although the latter term is not used at this point. There is nothing to 'He tries to bring it about that P'— Spinoza is implying—except 'His nature is such that he does tend to bring it about that P'. The virtue of this, in his eyes, is that what the person does is explained through his intrinsic nature, with no help from the concept of a possibly resultant P.

Let me take this seriously as Spinoza's account of what 'try' means in his system. It follows that when he credits people with trying to preserve themselves he means only that they are so built that they do behave in self-preserving ways. On the basis of this, let us run through the p4–5–6 argument again, now taking it that the conclusion is to be something like:

> People always do things which tend to keep them in existence.

We have a much smoother journey towards this conclusion than towards the other. We start with p4:

> If x does f, then the doing of f does not destroy x;

it is not unreasonable to think that that could be true only if:

> If x does f, then the doing of f does not tend towards x's destruction;

and it is not very bad behaviour to infer from this that

> If x does f, then the doing of f tends towards x's preservation.

And so, with two tiny stretches, we get from p4 to the version of p6 which is not tainted with teleology, the one in which the so-called 'trying' is 'nothing but the actual essence of the thing'.

4. Unfortunately, this harmless conclusion for which Spinoza has a tolerable argument is not what he deploys in the rest of the *Ethics*. What he regularly assumes is not that people have an austere Spinozist appetite for self-preservation but rather that they want it, seek it, pursue it, in the normal teleological senses of these terms. That is, he avails himself of the self-preservation doctrine for which he has only the terrible argument given in .2 above, not the much better one in .3.

The difference between the two is simple. The nonteleological doctrine could be put by saying, of any individual and any possible action:

> If he does it, it will help him.

That is as much as Spinoza can squeeze from p4–5–6 by any reasonable argument. It attributes a self-preserving tendency to individuals. A teleological statement, however, would attribute to them not a mere *tendency* but self-preservation as a *goal*, and according to the theory of goals presented in §53 that is to say, of the individual and the possible action, something like:

> If it would help him, he will do it.

Essentially, it is a matter of a conditional and its converse, and the difference is, though simple, enormous. The teleological statement supports positive predictions of behaviour: the man *will do F* because that will help him. In contrast, the other supports only negative predictions: the man *won't do F* because that will not help him. Similarly, the teleological statement can explain why the man did F, while the other can only explain why he didn't. It is easy to see why: the teleological statement has behaviour in its consequent, whereas the other doctrine has it in the antecedent and can move it over only through contraposition:

> If it wouldn't help him, he doesn't do it.

It is because the consequent of that is negative that the nonteleological doctrine lets us predict and explain only negative facts about behaviour.[6]

Here is a careful, scrupulous writer on Spinoza completely overlooking the difference I have been calling attention to:

From the fact that a thing cannot destroy itself, does it follow positively that it will try to preserve itself? . . . Yes, but on one condition: the thing in question must *act*. If its nature is to produce certain effects, it is certain that these effects will agree with its nature and therefore tend to preserve it: its non-self-destruction will be-

---

6. For an account of how to divide facts about conduct into positive and negative, see J. Bennett, 'Killing and Letting Die', in S. McMurrin (ed.), *The Tanner Lectures on Human Values* II (Salt Lake City, 1981), at pp. 53–61.

come self-preservation. *If* its nature is to perform certain actions, it is certain that its actions will be opposed to whatever excludes its nature.[7]

This takes the premiss 'x does nothing which harms x' and saves it from vacuity by adding the further premiss 'x acts'. That takes us to 'x does things, none of which harm x', and we might allow—though no case is made for it—a strengthening of this to 'x does things, all of which help x'. But this, which is the farthest point to which the argument can possibly be dragged, is well short of 'x tends to preserve x'. The latter involves a conditional running the other way: not 'All the things x does help x' but rather 'x does all the things that would help x'. The phrase 'opposed to *whatever* excludes its nature' makes this explicit in a satisfying way.

5. My evidence that Spinoza helps himself to a teleological doctrine of self-preservation comes in a crescendo. The very choice of the word 'try' is prima facie evidence. So also is the fact, which I have so far suppressed, that p6 says that each thing *'as far as it can'* tries to stay in existence. Let us remove 'try' from the picture, and then see if we can combine 'as far as it can' with each of the basic conditionals in turn. 'If it would help him, he will do it as far as he can' makes perfectly good sense, but 'If he does it, it will help him' has no plausible hook onto which 'as far as he can' can be hung.

There is more decisive evidence in p9s, where Spinoza says: 'From a man's nature there necessarily follow those things which are conducive to his preservation'—which literally means that he does all the helpful things rather than that he does only helpful things. After that, they come thick and fast: propositions which say 'If . . . , we try . . .' rather than 'Only if . . . we try . . . .', and 'We try to do whatever . . .' rather than 'We try to do only what . . .'.[8] In each case, the topic is not what we do but what we try, but forget that; I am contending that these propositions are teleological not because they contain 'try' but because they infer facts about conduct from facts about the results of the conduct, i.e., they have the form 'If it would lead to P, he will do it'.

6. In addition to 3p4–5–6 Spinoza tries again in Part 4 to make self-preserving egoism seem to stand to reason: 'No one can desire to be blessed, to act well, and to live well, unless at the same time he desires to be, to act, and to live, i.e. actually to exist.' (4p21) This affects the rest of the theoretical structure only through 4p22c which argues that one's own preservation must be the cornerstone of any value system, from which Spinoza

7. Alexandre Matheron, *Individu et communauté chez Spinoza* (Paris, 1969), p. 11.

8. There are eleven such propositions in Part 3, starting with p12. All are derived from p12 or p13.

infers that 'No one tries to stay in existence for the sake of anything else' (4p25). He wants us to say: 'Of course you are right! How could anyone want to be good without wanting to be? So how could there be a value system which did not have one's own survival at the heart of it?' This is doubly wrong. I have nothing more to say about the curious belief that an egoist cannot wish to die; but there is the separate error of assuming that all motivations must be egoistic. In 4p21 Spinoza tries to convince us of that, but he does so by *assuming* that any motivation, however high-minded, must aim at a state of affairs essentially involving oneself. He assumes that if I want to feed the starving, say, my basic objective is to bring it about that *I feed the starving*. But perhaps what I basically want is that *the starving be fed*. I think that this requires help from me and so I want to 'act well' in bringing it about; but what I ultimately want is a state of affairs which does not essentially involve me; if I thought the best route to it involved my not acting—or even my not existing—I should be prepared to stay still or to die. This is not true self-description: my point is just that this is intelligible, and Spinoza's attempt to show that it isn't assumes that it isn't.

7. Still, despite the failure of 3p4–5–6 and of this Part 4 attempt to make egoism look necessary, we may still wonder whether something like a doctrine of human egoism is true and deeply grounded. Can we attribute to some larger class of items—Spinozistic 'individuals', perhaps—some more general property of which egoism is a special case? In all of this I mean real egoism—i.e., egoism considered as truly teleological, not as mere Spinozist appetite.

We could provide a grounding of a sort for egoism in evolutionary theory, which gives reasons why a kind of egoism is almost inevitable among higher organisms. (Almost, but not quite; see §58.4.) But even if Spinoza had had access to that explanation, I think he would have objected that it does not go deep enough, or range widely enough, to satisfy his intuitions about the roots of egoism. Is there anything true that would come closer to satisfying him?

§58. *Other arguments for egoism*

1. Two of the best writers on Spinoza have thought so. Hampshire, having seen that Spinoza's teleological doctrine of egoism is not adequately supported in p4–5–6, offers other considerations which could reasonably lead him to the same conclusion. He has two main offerings, each of which was significantly foreshadowed by Pollock a century ago.[9] I shall discuss Hampshire's form of them, though I would not want to dissuade anyone from reading Pollock.

9. Pollock, *Spinoza*, pp. 218–221.

2. Hampshire notes Spinoza's emphasis on the different degrees in which things interact with their environments, associates that with differences in structural complexity, and aligns that with a scale from inanimate things through lizards up to humans: the difference between 'a human mind-body' and an animal, he says on Spinoza's behalf, 'is entirely a difference of degree of complexity'.[10] With that in the background he bases self-preservation on a perfectly general 'cohesion' or 'tendency to self-maintenance'. Some such tendency must be present even in 'the simplest mechanical systems as well as [in] organic and living systems', Hampshire says, the main difference being that in the latter it is more noticeable:

In the higher-order systems . . . the relative cohesion, or tendency to self-maintenance, in spite of internal change is the more noticeable, precisely because of the greater possible variety of internal change; in the study of organic systems, and even more in the study of living systems, the contrast betweeen internal diversity, arising out of the constant dissolution and replacement of sub-systems, and the persisting equilibrium and self-maintenance of the whole is much more conspicuous.[11]

In considering this, let us start at the simple end of the scale. When a rubber ball is dropped onto a hard floor, it is subjected to pressures which would shatter it if there were not a change of shape, a redistribution of forces, a release of energy enabling the ball to regain its former shape. And the continuing integrity of many physical things depends on their having something like elasticity and thus a 'tendency to self-maintenance'. But at best this is a weaker thesis than Spinoza would like, because there is no necessity about it: there is no obstacle to there being things which survive just by being tougher than their environments, with no need for anything like elasticity. Such things would tend to stay in existence; but would not tend to undergo changes which facilitate survival, which is what is needed for relevance to Spinoza.

Still, let us pursue Hampshire's idea up the complexity scale. In the organic realm there are many self-preserving happenings. The survival of an organism, and especially of a higher animal, requires an amazing amount of internal harmony, and so it requires the organism to be packed with devices which cause the events needed for survival: when the brain needs more oxygen a signal goes to the heart which pumps harder, when the body temperature is too high the sweat glands are triggered into activity, and so on. My self-preserving physiology is, as Hampshire implies, much more complex than that of the rubber ball, though I am not sure that the main

10. Hampshire, *Spinoza,* p. 76. Something similar is adumbrated in Matson's 'Spinoza's Theory of Mind' at p. 58.

11. Hampshire, *Spinoza,* pp. 78f.

significance of that difference is that it makes the survival value of my physiology 'more noticeable' than that of the ball's elasticity.

3. But never mind that. The analogy with elasticity is in any case not much use to us, because it provides an analogue for my physiology but not for my psychology, i.e., for chemical processes in my body but not for my behaviour. Let us consider these two:

(i) My heart pumps faster because that will give more oxygen to my brain.

(ii) I push the vase back an inch because I think that that will save it from falling.

It will be noted that (i) explains what my heart does, while (ii) explains what I do; but I shall not avail myself of that difference at the present stage. I want a deeper account of how (i) differs from (ii)—an account which will *explain why* (i) is about my heart while (ii) is not about my hand.

The chief difference is that (i) is a bad explanation and (ii) is a good one. I have explained in §53.3 why (ii) is legitimate: it brings my hand movement under a teleological generalization which is not co-extensive with any mechanistic generalization. But in just the cases where my heart beats faster 'because that will give more oxygen to my brain' it is also true that my heart beats faster because a neural signal of intrinsic kind K has reached it. That is why it would be wrong to say that my heart, in speeding up, has the sending of oxygen to my brain as a goal.

Of course there is something of a 'final cause' sort to be said about (i), namely that the *function* of the K signal's going to the heart is *to make the heart pump faster*. What that means is

(a) The K signal makes the heart pump faster, and

(b) It is because of fact (a) that the brain sends out a K signal when it needs more oxygen.

This beautiful analysis of the concept of function[12] allows evolutionists and special creationists to agree about what the functions are of various biological structures and processes: they disagree only about what underlies the 'because' in (b). It also lets a single concept of 'function' apply not only to organisms but also to artifacts.

Now, a ball's elasticity does not have the function of keeping it from shattering (unless the manufacturer elasticized it in order to stop it from shattering); and most of the self-preserving tendencies to which Hampshire

12. The analysis is Larry Wright's. See his *Teleological Explanations: an Etiological Analysis of Goals and Functions* (Berkeley, 1976). For more on the relation between functions and goals, see *Linguistic Behaviour*, pp. 78–80.

is calling attention do not engage the concept of a function. But that does not necessarily spoil the comparison he is making. Some artifacts have features whose intended function is to preserve them; organisms have features whose intended or evolved function is to preserve them; many other things have features which *do* preserve them, though in no good sense is that their 'function'. It may be that Hampshire's comparison depends only on what the three classes have in common, not on what separates them.

4. What does spoil his comparison is that it concerns only self-preserving physiology, not egoistic behaviour. It does not give us a purchase on the kinds of events that occur in a human body which we explain in terms of goals, desires or purposes, bringing events under teleological generalizations which do not correspond to mechanistic ones, and which have something cognitive in the antecedent—the person makes a certain move because of what *he thinks* its upshot will be. Hampshire's continuum, his slide from simple to complex, has at its complex end physiological features whose function is to preserve the organism; it does not stretch to behaviour with self-preservation as its goal.

A sense of the gap in Hampshire's account may be given by considering possible creatures which have a self-maintaining physiology but whose goals do not include their own survival. Imagine a tough leathery animal swimming in an ocean of nutrient broth, which contains no predators. The animal, which prefers some nutrients over others, uses its sensors to pick up evidence about these in the form of concentration gradients and other subtle indicators, and it swims accordingly. It does not sense gradients in the concentration of sodium chloride, so that none of its swimming relates to the avoidance of salt as a goal. Yet the only thing which can destroy our animal is its entering one of the rare salty regions in its ocean. When close to such a region, it continues to dart about in pursuit of its favourite nutrients, and it's a matter of chance whether this brings it to a lethally high concentration of salt. This organism is not merely logically possible—I can invent an evolutionary history for it: a million years earlier the different nutrients were associated with different kinds of predator and thus, through natural selection, with different behavioural dispositions; then the predators died off, and the dispositions lingered on in the genes as mere gustatory preferences.

5. Hampshire's other attempt to provide foundations for the self-preservation doctrine is quite different. It is the suggestion that self-maintenance may be involved in the very concept of an individual. That might be what 3p4 means: not that when you know which bits of the world are parts of x you will find that none of them hurts x, but rather that when you are trying to decide which bits of the world are parts of x you must exclude anything which hurts x. In Hampshire's words:

This striving towards . . . the preservation of its own identity constitutes the essence of any particular thing. . . . Its character and individuality depends on its necessarily limited power of self-maintenance; it can be distinguished as a unitary thing with a recognizable constancy of character in so far as, although a system of parts, it succeeds in maintaining its own characteristic coherence and balance of parts.[13]

How do we decide whether a given bit of the world constitutes a single individual? My body is a single individual, whereas the inch-thick horizontal slice of it centered on my navel is not, nor is the bit of the world consisting in my body and yours; and there is a question about what makes these things true. Spinoza's 'same proportion of motion and rest' is not relevant: it concerns the diachronic counting of individuals, whereas we are asking about synchronic counting.

Hampshire's remarks cannot be the whole answer to our question. We are to decide what counts as a part of x by finding out which bits of the world help to preserve x; but how can we decide what is x-preserving unless we already know what the limits of x are? The proposed criterion for individuality looks circular.

Still, Hampshire is right to this extent: the criteria for individuality, for a large class of individuals, do involve the concept of self-preservation; claims of the form 'x is an individual' can sometimes be rejected as failing certain self-preservation tests. Thus, the part of the world consisting of my body and yours does not count as 'an individual' because there is not enough teleological interplay between the two bodies, that being more important than their mere spatial separateness. And it is because of teleological considerations that we do not find it absurd to suggest that a colony of ants is one individual.

Furthermore, Spinoza seems to have had thoughts along this line. Having introduced the phrase 'particular thing' in a weak and undemanding way, he adds: 'If a number of individuals so concur in one action that together they are all the cause of one effect, I consider them as being to that extent one particular thing.' (2d7) Taken with slavish literalness, this implies that the people whose combined breathing is fouling the air are to that extent one thing. But perhaps he meant something like the thought I have taken from Hampshire, namely, that our decisions about which bits of the world count as single individuals depend in part not on common *effects* but on common *goals*. Spinoza virtually says as much, after he has overcome his shyness about teleology:

If two individuals are joined to one another, they compose an individual twice as powerful as either one. A man can wish for nothing more helpful to his staying in existence than that all should so agree in all things that the minds and bodies of

13. Hampshire, *Spinoza*, pp. 76f.

everyone should compose, as it were, one mind and one body; that all together should try as far as they can to stay in existence; and that all together should seek for themselves the common advantage of all. (4p18s at 223/6, quoted with omissions)

I conclude that Hampshire has here got hold of something Spinozistic and probably true; and, unlike his other proposal, this one really does concern teleology—shared *goals*. But it does not suffice to justify Spinoza's egoism doctrine. As I remarked earlier, our judgments of the form (i) 'x and y are parts of a single individual' cannot depend solely upon ones of the form (ii) 'There is something to whose preservation x and y both contribute', because (ii) requires us already to have some handle on what individuals there are and thus to know (i) already. And that point can be illustrated in a manner which dooms this as a basis for Spinozistic egoism. We have a pretty secure grip on the idea of what constitutes a single human being; it does have some teleological and self-preserving content, no doubt; but if we encountered an organic configuration which passed all the tests for being one human being except that it did some things which were not conducive to its survival, we would not take that as proof that it was not a single individual. If Spinoza thinks that we ought to do so, he owes us reasons which he has not given. And he also should admit that his doctrine of individual egoism is true only because of how he defines 'individual', and that it may well be false when understood in terms of our normal concept of a single individual, person, or the like.

Spinoza's substantive morality rests on a psychological theory, not all of which has been expounded. In chapter 7 I presented his views about the cognitive side of the human mind—belief, perception, etc. In chapter 10 I have approached his theory of conation—wants and intentions and try-ings—by considering the two most basic questions it raises: How does Spinoza try to show that egoism is true? And how does he try to reconcile it with his rejection of teleology? In the present chapter I shall dig further into the conative side, while also taking in the affective aspects of the human condition, i.e., those pertaining to feeling and emotion. I have just been using 'cognitive', 'conative' and 'affective' in their standard meanings, but Spinoza's terminology is different. He classifies as 'affects' a large group of items which—roughly speaking—include all the emotions and all the immoderate desires. He has no common definition for the whole genus of affects, only definitions of the two species. The unity of the genus lies only in the toxicity of all the species—how damaging they are to happiness and health.

§59. *Pleasant and unpleasant affects*

1. Spinoza says there are three primary kinds of affect—pleasure, un-pleasure, and desire—of which all other kinds are subspecies. The first two jointly comprise the emotional affects, the ones which essentially in-clude a component of feeling; the third item, desire, needs to be treated separately.

I am using 'pleasure' for Spinoza's *laetitia*, and 'unpleasure' for his *tristitia.* His two words are clearly meant to contrast pleasant and unpleasant states of mind (and body), and in a commentary it is best to give them names which reflect that fact. Although Spinoza's two terms do not wear their polarity on their faces as mine do, he says explicitly that they stand for polar opposites; so that is all right. It is a mild nuisance having to remember that I am using 'pleasure' to stand for every pleasant state of mind—not merely bodily pleasures—but the alternative is to render *laetitia* by 'joy', as White and Curley have done, and that is even further off track.

Unlike translators who have put 'pleasure' for *laetitia*, however,[1] I do not

1. George Eliot, A. Boyle, Samuel Shirley.

render *tristitia* by 'pain'. As a label for every unpleasant state of mind, 'pain' is hopelessly wrong. And 'sorrow' (White) and 'sadness' (Curley) are too specific, in about the way that 'joy' is on the other side. So is 'displeasure', which suggests disapproval, or the frowns of someone in authority. These drawbacks are not found in the seldom used 'unpleasure'. This good word is listed in the OED, with examples where it has the kind of meaning I am giving it. Its principal twentieth century use is when 'pleasure' and 'unpleasure' are used to render Freud's *Lust* and *Unlust*. That is a comforting precedent, since Spinoza's polarity is like Freud's, and in a current German translation of Spinoza (Jakob Stern's) the terms *laetitia* and *tristitia* are rendered by the Freudian *Lust* and *Unlust*.

2. Although I have put this in terms of pleasant and unpleasant states of mind, Spinoza's notion of an affect is a psycho-physical one. Specifically, he says that pleasure and unpleasure are what I shall call upward and downward moves, i.e., changes to a greater or a lesser degree of vitality and self-sufficiency, shifts away from or towards death: 'By affect I understand the states of the body in which the body's power of acting is increased or diminished, aided or restrained, and at the same time the ideas of these states.' (3d3) This is not one of the cases where Spinoza understands what he is saying in its physical application, and throws in the mental counterpart as a sheerly theoretical entity on the strength of the parallelism. On the contrary, he knows very well what the idea of a change in my level of physical vitality is, namely, a change in my level of mental vitality. The point is that the notion of a decrease or increase in *health* (my word, Spinoza's concept) is a trans-attribute one. To say that x has pleasure, or is becoming healthier, is to say that x is becoming less likely to be acted on by outside causes in a manner which threatens its continued existence; and that could be said univocally if x were physical or if it were mental, since it involves only concepts belonging to logic, cause, and time (see §12).

The 3d3 account of what affects are bifurcates in AD 2 and 3, that is, in the second and third affect-definitions at the end of Part 3. It may be noted that those definitions speak not of bodily changes and the ideas thereof but just of changes in 'a man'. Thus: 'Pleasure is a man's passage from a lesser to a greater perfection', 'Unpleasure is a man's passage from a greater to a lesser perfection.' These two exhaust the content of d3, which means that the official definition of 'affect' excludes desire! That is a sign of trouble, to which I shall return.

In p59d Spinoza implies that pleasure and unpleasure *cause* the upward and downward movements, but his usual view is that they *are* those movements. (That is why I render d3 with 'in which the body's power' etc. rather than 'by which the body's power' etc.) In a note on AD 2 and 3 Spinoza comments on his view that pleasure and unpleasure are kinds of change, but defends it only for unpleasure, as follows:

Unpleasure consists in a passage to a lesser perfection, not in the lesser perfection itself, since a man cannot be unpleased insofar as he participates in some perfection. Nor can we say that unpleasure consists in the lack of a greater perfection. For a lack is a nothing, whereas the affect of unpleasure is an actual happening [*actus*], which can therefore be no other happening than a passage to a lesser perfection. (Note on AD 3)

This is one of those stratospherically abstract arguments of Spinoza's which look so strange at first but which, when properly understood, show him at his best. There are two points in it.

He is assuming that however down or unpleased someone is, he does have some 'perfection', i.e., something about his state is good as far as it goes. So there sits our unpleased man with his perfections, and Spinoza's first point is that the unpleasantness of his condition cannot arise from or consist in his having those perfections. Unpleasure pertains to bads, and perfections are goods.

The second point is that the man's unpleasure cannot consist merely in the fact that those perfections are not greater, i.e., that there are levels of perfection which he has not attained. Spinoza calls this fact a 'nothing', which is extravagant; but he probably means only that it is a negative fact whereas the man's being unpleased is positive. However, since there is no well-founded general distinction between positive and negative facts, even this more cautious rendering of the argument does not save it. One last try: unpleasure is an *actus* in the sense of being not just actual but an actual happening, something going on in the man, whereas a mere relation between his level of perfection and some other level is not a happening in him, and so is not what his unpleasure consists in. That is a cogent argument, but its premiss—namely, that unpleasure is an actual happening— would probably not be conceded by someone who needed to be convinced of the final conclusion that unpleasure is a change for the worse.

However, let us take someone who questions that premiss and try with Spinoza's help to persuade him of it. If unpleasure is not an *actus*, what is it? It cannot consist merely in having a level of perfection which could be higher, for then all pleasure would be maximal, i.e., there would be almost no pleasure. There might be some level L of perfection such that unpleasure is being below L; but we can ignore this until someone suggests a plausible candidate for L. The only remaining possibility seems to be that unpleasure is the having of a certain kind of thought about one's level of perfection. There are two obvious candidates: I am unpleased if I think that my level used to be higher, or I am unpleased if I had expected my level to be higher. Spinoza does not discuss the latter, and really he ought to. He does mention the former on the last page of Part 3, where he says that in pleasure and unpleasure it is not that 'the mind compares its body's present constitution with a past constitution' but rather that it 'affirms of the body something which really involves more or less reality than before'. We must agree that unpleasure is not the same as disgruntled nostalgia, but I am not convinced that it must be the mental side of an actual medical decline. (Notice, incidentally, that Spinoza here describes the (un)pleasure in terms not of how it feels but of what the mind 'affirms'. He is trying to make the attribute of thought as cognitive as possible.)

3. In support of his thesis that pleasure is a process, all Spinoza does is to assert a consequence of it. Of a man who in fact has pleasure because he is passing to a higher level of perfection, Spinoza says that if he had been born with this level of perfection 'he would possess it without an affect of pleasure'. Perhaps we are meant to find this obviously right, and thus to be disposed to accept the theory which implies it. I am inclined to think that it is right, though not obviously so. Some philosophers have thought that the best frame of mind would be a static one in which everything is so perfect that there is no room for any change except for the worse; but it seems to me that Leibniz is right when he says that that is not experiencing pleasure but rather being 'insensate and stupefied'.[2] That is not necessarily to agree with Spinoza's AD 2, and indeed with Leibniz, that pleasure must involve *improvement* along some dimension.

That unpleasure involves process seems less sure to me than that pleasure does. This is because uniformity through time seems to be an enemy of pleasure but not of unpleasure. If the content of my mind is enjoyable but does not change, it will in time become unenjoyable just because of its unvarying quality. That is what boredom is—a loss of pleasure through sheer lack of variety. I cannot see that anything relates to unpleasure as boredom does to pleasure, but the point is controversial, and I am not in a position to insist upon it.

4. For most of Spinoza's purposes he needs only that pleasure and unpleasure are opposites, and that each is at root a medical or biological phenomenon. Indeed, some details in his theorising will be in trouble unless he backs down from the definition of them purely in terms of upward and downward movements. For example, when he defines 'love' as 'pleasure accompanied by the idea of an external cause' (AD 6), and 'hate' as 'unpleasure accompanied by the idea of an external cause' (AD 7), he implies that nobody can love and hate at the same time. But this is false, not just when construed in terms of dispositions to love and hate but also when taken episodically. I can fill my mind with my hatred for y and at the same time my love for x, perhaps loving x the more because he too hates y. And in p17,40c1 Spinoza himself allows something even stronger, namely, that I can at once love and hate the same object. He tries to make some room for himself by distinguishing upward and downward moves of the entire organism from partial unbalancing improvements and deteriorations.

2. *New Essays*, p. 189.

But really I think he should drop the entire upward/downward idea and look for a more complex account of the essential nature of pleasure and unpleasure.

5. Still, the up/down theory is at work in one important aspect of Part 3, which I now expound. Spinoza holds onto his view that nothing actively harms itself, from which it follows—given that unpleasure is a move downwards, a lowering of vitality, a harm—that all the unpleasant affects are passions, i.e., are caused from outside the organism. Pleasant affects, on the other hand, may be either active or passive: whatever I do unaided will be pleasant, according to Spinoza, but pleasant changes may also be caused from outside.

Yet when he first introduces pleasure, he defines it as 'that *passion* in which the mind passes to a greater perfection' (p11s); and some other passages also imply that there is no active pleasure, i.e., pleasure caused by the organism which has it. Here are the textual facts.

In most appeals to the p11s definition of pleasure, in Part 3, the 'passion' part is ignored: all that is used is pleasure's being an upward movement of mind and body—thus p15,19–21,23,34. Also p53: this concerns an affect which could not be passive, namely, the pleasure which occurs 'when the mind contemplates itself and its power of acting', which Spinoza later adduces to prove that there are active pleasures as well as passive ones (p58)—a view which is confirmed when p59,d say that pleasure can be active while unpleasure cannot, and is finally enshrined in AD 2.

But two demonstrations in Part 3 depend on pleasure's always being caused from outside. One of them is p56d which argues that 'there are as many kinds of pleasure as there are kinds of object by which we are affected', and the argument assumes, on the strength of p11s, that all pleasures are caused by the action of external objects on the person. Still, if the argument were otherwise all right it would show that there are as many kinds of *passive* pleasure as there are objects etc.; from which it follows, *a fortiori*, that there are at least as many kinds of pleasure as there are objects etc. The progeny of p56 are harmless too, because they all flow through the bottleneck of 4p33 which speaks only of 'affects which are passions', not implying that all affects are passions.

Then there is the peculiar case of p57. It may not matter much in itself, since it is not heard from again; but we should notice that its demonstration seems to depend entirely on the premiss: 'Pleasure is desire or appetite insofar as it is increased [or] aided by external causes.' The one clear fact about this obscure argument is that it will collapse unless all pleasure is passive.

6. Just after the two episodes which confine pleasure to passive pleasure, Spinoza writes: 'This will be enough concerning the affects which relate to a man insofar as he is acted on. It remains to add a few words about those which are related to him insofar as he acts' (p57s), and then proceeds immediately to p58 which says that there is active pleasure. 'This will be enough . . . ' *What* will be enough? The whole of Part 3 up to there, or just p56,57? Either way, if there is active pleasure then why is pleasure defined in p11s as a passion?

It is pretty clear that at some stage in the development of his views Spinoza did think of all pleasure as passive, and that when he changed his mind about this he made an imperfect job of cleansing his text.[3] The impurities that remain, like the p11s definition, are not to any significant degree taken up in demonstrations and insinuated into the doctrinal structure. As I have mentioned, p56 remains all right even if some pleasure is active, and p57 has no progeny. The later consequences of the p11s definition of 'pleasure' all occur in Part 4, and five of them are harmless. The one which puts to work the idea that all joy is passive is 4p18d, which purports to show that 'A desire which arises from pleasure is stronger, other things being equal, than one which arises from unpleasure'. Spinoza's argument for this relies on the notion that pleasure and desire both involve changes in the same direction, while unpleasure involves a change in the opposite direction, so that our desires are reinforced by our pleasures and damped down by our unpleasures. Never mind all the corners that are being cut here. For present purposes what matters is a decorative touch which Spinoza adds to his account of pleasure and desire as collaborators: he says that in pleasant desire there is not only the thrust from 'human power' (desire) but also a thrust from 'the power of the external cause' (pleasure), whereas in unpleasant desire 'human power alone' has to give the desire its force. The argument did not need thus to tie pleasure to external causation, but on analysis that is what it turns out to do.

This is relatively harmless too. Still, although the demonstrative structure is little damaged by the lingering traces of the thesis that all pleasures are passions, this thesis is still powerfully present in the work in two other ways. One will be explained in chapter 13, the other in my next section.

§60. *Desire as an affect*

1. Affects include not only pleasures and unpleasures but also desires. Spinoza is thinking of desires which are harmful because immoderate or unbalancing or unsatisfiable; he holds that the pleasant and unpleasant affects tend to be harmful in similar ways. The way of life approvingly exhibited in Parts 4 and 5 is free of conduct which is engaged in 'from an affect'—e.g., conduct in which one is enslaved by hope (pleasure) or fear (unpleasure) or greed (desire). The three kinds of affect have, then,

---

3. Further evidence that the p11s definition is a leftover: it says that in pleasure the mind—not the man—passes to a higher perfection. This misrepresents the mature doctrine.

some unity at the moral output end of the theory; but that does not give them an intrinsic similarity, unifying them at the input end, and Spinoza does not face that fact. It is as though, needing the concept *weed* in our gardening, we assumed that it belongs in our botanical theory.

It is an eloquent fact that Spinoza twice undertakes to say in general what an affect is, in d3 and in the General Definition near the end of Part 3, each time confining himself to pleasure and unpleasure, omitting desire.

The situation is not, however, that Spinozistic desire sits at an uncomfortable distance from pleasure and unpleasure. On the contrary, if we take the latter two as defined in AD 2 and 3, and desire as defined in 3p9s, desire is a species of pleasure!

Eventually we shall drop Spinoza's theory of desire and take him to be using the term in a fairly normal, teleological manner. But his official p9s account of it does influence Part 3, especially by implying that desire is a species of pleasure. The dangers and stresses and avoidances which flow from this are not philosophically instructive; but we need to identify them and set them cleanly aside if we are to grasp what is valuable in the text. That is my aim in the present section.

2. Desire is 'appetite together with consciousness of it' (p9s), meaning 'appetite of which one is conscious'; and Spinoza says that consciousness is relevant to whether 'desire' is the right word, but has no substantive import: 'I recognize no difference between human appetite and desire. For whether a man is conscious of his appetite or not, the appetite still remains one and the same.' (AD 1, explanation) No fact about the content, direction, strength, causes or effects of an appetite will depend on whether it is a desire.

Add to that Spinoza's account of appetite (see §52.1), according to which my appetite for P's being the case is that part of my nature which makes me behave in P-producing ways. According to this analysis, the truth value of 'x now has an appetite' will always be the same as that of 'x now undergoes a change whose causes lie within him'.

Then add Spinoza's doctrine (see §57.3) that whatever a person actively does must raise his level of health and vitality.

When these ingredients are combined, we get the result that whenever someone has a desire he is caused to move upwards, i.e., to change in the direction of greater health, 'perfection' and so on. But that is just how Spinoza defines 'pleasure'! In short, he has left 'desire' with no work to do. He has tied it to 'appetite', and has supplied premises which entail that there is appetite when and only when there is active pleasure, i.e., pleasure caused from within. Admittedly, pleasure is the upward movement, while appetite is the causal basis for it; but Spinoza is not sensitive to such differences, and makes no attempt to use this one to prevent a collision. It is as though he had defined appetite not as the person's nature insofar as it causes upthrust, but just as upthrust—progress towards greater vitality— itself. For simplicity's sake I shall take it in that way throughout this section.

3. Much of the time throughout p14–59 there is no trouble from the fact that Spinoza ought to include desire within pleasure. Some propositions, such as p14,27,51, generalize about all the affects, without distinguishing amongst them. Others, including p16–26, speak only of pleasure and un- pleasure, not of desire. Some remarks about desire or about 'trying', in- cluding several in propositions and scholia from p28 onwards, run smoothly because they do not clearly tie desire to Spinozistic appetite, or do not ex- plicitly lay it alongside pleasure in the trio of affects, or both. Thus, sheer casualness helps to keep Spinoza out of trouble, as in p15d where he de- fends the thesis that anything can by sheer coincidence be the cause in someone of pleasure, unpleasure, or desire, arguing for it in detail for the first two kinds of affect and then adding airily: 'And in the same way it can easily be shown that that thing can be the coincidental cause of desire.' Trouble is also avoided in p59, which says that of the three affects only pleasure and desire can be active: Spinoza argues that unpleasure is always passive, and gets his result by remainder, without having to say how pleasure and desire relate to one another.

4. But there is trouble in p37: 'The desire which arises from unpleasure or pleasure . . . is greater, the greater the affect is.' The very wording of the proposition, taken seriously, implies that desire is not an affect. But even more revealing is the demonstration. If desire were taken to be Spinozist appetite, pleasant desire would be proportional to pleasure because pleasant desire *is* pleasure. Spinoza steers clear of that trouble spot: he argues that since pleasure is good for us, 'a man affected with pleasure desires nothing but to preserve it' etc. That relies on the teleological form of the egoism doctrine: not 'What a man does will give him pleasure' but rather 'What will give a man pleasure he does'.

The other half of the demonstration ought not to work at all. As I reported in §59.6, Spinoza argues in 4p18d that desire and unpleasure run opposite ways, which implies that the stronger the unpleasure the weaker the desire. But here in 3p37d he is arguing for the exact opposite: the stronger the unpleasure the stronger the desire. This switch depends essen- tially on the conversion into teleological form of the conditional which defines desire. The argument is that an increase in unpleasure, being a de- crease in vitality, is something against which the self-preserving desire will exert itself; and the greater the unpleasant challenge, the greater the desiring response to it. That depicts desire as rising to occasions, meeting challenges, doing what is needed for health and welfare, moving teleo- logically from 'It would help him' to 'He will do it' rather than conversely.

There is also trouble in p56, which I mentioned earlier. Having argued for a great variety among pleasures and unpleasures, Spinoza extends this result to desire, as follows. First he defines 'desire' in terms of those parts of the person's nature which cause him to act in a given manner, and then he continues:

Therefore, as each one [has] this or that kind of pleasure, unpleasure, love, hate, etc.—i.e. as his nature is constituted in one way or the other—so his desires vary, and the nature of one desire must differ from the nature of another as much as the affects from which each arises differ from one another. (185/11)

This argument takes desire to comprise *everything* that happens within the individual. If desire is less than that, a difference in two people's natures does not ensure that their desires differ. Spinoza has moved away from the teleological reading of 'desire' back to a broadened Spinozist reading—but it is so broad that instead of desire's falling within pleasure the danger is now that pleasure and unpleasure will both be swallowed up in desire. The demonstration, in short, does not comfortably juxtapose desire with pleasure and unpleasure as one of a trio.

In p57d there is trouble of yet another kind. Spinoza here stops desire from colliding with active pleasure by proceeding as though all pleasure were passive. This also happens in 4p18d; and I suggest that in each case Spinoza is enticed into making pleasure always a passion by the fact that this shrinks pleasure enough to give desire some ground of its own to stand on.

5. Summing up so far: in arguments where desire and pleasure come to grips with one another, we have found one where desire is blatantly teleological (p37d), one where desire remains unteleological but is so broad as to have almost no content (p56d), and one where room is found for desire through the pretence that all pleasure is passive (p57d).

After all this, there remains only the extraordinary p58: 'As well as the pleasure and desire which are passions, there are other affects of pleasure and desire which are related to us insofar as we act.' This announces active pleasure, after some suggestions that pleasure might always be a passion (see §59.6); and it also announces active *desire*—but have we been encouraged to think that perhaps all desire is passive? There may be a buried hint to that effect in p56d, but most of Part 3 gives no indication that any desire is passive, let alone all. In p58d Spinoza appeals to p9 as implying that we have desires 'insofar as' we are passive. But all he means by that, back at p9, is that we have desires even *when* we are passive, not that a desire can ever be a passive aspect of us; so it doesn't help us to understand Spinoza's thinking it worthwhile to say in p58 that not all desires are passions.

The inclusion of 'and desire' in p58 is not a mere slip. Although not properly introduced, the notion of passive desire does lurk in Part 3, as here: 'This affect can hardly be overcome. For so long as a man is gripped by any desire, he must at the same time be gripped by this one.' (AD 44, explanation) A man cannot be 'gripped' by his 'very essence'! When Spinoza speaks in this way of one's desires he is not taking them to be merely aspects of one's nature which cause one's behaviour.

That foreshadows an increasing tendency throughout Part 4 to countenance passive desires, and we shall see in chapter 13 that Spinoza has an acute need for some desires to be passive. If none are, then by his own 'no self-harm' principle no desire can be harmful to the desirer; but Spinoza is rightly sure that many of our desires are extremely harmful to us. This need of his is made explicit in the first three paragraphs of 4 Appendix, which clearly affirm that there are passive desires.

We must suppose, as I shall from now on, that Spinoza is mainly using 'desire' teleologically, taking it to mean what it ordinarily *does* mean, rather than what it is said to mean in 3p9s and AD 1. This will free us, as it does him, both from the equation of desire with active pleasure and from the implication that all desire is active and thus unharmful to the desirer.

§61. *Spinoza's list of affects*

1. Spinoza scatters definitions of many kinds of affect through scholia in p11–59, and then repeats them, sometimes altered a little, in the affect definitions with which Part 3 ends. I shall attend to the later versions, using unadorned numbers to refer to the affect definitions.

There are four dozen of them, starting of course with desire, pleasure and unpleasure. The next two, wonder and disdain, are cognitive states which Spinoza says he includes not because they are affects but because he will need them in later definitions. Wonder is the state in which your mind is flooded and brought to a halt by the impression of some object which you don't know what to make of—'this particular imagining has no connection with others'. And disdain, judging from 5 aided by its precursor p52s, is a negatively belittling attitude to something which has fallen short of one's expectations, so that 'the thing's presence moves the mind to imagining more what is not in it than what is'.

From 6 through 31, everything is defined in terms of pleasure and unpleasure and their derivatives, prominent among the latter being love and hate which are defined in 6 and 7 as pleasure and unpleasure, respectively, 'accompanied by the idea of an external cause'.

There are four affects which strictly speaking are defined not as pleasure or unpleasure or any derivative thereof but as thinkings—for instance 'Overestimation is thinking more highly of someone than is just, out of love' (21; the others are 22,28,29). But each of these is defined as a thinking which arises from an affect, and Spinoza is not the man to distinguish that from an affect which gives rise to a thinking.

2. After explaining AD 31, Spinoza announces that he is turning from affects defined through pleasure and unpleasure to ones relating to desire. The supposed 'desire' group, however, begins with six which do not comfortably fit into it. I propose to drop 32 as a minor item which we can do without, and 33 because it is not an affect at all. Then come 34–37 which I propose to elevate to membership in the pleasure-unpleasure group. They are all defined in terms of pleasure or unpleasure, or derivatives of them, as well as in terms of desire; and I shall argue later that what counts is not whether desire is present but rather whether pleasure/unpleasure is absent. I don't take that view of the use of 'love' in the final four affect definitions—e.g., 'Greed is an immoderate desire and love of wealth'— because those uses of 'love' strike me as perfunctory, and not as showing that the defined items are thought essentially to involve pleasure.

Three other members of the desire group are misplaced, namely 40–42. Of these, daring (40) is defined through desire, but back at p51s it is more plausibly defined as the lack of a certain restraint on one's desires; that makes it not an affect at all, and I propose dropping it. The other two are awkwardly handled versions of fear, which is already included as item 39; we shall lose little by dropping both, and letting their work be done in a blanket way by fear. I do not similarly drop fright (13), for an important reason which I shall give in .5.

3. Summing up, now: if we set aside *wonder* and *disdain* as not being affects, and elevate 34–7 from the desire group, we can arrange most of the affects of pleasure and unpleasure in fifteen pairs, the first member of each pair relating to the second as pleasure does to unpleasure:[4]

6. love	7. hate
8. inclination	9. aversion
10. devotion	11. mockery
12. hope	13. fright
14. confidence	15. despair
16. gladness	17. disappointment
19. favour	20. indignation
21. overestimation	22. scorn

4. It is a slight liberty to pair 10 with 11, and 35 with 36. The latter become a pair if in AD 35 we replace 'pity' by 'compassion'. See next footnote.

23. envy	24. compassion
25. self-esteem	26. humility
28. pride	29. despondency
30. self-exaltation	31. shame
34. gratitude	37. vengeance
35. well-wishing	36. anger

There remain only repentance (27), which could well have a polar opposite in boastful self-satisfaction, but happens not to; and pity (18), about whose status Spinoza is unclear.[5]

The desire part of the list, after the elevations and omissions I have proposed, is this:

38. cruelty	39. fear	43. courtesy
44. ambition	45. gluttony	46. drunkenness
47. greed	48. lust	

I am taking Spinoza to mean what he says in defining cruelty, namely, that we call a person cruel if *he* is ill-disposed towards someone whom *we* love. Curley and others conjecture that this is a slip, and that Spinoza meant . . . if he is ill-disposed towards someone whom *he* loves, thus representing cruelty as a love-hate affect. Both these views of cruelty can be found in p41cs, and one must have been dropped along the way. In deciding which, why choose the one which requires us to rewrite AD 38 on Spinoza's behalf? If I agreed with the rewriters, I would of course raise cruelty to the pleasure/unpleasure group.

4. Since kinds of affect are supposed to be as numerous as kinds of object that can act on us, there must be an infinity of them (see 3p56). What led Spinoza to pick out this four dozen rather than some other selection from the infinity? In p59s he says they are 'the main ones', but he does not explain that. It is not that these are the ones he badly needs in his demonstrations: of the affect names defined in Part 3, fewer than half appear in demonstrations in Parts 4 and 5; and fourteen of those appear only once each.[6]

The answer is that Spinoza's choice of affect kind is guided by the mean-

5. In explaining AD 18 Spinoza virtually identifies pity with compassion, though one is an unpleasure and the other a form of love and thus of pleasure.

6. The three basic kinds appear most often, followed by love and hate. The others appearing more than once are 13, 25, 28 and 30.

ings of affect names in ordinary language. In each case, he takes an ordinary word and lets its common meaning serve to locate a certain line, and then he undertakes to give a theoretically deep account of what that line consists in. If the line drawn by ordinary language is too disorderly to admit of any solid Spinozistic analysis, he will relocate it a little before going to work on it. That is what I think is happening here: 'I know that in their common usage these words signify something else. But my purpose is to explain the nature of things, not the meaning of words. I intend to indicate these things by words whose ordinary meanings come closest to the meanings I wish to use them with.' (19 and 20, explanation, lightly edited. I have followed the Dutch version at the end of the passage, preferring 'come closest' to the Latin version's 'are not entirely opposed'.)

This allows common meanings a role only in the selection of targets for analysis, not in determining the content of the analysis. Objection: 'You are still crediting Spinoza with giving weight to facts about ordinary language, which is something he would never do.' Not often, I agree, but in this area he does. He says for example, that there are some kinds of imitation which he won't count as emulation—'not because we know that emulation has one cause and imitation another, but because it has come about by usage that we call emulous only someone who . . . etc.' (33, explanation). He also says that he has introduced wonder because 'it has become customary' to call the three primary affects 'by other names when they are related to objects we wonder at' (192/8); he omits to define one pair of affects 'because no affects that I know of derive their names from them' (192/18); he re-locates longing 'because the word *longing* seems to concern desire' (200/5); he omits the definitions of certain other affects partly 'because most of them do not have names' (203/18).

I should say candidly that many of Spinoza's definitions do not fit the ordinary senses of the terms being defined and seem not to capture any interesting neighbours of them. There is a lot here which could be regarded as revisionary but is probably just incompetent. Examples will be given in due course, but we might note right away that several of the so-called 'affects of desire' are really character traits: they include dispositions to want, to feel and to behave in certain ways, and Spinoza's definitions do nothing like justice to their complexity.

5. The nonbasic kinds of affect which appear on the desire part of my list are not used in demonstrations. Spinoza's main interest is in pleasure and unpleasure, and so is mine. Still, we should ask what he thought he was doing in bringing both kinds of affect under a single label.

We know what unity there is supposed to be in the moral output of the theory. Affects in both genera can sour and twist and spoil our lives: we are threatened not only by fear, hate and self-exaltation, but also by greed, lust and ambition. That unity in the output requires one bit of unity at the input end of the theory, namely, the assumption that any affect can influence behaviour. That is clearly Spinoza's view, and surely he is right.

However, something may influence behaviour—and so help to explain it—without being much of a basis for predicting it: the information that someone is drunk may help one to explain why he behaved as he did, but generates no reasonable guesses about what he will do. With that fact in mind, look at my version of Spinoza's list. I submit that the members of the desire group, understood teleologically, are fairly rich bases for predictions of behaviour, while the pleasure/unpleasure affects are much poorer. On the other hand, the affect kinds which are thin in behavioural content are relatively rich in information about emotional tone, and conversely. Consider some examples—taking all the affect kinds in their dispositional rather than their episodic form, since this is the more natural way to understand the desire group. If we are told that Peter is proud (28) and Charles cruel (38), we know more about how Peter feels than about how Charles does, and can make better predictions about Charles's behaviour than about Peter's. Again, if we are told that Albert is ambitious (44) for professional success while Ernest is envious (23) of professional success, this tells us a lot about how Albert will behave but little about how he feels, and conversely for Ernest.

Or so I am inclined to think. And I conjecture that this double difference helped to guide Spinoza's sorting of items into two lists. That would help to explain what is going on when he distinguishes fright (*metus*, 13), which is 'a wavering unpleasure, arising from the idea of a future or past thing whose outcome we to some extent doubt' from fear (*timor*, 39), which is 'a desire to avoid a greater evil, of which we are frightened, by means of a lesser one'. Typically dry and abstract as these are, they support my conjecture. Spinoza is taking fright to be an episode of anxious dread about some outcome, with no implication of being able to do anything about it; and he is taking fear to be an occasion of willingness to put up with something nasty in order to avoid something worse. He says that we 'are frightened' of the latter, but I shall argue in §73.4–5 that when he puts his concept of fear to work the emphasis is less on emotional tone than on coercion of the will. Consider, for example, someone who lives sedately—hating it—because he thinks this is the way to stay out of hell. Even if he is so sure of success that he suffers no episodes of fright, I believe that Spinoza would describe his motivations in terms of fear. So I think that his concept of fear is much more informative about behaviour than about emotional tone, which is why I do not promote it to the pleasure/unpleasure category. Of course we must constrain our word 'fear' to make it mean only this; for in normal usage it sometimes names an emotional state ('He was paralysed with fear'), as well as sometimes standing for a fact about preferences ('He took his umbrella for fear that it might rain'). But 'fright' and 'fear' are the best labels I can find for 13 and 39; anyway, the concepts are important, not the labels.

Consider now the affect kinds 34–37 which I shifted out of the desire group. Each of them has quite strong implications about behaviour and about emotional tone. That someone is grateful (34) to me bears more specifically on his likely behaviour than does (say) his being indignant (20) towards me; on the other hand it tells more about how he feels than does (say) his being ingratiatingly polite towards me (43). And similarly with the other relocated kinds of affect: each seems to have more emotional content than the other affects of desire, and more behavioural content than the other affects of pleasure and unpleasure. That could explain why Spinoza and I disagree about which group they belong with.

Perhaps. I am not sure that my double conjecture is right and shall not rest anything on it in what follows. From here on my concern will be purely with the kinds of affects which I classify under pleasure and unpleasure.

§62.   *Spinoza's account of emotions*

1. Spinoza's pleasure/unpleasure group of affects—or my enlarged version of it—could be seen as a group of kinds of *emotion*. Let us consider them in the light of six items which Alston lists as having been given prominence in various theories of emotion:[7]

1. cognition

2. feelings of certain kinds

3. marked bodily sensations of certain kinds

4. involuntary bodily processes and overt expressions of various kinds

5. tendencies to act in certain ways

6. an upset or disturbed condition of mind or body.

Spinoza would presumably bracket (3) with the first half of (4), under the parallelism. We have seen that he describes the mind in a highly intellectualist way, and might prefer to speak not of sensations which parallel bodily upsets but rather of the mind's 'affirming' that the bodily upsets occur; but we ought to see him as making a place, even if grudgingly, for (3). He does not in fact talk about bodily upsets and sensations of them, and that is all right, because they don't help us to classify emotions into useful kinds, nor do they bear much on the role of emotional episodes in our lives. In the nineteenth century some theorists put bodily sensations at the

7. W. P. Alston, 'Emotion and Feeling', in Edwards.

centre, using them to classify emotions and even to explain what it is for a state to be emotional.[8] But that theory was not yet born in Spinoza's day and is dead in ours.

2. As for the other half of Alston's item (4)—overt expressions of certain kinds—Spinoza does not feature them either, but he does say something odd about them: 'As for the external states of the body, which are observed in the affects—such as trembling, paleness, sobbing, laughter, etc. —I have omitted them because they are related to the body only, without any relation to the mind.' (p59s at 189/28) This sounds like a backing down on parallelism, but I am sure it is not, and that Spinoza's point is as follows.

Corresponding to any decent classification of items under one attribute, there must be a classification under the other, but we may have one taxonomy without having the other. At the deepest scientific level, Spinoza must say that we do have physics but do not have psychology (see §33.5), but in the case of the affects the situation is reversed: we classify and understand and control our emotions through a taxonomy which has to do with how they feel and what cognitive states they involve. It is true that 'pleasure' and 'unpleasure' are defined in transattribute terms, but the fine-grained classification depends on associated 'ideas' with specified contents, as when love is defined as pleasure accompanied by the idea of an external cause. As I pointed out in §51.5, a classification of ideas by their representative features—meaning what they are indirectly of—cannot be mapped onto any classification of bodily states by their intrinsic features, i.e., their motion-and-rest structural properties. And so, having adopted a taxonomy of the affects in terms of idea content, Spinoza is cut off from a taxonomy of them in physical terms.

That is why he always describes the cures of the affects mentalistically. In 3 Preface he says he will supply what we have not hitherto had, namely, a theory of 'the power of the mind over the affects', an account of 'what the mind can do to moderate them'. And there is more to that effect in 3p56s. Of course he must hold that the power of the mind over affects is matched by a power of the body over them, so his view has to be that we have some grasp of the former power and none, yet, of the latter. See, for example, the sequence p11–13 in which we are made to move to the mental side in order to find levers that will budge our affects.

That explains Spinoza's omitting laughter and tears because 'they are related to the body only'. He means that the line between 'cries' and 'doesn't cry' does not coincide with any line we can draw in mental terms, and so does not mark a distinction that we are at present equipped to find useful in controlling our affects.

8. For a good discussion of this and related matters see William Lyons, *Emotion* (Cambridge, 1980), pp. 115–129.

That explanation does not carry over to this puzzling remark of Spinoza's: 'As for the definitions of cheerfulness, pleasurable excitement, melancholy, and pain, I omit them because they are chiefly related to the body, and are only species of pleasure or unpleasure.' (AD 3, explanation) But all the items on Spinoza's big list are species of pleasure or unpleasure! I suppose his point is that cheerfulness etc. are not marked off by anything he is interested in, i.e., any sort of cognitive component. Whatever it is that makes a feeling one of cheerfulness, say, rather than of some other kind of pleasure, is not essentially a matter of associated beliefs; it is just a difference in feeling tone, which is better thought of in terms of its bodily correlate than in terms of states of the mind.

3. Alston's item (1)—cognition of something as desirable or undesirable—must have a central place in any viable theory of emotion. To connect this with Spinoza we must split it into

1a. belief that P, for some P

1b. desire or attitude involving P.

For example, if I resent your treatment of me, my cognition of your behaviour as undesirable comprises a thought that you did x and a wish that you had not. The belief component is often hard to isolate cleanly; but still the two components must be present, and it suits my purposes to have a clean split.

Spinoza's definitions of the kinds of emotion—i.e., the kinds of affect in my first group—are strikingly cognitive, as I have already noted. In many of them the definiens contains 'love' or 'hate', and these are defined with help from 'idea', meaning 'belief'. All the rest appeal directly to the parent notions pleasure and unpleasure together with something about an 'idea' or about what the person 'considers' (25 and 26) or 'thinks' (29).[9]

I shall return in §63 to the place of belief in Spinoza's theory of the emotions.

4. He puts less stress on the role of desire, and we can see why. On the surface: he seeks to split the affects into two according to the absence or presence of desire, whereas I have done it according to the presence or absence of pleasure/unpleasure, which frees me to argue that desire is always involved. At a deeper level: his problem about how desire relates to pleasure (see §60.2) gives him a reason to insulate them from one another.

But desire *is* always relevant, I contend. There are elations and depressions which don't involve desire, but they also don't involve anything

---

9. The cognitive element in emotions is crammed into the *Ethics* at a curiously early stage, in 2a3. This axiom is a rich source of puzzles: about its wording (*animi* instead of *mentis*), its alluding to affects rather than to all modes of thought, and the peculiar way it is used in demonstrations.

cognitive; they shouldn't and don't occur on Spinoza's list because they are moods, not emotions.

And if desire is always part of the story, then there will always be behavioural tendencies—Alston's (5). Spinoza would agree, since his whole concern with affects comes from their ability to make us think and feel and act in harmful ways.

5. The place of feelings—Alston's (2)—in Spinoza's account is secured by the terms in which he divides emotions primarily into pleasant and unpleasant. We shall see, though, that the further refinements of his taxonomy do not depend on finer details about how emotions feel: in determining what kind an emotional episode belongs to, Spinoza will ask whether it is pleasant or unpleasant, but his next question will concern not how it feels but what thoughts go with it.

The pleasant/unpleasant polarity among feelings is matched by a positive/negative polarity among desires—matched and apparently produced by it. I feel good because what I wanted happened; I feel bad because what I wanted not to happen happened. In defining hope and fright (12 and 13), Spinoza mentions only the difference in feeling, but we naturally infer that the 'thing whose outcome we to some extent doubt' is wanted in the case of hope, and wanted not to happen in the case of fright.

6. Finally there is mental and physical upset—Alston's (6). I regard turbulence as essential to emotions, properly so-called, and I believe that Spinoza did too, and that his 'pleasure' and 'unpleasure' are meant to suggest a *rush* of pleasant or unpleasant feeling. He writes: 'We are driven about in many ways by external causes, and just like waves on the sea driven by contrary winds, we toss about, not knowing our outcome and fate.' (p59s at 189/5) He speaks of 'a strong affect, which cannot be calmed' (p2s at 143/19), of people who are 'assailed by affects which are passions' (4p33,34) and who are 'changeable and inconstant' (4p33). It is also relevant that the Latin for 'emotion' means 'turbulence of the soul', and that Spinoza seems not to distinguish emotions from affects of pleasure and unpleasure: see AD 27, explanation, and 5p2.

But although the theme of turbulence runs strongly through Spinoza's thinking about the emotional affects, it has no part in his official theory of them. That is a pity, because if he had openly given it a role he could have lessened some of his later difficulties. We shall find him contrasting the life of the affects with the life of reason, saying that they involve bondage and freedom respectively, and interpreting this in terms of his contrast between being acted on from the outside and being self-caused. It does not work at all well; and Spinoza might have done better to retain the affect/reason contrast and align it with bondage/freedom, with this being divorced from outer/inner and instead being understood in terms of the difference between being and not being in thrall to one's own emotional turbulence.[10]

§63.   *Emotion and belief*

1. Spinoza's emphasis on cognition in classifying emotions is uncontroversial these days, but it was not always so. It is absent from Descartes's *Passions of the Soul,* a work which Spinoza knew. Let us look into Descartes a little.

According to Descartes, the emotions or 'passions of the soul' are the mind's perceptions of certain happenings in the body: he calls them movements of the 'animal spirits', and his views about them constitute a speculative neurology. They may be actively performed, but the mental registering of them is passive because it is caused from outside the mind. What marks off a passion from a bodily sensation? Descartes seems to hold that the difference involves an illusion on our part: a fit of rage does not *seem* to be a perception of a bodily event as a hunger pang does, though really it is a perception of movements of the animal spirits.[11]

Descartes seems to regard each kind of passion as marked off intrinsically, by how it feels, and to have nothing cognitive in his considered theory about what the passions are. He does say that they can cause 'thoughts which it is good to retain',[12] but these 'thoughts' are acts of the will rather than beliefs. Something cognitive is involved when he says that we can alter the strength of a passion by forming suitable mental representations,[13] for it is hard to make this plausible unless the mental representations are beliefs standing in causal relations with the passions. But Descartes does not cash in on this cognitive implication of what he says. Even if Lyons is right that Descartes regarded a passion as a kind of 'knowledge',[14] that is only because they are perceptions of movements of the animal spirits. Descartes makes no proper place for beliefs about danger in the concept of fear, beliefs about self-related achievements in the concept of pride, and so on.

10. Michael A. Slote thinks that this better course was Spinoza's. In his 'Understanding Free Will', *The Journal of Philosophy* vol. 77 (1980), pp. 136–151, he attributes to Spinoza an idea of 'autonomy' in which 'calm' is the chief ingredient.

11. Descartes, *Passions of the Soul* §§24–5. For a different though related attempt to mark off the 'passions' ordinarily so-called from bodily sensations, see *Treatise*, p. 276.

12. *Passions of the Soul* §74; see also §§40, 52.

13. *Ibid.* §45.

14. William Lyons, *Emotion* (Cambridge, 1980), p. 4.

2. Hume is more forthright than Descartes about the lack of any essential cognitive element. He says: 'It is altogether impossible to give any definition of the passions of love and hatred . . . because they produce merely a simple impression.'[15] He is taking 'love' to be the name of a certain kind of feeling, not made up out of other kinds and therefore not explainable discursively. Similarly with the other kinds of emotion. He characterizes pride and humility in terms of 'their sensations, or the peculiar emotions they excite in the soul, . . . which constitute their very being and essence'.[16] Just before that he has remarked that pride and humility always have oneself as 'object'—by which he means that you can be proud only of something you connect with yourself, and humble only about your own talents, virtues etc. That you should be proud of the moon or humble about the size of Fiji is, he says, 'absolutely impossible from the primary constitution of the mind'. Why? Here is Hume's disastrous answer to this and other such questions: 'For this I pretend not to give any reason; but consider such a peculiar direction of the thought as an original quality.' Thus, it is a fundamental fact—a basic law of nature, presumably—that someone who has *this* kind of feeling has *that* kind of thought, namely, one about himself. And it will have to be another law of nature that someone who has that kind of feeling we call 'fear' usually also has a thought about danger.

There are two false theses here. One is that kinds of emotion can be delimited just by how they feel. Hume writes: 'A passion contains not any representative quality. When I am angry, I am actually possessed with the passion, and in that emotion have no more a reference to any other object than when I am thirsty or sick or more than five foot high.'[17] This clearly implies that my state can be identified as anger just by what it feels like, without attending to its cognitive or representative aspects. I submit that that is wrong.

The second false thesis is that the belief which goes with an emotion is caused by the feeling rather than causing it. Of the 'peculiar impression or emotion which we call pride' Hume says: 'To this emotion [nature] has assigned a certain idea, viz. that of self, which it never fails to produce', and he says that 'the passion always turns our view to ourselves'.[18] I contend, on the contrary, that our view of ourselves produces the 'peculiar

---

15. *Treatise*, p. 329.

16. *Ibid.*, p. 286. I should acknowledge that Neu's *Emotion, Thought and Therapy* is what first showed me the profit in contrasting Spinoza's account of emotions with Hume's.

17. *Treatise*, p. 415, quoted with omissions.

18. *Ibid.*, p. 287.

impression', i.e., produces the noncognitive element which Hume calls 'the passion'. When Hume does assign causes to emotions, they tend to be things like houses and people and their properties, rather than ideas or beliefs.[19]

3. A satisfactory theory of emotion must make cognition central and operative. For one thing, most of our words for kinds of emotion clearly *mean* something about associated cognitions: it isn't just a law of nature that I cannot be proud of the moon if I think it has nothing to do with me; it's a consequence of what 'proud' means. Similarly with gratitude and the belief that one has received a benefit, and so on with the others. The following is good but not quite strong enough: 'Some emotions might be different from moods in this regard: envy, resentment, and gratitude, for example, seem more likely to have a "representative" or "belief-like" component than do good cheer, boredom, or grouchiness. That is, there seems to be an aspect, or even constituent, of them that is either true or false, and likewise either rationally justified or not.'[20]

Notice the phrase 'rationally justified'. We do think that emotions can be justified or unjustified, and many writers have noted that this is hard to explain if emotions are just feelings, but easy if they essentially involve beliefs.

4. Above all, if we build beliefs into emotions we can make sense of the concept of the object of an emotion.[21] The objects of emotions belong to a dazzlingly varied range of categories—things, events, qualities, states of affairs, and others—and are relatable to their emotions with a great variety of prepositions. One is grateful *to* someone, or *for* a benefit; afraid *of* a tiger, or *that* the tiger will spring; angry *at* something or *because* of what he did; and so on. How are these items that we can be grateful to, angry with, anxious about, astonished by, afraid lest, etc. tied to the emotions in which they figure?

The tie cannot be causal, if only because nonexistent items cannot cause anything yet can be objects of hopes, fears, etc. The most plausible conjecture is that the object of an emotion is what the associated belief is in some sense 'about'. This has explanatory power. It is because I can believe I am in danger from a tiger, when there is no tiger, that I can be afraid of a nonexistent tiger. It also explains the great variety of objects

19. An exception to this at *Treatise*, p. 414, is a passing phrase and not considered doctrine.

20. John Haugeland, 'Author's Response', *The Behavioral and Brain Sciences* vol. 2 (1978), pp. 257f.

21. The most thorough exploration of this point that I know of is J. R. S. Wilson, *Emotion and Object* (Cambridge, 1972).

of emotions, since there is no limit to the categories of items that beliefs can be about.

There may be emotions which have no object, e.g., a generalized sense of dread. Since they are also not associated with relevant beliefs, they tend to confirm that the objects of emotions are constituents in the associated beliefs. They might seem to challenge the thesis that a good theory of emotion will put cognition at its centre, but if we drop that thesis and look for some unitary noncognitive account of what makes an episode an emotional one, we shall fail—or so far everyone has failed. Like many others, I agree with Kenny[22] that objectless dread and its kin are parasitic cases of emotion: we describe them as 'fear' or whatever because they look and feel like standard cases of fear, which are thus classified on the strength of their cognitive content.

5. There are powerful reasons for thinking not merely that emotions must include beliefs but that the belief must cause the rest of the emotion. For one thing, if we define the 'object of an emotion' in terms of *accompanying* beliefs, we shall have to assign many emotions objects which they obviously don't have. If you are angry while thinking about what I said to you and about the weather, what makes it the case that you are angry with me and not with the wind? This is nicely answerable if we suppose that the object of an emotion must figure in a certain way in a belief which *causes* the rest of the emotion.[23] Consider also what happens when someone discovers to his surprise that what he feels towards his brother is jealousy. He is not discovering how he feels or, in most cases, what he believes. He is probably discovering which of his beliefs has caused the way he feels.

Now, Spinoza defines most kinds of emotion in terms of pleasure and unpleasure and belief, but he wavers in *how* he relates the belief to the rest of the emotion. Seven of his affect definitions are fairly openly causal: they define a given affect as pleasure or unpleasure 'arising from' a certain kind of idea, and that is presumably meant to be causal (AD 11–15, 25–6). Of the remainder, a few are hard to describe, but most speak of pleasure or unpleasure 'accompanied by' an idea, or else they invoke love and hate which are themselves defined in terms of an 'accompanying' idea.

If Spinoza stands by his uses of 'accompanied by', he will be committed to an absurdly weak concept of the object of an emotion. I know of three places where he accepts that—3p33d, 3p40d and 5p15d which argues on the assumption that if I am in a pleasant condition *while* thinking of x then I love x.

22. Anthony Kenny, *Action, Emotion and the Will* (London, 1963), pp. 61f.

23. Thus W. P. Alston, 'Emotion and Feeling,' in Edwards at p. 485. I say 'figure *in a certain way*' because mere occurrence in the belief is not enough. You are angry with me because I hurt her: she figures in the belief which caused your unpleasure, but you are not angry with her.

But I do not think that that was Spinoza's considered opinion. In 4d6 he says that he has explained in the scholia to 3p18 what he means by an affect towards F things; but those scholia contain no such term as 'towards', though they do mention affects which 'arise from the image of' an F thing. That is a step in the right direction, tying the object of an emotion to something involved in its cause, though it is a bit awkward because 'images' are physical and Spinoza wants to handle affects under the attribute of thought.

6. I submit that he was groping towards the view that emotions are caused by beliefs, but failed to get it clear enough in his mind to express it properly. The affect definitions are supposed to repeat ones given in the scholia, but there are discrepancies, some of them bearing on our present topic. Sometimes the first definition is causal and the second uses 'accompanying', sometimes it is the other way around; and I can find no significant pattern in all this.[24] Spinoza was apparently not sensitive, in this context anyway, to the difference between 'caused by x' and 'accompanied by x'.

There is a special reason why he should have failed, in his definitions of love and hate and and in similar or dependent ones, to assign a properly causal role to the belief. It concerns a peculiar wrinkle in his definitions of love and hate—either will do. He defines hate as 'unpleasure with the accompanying idea of an external cause', which I take to mean ' . . . with an accompanying belief, concerning something external, that it is the cause'. So an episode of hate in me is an unpleasant frame of mind in which I believe, of something outside me, that it is the cause . . . of what? Spinoza's answer must be ' . . . of the unpleasant frame of mind'. He gives no hint of any other answer, and at least once he does give that one: 'To hate someone is to imagine him as the cause of one's unpleasure.' (3p39d)

But that is strange. At the core of my hatred of W there is an unpleasant state of mind and a belief about W's causing something—but not his causing my mental state! I could forgive that. What I will not forgive is the harm he caused to the American wilderness. I do think he caused my distress: I think he caused my beliefs about his actions, that those caused my unpleasure, and that causation is transitive; so, being rational, I think he caused the unpleasure. But that is because I have philosophical opinions about belief, emotion, and cause; it is not at the heart of my hatred towards W.

I think that that oddity in the definitions of love and hate impeded Spinoza's properly grasping the causal role of a belief in an emotion. My hatred for x involves an unpleasant condition which is caused by some belief about x, and that belief must be about x's causing something; there is just one belief, but the concept of cause is used twice—first in saying what the belief does, and again in saying what its content is. Spinoza

24. For example, compare 16 with p18s2, 18 with p22s, 25 with p30s, and 31 with p30s.

fastened onto the second of these, and got it wrong: he said that I must believe that x caused my unpleasure. This then helped him to overlook that a belief must have caused my unpleasure.

I still think that Spinoza mainly saw emotions as caused by cognitions. I have merely suggested a reason why he did not say this clearly enough and sometimes lost sight of it entirely.

7. If Spinoza thinks physics is part of basic science, and that psychology corresponds to it—concept for concept, law for law—then he should regard his main theorizing about the affects as unbasic. By couching it in terms of 'ideas (indirectly) of' things he ties it to the representative rather than the intrinsic features of ideas, which makes it conceptually immiscible with anything that could be mapped onto physics (see §51.5). I do not know whether he was aware of this implication of his position. If he was, he might have been nervous of saying outright that good and bad feelings are 'caused by' beliefs, preferring the less scientific statement that they 'arise from' beliefs. That is indeed how Spinoza *always* expresses the causal relation of belief to pleasure or unpleasure; the choice of terminology may be significant.

Objection: 'He has no reason to shy away from saying "My idea of Peter causes pleasure in me", since that merely refers to a cause through properties of it other than those which make it a cause. It is like "Johnny's bruise was caused by Mary's dropping her birthday present on him"—the object in question did cause the bruise, but not by virtue of its being a birthday present.' True, but Spinoza is not well placed to say it, since he tends to think of causes not as concrete particulars—objects or events—which have features other than those through which they are referred to, but rather as facts or states of affairs, propositionally structured items which have no undeclared features. On that way of looking at things, one should not say 'My pleasure was caused by my idea of Peter . . . ' to which could be added ' . . . though not by virtue of its being of Peter', but rather 'My pleasure occurred because I had an idea of Peter', which leaves no room for a disclaimer saying that the 'of Peter' aspect of the situation was causally irrelevant. So there is a real discomfort for Spinoza in this situation. He is committed to the causal irrelevance of certain features of ideas, and his unformulated assumptions about causes imply that they cannot have causally irrelevant features; and I have been suggesting that his use of 'arise from' rather than 'caused by' may be a response to this tension or conflict in his thought. But I don't insist on that. What matters most, of course, is that the conflict is there and is never resolved.

§64. *Some theory about how emotions work*

1. Spinoza 'demonstrates' a number of near-truths about the human condition: we like our enemies to suffer harm (3p20), our estimates of our own achievements mirror the estimates of others (p30), one's love for another person always involves the wish to be loved back (p33), hatred begets malice (p39), we like getting more than our due (p41), our friends' enemies are our enemies (p45), and so on. The picture is unflattering, coloured as it is by universal egoism, though the tones will be lightened when Spinoza argues in Part 4 that rational egoism requires generous co-operation.

If we are to be convinced of such claims as these, it must be by our observations of the human scene. That is surely where Spinoza started also; and if he came to think that his 'demonstrations' really did explain why these things are true, we ought to part company with him on that point.[25] I shall defend that judgment by examining Spinoza's 'demonstration' of one thesis. Less flattering examples could have been chosen.

In p25 he says in effect that the wish is often father to the thought. There is truth in this, and it does connect with the near-truths derived from it in p40s,41s. But his demonstration of p25 is an unconvincing affair. From (p6) the teleological thesis that we try to *do* what will improve our health, Spinoza has inferred (p12) that we also try to *imagine* what will improve our health, this being the mental counterpart of the other; and from that he further infers (p25) that we try to have beliefs about ourselves which are pleasant to have, since pleasure is a move towards greater health. Never mind detailed criticism of this. We just know that it is not always for this kind of reason that the wish is father to the thought, because we know that wishes and thoughts are not always as life-enhancing as that 'demonstration' makes them out to be.

From p25 Spinoza infers the roughly true thesis that people tend to think that they deserve to be liked and don't deserve to be disliked (p40s, 41s), but he also derives the obviously false thesis that people generally exaggerate the chance that good things will happen to them and to underestimate dangers (p50s). Many do have that tendency, but many have the opposite one, and some keep an even keel. There is much more spread in this matter than in beliefs about whether one deserves to be liked or disliked; so there is something wrong with how Spinoza is using p25, quite apart from what is wrong with his route *to* it.

2. Two doctrinal threads running through these demonstrations are worth following, however. They are a pair of theories about how our emotions depend (i) on meaningless coincidences and (ii) on the emotions we perceive others as having. Of these, (i) has no deductive progeny after Part 3, but (ii) is used a certain amount in Part 4. Apart from their subsequent uses, however, they serve to intensify Spinoza's warning that

25. This claim is made, and this whole aspect of Spinoza astringently discussed, in H. M. Gardiner *et al.*, *Feeling and Emotion: a History of Theories* (New York, 1937), at pp. 192–204.

affects make one vulnerable—apt to be 'driven about in many ways by external causes', and 'under the control not of oneself but of fortune'. They are presumably meant to linger in the reader's memory, darkening one side of the subsequent contrast between affects and reason. I shall examine these two doctrines in turn.

3. The first of them stems from p15 which says that anything may come, through chance associations in the mind of a particular person, to be the cause in him of any emotion you like. Spinoza puts this by saying that a thing may be a 'cause *per accidens*' rather than a 'cause *per se*' of an emotion, and that wording is dangerous. But the general idea is clear enough: it is that I may find a thing pleasant or unpleasant just because I previously experienced it while I was up or down—for example, loving apples above all fruit because I was happy on my uncle's apple farm in the 1930s. Spinoza says that this is why 'we love and hate certain things from no cause which is known to us' (p15cs), though he does not explain why I am more apt to know what caused my emotion if it had a 'cause *per se*' than if it had a 'cause *per accidens*'. Cognitive notions are present all through Part 3 in a sadly undigested form.

From this doctrine Spinoza also infers that an emotion can be evoked by something which merely resembles its usual object (p16,17), and that hope and fright are at the mercy of coincidence (p50). And there are conclusions about jealousy (p35), nostalgia (p36) and xenophobia (p46). All of this reinforces his theme of the turbulence, unpredictability, and waywardness of the emotions, and thus strengthens his case for saying that the wise person will opt out of the life of the emotions altogether.

4. Spinoza labours mightily to demonstrate p15. It is all rather a jumble, which is a pity because a much simpler and more cogent inferential route was open to him. I shall explain this briefly.

We start back at 2p18: 'If a human body has once been affected by two or more bodies at the same time, then afterwards when the mind imagines one of them it will immediately recollect the others also.' Spinoza's demonstration of this is weak: it cannot be extracted from the skimpy premises he provides. Still, something like 2p18 is apparently true, so let us concede it to Spinoza without fussing over its provenance.[26] It is in fact a version of that 'association of ideas' doctrine which was a commonplace in the seventeenth century and thereafter, was prominent in Locke's philosophy and pivotal in Hume's. Spinoza uses it a lot. He gets from it a thesis about association of imaginings in 2p18s and uses it in his theory of general terms (2p40s1), in relating imagination to contingency and to

---

26. He does better in the *Theological-Political Treatise* at III/58/3, where he says that it 'necessarily follows from human nature'.

time (2p44c1s, 3p11s, 4p13), and in devising techniques for achieving greater mental freedom (5p10s,12,13).[27]

And then there is the use of 2p18 to demonstrate 3p14 and, through that, 3p15. The trouble here is that 2p18 links imaginings with imaginings, 3p14 links affects with affects, and 3p15d tries to link affects with imaginings, and there is no legitimate bridge across either gap. Spinoza uses illegitimate ones: they are complex and hard to describe, and I shan't give the details. It is clear what he ought to have done instead. Whatever case he could make for the 2p18 thesis about links between *imaginings* would equally support a more general thesis about links between *states* of all kinds—imaginings being one species of state. That would be a premiss from which both 2p18 and 3p14 could be inferred, with none of the twisting and straining Spinoza goes through trying to derive 3p14 from 2p18. And he could also directly infer 3p15—if *states* are linked with *states*, then *affects* are linked with *imaginings*, since they are both species of states. That would have saved him from having to introduce the concept of a neutral affect—one which 'neither increases nor diminishes the power of acting'—just so as to have a so-called 'affect' which would behave like an imagining! It would also, incidentally, put 3p14 out of business, since its only use is in 3p15d.

Spinoza's handling of these propositions is powerful evidence of his being good at smelling out genuine relevances and bad at putting them into proper logical form. It does not take a highly skilled logician to see that 3p15 and 2p18 should have a common source, rather than one's being derived from the other.

5. The other doctrinal thread I mentioned in .2 above stems from the thesis (p27) that if I perceive someone else to be in a certain emotional state, I shall tend to acquire it myself. (This is said only for the case where I do not already have some affect towards the person: if I hate him already, then perception of his pleasure will be unpleasant, and so on.) This is a cooler and more clinical version of the thesis on which Hume founded his moral psychology, namely, that people are linked by a universal, basic, instinctive tendency towards sympathy for one another's joys and sorrows.

Spinoza infers from it that we try to do what pleases other people (p29), that everyone tries to make others love what he loves (p31c), that we hate people who hate us without cause (p40), that we are depressed by ingratitude (p42), that the natural response to congratulation is self-congratulation (p53c); and some others. The demonstrations are of uneven quality, and I shan't discuss them.

6. The doctrine about imitation of affects concerns how people respond to the emotions of other people. It is time for us to ask: How does the

27. I omit 5p1 and its progeny, since the appeal to 2p18 in 5p1d is idle.

concept of a person, or a human being, work its way into Part 3? Thirty-eight of its propositions are fairly explicitly about human beings, and yet Spinoza has implied that the concept *man* does not belong in basic metaphysics or serious science (see §11.3). He needs some way of introducing it cleanly at a less basic level.

He has two ways. Some of what he says about humans is mediated by special premises such as that a human being is finite, falls under two attributes, is richly sensitive to the environment, and so on. These broad facts are introduced as 'axioms' in Part 2; they generate some simple theory of humanity in 2p10–13, whence they flow into the body of the work—aided by some avowedly speculative 'postulates' about human anatomy and physiology just before 2p14, and some more after 3d3. Spinoza presumably thinks that those raw materials are safe enough, even if the concept of humanity is a fuzzy one. His other way of getting humans into the picture is to assert something about all things, or all individuals, and then apply it to humans as a special case—a clearly valid procedure, however unsatisfactory the concept of humanity may be. An example of this is the doctrine of human egoism, which follows from the p6 doctrine of thing-egoism.

Now, the theory of the imitation of affects brings in humanity in the latter kind of way. Spinoza argues that *people* imitate the affects of *other people* because *individuals* imitate the affects of *other individuals which are like them*. Spinoza's entire interpersonal morality is based on an interpersonal psychology in which the basic thought is not 'that individual is human'—with 'human' naming some natural kind—but rather 'that individual is like me'. Because similarity is a matter of degree, Spinoza can calmly handle borderline cases, allowing for creatures to which we would react in *almost* the typical interpersonal way. He would be equally imperturbable about the borderlines of his Part 4 morality of interpersonal conduct—a body of doctrine contrasting vividly with Leibniz's view about the proper treatment of creatures which neither clearly are nor clearly are not human.[28] Leibniz says that it depends on whether the creature has a rational soul—a question with a determinate though unknown answer. The moral and metaphysical chasm between the two philosophers is nowhere wider than here. Ultimately, it reflects a deep difference in their world pictures; but the immediate source is the difference between a cliff and a gentle slope, between Leibniz's 'It has a rational soul' and Spinoza's 'It is like me'.

This use by Spinoza of the concept of similarity is a brilliant metaphysical *tour de force*. It respects his continuing demand for abstractness and depth; and, without conceding metaphysical importance to mankind as such, it provides a basis for a humanistic morality centering on how people relate to people.

28. *New Essays*, pp. 311, 320.

7. That is praise for Spinoza's strategy. Tactically he does less well, because here as elsewhere he is too sparing with detail. He says nothing about how much similarity is needed to bring his theory into play. For all he says to the contrary, I might be greatly saddened by the perceived sadness of any vertebrate, or I might be almost untouched by the emotions of any but middle-aged, white, male philosophers. Spinoza wants a doctrine of the emotional brotherhood of *all mankind*; but nothing in his theory secures that result, or even rules out either of the absurd extremes.

One might hope that some light would be shed on this by the way similarity works in the demonstration of the doctrine. Unfortunately, it doesn't work. The doctrine of the imitation of affects, like so much of the Part 3 psychology, is not well demonstrated. It says: 'If we imagine a thing like us, towards which we have had no affect, to be affected with some affect, we are thereby affected with a like affect.' (p27) Here first is a simplified version of Spinoza's demonstration. When I imagine your body, e.g., by seeing it, my state 'involves' the nature of your body as well as of mine. So if yours is in state A then so is mine, and if A is an affect then I will have it too.

That misrepresents what is plausible in Spinoza's account of sense-perception, i.e., of what I call ideas 'indirectly of' things. Granted that if I see you my state to some extent 'involves' yours, that means only that my state depends on yours, not that they are alike (see §37.5). The argument confuses representation with imitation.[29]

That is not the whole argument, however. If it were, Spinoza would have to conclude that the imitation of affects holds between lizard and elephant, as well as between man and man. Here is all of his argument, streamlined a little but exactly following the text in all essentials:

My image of x is a state of my body, the idea of which (by 2p16) involves the nature of my body and at the same time the present nature of x. So *if the nature of x is like the nature of my body*, then the idea of x when I imagine it will involve a state of my body like the state of x. (p27d), adapted)

The clause I have italicized is needed to block the inference that lizards will pity elephants. Does it also help to rescue the argument from my criticism? I cannot see that it does. When I see a man I am more like the thing I see than when I see an ostrich; but it does not follow, and is not true, that my perceptual intake of the man's detailed features involves my becoming like him in those further respects. All the italicized clause achieves is letting Spinoza escape from 'Perceptual representation is always imitation' to 'Between individuals which are sufficiently alike to begin with, perceptual representation is always imitation'. It is still quite

---

29. As Broad points out in his fine diagnosis in *Five Types of Ethical Theory*, pp. 37f.

wrong, as well as conflicting with Spinoza's repeated assertions that these 'imaginings' *cause* the affects: if p27d were sound, the imagining would *be* the affect.

8. Incidentally, p27 is the source of the entire interpersonal element in Part 3, that is, of the eighteen propositions about how people relate to people. (I exclude p39, since its 'He who hates someone . . . ' could in theory be 'He who hates something . . . ' .) Of the interpersonal doctrines in Part 4, three follow from interthing premisses without help from 3p27, while the considerable remainder, starting at 4p34, lie in the deductive progeny of 3p27.[30] In Part 5, the only proposition descended from 3p27 is 5p20, which is indeed the only thing Part 5 says about relations amongst people.

§65. *Strength of emotions*

1. Spinoza's psychology of the affects runs on into Part 4, in which p2–4 assert that men are vulnerable to the universe and infinitely weaker than it, and p5–18 present a body of doctrine about the strength of the affects. It is only in 4p18s that Spinoza announces that he has completed his account of 'the causes of man's weakness and inconstancy' and is turning to the task of 'showing what reason prescribes'. His use of value judgments—their content being 'what reason prescribes'—will be my topic in chapter 12. But the preceding propositions can fitly be handled here.

This material is fairly smoothly continuous with Part 3, except in attributing strength, force and intensity to the affects. In Part 3 those terms are not used, but we do hear about size of the affects: one affect is said to be greater than another, or greater than it would have been if. . . . We are not told what it means for an affect to be large or small, and the propositions in which the concept of affect size occurs don't increase our grasp of it. Still, some of the demonstrations indicate that the size of a *pleasure* or *unpleasure* is the amount of change in level of vitality that it involves, though at the end of p51s Spinoza implies that the 'violence' of the change comes into it also. What is it for a *desire* to be large or small? That depends on whether we understand 'desire' teleologically or as Spinozist appetite (see §52), but I shall not pursue the question since the answer will not significantly affect our dealings with the text.

In Part 4 there is little about the size of affects, but much about their strength, force, intensity—these terms being synonymous for Spinoza. The concept they express is not that of size: it concerns the power of an affect, not the distance one travels in the course of it. In Part 4, indeed, he seems to think of affects themselves as pressures rather than as actual

---

30. I do not count 4p57—the proud man loves 'parasites or flatterers'—as interpersonal, because the demonstration of it goes through just as well if the fawning hangers-on are domestic dogs, say.

changes. When one affect is 'restrained' by an equal and opposite one, no change occurs but there are two affects. If these affects were upward or downward movements, they would cancel out.[31]

2. Spinoza's concept of affect strength grows out of the concept of causal power, which is used in Part 4's striking axiom: 'There is no particular thing in Nature than which there is not another more powerful. Given any one, there is always another more powerful by which the first can be destroyed.' This is fully employed only in 4p3d, in which it is inferred that each person is infinitely weaker than the universe. (That *nearly* follows. There is a small gap between premiss and conclusion, for it could be that x's strength is 1.1 times mine, that y's is 1.01 times x's, that z's is 1.001 times y's, and so on to infinity, with nothing being infinitely stronger than I am.) The trio 4p2,3,4 reminds us of what the odds are— that you cannot get your life on an even keel by becoming strong enough to withstand the buffeting of the rest of Nature.

That is about causal power generally. Affect strength enters at p5, which says that what defines the 'force and growth of any passion' is 'the power of the external cause compared with our own'. The demonstration of this reaches back to Part 2 propositions asserting that when someone is acted on from the outside he is in a state which reflects the outside causes as well as his own nature. All I can get from this demonstration is the picture it offers of a passive affect as the resultant of the universe's push one way and the person's push the other. I cannot turn this into something literally intelligible, even on generous Spinozistic assumptions.

Still, that is the picture Spinoza is working with, and it does imply that we can measure the strength of an affect by comparing one causal input with the other. Also, when combined with the p3 thesis that each person is infinitely outgunned by the universe, it yields the memorable conclusion that 'The force of any passion or affect can surpass the other actions or power of a man, so that the affect stubbornly clings to the man' (p6). This has no deductive progeny worth mentioning. It is another of those propositions which are primarily intended to lodge in the memory and heighten Spinoza's drama about the options confronting us. Notice, incidentally, his brazen phrase 'any passion or affect': he is well launched on his campaign of representing affects as all passive, so as to make the affect/reason line coincide with the passive/active line.

3. Affect strength is also treated in 4p9–13, each of which relates the strength or intensity of an affect to something cognitive: my affect is stronger if I perceive its cause as present than if I do not (p9); my affect towards x is more intense if I think x lies in the near future or past than

31. Admittedly, Spinoza uses affect size in 5p5 and affect power in 5p6d,7, and in that context he seems to equate the two. But that is a mistake on his part, connected with his mistaken attempt to derive 5p5 from 3p49.

if I think it is remote in time (p10), and if I imagine it as necessary than if I do not (p11); if I know that x does not exist now, my affect towards it is less intense if I take x to be merely contingent than if I take it to be not inevitable (p12) or to lie in the real past (p13).

In those propositions the concept of affect strength is somehow extracted from the materials of Part 2, but none of the demonstrations is satisfactory. Consider 4p9d, for example. Spinoza has said in 2p17 that if x causes me to imagine it, and then absents itself without its departure affecting me, I shall go on imagining it as present. In 4p9d this is taken to imply that while I haven't registered x's departure my imagining of it 'is more intense' than if I did know it was absent; but 2p17 does not contain the concept of intensity or anything like it.

Of the other four 'affect strength' propositions, three are derived from 4p9 and inherit its frailty. The exception is 4p12 which finds other broken reeds on which to rest its weight.

§66. *Cognition of good and bad*

1. In 4p8,14–17 Spinoza presents a body of doctrine about what he calls 'cognition of good and bad'—a phrase which occurs only three more times in the whole work.[32] Its main thesis is that knowledge or beliefs about good and bad are not especially helpful in controlling one's affects.

In this area Spinoza is using 'good' and 'bad' in what he thinks are the plain man's senses of the terms, rather than in the revised senses he has proposed in 4 Preface. His real topic here is so-called thoughts of so-called good and bad, what passes for moral knowledge in cafés and nurseries and bedrooms, as condescendingly described in 1 Appendix, 3p39s, and 4 Preface. His central point is that the unreformed value judgments of the man in the street are made under no guidance but that of the feelings and attitudes of the speaker. He writes:

By good here I understand every kind of pleasure and whatever leads to it, and by bad every kind of unpleasure. For we have shown in 3p9s that we desire nothing because we judge it to be good, but on the contrary we call it good because we desire it. So each one, from his own affect, judges or evaluates what is good and what is bad. (3p39s, quoted with omissions)

This reflects the problem about how desire relates to the other two basic kinds of affect, but never mind that. The main point is clear enough: the plain man's judgments about good and bad are not made under the discipline of facts about objective value, but only under the influence of his feelings.

2. When he comes to 4p8, however, Spinoza has flattened the plain man's value judgments even further: 'The cognition of good and bad is

---

32. They are 4p19d, 4p62s at 257/28, and a biblical reference in 4p68s at 261/30.

nothing but an affect of pleasure or unpleasure, insofar as we are conscious of it.'[33] This could mean either that an unreformed value judgment expresses one's knowledge that one is in a pleasant or unpleasant state, or that such a value 'judgment' really consists in nothing more than conscious pleasure or unpleasure—a state of wellbeing or illbeing accompanied by a glow or gloom of consciousness, whatever that might be. In p8d the former reading is encouraged, but Spinoza's subsequent uses of p8 strongly suggest the latter reading, according to which the phrase 'cognition of good and bad' is being used ironically for something with no cognitive content.

On either reading, I think he is less than fair to ordinary so-called moral knowledge. Even if it is speaker relative, not knowledge of objective external facts, perhaps not knowledge at all, it is still not as transitory, unprincipled and vulnerable to the whims of the moment as Spinoza makes it out to be.

With the help of this account of what 'cognition of good and bad' really is, Spinoza easily shows that desires arising from such cognition can be vanquished by other desires in various ways: for example, the present has a stronger grip on our affects than the future (p9c), and that remains true even if an affect relating to the future 'arises from a true cognition of good and bad' (p16). In brief, our thoughts about good and bad have no special privilege in our emotional life.

This part of the *Ethics* is presumably aimed at Descartes, perhaps among others. Descartes says:

Some people . . . never let their will fight with its own weapons, but only with ones which some passions provide as a defence against other passions. What I call its own weapons are firm and determinate judgments concerning the knowledge of good and bad, with which the will has resolved to regulate the actions of its life.[34]

In p8 Spinoza is replying that that is a false antithesis, and that the so-called 'knowledge of good and bad', far from standing over against our emotional life, is part of it: if it does ever help to restrain an affect, that will be an instance of that 'passion against passion' which Descartes deplores.

3. Spinoza's attack on the quoted Cartesian position is further developed in p14–17, which rely on p8. A striking feature of the extended attack is that Spinoza moves from 'cognition' in p8 to *true* cognition' in the other four propositions. This suggests that he really does see ordinary value judgments as having cognitive content, and as being sometimes false. But I doubt that. In three of the four the qualification 'true' is idle: something is asserted of every affect, and thus of every cognition of good and bad, and

33. I shall not explore the troubles in the demonstration of this, except to remark that it invokes ideas of ideas—a rare event.

34. Descartes, *Passions of the Soul* §48.

thus *a fortiori* of every 'true cognition of good and bad'—whatever that might mean.

The occurrence of 'true' in p14 is not idle—it works hard. But it presupposes no view about what it would be for a 'cognition of good and bad' to be true. The chief premiss in p14d is p1, which says that the truth as such has no corrective power on the mind: when you tell me something surprising, its effect on me depends purely on whether I believe it and not on whether it is true. This is right, and important, though I don't endorse Spinoza's derivation of it from his doctrine that error is a sort of ignorance. From 4p1 it theoretically follows that the sheer truth of a 'true cognition of good and bad' will not strengthen its grip on its owner's emotions, but this is hardly an interesting result when we have no idea of what it would mean for a 'cognition of good and bad' to be 'true'. It is odd that 4p1, which on any showing belongs in Part 2 and deserves prominence there, should be withheld until Part 4 and then used only to add a verbal flourish (4p14) to the attack on Descartes, with neither it nor the flourish being heard from again.

4. We are not quite finished with p14. Here is the whole of it: 'No affect can be restrained by a true cognition of good and bad insofar as it is true, but only insofar as it is considered as an affect.' I have not yet attended to the last part of this. It is based on p7: 'An affect cannot be restrained or taken away except by an affect opposite to and stronger than [it].' That is a further shaft aimed at Descartes. He said that misguided people fight their passions with passions, and Spinoza replies that there is no other way to win.

I cannot reconcile that with Spinoza's view that emotions can be restrained through cognitive therapy. See for example 3p48,49, and 5p3, and also this: 'If we separate an emotion or affect from the thought of an external cause . . . , then the love or hate towards the external cause is destroyed, as are all the vacillations of mind arising from these affects.' (5p2) In his contemptuous rejection of Descartes's kind of moralizing control over the emotions, Spinoza has let himself be swept on into rejecting every use of cognitive levers to shift emotions.

He is not carried there by his own doctrines, for 4p7d is weak. The heart of it concerns affects considered as physical. Such an affect, the argument says, 'can be neither restrained nor removed except by a corporeal cause (by 2p6), which affects the body with a state opposite to it (by 3p5) and stronger than it (by 4a)'. All Spinoza is entitled to mean by this is that the affect can be quelled only by a bodily happening which is 'opposite' to it in the sense of being able to quell it; but he quietly turns 'opposite state [*affectio*]' in the demonstration into 'opposite affect [*affectus*]' in the conclusion, thus concluding that an uprush can be quelled only by a downrush and conversely.

5. I don't know why it is that Spinoza, in 4p7d and again in p7c, carefully lets the physical side of the affect carry the argument, while the mental side tags along. He did not need to. Since the argument deals purely in the notions of 'power' and 'direction of change', which are equally applicable under both attributes, it could have been stated mentalistically. Most of what we can say about mental items concerns their (indirect) representative features, which do not map onto anything physical; but we can also describe them in terms of strength of feeling and (un)pleasantness of feeling—or, digging below the latter, in terms of changing levels of mental health—and that is enough for p7d,c.

But much of Part 3 does speak of affects in terms of their causation by ideas (indirectly) of things. Before bringing this chapter to a close, I want to look back at that material in the light of the thesis that the (indirect) representative features of ideas do not contribute to their causal powers—'the Thesis', for short. Although Spinoza does not assert it, and probably was not explicitly aware of it, he is deeply committed to the Thesis, and we should consider how much harm is done to various parts of the *Ethics* by adding it to what is already there.

I have suggested that Spinoza's subliminal awareness of it may explain his speaking of affects as 'arising from' rather than outright 'caused by' ideas; but that is just in the definitions. What about the demonstrative fabric of Part 3? Getting a full answer to that is a research project which I have not carried out, but I can answer the question for the two bits of argument I have attended to separately.

6. The case for 3p15 is a muddled affair, as I pointed out in §64.4, but we can generalize it into this: by 2p18d, if an individual is in a pair of states at the same time, then if it later comes to be in one of them it will tend also to be in the other; from which it follows that if someone is in a certain imaginative state x while also having an affect y, then when he is later in x he will tend also to have y. That argument says nothing about the (indirect) representative features of ideas, and so it can be regarded as sternly causal without threat from the Thesis that such features are causally impotent.

But that safety was achieved by departing a little from Spinoza's own position. Suppose that I have affect y while looking at Paul, and that my seeing of Paul involves my being in intrinsic state x. The argument I have given implies that I shall tend to have y when I am next *in state x*; but Spinoza thinks, and says explicitly in 3p15cd, that I shall tend to have y when I am next *seeing Paul*. He thus assumes that different 'imaginings' of a single thing involve intrinsic states which are alike enough to bring the 'association of states' thesis into effect; that assumption visibly comes into play in 2p18d, which is the source of 3p15. Still, it is not a large assumption, and it does not clash with the Thesis. Analogously, reverting to an example I used in §51.5, even if the causal powers of a piece of paper owe nothing to its being a map of Sussex, it *could* be the case that maps of Sussex are so intrinsically alike that some kinds of causal interaction will have the same upshot with all of them.

7. The doctrine about imitation of affects depends on the idea that 'imagining' involves imitation, i.e., that when I observe your misery I am miserable. This is false, but it does not conflict with the Thesis, since it is not causal. It does not say that my seeing your misery causes misery in me, but rather that it is misery in me.

8. If Spinoza somehow made room for the view that a cause is a concrete item—an object or event—which can have causally irrelevant features (see §63.7), then I think his whole Part 3 project would be safe from any serious damage at the hands of the Thesis. Even if the concept 'belief that someone has harmed me' is not reducible to any that belong in basic mental science, an unpleasant state of my mind may nevertheless be caused by a belief that someone has harmed me, and I might have reason to think that this was so. There might even be fairly reliable generalizations about what kinds of beliefs cause what kinds of feelings. But they could only be inductively established, and Spinoza ought to admit this, and to concede that any particular identification of an emotion—'He feels bad because he believes that P'—should be somewhat tentative. However confident he is about his theory of emotions, he should be cautious about which human episodes, if any, are emotions.

12 *Value*

§67. *The common man's evaluations*

1. Spinoza is not an admirer of the way in which the common man arrives at value judgments. He condescends, he distances himself:

After men persuaded themselves that everything which happens, happens on their account, they had to judge that what is most important in each thing is what is most useful to them, and to rate as most excellent all those things by which they were most pleased. Hence they had to form these notions, by which they explained natural things: *good, bad, order, confusion, warm, cold, beauty, ugliness*. And because they think themselves free, these notions have arisen: *praise* and *blame, sin* and *merit*. (1 Appendix at 81/25)

The first list falls into four pairs of opposites. What they have in common, in Spinoza's view, is being speaker relative: I call something confused if I cannot grasp it, warm if it affects my body in a certain way, and so on. We are concerned only with the first pair, good and bad.

Good and bad can occur in the foundations of a system of further moral concepts. Consider:

    (1) The occurrence of x would be a good thing to happen.
    (2) I ought to try to bring about x.
    (3) I ought to have tried to bring about x.
    (4) I am to blame for not having tried to bring about x.

Each kind of judgment presupposes the ones above it. We could not blame people unless we had views about what they ought to have done; that depends on sometimes judging what a person ought to do, which in turn requires that we sometimes distinguish good from bad results of actions. But the converse does not hold: one could go any distance down the list and then stop.

Spinoza's second list—'praise and blame, sin and merit'—pertains to my item (4). He rejects (4), partly because he thinks it presupposes a belief in radical freedom, i.e., the falsity of determinism. And he ignores (3), presumably because he thinks that a rational person always looks ahead. But he is willing to make judgments of kinds (1) and (2), forward-looking ones about the goodness of states of affairs and about what we ought to do.

2. These are not in conflict with determinism: the opinion that what you do is wholly causally determined need not discourage me from having and voicing opinions about what you ought to do—rather the contrary. Objection: 'If my utterances merely *cause* you to behave differently, then they are not serving as moral principles which give you *reasons* for altering how you behave.' That is a false antithesis if the operation of reasons on the will is a special case of causation, as I think it is. New objection: 'If determinism is true then when we engage in practical deliberation we must be essentially deluded: we think that the question of what we are going to do is still radically open, and that our deliberation will close it; but determinism implies that it is closed already, because the world is already in a state which makes only one outcome causally possible.' Do plain thoughtful people think that when they are deliberating, the question of what they will do is in no sense closed? That is a rather fancy opinion to attribute to someone who is not philosophising about determinism. We can perhaps credit the plain man with a confidence that in deliberating he is tackling questions about his own future conduct in the right way, indeed the only possible way. But he is right about that, and is not thereby committed to denying determinism. Determinism does not imply, as some philosophers seem to have thought it does, that if I knew enough I could confront every question about my own future as a predictor rather than as a deliberating agent.[1]

That is enough about that. In working our way into Spinoza's moral philosophy, we need not keep remembering that he is a determinist. The thesis that determinism can be combined with morality has been held by many and is true; and although Spinoza relied on its truth, he contributed nothing directly to the case in its favour. So let the determinism fade into the background.

3. Spinoza holds that when common people call things good or bad, they go by how they feel and what they want: they 'call the nature of a thing good or bad as they are affected by it' (1 Appendix at 82/20). This theme is developed at length in 1 Appendix and 3p39s; I have treated it in §2.1, and need not go through that again. At present, what matters is Spinoza's view that ordinary untutored value judgments are unprincipled, undisciplined, erratic—guided by how the speaker feels and what he wants at the moment of speaking.

Ironically, this instability in value judgments is accompanied by the belief that there are objective value properties—that goodness and badness are 'chief attributes of things'. Spinoza thinks they are not. He is sure that no sense attaches to the idea of any natural item's being in itself bad or wrong: this is his rejection of pathology of Nature, which is expressed also in his view that no actual belief can be in itself false (see §41.1). Why

1. For a defence of that see J. Bennett, *Kant's Dialectic* (Cambridge, 1974), §§68-9.

doesn't the belief in objective value properties lead to value judgments which are stable and regular to the point of being ossified? Spinoza has an answer to that, but I shall not go into it now.

4. In 4 Preface Spinoza offers 'a few words on perfection and imperfection, good and bad', and now a new emphasis enters his account of the plain man's value judgments.

He says that the 'first' meanings of 'perfect' and 'imperfect' are nonevaluative, for they primarily mean 'finished' and 'unfinished'. (The Latin words do have those meanings as well as evaluative ones.) In those senses they are applicable only to artifacts: to call something (im)perfect is to relate it to the mind of its maker, saying that he has (not) completed his project. But, says Spinoza, 'men began to form universal ideas' on the basis of which they would judge artifacts to be (im)perfect without knowing what the maker intended, judging of (im)perfection on the basis of how the things related to the speaker's view about what such kinds of things ought to be like. Thus judgments about (in)completeness were transmuted into value judgments. And the same mechanism seems to be at work, Spinoza says, when value judgments are passed on things 'which have not been made by human hand':

Men commonly form universal ideas of natural things as much as they do of artificial ones. They regard these universal ideas as models of things, and believe that Nature (which they think does nothing except for the sake of some end) sets them before itself and looks to them as models. So when they see something happen in Nature which does not agree with the model they have conceived of this kind of thing, they believe that Nature itself has failed or erred, and left the thing imperfect. (4 Preface at 206/11)

I shall state in my own way what I take to be Spinoza's analysis of, and objection to, the procedure described in that passage.

If universal ideas are to serve as the basis for value judgments, some subset of them must do this work for us. Lacking a privileged subset, we shall have too many judgments: a hydrocephalic baby is good (i.e., a good specimen of a hydrocephalic baby), a healthy baby is bad (i.e., a bad specimen of a sick baby). With the aid of a privileged subset of what we may, following Spinoza, call 'models', we can be selective in our value judgments. For although any particular exactly fits many universal ideas, it may not exactly fit any model, and so we have a working notion of degree of (im)perfection.

Spinoza protests that there is no objective basis for selecting universal ideas to serve as models. We might hope to select on the principle: Idea I is a model for judging the perfection of x if and only if Nature intends that x should conform to I. But Nature intends nothing.

This is quite independent of the 2p40s1 thesis that most of our universal notions are too fuzzy to carve up reality at its joints (see §11.2). Even if they were sharp and deep, they still could not generate value judgments because they are too numerous, and we have no sound way of selecting from among them.

The thesis that our value judgments are based on models is not in conflict with the earlier thesis that they are guided by our feelings and desires. Rather, the two are aspects of a single unified account, the unifying factor being the view that our feelings and desires guide our value judgments *by* guiding our selection of models. Spinoza says this in a typically compressed way:

> But after men came to form universal ideas, and devise models of houses, buildings, towers etc., and to prefer some models of things to others, it came about that each called perfect what he saw agreed with the universal idea he had formed of this kind of thing ... etc. (4 Preface at 206/2)

The crucial phrase is 'prefer some models to others': we base our value judgments on our own personal attitudes, by basing them on models which are selected according to our likes and dislikes. The procedure starts with models of artifacts such as houses, but we extend it to the selection of models of unartificial objects, Spinoza says. And we tell ourselves that our procedure is objective because our chosen models represent Nature's intentions: the line around what we like coincides with the line around what Nature intends, we think, because everything is intended by Nature for our benefit.

5. After Spinoza has presented most of his account of common value judgments in Parts 1 and 3, why does he return to the topic in Part 4 and add the extra bit about models? I shan't be in a position to explain this properly until I reach §68.4.

§68. *Spinoza's revisions of value concepts*

1. In 4d1,2 Spinoza offers new, improved senses for 'good' and 'bad', saying that he will take good to be 'what we certainly know to be useful to us' and bad to be 'what we certainly know prevents us from being masters of some good'.[2] What is the force of these definitions? How will our value judgments alter if we move from being 'ignorant' people as described in 1 Appendix and 3p39s to judging in accordance with 4d1,2?

Well, our judgments will still be speaker relative. The definitions speak of what is useful 'to us', suggesting a notion of collective welfare; that would make value judgments relative not to the judger but to his community or his species. That is where Spinoza is heading, but not by definition: starting at 4p29 he will *argue* that what is good for one is good

---

2. They are the first two future-tense definitions ('By good I shall understand . . . '). But that is not strong evidence of revisionary intent, since 4d5,6 are also future-tense.

for others—that is a defended theorem and not an element in the revised meaning of 'good'. So speaker relativity is still with us.

But we now have it in a different way, for under the revision my value judgments straightforwardly *are* statements about how things relate to my welfare: speaker relativity is not now a hidden guiding force, but rather a consciously meant propositional content. Also, my value judgments will no longer be encrusted with metaphysical errors about objective value properties or divine or cosmic purpose.

I think Spinoza intends his revision to effect those benefits, but they are not all. He also thinks that the reformed Spinozist evaluator will differ from the ignorant plain man not only in the conceptual health of his mind when he makes value judgments, but also in what value judgments he makes.

2. One source of this further difference comes from the contrast between the plain man's momentary feelings and desires and the Spinozistic man's prudent, foresighted, informed opinions about what will serve his interests. Spinoza expresses this, in an unusual formulation which he seems to be using for special emphasis, when he derives from the 4d1,2 way of thinking the demand 'that everyone love himself, seek what is useful to him, what is really useful, and want whatever really leads a man to greater perfection' (4p18s at 222/18). The repeated 'really' here stands in contrast to the plain man's unacknowledged 'apparently'.

This same emphasis is meant to be carried by the inclusion of 'what we certainly know' in the definitions of good and bad. This is clumsily done: it ought to mean that for something to count as good it must not only be advantageous to us but must be certainly known to be so; but Spinoza never uses it like that. His intent seems to be merely to emphasize that under his revision the question of whether x is good for y is objective, factual, and far-reaching—a possible subject for knowledge, ignorance, or error—whereas the value judgments of the man in the street are answerable only to the speaker's evanescent feelings and momentary impressions of where his interests lie. Relativity to a person at a time has been replaced by relativity to a person. Or so I understand Spinoza's position. This does not sit happily with his saying, in the context of unrevised value concepts, that 'By good here I mean every kind of pleasure and whatever leads to it' (3p39s). I suppose that the phrase 'whatever leads to it' acknowledges that the common man does exercise some foresight, giving thought to his long-term welfare as he conceives it; the miser, for example, thinks about how to become richer. But Spinoza sees the plain man as not prudent *enough*, as well as having wrong views about what his welfare consists in.

If unreformed value judgments are hasty and imprudent, why does Spinoza say that plain men have called good 'whatever conduces to health'? The answer is that he is not using 'health' to stand for long-term welfare. Here is how he uses it a few sentences later:

> They call the nature of a thing good or bad, sound or rotten and corrupt, as they are affected by it. For example, if the motion the nerves receive from objects presented through the eyes is conducive to health, the objects by which it is caused are called beautiful; those which cause a contrary motion are called ugly. (1 Appendix at 82/20)

It is pretty clear that 'health' here refers only to the physical counterpart of a momentary pleasure.

3. Suppose that I judge something to be good, meaning that it really is conducive to my health and survival (here and always I use 'health' to refer to health in the long run). How might I have judged it differently if I were not guided by 4d1,2? There are two possible answers, each given by Spinoza. One forces him to change his position a little, since it clearly conflicts with his stance up to here in the *Ethics*; the other is a less obvious source of trouble, but the trouble it does involve is deeper and more serious.

(i) I might judge the good thing to be bad. Spinoza thinks that judgments based on present feelings and desires can take us in exactly the wrong direction. Some unpleasant states are not harmful, he now tells us, and some pleasant ones are not healthful; that is, in his revised terminology, there is good unpleasure and bad pleasure. I shall discuss this in §71.5–7.

(ii) I might judge the really good thing to be neither good nor bad. That sounds harmless: the common man judges and acts on the basis of less information than does the Spinozistically alert man, and so he sometimes judges a good or bad thing to be merely neutral, because he leaves out relevant facts about its long-term bearing on his true welfare. But really Spinoza has no room for any such contrast in his system: the contrast concerns the information in the light of which a person makes value judgments, and thus in the light of which a person acts (how value judgments relate to actions will be the topic of §70); and Spinoza has no account of what it is to act in the light of information or on the basis of beliefs.

His self-preservation doctrine ought to have been the thesis that everything I actively do is helpful to me, but we have seen him assume its teleological converse, that if something would be helpful to me I shall do it (see §57.4). Spinoza might be able to entitle himself to the teleological form of the doctrine through an open appeal to observed facts, together with—perhaps—something of one of the sorts discussed in §58. But no such rearrangements of his premises can entitle him to move not merely to 'If it would help him, he will do it' but further to 'If he thinks it would help him, he will do it'. Of course the teleological form of the self-preservation theory has been too strong from the outset: it is never true of any interesting individual that it does *whatever* would help it to survive. Some restrictions are needed, and surely they must include a move from 'what would help it' to 'what it thinks would help it' or the like. But this lacuna in Spinoza's account has never mattered as acutely as it does now, when he is advocating the pursuit of what we soberly and reliably, rather than impulsively and carelessly, think will help us. This is a choice within the framework of ' . . . what we think will help us . . . ' ; Spinoza writes as though he had already constructed that framework, but he hasn't.

He sometimes pretends to have done so, as when he says that 'We try to further the occurrence of whatever we imagine will lead to pleasure' (3p28), which has the teleological-cognitive form of 'If he thinks it would help him, he will do it'. Where does this come from? Well, the demonstration includes this: 'We try to imagine what we imagine to lead to pleasure (by 3p12)', but 3p12 is: 'The mind tries to imagine those things which increase or aid the body's power of acting.' Spinoza has without any warrant moved from 'If it would help him . . . ' to 'If he imagines it would help him . . . ' .

This trouble is part of the general failure to introduce the concepts of belief and desire in the right way, namely, as partners in a teleological account of the explanation of behaviour (see §39.4). That failure was encouraged by Spinoza's good insight that teleological explanations—'final causes'—are puzzling and prima facie objectionable; but it was a failure nevertheless. We have not finished reaping its bitter fruit, but I shall not pursue this theme further at present.

Let us now allow Spinoza his doctrine of egoism, construed teleologically and cognitively—not as explained or justified by his principles but as warranted by observation of human conduct. This will be in the spirit of his saying confidently that egoism is common knowledge (1 Appendix at 78/14). Even if we think that it is an overstatement, that does not remove all interest from a system of morality based on it. If we think it wrong to ask 'How can we have an acceptable morality when there are only egoistic motivations?', we can at least ask 'How much of an acceptable morality can we construct without having to appeal to altruistic motivations?' The latter is of great importance, given what most of us are like most of the time.

4. In §67 I discussed two strands in Spinoza's account of the common man's value judgments, (i) their basis in feelings and desires, and (ii) their use of 'models'. I sewed these together as well as I could, but remarked on the oddity of Spinoza's procedure in which (i) is the whole story until 4 Preface, when suddenly (ii) is thrust upon us. Now, the 4d1,2 revision of value concepts is a response to (i), and that is how I have handled it. It is now time to remark that Spinoza also offers a revisionary proposal aimed rather at (ii). After explaining how untutored people call things 'good' or 'bad' according to how they fit certain models which are not selected according to any objective criteria, Spinoza continues:

But we still must retain these words. For because we desire to form an idea of man, as a model of human nature which we may look to, it will be useful to us to retain these same words in the sense I have indicated. In what follows, therefore, I shall understand by good what we certainly know is a means by which we may approach nearer and nearer to the model of human nature which we set before ourselves. By bad, what we certainly know prevents us from becoming like that model. Next, we shall say that men are more perfect or imperfect to the extent that they approach more or less near to this model. (4 Preface at 208/14)

That is the last we hear of this 'model of human nature which we set before ourselves'. This passage must be a relic of a time when Spinoza planned to make the concept of a favoured model of mankind do some work for him in the body of Part 4.[3] That also solves the puzzle about why he tacks (ii) his 'model' account of common value judgments onto (i) his earlier 'feeling and desire' account. What we have here is a palimpsest, bearing traces of earlier stages in Spinoza's thought: he planned to put 'models' at the centre of everything, then changed his mind, but omitted some of the needed repairs. As for his two revisionary proposals, the one in 4 Preface and the one in 4d1,2: they are both cast in the future tense, and both speak of 'what we certainly know'; but they differ greatly in content, and it was careless of Spinoza not to see this and do something about it.

5. As well as failing to sort out his revisions for us, Spinoza also fails to hold onto the difference between revised and unrevised value notions. His account of the 'cognition of good and bad' rests on ordinary unrevised notions of good and bad. This is made clear by p8 and its progeny, in which a cognition of good or bad is said to be nothing but 'an affect of pleasure or unpleasure insofar as we are conscious of it' (see §66.2). Yet p8d invokes the revisionary d1,2—as though a definition in terms of 'what we certainly know to be useful to us' could imply that a so-called cognition of something as good is just a pleasurable affect! Perhaps Spinoza in speaking of the *so-called* cognition of *so-called* good and bad is muddled about how far he is using and how far merely talking about the common man's value notions.

But the trouble does not stop there. Throughout Part 4 Spinoza says many things about what is good and what bad, anchoring them sometimes in the revisionary d1,2 and sometimes in the unrevisionary p8, the distribution apparently being random. The philosophical fact is that three of the five invocations of p8 from p19d onwards are nonsense which become sense when construed as references to d1,2.[4]

3. He did take that approach in the *Emendation* §13 (II/8/17).

4. They are in the demonstrations of p19,29,30. The other two are the demonstrations of p63c,64. For a detailed discussion of 4p8, kinder than mine yet aware of the problems, see Frankena, 'Spinoza on the Knowledge of Good and Evil'.

6. I left the notions of perfection and imperfection dangling in §67.4; it is time to complete Spinoza's account of them in 4 Preface (207/18). Having described how ordinary people make judgments of (im)perfection on the shoddy basis of assumptions about what Nature intends, Spinoza describes a better way of using 'perfect' and 'imperfect'. He seems to imply that he is still describing what the common man does, but I think his intent is revisionary.

In 2d6 he has said 'By reality and perfection I understand the same thing', and now he is trying to explain and justify that. In the background is the notion of value judgments based on models. Spinoza says that judgments of (im)perfection are based on taking as a model 'the notion of being, which pertains to absolutely all individuals'. Because everything falls under *being*, it is not an arbitrarily chosen model: there could not be an actual thing which was not fit to be related to the idea of being, and so in calling something imperfect by this standard we are not, as it were, treating a duck as a poor specimen of a swan. But Spinoza needs it to be the case that although every thing falls under the concept of being, different things fall under it more or less completely. He thinks that that is all right:

We find that some individuals have more being or reality than others, and so we say that some are more perfect than others. And insofar as we attribute something to them which involves negation, like a limit, an end, lack of power etc., we call them imperfect, because they do not affect our mind as much as those we call perfect. (4 Preface at 207/27)

The crux of that is 'lack of power'. I think Spinoza is trying to tie 'perfect' to 'powerful' by tying each to 'real': that seems to be how 2d6 is used here and in 5p40d, its only two significant reappearances in the *Ethics*. In Spinoza's moral philosophy, fortunately, we need attend only to the equation of perfection with power: that is what does all the work, without any direct appeal to the underlying view that weak things are less real than strong things (which is presumably associated with Spinoza's view that contingent things are weaker than necessarily existing things; see 1p11d3). That is what we carry with us into Part 4, then—the idea that to call a thing 'perfect' is to speak of how powerful it is. Combining this with d1 we get the result that I should call a thing good if it is 'useful' to me, i.e., conducive to my survival and strength, i.e., apt to increase my own perfection. Thus, the revised use of 'perfect' fits well enough with the d1 revision in the use of 'good'.

7. What does Spinoza hope to achieve by the proposals embodied in d1,2? As mere declarations of how he will use value terms from then on, they do not give us any reason to follow suit while also still giving the words a role in guiding our conduct. Similarly with the definition of 'virtue': 'By virtue and power I mean the same thing.' (d8) Some of what Spinoza says about virtue amounts to a mere attempt to get the word used his way. In p20d, for example, he ties 'virtue' to 'power' through d8, links power with the pursuit of one's own survival, and concludes that the more persistently someone tries to stay in existence 'the more he is endowed with virtue'. Nothing is done here to give the word 'virtue' any evaluative force.

But in the bulk of Part 4 it is supposed to be an evaluative, action-guiding term, as are 'good' and 'bad'. If they are to have such a force, while also being used in conformity with d1,2,8, then arguments are needed; the definitions alone cannot do the job.

Really, there is just one argument, lurking below the surface of the transition from p21,22 to p24–28 (jumping over p23, which connects Spinoza's morality with his epistemology). Those seven propositions constitute a tightly packed and weighty cluster which argue, in effect, that since the only possible value system is egoism, the only rational value system is informed egoism. That implies that the rational man will pursue the things he could truthfully call 'good' in Spinoza's revised sense. That move from psychological necessity to value judgment can be seen in the scholium which heralds this segment of Part 4:

Since reason demands nothing contrary to Nature, it demands that everyone love himself, seek what is useful to him, what is really useful, want whatever really leads a man to greater perfection, and absolutely that everyone should try to stay in existence as far as he can. This, indeed, is as necessarily true as that the whole is greater than its part—see 3p4. (p18s at 222/17)[5]

The general line of thought is clear enough: egoism is necessary, so it is no use advocating any mode of life which is not egoistic; and all that is left is to set oneself and perhaps others to seek what is *really* useful, what *really* leads to greater perfection.

On the face of it, the argument is reasonable, given the premiss of egoism. But let us not forget that its reasonableness depends partly on construing the egoism as teleological and cognitive, i.e., as saying that necessarily a man will do what he thinks would promote his survival, and that Spinoza has laid no foundation at all for that.

8. Spinoza is trying to alter how we live. I see him as presenting a morality which *enjoins* us to be informed, to use our heads, to pursue what is really in our interests instead of going by momentary feelings or careless calculations. Although I have spoken of 'value judgments', he is concerned with good and bad only because of their bearing on what we ought to do. He usually words these moral injunctions as statements about what 'reason demands' or about what will be done by one who is 'led by reason', as here:

5. Just as in the causal sphere the possible is equated with the necessary, so in morality Spinoza equates the permissible with the mandatory. Compare this p18s passage with 4 Appendix 8.

We shall easily see what the difference is between a man who is led only by an affect, or by opinion, and one who is led by reason. For the former does those things he is most ignorant of, whereas the latter does only those things he knows to be the most important in life. (p66s, quoted with omissions)

There can be no doubt that this has an injunctive, moralising intent. What now has to be seen is the content of the morality which Spinoza offers us.

§69.   *The case for community of interest*

1. Spinoza's only moral premiss is individual egoism: the notion of good is that of what is good for, or conducive to the survival of, whoever is using the notion. Much of p29–60 draws conclusions from this, e.g., that pity is bad (p50) and humility is not a virtue (p53). Those two are natural enough, but Spinoza also draws some morals which we might not have expected. When he argues that we should try to secure for others the goods that we want for ourselves (p37), and should repay others' hatred with love (p46), he seems to be getting enormously conservative conclusions from a drastically radical premiss. How it is done?

Spinoza does it by arguing that the thoughtful egoist will be led by his egoism to care as much for the welfare of others as for his own. Other moralists have said as much, but usually by appealing to civil society: the egoist is coerced by the thought that if he is not cooperative the state will make him pay. Spinoza agrees that this can be effective, but says that it involves the restraint of anger, greed etc. 'by threats', whereas his argument shows how men can live 'by reason' (p37s2 at 238/13); and I suppose he also prefers arguing through abstract metaphysics to relying on the historical fact that men have invented governments and prisons.

2. The entire interpersonal morality of Part 4 flows from p30,31. Here, as in the interpersonal psychology, the key concept is that of an individual which is *like* another individual: my fellow man appears in the form of an individual with the same nature as myself. Here are the two crucial propositions:

No thing can be bad through what it has in common with our nature; but insofar as it is bad for us, it is contrary to us. (p30) Insofar as a thing agrees with our nature, it is necessarily good. (p31)

Putting these together: if a thing is bad for me, it must be unlike me; to the extent that a thing is like me, so far is it good for me. It will be easier to comment on the case for p30 if we first look at how Spinoza derives p31 from it. He argues that if p30 is true, then a thing which is like me must be either neutral or good for me; but if it were neutral with respect to my welfare it would be neutral with respect to its own, which is absurd (by 3p6, the self-preservation doctrine); so it must be good for me.

That argument assumes that if x and I are alike then x could be neutral for me only if it were neutral for itself. If that is all right, then here is a simple argument for p30: if x and I are alike, then if x were bad for me it would be bad for itself, which is absurd (by 3p4). Really, that *is* what happens in p30d, but Spinoza decorates it, making it hard to follow. I shall return to that in a moment.

In p31cd Spinoza argues for the converse of p31: a thing's dissimilarity makes it likely not to be useful to me. If x and I have different natures within the same shared attributes, then those natures are mutually 'contrary', so x's nature is contrary to mine and to what agrees with mine; so it is contrary to what, according to my value system, is good; but what is contrary to something good is bad. That last step equivocates with the term 'contrary', which at first meant 'dissimilar' and now means 'hostile' (compare 3p6d, discussed in §57.2). But this fiasco does not matter much, since Spinoza cannot have seriously believed that only what is like me can be good for me. Most of his appeals to p31c could be appeals to p31, and I shall ignore the corollary from now on.

3. The credentials of p31 must be examined, however, since it is the foundation of Spinoza's interpersonal morality. In arguing for p30,31 he is relying on something like this:

> To the extent that two things are qualitatively alike, the things which help (harm, are neutral with respect to) one of them are all and only the things which help (harm, are neutral with respect to) the other.

What leads Spinoza to this remarkable conclusion is the assumption that the relations ' . . . is helpful to . . . ' and ' . . . is harmful to . . . ' are between helping or harming items on the one hand and *natures* on the other. To be harmful to a thing is to relate in a certain way to its nature, to its totality of properties, to how it is; and so if two things have the same nature, you can't be harmful to one and not to the other. Similarly for helpfulness. Thus, since I cannot be harmful to myself (3p4), nothing which is like me can be harmful to me. And anything helpful to something like me is helpful to me, which implies that by helping those who are like me I can help myself. Thus out of utter egoism flows a collaborative morality, without help from politics.

Even if we accept the premiss about the logic of the helping and harming relations, this argument won't do. The premiss entails that what helps or harms me must help or harm anything *exactly* like me; but that conclusion is useless to Spinoza. He needs to speak of how something helpful or harmful to me relates to individuals which resemble me fairly closely though not exactly, and that requires a further premiss which I cannot devise.

4. Anyway, the premiss about the logic of helping and harming is false. A thing's being a threat or a help to me depends not only on how it relates to my nature but also on other factors—e.g., on its spatial relation to me. However alike you and I are, the thing in question may relate to us— not to *our natures*, but to *us*—quite differently, and thus bear differently on our welfare. That one small point brings Spinoza's collaborative edifice tumbling down. Suppose that you and I are alike, that x could harm either of us, and that to avoid the harm what is needed is to keep at a distance from x; and suppose that we cannot both do this—the floodwaters are rising in the mine and there is room for only one in the elevator which is starting up for the last time. Here the similarity between us is no help at all. And it can contribute to conflict, as when we compete for limited food: the rivalry would vanish if we didn't need the same kinds of food. (The food example, incidentally, is fatal to Spinoza's remark that 'Wrongs, suspicions and enmities arise only from love for a thing which no one can really possess' (5p20s at 294/4). This strange statement, for which no reason is given, is clearly refuted by the fact that food scarcity can create enmities; for a person does in the fullest sense 'really possess' the food which he eats and digests and absorbs into his own fabric.)

The point about differing spatial locations reminds us of the deeper fact that two things, however alike, are still *two*; so their interests can conflict because they each need something which can be had by only *one*— the last bit of food, the last place in the elevator. Spinoza knows this: 'If we imagine that someone enjoys something of which only one can get possession, we shall try to bring it about that he does not get it.' (3p32) The phrase 'only one' shows him to be thinking in terms not of natures but of their instantiations: the rivalry comes about because the coveted item can be possessed by only one person—not by only one kind of person. But in his collaborative morality in Part 4 he forgets 3p32, and the concept 'not enough to go around' is conspicuously absent. It should put in an appearance when Spinoza acknowledges a problem created by his previous treatment of sexual jealousy:

I have said that Paul hates Peter because he imagines that Peter possesses what Paul himself also loves. At first glance it seems to follow from this that these two are injurious to one another because they love the same thing, and hence because they agree in nature. If this were true, p30,31 would be false. (p34s)

But instead of discussing competition generally, Spinoza confines himself to the harmless special case of it which he treated in 3p35. It is the case of the jealous, jilted lover: Paul hates Peter because the lady has transferred her affections from Paul to Peter. From this Spinoza infers that Paul is sad while Peter rejoices, and that their antipathy stems from this difference between them and not from the love which they share! But what if neither Peter nor Paul has been specially favoured by the beloved person, they are alike in their emotional states and their desires, and each knows that if his desires are satisfied his rival's cannot be? This conflict of interest arises in part from the similarity between the two rivals, and it does refute p30,31.

Spinoza's failure to tackle the problem in its general form was presumably an honest oversight. Despite the refreshing occurrence of 'only one' in 3p32, he usually pays little attention to particulars as distinct from the natures they instantiate. He seems always to pick them out descriptively as 'the thing which has nature N', rather than indexically as '*that* one' or 'the one in front of *me now*'. That helps him to overlook the difference between 'inimical to the likes of me' and 'inimical to me'. This, by the way, shows how perfectly wrong it is to call Spinoza a nominalist, if this means that he rejected universal items in favour of particulars (see §11.2). Usually he makes room for nothing but universal items—natures or essences—and has no particulars except for the grand all-encompassing one, God or Nature.

5. From his indefensible doctrine of harmony through similarity Spinoza infers that if I am reasonable I should look for my allies among other reasonable people. But he does not infer that if I am unreasonable I should look to others who are like me in this regard. On the contrary, he holds that the prospect of harmony through similarity is available, as something predictable and reliable, only to reasonable people: 'Only to the extent that men live in accordance with the guidance of reason do they necessarily always agree in nature.' (p35) He does not mean: 'For certain: they are similar only to the extent that they are reasonable', but something weaker: 'They are certain-to-be-similar only to the extent that they are reasonable.' But this is still too strong to be plausibly defended.

Spinoza argues for it through p32–34, the argument depending on the idea that the alternative to being guided by reason is being 'assailed' by passions, so that what has to be shown is that passionate people can never be assured of having a shared nature.

The first part of the argument (p32) contends that the mere fact that x and y are both subject to passions is not in itself a point of similarity between them. This is because to say that something is passionate, or passive, is to say that it is *not* the sole cause of what is happening in it; that is a negative fact about it; and negative facts do not generate similarities: 'If someone says that black and white agree only in this, that neither is red, he affirms absolutely that black and white agree in nothing.' (p32s) I don't think that there is any clean objective line between positive facts and negative ones, and I do think that 'Neither x nor y is the sole cause of what happens in it' reports a similarity between x and y. Still, Spinoza might plausibly have said that if passionateness as such is a respect of similarity, it is so thin and abstract as to be without moral significance.

In p33,34 he carries the argument further. If x and y are both passionate, might there be other facts about them which guarantee that they 'agree in nature' in a morally relevant fashion? In reply to this, Spinoza points to how varied passions are, and to how they can set men against one another, and infers that if x and y are both passionate they can 'disagree in nature' and 'be contrary to one another'. The argument is flatly invalid. It shows that 'x and y are both passionate' does not rule out 'x and y are unalike and mutually hostile', but Spinoza needs something much stronger, namely, that if x and y are both passionate then no *further* fact about them can rule out their being unalike and mutually hostile.

6. That concerns the first sentence of p35d, which is addressed to the claim that to the extent that people are unreasonable they are debarred from having any guarantee of agreeing in nature. The large remainder of p35d aims to establish the converse conditional (which p35 does not assert but which Spinoza clearly intends), namely, that to the extent that people are reasonable they *can* be sure of agreeing in nature. I shall not analyse this taxing argument in detail, but merely call attention to three of its features. One is that it revives that conflation of 'good for me' with 'good for (whatever has) my nature' which I discussed in .3 above. The second is that it blocks Spinoza from using p31,35 in the manner that seems most natural, namely in this argument:

> If x and y are reasonable, they are alike (p35)
> If x and y are alike, they are in harmony (p31,c)
> ∴. If x and y are reasonable, they are in harmony.

That argument is not available to Spinoza because an intermediate step in p35d says that if x and y are reasonable they must both do what is good for each of them, which is tantamount to the conclusion of the above argument. So Spinoza cannot use the argument, since his only route to its first premiss is through its conclusion. I suspect that at some stage he intended to use p31,c in an argument tying reasonableness to harmony through similarity; but in fact no such argument occurs in the *Ethics*, and p31,c are directly used only in demonstrating p35,c1.

The third feature of the argument is the most significant. It concerns a subargument for the thesis that each reasonable person tries to do what is good. Never mind exactly what this means: what is interesting in it does not depend on fine details.

In the background are Spinoza's two principal theses about reason. (i) A person is reasoning in proportion as he is active. (The Latin strictly means only that activity implies reasoning, but the argument requires that Spinoza also means that reasoning implies activity.) (ii) In reasoning one commits no errors. And he also avails himself of p19 which says that everyone's active or inner-caused conduct is aimed at doing whatever he thinks to be good. Put those three together in the right way and you get the following argument:

x is reasoning (Hypothesis)
∴ x is active (by thesis (i))
∴ x does what he judges to be good (by p19)
∴ x does what is good (by thesis (ii)).

What is striking about this is its reliance on a version of the self-preservation doctrine which is cognitive as well as teleological. Spinoza has helped himself to this in moving from 'those things which aid the body's power of acting' in 3p12 to 'whatever *we imagine* will lead to pleasure' in 3p28, from which it is an easy step to 'what *he judges* to be good' in 4p19. A couple of other demonstrations also cite p19, but they do not put its cognitive element actively to work. That is what this episode in p35d does, because it turns on the difference between 'is helpful' and 'is thought by x to be helpful'. Starting with a premiss of the form ' . . . he thinks it would help him . . . ', the argument says that if that premiss is true and he is reasoning then we get the corresponding proposition of the form ' . . . it would help him . . . '.

This is not valid if it, like p19, is using the teleological doctrine of self-preservation. From 'If he thinks that it would help him he will do it' and 'If he thinks it would help him it would help him', we cannot infer that if it would help him he will do it. But perhaps the argument concerns only the converse conditional, the one involving not teleology but Spinozist appetite; and then it is valid though not properly related to p19.

However, my main interest is not in whether the argument is valid but in the essential role of cognition in it. The cognitive form of the premiss connecting action with what the person *believes* will help him is structural in the argument, not a mere accident of its wording.

See what has happened on the large scale. Having started with conditionals linking what is done with what is helpful, Spinoza has *drifted on* to conditionals linking what is done with what is thought to be helpful; and now he is *arguing his way back* to what he started from, in the special case of someone who is reasoning.

7. Later he defends the conclusion that reasonable people must be in harmony, against the objection that they may have to compete for a scarce commodity. He contends that for reasonable people the only really valuable thing is understanding (p26), and that this 'can be enjoyed by all equally' (p36). His troubling to make the latter point suggests a lack of confidence in the arguments I have been examining. But the new attempt is no better.

It starts in p26, which includes the claim that 'On the basis of reason [*ex ratione*] all that we try to do is to understand'. The demonstration of this, stripped down a little, goes thus:

A thing's trying to stay in existence is (by 3p7) nothing but its essence. But the essence of reason is nothing but our mind, insofar as it understands. Therefore, all that we try to do on the basis of reason is to understand. (p26d)

There are other details, but I cannot see that they help the main line of argument, which seems to be as follows. Any thing's essence must cause it to do whatever will most strongly tend to keep the thing in existence and thus keep it possessed of that essence (this is based on the Part 3 self-preservation doctrine); the essence of reason is understanding; and so reason is suffused by a force which drives it always towards greater understanding.

It is a bad argument, because it treats reason as a thing, an individual, a particular. In writing as though reason were a thing to which 3p6 etc. apply, Spinoza is doing what he sometimes condemns, namely, hypostatising a faculty or capacity, treating our ability to reason as though it were a part of us. We can throw back at him his own words: 'We are easily deceived when we confuse abstractions with real beings.' (2p49s at 135/22)

He may be trying to forestall that objection when he speaks of reason as 'our mind, insofar as it understands'. This amounts to saying that reason is a thing, namely a mind, considered in respect of its reasoning activities. But I cannot see how to make clear sense of the argument on that reading of it. Is it of the essence of my body insofar as it swims to try to spend more time in water? If Yes, then the whole position is ludicrous. If No, then what is the relevant difference between reasoning and swimming?

(Bad as p26d is, it is not wildly out of character for a philosopher who is not a skilled logician and who is independently assured of the conclusion (see §7.4). 'It is obvious that reasonable men value understanding above all else. How is this to be explained? Well, presumably it is necessarily true, the necessity stemming from the double fact that they are men who use *reason* and that to understand is to exercise *reason*. Indeed, understanding is the essence of reason—isn't that relevant? Yes it is! I have already shown that everything is suffused by a drive to preserve and aggrandize its own essence, which implies that reason must be suffused by a drive towards ever more understanding. Or, anyway, the mind *qua* reasoner must have such a drive. Isn't that just a way of saying that reasonable people will put the acquisition of more understanding above all other goals?' I offer that as the kind of informal thinking which could lead Spinoza, once he was sure of p26, to fabricate p26d.)

From the premiss that what we try to do on the basis of reason is to understand (p26), Spinoza infers that 'Cognition of God is the mind's greatest good; its greatest virtue is to know God' (p28), and from that he derives a significant claim about the possibility of harmony: 'The greatest good of those who seek virtue is common to all, and can be enjoyed by all equally.' (p36) This might be defended on the ground that knowledge is not a depletable resource, though there is the counterargument that knowledge requires education and leisure, and there can be competition for those.[6] But Spinoza argues quite differently: he says that all men *can* have knowledge of God because all men *do*, this being based on 2p47: 'The human mind has an adequate cognition of God's essence', and its scholium which says that God's essence is 'observed by all'. This is a terrible argument. Back in Part 2 Spinoza has argued that any cognitive state must include some cognition of God; now in Part 4 he is supposed to be talking about a greater understanding of God to which all reasonable men aspire. Because all men have the lesser possession, Spinoza argues in p36d and again in p36s, they can all have the greater. This is on a par with arguing that because all men eat, it is possible for them all to eat well.

8. I am afraid that Spinoza fails at every step in his journey towards his collaborative morality—towards the theses aligning harmony of interests with sameness of nature, and both of those with reasonableness. Any truth those theses contain must depend on contingent facts about human nature and perhaps about human societies; it cannot be derived in a few short steps from basic, abstract metaphysics, as Spinoza tries to do.

In these doctrines of his, Spinoza is trying to give metaphysical support for a certain moral vision. Part of his trouble arises, I think, from his not being clear about what vision it is. Here is his grandest statement of it:

> If two individuals of entirely the same nature are joined to one another, they compose an individual twice as powerful as either one. To a man, then, there is nothing more useful than man. A man, I say, can wish for nothing more helpful to his staying in existence than that all should so agree in all things that the minds and bodies of everyone would compose, as it were, one mind and one body; that all together should try as hard as they can to stay in existence; and that all together should seek for themselves the common advantage of all. (p18s at 223/6)

Impressive as this is, it contains a deep incoherence, reflecting a split in Spinoza's thinking. The picture of men as composing a single individual, and together seeking the common advantage of all, suggests a single organism each of whose organs preserves itself through its special contribution to the survival of the whole. But that conflicts with the idea that men should be 'entirely of the same nature': they may have the common goal of preserving the whole individual, but if they 'agree' in the sense of being extremely alike that will prevent them from interrelating as organs do within an organism.

6. This point is developed by Broad, *Five Types of Ethical Theory*, pp. 43f.

Spinoza seems not to have noticed this difference between two kinds of harmony—the harmony which relates my lungs to my heart and both to my blood etc., and the harmony of a school of fish peacefully swimming in the same direction. He wants us to interrelate like the former, but his arguments all point to the latter.

§70.   *The guidance of reason*

1. When Spinoza says things about people who reason, or are reasonable, he says that they act under the guidance of reason, or conform to its dictates. Let us consider this.

Many philosophers have held that reason cannot prescribe, i.e., that you cannot reach practical conclusions by sheer thinking unaccompanied by some input of wants or urges or value judgments. Hume, for instance, said that 'Reason is, and ought only to be, the slave of the passions', meaning that reason can help you towards your goal but cannot help you to select a goal; and his basic thesis, if not his way of putting it, is widely accepted. Spinoza would have accepted a form of it too, agreeing that a practical conclusion can be derived from reason only in combination with something which is already practical; but for him the practical input would come not from anything he would call a 'passion' but rather from the necessary drive towards self-preservation.

This is my guess about how, in the informal margins of his thought, Spinoza viewed 'the dictates of reason'. I conjecture that he thought of our necessary egoism in a teleological and cognitive way, i.e., as described by the statement that we shall always do what we think would be in our interests. Given that form of egoism, people's conduct can be affected by cognitive input, which might be said to constitute 'dictates' or 'guidance'. Of course any bit of information may affect someone's conduct, yet we don't count all information as prescriptive. But Spinoza is concerned with information which he thinks *must* have the same effect on *everyone* who believes it, and that entitles him to call it 'prescriptive' in a fairly strong sense. In this I am following Curley:

His prescriptions are hypothetical imperatives with necessary antecedents, and so, in effect, categorical. If you want to 'preserve your being', strive to hate no one. Well, you do want to preserve your being, and it is not a contingent fact that you do. So the command is not in any way conditional.[7]

It is a further question whether Spinoza is entitled to regard the dictates of reason as *moral* principles. I think he is, because I count as a morality any set of universal principles offered as something to live one's life by. Those who have a stricter concept of morality than that may deny that

7. Curley, 'Spinoza's Moral Philosophy', p. 371, quoted with omissions.

Spinoza has a morality at all; but that difference between us has no effect on any of the details, and I shall not discuss it.[8]

2. I have suggested a way for Spinoza to maintain that the deliverances of a cognitive faculty could count as practical 'dictates'. But if he accepted and developed this suggestion, he would run into trouble, because he cannot explain how reason could tell us what is really in our interests. In Hume's slogan about reason and the passions, 'reason' stands for everything cognitive; but it is essential to Spinoza's strategy that 'reason' excludes everything sensory. This makes it a poor source of knowledge of what is in our interests.

Am I being too strict in holding Spinoza in Part 4 to the sense he gave to 'reason' back in Part 2? No. In each Part the word is essentially tied to *activity*—to mental and physical changes which are caused purely from within oneself. In Part 2 the contrast is with sense-perception, in Part 4 it is with the passions—these being the affects, now more openly than ever being viewed as passive (see §59). I doubt if Spinoza was clear about how he wanted to relate the sensory to the emotionally passionate, but he certainly opposed both of them to (active) reason; so he must take the 'reason' of Part 4 to be free of all passivity, and thus not to involve anything empirical. In 3p3 he connects active/passive with adequate/inadequate, thus linking his moral psychology with his epistemology. This pivotal proposition hardly matters in Part 3, but starting at 4p24 it is woven intricately into the fabric of Parts 4 and 5. This creates a profound problem for Spinoza, which I shall address fully in §74. Now I shall attend only to its bearing on what he says about the 'guidance' or 'dictates' of reason.

3. He might say that a strictly nonempirical faculty can indeed tell us what is in our interests, because a lot of information about this is demonstrated *a priori* in the pages of the *Ethics*. I would not accept that because, as I shall show in my next chapter, those demonstrations don't work—and could not work unless we already understood how reason can tell us how to live. Anyway, that is not in fact how Spinoza brings reason's 'guidance' and 'dictates' into the story. Let us examine his actual procedure.

4. The concept of reason's dictates first occurs in two definitions in 3p59s and is next heard from in 4p18s where Spinoza announces his plan to 'show what reason prescribes to us'. It is first put to work shortly after that and is fairly active throughout the rest of Part 4: I find it in twenty-one propositions, either explicitly or by implication through Spinoza's equation of 'free' with 'living according to the dictates of reason'. None of these

---

8. Curley, *op. cit.*, thinks that Spinoza is offering a morality; Frankena, in 'Spinoza's "New Morality": Notes on Book IV' thinks that Spinoza wants us to 'kick the moral habit'; and Eisenberg adjudicates in 'Is Spinoza an Ethical Naturalist?'

propositions gives the so-called dictates of reason any identifiable prescriptive content. Their demonstrations are all powered by such doctrines
as that while reasoning you do only what is good for yourself, are causally
self-sufficient, are free from error, and so on; and they add to these doctrines a silent assumption that what you do *while reasoning* is what you do
under the guidance of reason. They fall into two groups: those that rashly
assume that if you reason you are guided by reason, and those that assume
more safely that if you are guided by reason you reason. Let us look at
them separately.

5. One group is headed by p24, which says that acting 'from virtue' is
acting self-interestedly 'by the guidance of reason'. The demonstration is
drastically compressed, and I now give an expanded form of it. From his
definition of *virtue* in terms of *power* (d8) Spinoza infers that acting
virtuously is acting in a causally self-contained way, one 'which can be
understood through the laws of one's nature alone'. It follows that if you
act from virtue your movements are caused from within your body and
your ideas from within your mind; so your ideas are adequate; so you are
using reason. The argument up to here is valid, however little charmed we
may be by its premisses. But now Spinoza makes the move which introduces
'the guidance of reason' into the argumentative structure of the *Ethics*:
it is the wild leap from 'done while using reason' to 'done by the guidance
of reason'. It lets him introduce 'the guidance of reason' without explaining
how reason can be prescriptive or what its prescriptions are.

From that proposition flow p36,56,67,72, and it ought to be cited in
p59d as well. Where the concept of the guidance of reason occurs in the
demonstrations of these, it always does so in the consequent of a conditional: if someone is F he lives under the guidance of reason. (In p37d
there is a conditional relying on p24 and running the other way, from
reason to virtue.) But we do not find out how reason can be prescriptive
by looking at the various values of F. For in each case Spinoza argues
from 'He is F' to 'He employs reason' and then leaps on to 'He lives by the
guidance of reason'. That leap prevents these propositions from enlighten-
ing us about reason as prescriptive.

6. The second group of propositions relies on the converse inference:
If someone lives by the guidance of reason, then he reasons. Since nothing
is done with 'He lives by reason' except through its implying 'He employs
reason', we again learn nothing about reason's prescriptive role.

This group starts with p35. When I expounded this in §69.6 there was
no need to mention living by the guidance of reason: to explain the argument I needed only to say that if you and I do employ reason when we act
egoistically, then . . . etc. The argument is worded in terms of 'living according to the guidance of reason', as though it had to do with acting on
good advice from reason; but there is nothing like that in the demonstrative

structure. The same goes for some of p35's descendants—p37,46,50,73—and also for a further septet of propositions, all within p59–68, which do not come from p35 but resemble it in how they pretend to use the notion of living by the guidance of reason.

7. The dismal conclusion is that Spinoza has no suggestions at all to offer us regarding how reason can be prescriptive. His phrases suggesting that it can be are all launched through conditionals which are either too wild or too tame to be helpful.

§71. *Bodily versatility*

1. A persistent theme in the later parts of the *Ethics* is the value of bodily versatility. Spinoza's central claim about this is one half of p38, namely: 'The more [something] renders a human body capable of being affected in a great many ways, or of affecting other bodies in a great many ways, the more useful it is.' (p38)

2. This may be a proposition about the advantages of being perceptually acute and physically dextrous. Thus construed, it can be argued for from the self-preservation doctrine in its cognitive, teleological and qualified form:

> For all x, if he thinks that x would help him, then
> he will do x if he can.

With that in mind, consider two familiar truths. (i) A goal-pursuing person is better off if he does not have relevant ignorance or error, i.e., if 'He thinks x would help him' is true just when 'x would help him' is true. Ignorance leads to missed opportunities, error to wasted effort, and it is good to be free of both. (ii) The person is also better off if he can do whatever would further his interests, i.e., if 'He will do x if he can' always has, for relevant values of x, the same truth-value as 'He will do x'. From those together it follows that when the above formula is true of someone, it is good for him if the following simpler version:

> For all x, if x would help him, then he will do x

is true of him. Of course it never will be; but the closer he gets to it the better, and so he has reason to value anything that moves him in that direction, e.g., (i) anything that makes him perceptually sensitive ('renders his body capable of being affected in a great many ways') and (ii) anything that increases his motor skills ('renders his body capable of affecting other bodies in a great many ways').

This general line of thought is presented by Spinoza in p18s at 222/34, and it is explicitly linked with p38 in 4 Appendix 27. It can hardly be doubted that p38 is intended partly as a thesis about acuity and dexterity.

3. But it is more often treated as though bodily versatility were a help not towards being sharp and nimble but rather towards being wise and contemplative. This happens in 5p39d where 4p38 is adduced as a reason for saying that 'He who has a body capable of doing a great many things is least troubled by bad affects'. This has to rest on the assumption that bodily versatility helps one to use reason, to have adequate ideas, to be causally self-contained; there is no other route to freedom from bad affects. But that has nothing to do with manual skill and strength, and it is positively opposed to sense-perception since this involves passivity. That opposition is clearly stated by Spinoza in 5p39s where he says that in giving a child 'a body capable of a great many things' we would be making its sensory intake 'of hardly any importance in relation to the intellect'. Whatever those last five words mean, they cannot free the passage of its anti-empirical tendency.

4. So there are two readings of 4p38: one would have us be clever, the other would have us be wise. Which of them better fits its demonstration? Well, p38d runs as follows. Start with the hypothesis that

> x makes a lot happen in my body;

from that it follows by 2p14 that

> Because of x, a lot is perceived by my mind;

Spinoza quietly and without justification equates that with saying that

> Because of x, I understand a lot;

and from that he infers by p26 that

> x is useful to me.

So the argument as a whole concludes that if something increases how busy my body is, it is useful to me.

It is a poor argument. The 'perceivings' dealt with in 2p14 are perceivings directly of happenings in my own body; an increase in their number and variety should not be equated with an increase in that 'understanding' which p26 says is my chief good.

Which interpretation of p38 does its demonstration favour? Well, the invocation of 2p14, though it concerns ideas 'directly of' bodily happenings, suggests acuity rather than wisdom, whereas the invocation of 4p26 suggests the reverse. In short, p38d faithfully reflects Spinoza's uncertainty about what sort of proposition p38 is supposed to be. Read them in succession—2p14, 4p38, 5p39—and you will see Spinoza moving from sensory acuity to contemplative wisdom, modulating on the pivot of the fiercely ambiguous 4p38.

5. Spinoza's only weighty use of p38 in Part 4 connects it with a third factor—neither acuity etc. nor wisdom etc. This is in demonstrating p43, which says that '*Titillatio* can be excessive and bad, whereas pain can be good . . . ' . In §62.2 I put 'pleasurable excitement' for *titillatio*; that is reasonably accurate, though it gives an odd appearance to Spinoza's reminder that *titillatio* is a kind of *laetitia*, since we do not need to be told that pleasurable excitement is a kind of pleasure. Pain, of course, is a kind of *tristitia*.

It is remarkable that Spinoza should say that there is bad pleasure and good unpleasure, given his initial explanations of these in terms of movements towards health and ill-health, and thus good and bad, respectively. Still, we can at a small cost extricate him from the contradiction. He is entitled to hold that the fundamental pleasure/unpleasure polarity comes from or has to do with a biological or medical polarity, while still maintaining that some pleasant feelings go with medically bad happenings and some unpleasant ones with good happenings. Where he went wrong was in saying, in a characteristic simplification, that the contrast between pleasant and unpleasant *is* just that between moving towards and moving away from health and vitality. Let us excuse him from that too strict account of the relationship, and examine his treatment of bad pleasure and good unpleasure in its own right.

6. It starts with the notion of partial pleasure and unpleasure: 'Pleasurable excitement and pain are ascribed to a man when one part of him is affected more than the rest, whereas cheerfulness and melancholy are ascribed to him when all are equally affected.' (3p11s at 149/7) Most actual changes in level of vitality are partial, Spinoza thinks: 'Cheerfulness . . . is more easily conceived than observed. For the affects by which we are daily assailed are generally related to some part of the body which is affected more than the others.' (4p44s)

Granted that there are partial pleasures and unpleasures, how does that help to show that some pleasures are bad and some unpleasures good? One might expect Spinoza to defend the first half of that as follows: every partial change alters the proportion of motion and rest, and thus tends towards the individual's destruction, which means that it is bad. In p39 he seems to be preparing for just such an argument, but in the upshot he makes no serious use of that proposition.[9] Perhaps he intended to give the argument I have sketched, and then backed away when he noticed that it would imply that all partial pleasures are bad (which is stronger than p43) and that all partial unpleasures are bad (which contradicts p43).

7. His actual argument for p43 involves an undeclared concept which I shall call the concept of *balance*. The assumptions are these: it is always good to become more balanced, and bad to become less so; a partial upward or downward move can affect one's balance; a nonpartial change cannot

---

9. Its only use is in p42d, which says nothing about bad pleasure or good unpleasure.

alter one's balance. That gives Spinoza what he wants: there can be bad pleasurable excitement and good pain, but there cannot be bad cheerfulness or good melancholy, because these are nonpartial pleasures and unpleasures. (Incidentally, Spinoza makes things needlessly obscure when he says in p43 that pain can be good 'insofar as the *titillatio* or pleasure is bad'. The goodness of the pain should be explained through its improving the person's balance, not through the badness of 'the pleasure'—whatever that means. Spinoza may be thinking of the 'pain' of being denied some harmful pleasure such as a dose of morphine; but he has made no place for such a thought as that.)

A person is unbalanced to the extent that his thoughts are lopsided, obsessively fixed in one direction, making him insensitive to other inner or outer stimuli. As Spinoza says, pleasurable excitement can be bad because 'The power of this affect can be so great that it surpasses the other actions of the body (by p6), remains stubbornly fixed in the body, and so prevents the body from being affected in a great many other ways. Hence (by p38), it can be bad' (p43d). Although this is about bodily balance, Spinoza is mainly interested in its mental counterpart. Thinking of affects mentalistically, he calls the unbalancing ones 'excessive', explicitly links this with p43 in p44d, and writes in the scholium to that: 'The affects by which we are daily assailed are generally related to some part of the body which is affected more than the others. Generally, then, the affects are excessive, and occupy the mind in the contemplation of only one object so much that it cannot think of others.' (p44s) And in Appendix 30 he says that 'most pleasurable affects in which reason and alertness are not present are excessive'.

So the enemy is obsessive thinking and feeling. 'Spinoza's morality has as its terms of evaluation freedom of mind and independence, which are to be contrasted with confusion, obsession, and inner conflict.'[10]

This gives us a third answer to the question about what sort of bodily versatility p38 is talking about—namely, that it is about whatever sort of versatility is opposed to mental fixations and obsessions. I cannot see how to reduce this to either of the other two.

8. The notion of an affect which arises 'from reason' runs through p51–54,58 without doing much work. These propositions all assume that an affect arises from reason if it is active; so this is just Spinoza's routine association of 'from reason' with 'while reasoning' and of that with 'while not being acted on from the outside'. But there is a peculiar turn in p61d, which I shall now expound.

According to p61, 'A desire which arises from reason cannot be excessive' —this being something Spinoza must accept if reason is to be the guaran-

---

10. Hampshire, *Two Theories of Morality*, p. 67.

teed rescuer from all kinds of bondage, including that of excessive affects. But why should we believe it, if all we know about reason is what follows from its consisting in the having of internally caused ideas? Why cannot a purely internally caused upthrust of an individual create an unhealthy obsession in him? Spinoza could answer by appealing to 3p4–6 which say that no internally caused change can be harmful, but perhaps by now he is unwilling to put all his eggs into that basket, for he offers a fresh argument. Here is the core of it:

A desire which arises from reason, i.e. (by 3p3) which is generated in us insofar as we act, is the very essence or nature of the man insofar as it is conceived to be determined to doing those things which are conceived adequately through the man's essence alone (by 3d2). So if this desire could be excessive, then human nature considered in itself alone could exceed itself, or could do more than it can. This is a manifest contradiction. Therefore this desire cannot be excessive. (p61d)

The term 'excessive' seems to have shifted its meaning. Earlier, something was excessive if it led to mental fixations; but now an excessive item is one which *exceeds* something or other. But if we ask 'If x is excessive then it exceeds what?' and 'What does it mean to say that x exceeds y?', we must gather our answers from the intensely unhelpful remark that if there were an excessive desire human nature would 'exceed itself'. Let us move on from this mystery to the next episode in the argument, and ask why it is a manifest contradiction to suppose that human nature could do more than it can do. This looks alarmingly like an elementary modal fallacy—like that of equating 'If he practised harder he could run faster than he can' with 'If he practised harder it would be the case that: he can run faster than he can', and declaring the former to be contradictory because the latter is. Something like that does occur in 5p37d, suggesting that Spinoza is not only uncomfortable but also incompetent in handling counterfactual conditionals (see §41.3). But perhaps this part of p61d is not committing that fumble. The point could be that human nature is not the sort of entity about which there can be counterfactuals: we can say that if P were the case then Peter would have been different; but human nature is an eternal entity, something which is necessarily just as it is, and so it is a contradiction to say that if such and such occurred human nature would be otherwise than how it actually is. I can see no other way of rescuing the 'manifest contradiction' move. This rescue, however, reminds us to ask by what right 'human nature' has been pushed into the argument in the first place. I do not think Spinoza could answer that.

314

13 *Freedom*

This chapter will explore Spinoza's account of 'freedom', and especially of what it does for its possessor, with special attention to the last section of Part 4.

§72. *Spinozistic freedom*

1. Part 5 of the *Ethics* is called 'Of the Power of the Intellect, or of Human Freedom', a title reflecting Spinoza's belief that we can achieve a measure of what he calls 'freedom' through the cultivation of intellect, i.e., the use of reason. In contrast, Part 4 is called 'Of Human Bondage, or the Strengths of the Affects'. The affects have strengths, stubbornness, making them hard to resist or dislodge; the intellect has power, potentiality for liberating us.

Oddly, it is in Part 4 that Spinoza tells us what the effects are of being free. What Part 5 adds are some intellectual techniques for increasing one's freedom; these will be the topic of my next chapter.

2. Let us start by examining how 'free' is used in the *Ethics* generally.

In Part 1 there are only three relevant occurrences. The first is a definition: 'That thing is called free which exists from the necessity of its nature alone, and is determined to act by itself alone. But that is called necessary, or rather compelled, which is determined by something else to exist and to produce an effect in a certain and determinate manner.' (1d7) This is used in two demonstrations in Part 1, one arguing that the only 'free cause' is the universe (1p17c2), the other that 'the will cannot be called a free cause' (1p32).

The will cannot be called a free cause because it is acted on from the outside. But usually when Spinoza rails against the common belief that the will is free, he is using 'free' to mean 'not caused' rather than 'not caused from the outside'. Of course he doesn't think that the will is 'free' in either sense, but the two should not be conflated. Even their extensions are different, in Spinoza's philosophy, because 'not caused' is true of nothing whereas 'not caused from the outside' is true of Nature. Also, there is a matter of degree associated with the 1d7 sense but not with the other: a thing can be more or less self-sufficient, but not more or less uncaused.

It is the belief in uncausedness which Spinoza sees as so damaging, as when men think they are free because they don't know the causes of their behaviour. He explicitly distinguishes this from 'free' in the 1d7 sense of 'self-caused':

Things could have been produced by God in no other way than they have been produced. Many will reject this opinion as absurd because they have been accustomed to attribute another freedom to God, far different from what we have taught (1d7), viz. an absolute will. But if they are willing to reflect on the matter, in the end they will utterly reject the freedom they now attribute to God, not only as futile but as a great obstacle to knowledge. (1p33 and 1p33s2 at 74/28, both quoted with omissions)

The freedom that God does have is the 1d7 freedom of self-causedness; the 'other freedom' is that of 'an absolute will', meaning a will which is not caused at all and so acts without antecedents, unconditionally, 'absolutely'. When arguing in 2p48d for his denial that human beings have 'free will' in the common man's sense, Spinoza implicitly appeals to 1d7. I think that that is a mistake. He does better when he goes on to infer the will's unfreedom from the 1p28 assertion of universal determinism.

I have just mentioned the only occurrence of the concept of freedom in Part 2. In Part 3 a few affect definitions mention the belief that something or other is free, in some sense; but this does not help us to understand what Spinozistic freedom is. The same applies to the two mentions of beliefs about freedom in Part 5 (p5d and p41s at 307/7). Part 5 also equates 'free' with 'blessed', and uses the latter several times; but it has a special content, involving a supposed 'intuitive knowledge' of God that is irrelevant to our present concerns.

3. Freedom is prominent in the final seven propositions of Part 4. It also occurs in 4 Appendix 19 and 20, and helpfully in two scholia from which I now quote, along with a couple of other fragments:

In the end they may live from the guidance of reason, i.e. may be free and enjoy the life of the blessed. (p54s)

We shall easily see what the difference is between a man who is led only by an affect, or by opinion, and one who is led by reason. . . . I call the former a slave, but the latter a free man. (p66s)

A free man, i.e. one who lives according to the dictate of reason alone. . . . (p67d)

I call him free who is led by reason alone. Therefore, he who is born free and remains free has only adequate ideas. (p68d)

These use a single concept of freedom, which operates throughout p67–73. One might wonder how it relates to the 1d7 concept, especially since that definition is not invoked anywhere in Part 4.

The answer is that Spinoza is still using his Part 1 concept of freedom, or at least one interdeducible with it. My being 'free' in the 1d7 sense is my being the cause of all that happens in me, i.e., having adequate ideas;

i.e., using reason; i.e., living by the guidance of reason; i.e., being 'free' in the Part 4 sense. So we can get from the 'freedom' which opens Part 1 to the 'freedom' which closes Part 4, and back again, through a chain of Spinozistic biconditionals. Two of them (linking self-caused with adequate, and that with reason) are doctrines of Spinoza's; the third (linking use of reason with living by its guidance) is not an announced doctrine, but it controls all Spinoza's arguments about living by the guidance of reason (see §70). So from now on I shall take Parts 1 and 4 to be employing a single concept of freedom, and shall move freely between 'self-caused' and 'living by the guidance of reason'.

It may seem a problem that whereas Part 1 says that only the universe is free, Part 4 speaks of free men. Without actually saying that there are any, it speaks of what free men are like, how they act and think, and so on. Spinoza must be talking about degrees of freedom: when he says that a free man is F, he must mean that a man is F to the extent that he is free. Part 4 tells us how to move towards greater freedom, whereas Part 1 reminds us that we cannot go the whole way. Within that framework, we might see the concept of 'the free man' as a theoretically convenient limiting case, like the concept of an 'ideal gas'—one whose molecules have zero volume.

§73.   *The psychology of the free man*

1. Spinoza's account of what it is like to be free, i.e., of what difference an increase in freedom makes, starts at 4p61. It is spread throughout p61–66 which speak of living by the guidance of reason, as well as p67–73 which use the term 'free'. I have already discussed the strange demonstration that desires arising from reason are never excessive (p61); and I have nothing helpful to say about the propositions that the free man is prudent as well as brave (p69); that he tries not to need help from the ignorant (p70); that he is especially grateful to other free men (p71); and that he is freer as a citizen than he would be as a hermit (p73). The demonstrations of these are all open to criticism, but the defects are easy to find.

I should mention the treatment of honesty in p72s, where Spinoza implies that if reason once told a man to lie it would have to tell all men to live by lies. It is puzzling that the wrongness of this was not apparent to Spinoza, or to Kant who repeated the error a century later. Granted that reason is supposed to dictate in the same way to everyone, and to speak only in general terms with no reference to *particulars*; but why can it not address itself to *special kinds* of case? It cannot say 'A lie is permitted this once—just for you'. But must it be so grandly programmatic that it cannot manage a subordinate clause? Why can't it say, for instance, 'No one should lie except to save his life'? For the rest, this segment of Part 4 contains three doctrinal clusters which I shall discuss, each embodied in a trio of propositions.

2. There is a strange trio saying that cognition of the bad is inadequate (p64), so that if one had only adequate ideas one would have no notion of the bad (p64c), from which Spinoza infers that 'If men were born free, they would form no concept of good and bad so long as they remained free' (p68). He moves from 'bad' to 'good and bad' because 'good and bad are correlates', presumably meaning that they are complementary notions neither of which can be had except in contrast to the other. That is plausible; but what about the rest of the argument?

The argument starts with cognition of bad, bringing in good only through the thesis that good and bad are correlates.[1] Its foundation is the claim that 'cognition of the bad is unpleasure itself', asserted on the strength of p8. That is a throwback to the unreformed plain man's so-called thoughts about bad, which are really just feelings, with no cognitive content (see §68.5). If that is all that Spinoza means here by 'cognition of the bad,' then he has no reason to say that without it you can't have cognition of the good either. Somehow, he must allow these so-called cognitions actually to have some cognitive content and not to consist merely in pleasant or unpleasant feelings.

Then his argument will have to run as follows. Thoughts about good and bad involve both cognition and affect—judgments and feelings—and so the free man cannot have thoughts about what is bad because he cannot have the unpleasant feelings that they involve. Somehow, that debars him even from having the cognitive element in such thoughts, i.e., forming judgments with the concept of badness; and so, by the argument from correlates, he cannot make judgments about goodness either; which means that he can have no concept of the good. He can of course have the pleasant feelings that would accompany the use of such a concept.

That is an argument, all right, but it has a weak spot. Why is someone who never has bad feelings debarred from judgments about badness? We might reply that judgments about badness involve the concept of unpleasure, which could not be had by someone who had never been in an unpleasant frame of mind (remember that Spinoza is talking about someone who was born free and has remained so). But this line of argument is really not available to him. He should say that a judgment about badness requires only the concept of a *move towards death*, and there is no reason why it should not be made by someone who had never participated in such a move.

1. Broad, *Five Types of Ethical Theory*, p. 52, gets the argument wrong because he thinks it applies evenhandedly to good and bad.

I doubt that my suggested argument is what Spinoza is actually getting at. I suspect that he has simply drifted from a p8 affective sense of 'cognition of the bad' (in p64d) to a d1,2 cognitive sense of it in p68. It is distressing not to know why p68 is supposed to be true, since that might explain why Spinoza wanted in his system this proposition in which he permits himself a rare counterfactual luxury: it is the only proposition in the *Ethics* whose antecedent is explicitly declared to be impossible (see p68s).

3. There is no such problem about the trio of propositions saying that reason ignores temporal direction and distance (p62), tells us to seek the greater of two goods when we have to choose (p65), and therefore tells us to prefer a greater future good to a lesser present one (p66). This is to be seen against the thesis, advanced in p9,10 and developed in several later propositions, that affects are more intense when their objects lie in the present or the near future.[2]

Most of the edifying moral philosophies deplore the inclination to give less weight to goods and bads which lie far in the future, and say that it is reasonable to be *prudent*—using this word in its proper sense of 'taking the long view of one's interests'. No doubt it is reasonable to be prudent, but one would like to be told why. Thomas Nagel has compared prudence with altruism, arguing in effect that since it is unreasonable to be moved by 'This is good for me now' but not by 'This will be good for me later', it is similarly unreasonable to be moved by 'This is good for me' but not by 'This is good for him'.[3] The comparison has been challenged, but it suits me to accept it and run Nagel's conditional contrapositively: since it is obviously fair to ask 'Why should *his* welfare count with *me?*', it is also reasonable to ask 'Why should *my later* welfare count with *me now?*' To the latter question it may seem sufficient to reply: 'If you are not prudent, you will come to regret it!' But then to the former question we can reply 'If you aren't altruistic, others will regret it!' In each case, the relevance of the reply—the relevance of others to me, or of me later to me now—is precisely what is at issue.

The question of why we should be prudent is hard and interesting. It can be made to arise out of Nagel's work, but it first arose for me from thinking about Spinoza's p62,65,66, which constitute the only attempt I know of to answer it.[4]

2. This theme is worked out through 4p12c,13,16,17,60s and 5p7, which constitute most of the progeny of 4p9,10.

3. Thomas Nagel, *The Possibility of Altruism* (Oxford, 1970), pp. 15–17.

4. John Perry's 'The Importance of Being Identical', in A. Rorty (ed.), *The Identities of Persons* (Berkeley, 1976), pp. 67–90, answers a related question at pp. 74f, but not quite this one.

The question is a wonderful one. That Spinoza saw that it needs an answer is yet another sign of his greatness. But his own answer, though typically ingenious, is unacceptable. Rather than asking what makes prudence 'reasonable' in some broad sense, he asks what is dictated by 'reason' in his narrow sense. And he answers that reason is time-blind: it can pay no attention to the difference between 'five minutes hence' and 'five years hence', and so its dictate 'If A would be a greater good than B, seek A . . . ' cannot be qualified by the rider ' . . . unless A is only slightly greater and is much more remote in the future'. This is an ingenious argument, but its conclusion is too narrow to be of much service to us. We need to know whether prudence is 'reasonable' in a broader sense than merely 'consistent with everything we could learn by *a priori* reasoning'. In fact, we ought not to grant him that our 'reason' in his sense can issue moral dictates of any kind, time-blind or not. And even if it could, they would surely have to be supplemented by moral input from a more worldly-wise source—some faculty which could distinguish five years hence from five minutes hence *and from five years ago*.

Why is reason time-blind? Well, 2p44c2 says in effect that when reason says that P it announces that *eternally* P, meaning that *necessarily always* P. This leaves no foothold for any concept involving *tempus*, i.e., involving past-present-future or temporal measure (see §47). And what justifies 2p44c2? The best argument for saying that *a priori* inquiries can establish only truths which are true at all worlds, and thus at all times, is this: If the set of possible worlds contains some at which P is true, and some at which it is not true, it is impossible to discover which subset the actual world belongs to without attending to the actual world; so P can be established only *a posteriori*. Thus, what can be established *a priori* must be true at all worlds, i.e., necessarily or eternally true.

Spinoza, however, does not argue in that way. Rather, he says that everything is necessary and nothing contingent (1p29), and reason perceives things truly (2p41), and so perceives them as necessary (2p44), and thus brings them under thoughts of the form *Eternally P* (2p44c2). This argument presupposes that 1p29 means that nothing is 'contingent' in our sense of the word, i.e., that this is the only possible world. Nothing short of that will get Spinoza to his conclusion. But 1p29d gives no support for that reading; and when in Part 1 Spinoza calls something necessary, as against contingent, he generally means only that it is either necessary in our sense or else inevitable (see §29.4). In short, his argument for 2p44,c2 is broken-backed.

4. All that remains to be considered in Part 4 is the trio p63,c,67, concerning the avoidance of bad things. On the face of it, p63 is plain sailing: 'He who is led by fright, and does good to avoid bad, is not led by reason.' Spinoza defends this on the grounds that reason is antithetical to all unpleasure, and thus to fright (*metus*, AD 13). At the end of p63d he speaks instead of the person who 'does good from fear of bad'.[5] He has so defined 'fear' that it essentially involves fright: it is the disposition to settle for something nasty so as to avoid something nastier of which one is frightened (AD 39). It looks, then, as though the pieces hang together nicely.

The clause 'and does good to avoid bad' or ' . . . from fear of bad' contributes nothing to the validity of p63d, which applies to anyone who is guided by fright, whatever it leads him to do. But Spinoza might say that he has included 'and does good to avoid bad' as a reminder of the role fright mainly plays in our practical deliberations, namely, as a deterrent from certain courses of action. In AD 39 he has defined fear in terms of avoiding 'a greater bad by a lesser *bad*', whereas now his topic is 'doing *good* from fear of bad'; but 'good' is here meant ironically. The topic is the person who acts in approved ways not because they are inherently attractive to him but because he is terrified of the consequences of not doing so.

In an eloquent passage in Part 5 Spinoza writes about people whose conduct is governed by the fact that they are frightened of hellfire:

They hope after death to receive a reward for their bondage, that is for their morality and religion. They are induced to live according to the rule of divine law not only by this hope but also because they are frightened that they may be punished horribly after death. If men were not thus hopeful and frightened, but believed instead that minds die with the body, they would return to their natural disposition, and would prefer to govern all their actions according to lust. (5p41s at 307/11, quoted with omissions)

Now, suppose that I am naturally disposed to be cruel, selfish and destructive, that only the thought of damnation makes me behave well, and that I am quite sure that my conduct will keep me out of hell. In that case, the thought of the afterlife will not frighten me. It will not cause in me any actual emotional down-draught of the sort that defines 'fright', because my fate in the after life is not something 'whose outcome I to some extent doubt' (AD 13). Is 4p63,d relevant to my way of life on this description of it? Strictly speaking, it is not; for Spinoza's argument and his wording require a confinement of attention to coercion through *actual*

---

5. The Latin is *bonum timore mali agit*. Curley and Shirley both render *timor* here by 'fear', although in Part 3 they use that for *metus*, not for *timor*. Boyle, Elwes and George Eliot dodge it altogether, pretending that Spinoza has merely repeated his p63 phrase meaning 'does good to avoid bad'. These translators have had to mishandle this passage because they all render *timor* in Part 3 by 'timidity', being forced into this by their rendering of *metus* by 'fear'. Even at AD 39, 'timidity' is unconvincing, and in 4p63d it is impossible. My rendering of *metus* by 'fright' and of *timor* by 'fear' seems to be a tolerable solution.

fright and do not stretch out to cover cases where a person *would* be frightened of something if he were not so sure of avoiding it. I am sure, however, that Spinoza does not intend his target to be so restricted. In the passage last quoted, and also here: 'The superstitious know how to reproach people for their vices better than how to teach them virtues, and they try not to guide men by reason but to restrain them by fright' (p63s), I do not think that 'fright' is the heart of the matter. Rather, Spinoza is protesting against the whole coercive approach to morality. (That is why in §61.5 I chose to construe 'fear' as the difficult avoidance of a strongly unwanted consequence, whether or not one is actually frightened by the thought of it.) Although his formal arguments do not secure it, we are here confronted by a strenuous moral attitude of Spinoza's which I want to explore a little.

5. What attitude is it, exactly? In p63c,d Spinoza says that the reasonable man will 'directly follow the good' and 'only to that extent flee the bad'. That has nothing to do with fright, but what does it mean? Apparently this: The reasonable man will try to achieve good states of affairs; that will bring in its train an avoidance of bad ones, but such avoidance will not be part of what he is directly pursuing. If that is Spinoza's position, though, then he has made a mistake. To want to bring it about that P *is* to want to prevent it from being the case that not-P: there is, for instance, no psychological or even logical difference between wanting to stay alive and wanting to avoid becoming dead. So it is impossible to follow the advice 'Don't try to avoid what is bad—simply pursue what is good and let the avoidance of bad follow naturally.' Also, that advice conflicts with Spinoza's saying in p65 that 'by the guidance of reason we . . . pursue the lesser of two evils', and adding in p65c that a lesser bad is a good.

I do not think we can clear Spinoza of the charge of being in error, and in conflict with himself, in what he says about directly pursuing good and only indirectly avoiding bad. But he may also have in mind two theses which are more defensible, though I doubt if he had them properly separated from the mistaken thesis or from one another.

6. One is an opposition to every kind of morality which does not train, educate and develop people's inclinations, but merely keeps them in check by adding inducements. In the passage about the 'burden of morality and religion' Spinoza deplores the inducements of hope as well as of terror, of heaven as well as of hell. He thinks it possible, and better, that men should become naturally and uncalculatingly inclined to act well. (See 5p10s at 287/24 for a connected point.)

This must be what he is getting at in his contrast between 'the sick man [who] from fear of death eats what he is repelled by' and 'the healthy man [who] enjoys his food'. The latter, Spinoza says, 'enjoys life better than if he feared death and directly desired to avoid it' (p63cs). If the sick man really needs repulsive medicines in order to survive, that is bad luck and Spinoza cannot be criticising him for that. I take Spinoza's point to be that we should become as much like his healthy man as possible, acquiring *tastes* for what is good for us, e.g., for healthy, nourishing food. If we fail to do that—if we eat properly only in the interests of health—we are in the same boat as the wretched invalid who has to force disgusting potions down his throat as a condition of survival.

This thesis does not fit comfortably with its immediate surroundings. The contrast is not between a sick man brooding on death and a healthy one thinking about life, but rather between a sick man who eats with a view to long-term consequences and a healthy one who eats happily, hedonistically, without calculation. When Spinoza says that the healthy man enjoys life more than (and preserves his life as well as?) he would 'if he directly desired to avoid death', what exactly is he saying? This sounds like that suspect contrast between directly pursuing what is good and only indirectly avoiding what is bad, but really it is not that at all, but rather a contrast between enjoying doing what will in fact bring a certain result and trying to bring about that result. The word 'directly', in the phrase 'directly desired to avoid death', seems to have no work to do.

The sanity and decency of this moral position of Spinoza's does not need to be proclaimed by me. It must be admitted, though, that it is not an all-purpose recipe for life. Spinoza may well urge us to do what we can to create in ourselves and others tastes and inclinations which will lead us to ways of life that are healthy, life-enhancing and cooperative, but he cannot deny that there are limits to how far this could go. No course of training could possibly ensure that the movements one needs to make to avoid being run over on the street are always just the movements one is incited to make by purely balletic impulses.

7. Spinoza may also be getting at something shallower, namely, that when we do act with a view to consequences we should not dwell on thoughts of what it would be like if we failed. This is not the impossible injunction 'When acting to produce a good result, stand in no cognitive relation to anything bad', but rather a bit of advice about the conscious phenomenology of risk: 'When acting to produce a good result, don't make things unpleasant and distracting for yourself by filling your mind with vivid imaginings of the consequences of failure.' Something like that is said in a bit of 5p10s which actually invokes 4p63.[6] Spinoza writes there: 'If someone sees that he pursues self-exaltation too much, he should think of its correct use, and of the end for which it ought to be pursued . . . ,

---

6. This is the only mention of any of 4p63,c,67 in a scholium; and they have no significant use in demonstrations.

not of its misuse and emptiness . . . or other things of this kind, which only someone sick of mind thinks of.' (288/23)

It is not bad advice. But it is not deep or original or specifically Spinozistic. Spinoza's reasons for it seem mainly to come from observations of human behaviour, plus hints of the other theses I have attributed to him in this section. If he did accept each thesis, he certainly tended to conflate them with one another, and 5p10s confirms that.

I should add that Spinoza is relying on the worst of the theses in his famous statement that 'A free man thinks of nothing less than of death, and his wisdom is a meditation on life, not on death' (4p67). That could come from the humdrum advice to accentuate the positive, thinking always about success rather than failure. But if p67d makes sense at all, it depends on the absurd thesis that we should try directly to make it the case that P and should not try directly to prevent it from being the case that not-P.

§74. *Spinozistic freedom: its incoherence*

1. Spinoza is in a bind about the place of sense perception in the life of a free man. On the one hand, a free man is intelligently self-interested: he does what will in the long run be best for himself, given the prevailing circumstances; and so he must inform himself about how he is situated in the actual world. On the other hand, his freedom—like his reasonableness—consists in his being self-caused, and that requires his not using his senses. The link between 'passionate' and 'sensorily receptive' is explicitly stated in 3p1,3.

Furthermore, the account of reason in terms of self-causedness is integral to the whole system: it works busily in many demonstrations, and, above all, it combines with the self-preservation thesis of 3p4–6 to bear the entire weight of the doctrine that reason is our route to staying in existence and leading the good life.

And Spinoza does not always shrink from the extraordinary consequence that the free man will not have recourse to his senses: a tendency to denigrate the senses is visible throughout Parts 4 and 5. Even in the course of admitting that we must learn about our surroundings if we are to survive, Spinoza witheringly characterizes such information as abstract and imaginary. Because it depends on temporal facts—the apple will go bad soon, so I had better eat it now—it cannot be handled by reason:

We can have only a quite inadequate cognition of the duration of things, and we determine their times of existing only by the imagination, which is not equally affected by the image of a present thing and the image of a future one. That is why the true cognition we have of good and bad is only abstract or universal, and the judgment we make concerning the order of things and the connection of causes, so that we may be able to determine what in the present is good or bad for us, is imaginary rather than real. (4p62s at 257/24)

I do not know what is supposed to follow from this about how we should live. But it is hard not to see Spinoza as committed to offering sensory deprivation as an ideal. We are familiar with the idea that there is something healthful and restorative in having long periods of meditation with as little sensory input as possible; but Spinozistic freedom is offered as an ideal way of life, the whole of life; it is not to be compared with the sensory deprivation proposals of Yoga, as is clear from 4p45c2s.

2. Here are a couple of suggestions for things that Spinoza might be saying about independence of the external world—things that stop short of denigrating the senses. One fails, the other has a limited success.

(i) Perhaps Spinoza is urging us to reduce our chances of frustration by trying not to have desires other than the basic one for survival, on the grounds that all other desires expose one to the risk of disappointment and frustration because of external factors. But really this doesn't involve the line between inner and outer causes: it is a strategy for reducing all inessential desire, not merely desires for external things; Spinoza's desire to write the *Ethics* laid him open to bitter frustration because his powers might have proved unequal to the task. Furthermore, the proposal is morally objectionable. It says that we should avoid hope and fear by sheer conative contraction; that is to achieve security by strategic retreat, and that is pusillanimous. I am glad that it was not Spinoza's own moral stance, as is shown by his years of labour at philosophical works which did not help him to stay in existence.

(ii) Perhaps he is partly deploring our habit of uncritically caring too much about the attitudes and opinions of others. He does hold that the free man will not let the thoughts and desires of others dictate what he thinks and wants. See his treatment of self-exaltation and shame in AD 30 and 31, his eloquent description in p58s of the anxious instability of the person 'who exults in the opinion of the multitude', and this: 'Judgment can be biased in many ways, and to an almost incredible degree, so that even though not directly controlled from the outside it may be so dependent on another man's words that it can be said to be ruled by him.' (*Theological-Political Treatise* at III/239/19)

This is an excellent theme of Spinoza's, but a triply limited one. It goes no further than that one should not uncritically adopt the opinions and attitudes of other people, i.e., relate in one special way to one special kind of output from a special group of individuals. We could remove one limitation by enjoining that we should pay no attention at all to others' attitudes and beliefs. But that would be foolish, and is not Spinoza's opinion;

he certainly thinks that the views of 'ignorant' people are a datum to be taken into account by the free man—see for instance p70s. Or we might remove another limitation instead by enjoining that we not take over uncritically the opinions and attitudes of other things, human or otherwise. Does Spinoza think there are any other opinions which could influence us? I suppose not. Yet sometimes he writes as though the whole world were clamouring with commands and opinions. That, at any rate, is all I can make of a remark about the unfree man who 'allows himself to be guided by things outside him, and to be determined by them to do what the common constitution of external things demands' (p37s1 at 236/29).

3. That was an attempt to salvage something from Spinoza's doctrine that the key to the good life is to be self-caused. Given that he seems committed to saying that ideally we should not use our senses, I have said, in effect, 'Let us ask how far along that road Spinoza might go without absurdity, forgetting that he is committed to going all the way.' We couldn't take him far, and what we found on that short journey was hardly worth the trouble. Now let us try a different tack.

I have been supposing that if something in my mind is externally caused, its cause lies outside my mind; and analogously for my body. Let us now suppose that for Spinoza what really matters is whether a change in me is caused from outside my *will*, i.e., caused in such a manner that it would have happened even if I hadn't wanted it to, no matter what bribes or threats had been offered to me, etc.

We do not find Spinoza talking like that about externality in the *Ethics*, but he did so earlier on: 'Every change comes either from external causes, whether the subject wants it or not, or from an internal cause by the subject's own choice.' (*Metaphysical Thoughts* I/256/8). That clearly ties internal/external to the line between what is and what is not under voluntary control. I conjecture that *that* internal/external line is lurking in the background of the *Ethics*, still exerting influence on Spinoza's thinking. If that is right, it has explanatory power.

4. It explains some textual details. (i) In p66s Spinoza says good things about the free man, including saying that 'he complies with no one's wishes but his own'. He does not explain whose wishes the unfree man complies with, and I don't think he could. But his point about the free man could be not that he obeys *only* his own wishes but that he *does* obey his own wishes, i.e., that his conduct is under firmer voluntary control than is that of the man driven by affects. (ii) Spinoza says that if unfree men did not believe in hell they would 'prefer to govern all their actions according to lust, and to obey fortune rather than themselves' (5p41s). This is enormously strange. If those men did not believe in hell they would prefer to obey fortune rather than themselves—so as things are they *do* obey themselves? I suggest that Spinoza's point is this: given their belief about postmortem punishment, their conduct does proceed from their will —they do what they think it best to do, all things considered—but only because the stakes are so high; if they did not think they had so much to lose, they would give themselves over to impulse, obsession, and addiction, no longer obeying themselves. This brings out once again the value Spinoza places on having one's life under voluntary control. Of course he prefers that it should be controlled by a will which is not strenuously coerced, but that is beside my present point. (iii) Of one of his techniques for emotional control he says that it is the best of all those 'which depend on our power', i.e., which are under our voluntary control and can be turned on or off at will (5p4s at 283/35). Internality to the will is highlighted once more.

If Spinoza is thinking of internality to the will, then he has a case for his eventual assumption that affects are all passions, i.e., changes which the person does not bring about voluntarily, instead of having to mean by this that they are all caused from outside the person. Furthermore, he can regard them as causes of further unfreedom, on the basis of that emphasis on emotional turbulence which I noted in §62.6. Being in the grip of an emotional upset is one way of not being properly in control of oneself, not doing what one wants to do. Spinoza can regard that as a loss of freedom in our present sense, without having to pretend that it involves causes from outside one's whole self.

This conjecture could also explain why, when Spinoza is defending 3p4 against apparent counterexamples, the latter concern suicide and not fatal diseases. The question of whether an organism might be killed by a purely endogenous cancer is not even mentioned, though it should be just as much a threat to the 'no self-destruction' thesis as suicides are. That could be because Spinoza has come to think of that thesis in terms of voluntary self-destruction, destruction by causes internal not merely to the whole organism but to the will.

Above all, on this account of Spinoza's position he is no longer committed to denigrating the senses. We are urged to be active, free, self-causing; but now this is to mean that what we do should be voluntary, and it need not imply that we should not use our eyes and ears and hands to investigate our environments. Quite the contrary: voluntary action, properly understood, must proceed from desires and beliefs (see §53.2); so this new position requires that we have beliefs on which to act, and our senses will help us to acquire them. The fact that the senses involve happenings in us of which we are not the sole causes no longer counts against them; for we are not now told to be causally self-sufficient, but only to avoid making movements and thinking thoughts which don't arise from our beliefs and desires. I still should not believe something just because you do (and I have a habit of acquiring your beliefs), but it is all right for me to believe something because I had a certain sensory experience (and cognitively processed it in the light of my other beliefs). Thus room is made for 2p14 and 4p38 on their most natural interpretations, and for all the other things Spinoza says implying that we should attend intelligently to our surroundings.

5. In short, many textual details plus much of the broad outline of Spinoza's moral theory can be nicely explained on the conjecture that it is a morality not of causal self-sufficiency but rather of completeness of voluntary control.

It is a pity, therefore, that this revised theory was perfectly unavailable to him. For one thing, it undercuts the argument of 3p4–6 for egoism. That argument stems from the idea that an individual's destruction cannot proceed from its essence; we have seen in §55 that it is hard to know what 'essence' means in this context, but there is no chance of making it mean 'will' or having anything to do with the notion of voluntary control. Furthermore, the present proposal abolishes most of the demonstrations in Part 4: their appearance of being arguments at all depends on the morality's being based on the dictates of 'reason', with this understood in terms of causal self-sufficiency; take away that last concept, and the elaborate structure of mostly invalid arguments collapses into a shapeless pile of rubble. Also, the revised morality takes as central two concepts, belief and desire, for which Spinoza has no remotely satisfactory theory. He was steered away from seeing the need for a theory of belief by his view that all ideas are beliefs, which he may have muddled with the thesis that they are propositionally structured; and his profound insight that there is a problem about actual false beliefs (§41) did not spur him to a theory of belief because he thought he could get by with the thesis that error is a species of ignorance. Then also his insight that there is a problem about teleological explanations (§51) and his thinking he had a sanitized replacement for them (§52) prevented him from knuckling down to a theory of desire. So if in Part 4 he is largely thinking in terms of what is internal or external to the will—as I think he is—this is something for which he has not even the pretence of a foundation earlier in the *Ethics*.

It is an oversimplification, but perhaps a helpful one, to say that two internal/external lines are hard at work in Parts 3 and 4: the line between internal and external to the organism gives the arguments their structure, and the line between internal and external to the will gives the conclusions their plausibility.

14 *Psychotherapy*

In 5p1–13 Spinoza presents techniques for controlling and damping down one's emotions. He says that these are procedures which 'everyone knows by experience' (5 Preface at 280/23), but that they are neither assiduously practised nor generally understood. He undertakes to tell us not only what they are but why they succeed. These explanations are the topic of the present chapter.

§75. *The mind's power over the affects*

1. Spinoza's psychotherapeutic proposals can be seen as an account of how to become more 'free' in the sense of being in control, behaving under the guidance of thoughts and desires rather than obsessions and impulses. It also concerns 'freedom' in his official sense, if we accept the pretence that all the affects are passions.

Anyway, whether or not 'freedom' is brought in, we are now to be told how to bring our affects under control by the use of 'the mind' or 'reason'. Reason is doing double duty, then. Just as in a revolution where the new president is also the man who led the coup, so reason whose 'dictates' replace the influence of the affects in our lives is also the faculty which dislodges or quietens the affects in the first place. No more now about the dictates of reason: we are to be concerned with techniques for stilling the affects which scream in our ears, not with the new morality which is to fill the ensuing silence.

It is about time! Spinoza has often said that reason or 'the mind' can quell or dislodge the affects: for example, he calls mercy 'a power of the mind, by which a man governs anger and vengeance' (AD 38, explanation), and refers to 'the power of reason over the affects' (4p17s). Now, at last, he undertakes to 'show how great the mind's dominion over the affects is, and what kind of dominion it has for restraining and moderating them'.

2. That clause comes from 5 Preface (at 277/16). This contains an attack on Descartes's account of the mind's control over the emotions, with most of the fire aimed at his view that the mind acts on the animal spirits which in turn influence the emotions. Spinoza of course rejects this interaction between the mental and the physical, subjecting it to criticisms which really belong back in Part 2 (see §33.4). He also has another complaint against Descartes and others, resting on his (Spinoza's) view that what a given mind can do depends on its condition, how it is structured and whether it is healthy, and so on. He opposes philosophers who hold that the mind just can do this or that, that it has an 'absolute' power to achieve such and such feats, so that if they are not achieved that shows not an incapacity in the mind but a moral defect in its owner. Thus:

> I shall treat only of the power of the mind, or reason, and shall show what kind of dominion it has for restraining and moderating the affects. It does not have absolute dominion over them. Yet the Stoics thought that they depend entirely on our will, and that we can command them absolutely. But experience cries out against this, and has forced them to confess that much practice and application are required to restrain and moderate the affects. Descartes was [also] rather inclined to this opinion. (277/16, quoted with omissions)

Spinoza is not primarily complaining that Descartes and the Stoics exaggerate the mind's power over the emotions. His main charge—a deeper and subtler one—is that they are wrong about what it is for anything to have a power. Rather than holding that the mind can control its owner's emotions *by virtue of* its own structure and the laws it obeys, *while* it is healthy and energetic, *to the extent that* it is well disciplined, and so on, they hold that the mind has its controlling power without conditions, has it 'absolutely', has it, period. In this as in other contexts, 'absolute' contrasts with 'conditional' and with 'qualified', and the objection Spinoza is levelling is to crediting anything at all with an absolute power, a power which comes from nowhere and is possessed by virtue of nothing. That this is different from any point about how much power the mind has is shown in 1p32d, where Spinoza says something implying that the will's powers are not absolute, but depend on how the will fits into the causal scheme of things, and explicitly adds that this would be true even if those powers were unlimited.

Spinoza objects to absolute powers, of course, because they would be inexplicable, and he thinks there is an explanation for everything. He also has another objection, implicit in his phrase about 'practice and application'. We understand how a thing can enlarge its capacities by going through certain procedures, because the procedures can alter the thing's structure, and thus increase its powers: practice begets power in athletics, for instance, because it alters muscles and arteries and so on. Spinoza's point, I take it, is that the Stoics and Descartes could not intelligibly explain how the mind can improve its performances through practice.

He does not say all this in 5 Preface; but the *Ethics* as a whole is suffused with his own view that the mind no more has absolute powers than does the body, and that increasing its powers is not a formless exercise of moral effort—the mind's doing something 'just because it wills' (278/7)—but rather a feat in applied medicine or engineering. Spinoza would have liked Leibniz's sarcastic remark about 'inexplicable "faculties"—helpful goblins which come forward like gods on the stage to do on demand anything that a philosopher wants of them, without ways or means'.[1]

Spinoza's rejection of 'helpful goblins' generates his Part 5 project of saying *how*—with what 'ways and means'—the mind must go about getting leverage on the affects.

3. This project does not betray the parallelism thesis. Affects are introduced as psychophysical episodes or dispositions, and Spinoza is free to say that therapy under one attribute has its automatic counterpart under the other.

Indeed, he launches Part 5 with a reminder of parallelism, a virtual repetition of 2p7: 'In just the same way as the thoughts and ideas of things are ordered and connected in the mind, so the states of the body or images of things are ordered and connected in the body.' (5p1). His only use of this is in demonstrating that 'So long as we are not assailed by affects contrary to our nature, we have the power of ordering and connecting the states of the body according to the order of the intellect' (5p10). All I can get out of that and its demonstration is that if Spinoza's psychotherapy succeeds on the mental side, then the physical side will automatically be taken care of. Use reason to control turbulent feelings and obsessive thoughts, thus increasing your mental health, and p10 promises that you will thereby improve your physical health also, curing stomach cramps or high blood pressure or a tendency to cancer.

In p10s Spinoza refers to 'this power of rightly ordering and connecting the states of the body' as though he had described a physicalistically conceived method of intervening in bodily processes. But he has not, and perhaps he does not mean to suggest that he has. In the rest of p10s the main topic is the practice of mental disciplines.

I am here relying on the fact that although each lever on our affects bears on them equally under both attributes, we can approach a given lever only under one attribute or the other. In psychotherapy, when I set myself to remember certain things and to push certain things out of my imagination, something goes on in my brain; but my only way of making those cerebral events occur is to do those mental things. That is because—as Spinoza has to admit—our epistemic relations to the two attributes are different.

4. In the context of basic science, that asymmetry shows up in our knowing little about the mental realm—hence the need for the physical interlude between 2p13 and 14. What we *do* know about the mental realm mostly concerns its indirect representative features, i.e., the contents of beliefs; but those are central to Spinoza's techniques for emotional control, and so in this area the emphasis is on the mental.

---

1. *New Essays*, p. 382, quoted with omissions.

(14) PSYCHOTHERAPY

Consider a simple example: the injunction 'When you are angry with someone, think about something else instead.' That involves thought content, and so it does not correspond to anything that could be said in physical terms. Whenever a person obeys that injunction something physical will happen, but there is no one kind of physical event E such that an E occurs when and only when a person shifts his thought from an object of his anger to something else (see §51.5). That is why the general mental injunction could not be replaced by a general physical one.

What about injunctions in particular cases? If *this* person *now* went through the desired kind of thought shift, there would be a corresponding F event in his brain. Can we utilize that fact by enjoining him to make an F event happen in his brain, instead of enjoining him to think about something else? In practice we cannot, because we never know what the relevant brain event is. But if in a given case we did know that, and if the person in question could somehow make an F event occur in his brain (other than by shifting his thoughts and letting parallelism do the rest), then there is no reason why he should not comply with it. I think Spinoza would agree about this.

5. Spinozist psychotherapies, then, focus on thought content. This fact, while it allows us access to the therapies under the attribute of thought, implies that they cannot be scientifically fundamental. There cannot be securely based causal laws which use the concept of 'thought about x' or 'belief that P'. That does not matter much, though, since we shall find that Spinoza's psychotherapies are not causal in nature, or not clearly so. 'How could there be a sound therapeutic technique which was not causal?' How indeed? But Spinoza's are not sound. To put it brutally, his account of them is not coherent enough for us to be able to say what causal elements, if any, they contain.

To the extent that they are causal in nature, they may still be secure enough in themselves. I explained in §66.8 how Spinoza's psychology of the affects might be secure as a set of general theses, and insecure only in its application to particular cases. The same might be true of the therapies, insofar as they are causal. But I cannot work that line of thought out in detail, because the therapies are not well enough worked out by Spinoza to admit of such treatment.

6. Some of the propositions early in Part 5 are remarks about therapy rather than recipes for doing it. I have already mentioned two such, namely 5p1,10, which amount to little more than expressions of optimism about Spinoza's methods. Another is 5p7; but this also has a special feature which should be discussed. It concerns the 4p7 thesis that an affect cannot be restrained except by another affect (see §66.4). It is natural to take that as implying things like this: 'If a person be obsessed by jealousy the mere conviction that this emotion is irrational and degrading will have

332

no tendency to overcome his jealousy unless the thought of himself as irrational and degraded stirs an emotion of disgust in him.'[2] But how unSpinozistic that sounds! And it conflicts with the thesis that the affects are to be restrained by reason. Spinoza explicitly restricts himself to cognitive therapies when he says: 'We shall determine by the mind's cognition alone the remedies for the affects.' (5 Preface at 280/24)

The only way both stories could be true would be if reason worked through affects. In the 4p50's Spinoza speaks of 'affects arising from reason', but he gives to that phrase only the content of 'affects which one has while reasoning'; and he does not try to show that reason controls the affects only through the mediation of affects of its own. Just once, however, he does tell both affect-calming stories together—namely, in 5p7,d.

The proposition says that affects arising from reason must eventually prevail over certain others to which they are opposed. Spinoza opens p10s with a cheerfully optimistic remark based on this; and in p20s at 293/10 (an especially obscure and confusing sentence) it is wrongly treated as though it were the source of a therapeutic technique. But we need not linger on that, since p7d is quite unconvincing, and there seems to be no prospect of getting nourishment from p7 by peeling it off its demonstration and chewing it on its own.

The demonstration says in effect that in a conflict between a reasoned affect and an unreasoned one, the former is an immovable object—because it must 'always' be present—while the latter is a resistable force, and so in the long run the reasoned affect must win. It would be no pleasure to report Spinoza's grounds for those premises.

§76.   *First technique: separating and joining*

1. The first technique we are offered is presented and defended in p2,d:

If we separate an emotion or affect from the thought of an external cause, and join it to other thoughts, then the love or hate toward the external cause is destroyed, as are the vacillations of mind arising from these affects. *Demonstration*: For what constitutes the form of love or hate is pleasure or unpleasure accompanied by the idea of an external cause (by AD 6 and 7). So if this is taken away, the form of love or hate is taken away at the same time. Hence these affects and those arising from them are destroyed.

The argument fails. Unpleasure does not count as hate unless it is accompanied by the idea of an external cause, but all that follows is that if from an instance of hate the causal thought is removed, then what remains does not qualify as hate; it may still be unpleasant and may continue to arouse the same 'vacillations of the mind' that it caused when it was harnessed to the causal thought.

2. Broad, *Five Types of Ethical Theory*, p. 33.

The same defect occurs in the strikingly similar 3p48d, where Spinoza says that 'hate towards Peter is destroyed' if the thought of Peter is replaced by some other thought, because 'this unpleasure is called hatred of Peter only because Peter is considered to be the cause of the affect'— the give-away being the words 'is *called* hatred of Peter'. In fact, 3p48d is even weaker than 5p2d, because it deprives the affect of the title 'hatred towards Peter' but not of the title 'hate', whereas 5p2d gets rid of 'hate' altogether.

But returning to my main point, the argument as given does not show how banishing the relevant thought can quell the unpleasure, 'vacillation', and so on. For that to be achieved, the 'thought of an external cause' must cause the unpleasure and turbulence, for then its removal might abolish them.[3] Spinoza does sometimes define kinds of affect in terms of cognitive causes rather than mere accompaniments (see §63.5), and we must suppose that that is the line he is taking here.

2. Let us interpret p2 as though it were based on the view that hatred consists in a bad state *caused* by the thought of a certain object. And let us assume that to 'separate' the state from one thought and 'join' it to others is to bring it about that when one is in the unpleasant state the former thought is displaced from one's mind by the others (what else could separating and joining be?). Then p2d is saying that hatred towards W is an unpleasant frame of mind caused by thoughts of W, so that when it occurs it can be abolished by getting rid of the thoughts. How useful a technique is this?

Well, the 'thoughts' are supposed to be ideas, i.e., beliefs: my bad feelings about W are caused by my belief that he caused my bad feelings (according to Spinoza) or that he caused the destruction of the forests (according to me; see §63.6). So the proposed technique would be wonderfully effective: many harmful emotions would indeed disappear if we were to rid ourselves of the beliefs on which they rest! Unfortunately, sure-fire techniques are usually hard to apply. This one is inapplicable because, as Spinoza knows, belief is not under the command of the will (see §38.3).

3. Perhaps I am not being told to *lose* the harmful belief, but just to put it out of my conscious mind, thus reducing mental nastiness and vacillation by an operation not on cognitive content but merely on conscious phenomenology. That would not sit well with Spinoza's apparent view that the causal powers of ideas do not depend upon whether they are

---

3. Neu in *Emotion, Thought and Therapy* praises Spinoza for showing how we might 'alter emotional life by changing beliefs' (p. 2). But the mere fact that 'thoughts are of greater importance than feelings in the classification . . . of emotional states' (p. 1) is not in itself therapeutically helpful, and Neu sometimes slips into implying that it is.

accompanied by consciousness. But it would offer a manageable technique: I am to destroy the unpleasantness and upset involved in my hatred for W by arranging that when a bout of it comes over me I stop thinking about W and flood my mind with thoughts of a Chardin pastel or a Mozart quartet or Verona or my father—something that fills me with pleasure.

This would probably succeed, not in abolishing my hostile disposition but in calming the feelings that go with it. And as a technique it is theoretically practicable: it makes sense to try to rid oneself of certain thoughts; it will often be hard to do, but it is not like trying to rid oneself of a belief.

And it might be made easier by practice. In p10s Spinoza recommends acquiring disciplined habits of mind which will bring us smoothly through life's rough passages. For example, of his Part 4 thesis that 'hate is to be conquered by love or by nobility' he says:

> In order that we may always have this rule of reason ready when it is needed, we ought to meditate frequently on the common wrongs of men, and how they may be warded off best by nobility. For if we join the image of a wrong to the imagination of this maxim, it will always be ready for us (by 2p18) when a wrong is done to us. Anger will be overcome in far less time than if we had not considered these things beforehand in this way. (287/32, quoted with omissions)

This is not said with reference to p2 in particular, but presumably it is meant to be applied wherever it fits. So it could suggest how the p2 technique could become easier to apply, namely, by practice in making a turbulent emotion a trigger for filling the mind with some calming thought. But although I have found in my own experience that this can be done, I do not agree with Spinoza that 'He who will observe these rules carefully—for they are not difficult—and practice them, will soon be able to direct most of his actions according to the command of reason' (289/10), and I would bring against him the famous closing cadence of the *Ethics*: 'All excellent things are as difficult as they are rare.'

§77.   *Second technique: turning passions into actions*

1. The second technique comes from Spinoza's thesis that 'An affect which is a passion ceases to be a passion as soon as we form a clear and distinct idea of it' (p3). Here as always 'clear and distinct' means 'adequate', and that is crucial: an idea which is adequate in my mind is caused from within, and is therefore an action of mine, not a passion; so its bodily counterpart is also an action, not a passion. So I cannot have an adequate idea of any of my passions, from which Spinoza infers that if I do form an adequate idea of one of my states it must cease forthwith to be a passion.

Why not infer instead that I cannot form an adequate idea of any of my passions? Spinoza answers in p4 that there is no state of the body of which we can't form some adequate idea; but his reason is that we have adequate ideas of certain aspects of all our bodily states. This is another of his moves of the form 'We *do*, so we *can*', with the conclusion being taken to mean that we can more than we do (cf. §69.7). It is invalid, and its failure ruins this entire line of thought.

Not that that is the worst of its troubles. Spinoza really does think this is a technique for emotional self-control:

> Each of us has—in part at least, if not absolutely—the power to understand himself and his affects, and consequently the power to bring it about that he is less acted on by them. . . . It is not possible to devise any other remedy for the affects which both depends on our power and is more excellent than this one which consists in the true cognition of the affects. (p4s at 283/8,34)

This 'excellent' procedure comes first in Spinoza's retrospective list of techniques in p20s. He clearly thought well of it. But really it is non-sense, for no one could possibly acquire an adequate idea of an event after it has occurred. If x now exists and is a passion in me, then its cause y was outside my body; so $I(y)$ was outside my mind, and thus $I(x)$ is inadequate in my mind. And that's that! I can no more make $I(x)$ adequate by bringing it about that $I(y)$ was inside my mind than I can become royal by altering who my parents were.

The absurdity remains if we set aside adequate ideas and attend merely to the notion of turning a passion into an action. That means making a change in what the cause of the event *was*, and once the event has occurred it is too late for that.

It might not be too late if the topic were not a past event but an ongoing process, whose causes could be altered as it continues—like altering the causes of a draught by gradually closing a window while uncovering a fan. But I cannot imagine what it would be like in this way to alter the causes of an ongoing emotional process.

Or Spinoza might be offering not a cure for present troubles but rather a prophylactic against future ones, telling us to ensure that our affects, when they occur, are as active as we can make them. I don't know what this would be like either.

2. I conjecture that what he had in mind in offering p3,4 was not nonsense, but rather the view that sufferings can be somewhat lessened by an understanding of their causes. That is all right as a bit of worldly wisdom, but p3d is irrelevant to it. Suppose that some episode x occurs in my body, and was caused by an external event y. If I inquire into the causes of x, and am successful, I shall acquire ideas of y. But those ideas will not include $I(y)$—the idea directly of y, its 2p7 counterpart—but only ideas indirectly of it. So the cause of $I(x)$, namely $I(y)$, will continue to be outside my mind; so $I(x)$ will remain inadequate and x will remain a passion. Thus, Spinoza's demonstration of the efficacy of this technique is to no avail. There is no guarantee that understanding will reduce suffering, and Spinoza is not entitled to say: 'To the extent that we understand the causes of an unpleasure it ceases (by p3) to be a passion, i.e. (by 3p59) to that extent it ceases to be unpleasure. And so to the extent that we understand God to be the cause of unpleasure, to that extent we are pleased.' (p18s)

In place of this pretence of an understood and guaranteed mechanism for reducing unpleasant emotions, we need something humbler and more interesting—namely, the observation that a knowledge of causes sometimes has healing power. This is now the common property of the schools of psychotherapy descended from Freud, though they disagree in how they explain it and what they do with it. None regards it as a proven necessity as Spinoza pretends to.

3. Hampshire disagrees with the usual reading of p3,4 which I have followed:

Spinoza is often represented as implausibly asserting that knowledge of the causes of suffering by itself brings liberation from suffering. This is a double over-simplification. [a] First, the liberation consists in the substitution of a free activity and of self-assertion, which is as such enjoyable, for a passive reaction, which is as such depressing and frustrating. [b] Secondly, in the definition of any of the passions the pleasure or suffering, and the thought of its cause, are indissolubly connected. [c] If the confused thought, or imagination, of an external cause is replaced by thought in an intellectual order, an active emotion replaces a passion.[4]

(a) makes the point that one can quell an unpleasant passion by embarking on active thinking. So one can, sometimes; it can also be done by swimming or listening to Wagner or having a good sleep. Did Spinoza contribute anything to discovering or explaining this? If so, where? What does he actually say that points towards it? Certainly nothing in p3d. Hampshire's (b), though apparently offered to correct the usual account of p3, reads like the premiss of p2, namely, a thesis about the meanings of certain words. And in moving on to (c) Hampshire seems to follow Spinoza in drawing therapeutic conclusions from semantic premises, in the manner of p2d on its least flattering interpretation. As for the content of the conclusion (c): I do not understand that well enough to comment on it.

§78. *Third technique: reflecting on determinism*

1. The third technique—oddly omitted from the list in p10s—is given in p6. Let us examine Spinoza's argument for that proposition.

We should start at 3p48. This is about love and hate, but I shall take it in terms of hate only, for brevity. The central claim is that my hatred for Peter will be lessened if I come to think that he was not the only cause

4. Hampshire, 'Spinoza and the Idea of Freedom', p. 308.

of . . . whatever it may be. The argument assumes that I have a fixed quantity of hate to distribute among its objects, and so the more there are, the less I hate each.

This is just wrong. Hate is not like that. If I come to believe that Paul as well as Peter contributed to my unpleasure (or to burning down my house) that will reduce the *proportion* but not necessarily the *amount* of my hate that is aimed at Peter. For he may move from receiving all my hate to receiving half of it simply because I add an equal hatred for Paul.

The unjustified conclusion of 3p48 is carried further in 3p49: 'If we imagine a thing to be free, then our love or hate towards it must, for the same reason in each case, be greater than it would be towards the thing if it were imagined to be necessary.'[5] The idea is that if my hatred for Peter is lessened by my thinking that Peter's causal role was shared, then so it will be by my thinking that what Peter did was causally determined. For that involves a thought of other causes of what Peter did to me; whereas if I think his behaviour was radically free I cannot share out the responsibility, and so the whole odium attaches to Peter.

Notice that Spinoza is now talking about reducing hate through the belief in other causes, not necessarily other collaborating causes. Whether Peter and Paul jointly harmed me (they were hooked up in parallel) or Paul caused Peter to harm me (they were hooked up in series), my belief that Paul was involved lessens my hatred for Peter. Furthermore, 3p49 implies that the lessening requires only the belief that his conduct had some cause—it needn't be a *de re* belief about the particular cause that it had (though 5p6s implies that a *de re* belief will have a greater emotional effect than the mere belief that something was the cause). It follows, apparently, that if I think that Peter's conduct resulted from an infinite causal chain, my hatred for him is reduced to something infinitesimal, i.e., is abolished.

3p49 is used in 5p5d, a difficult demonstration most of whose complexities we can avoid. In a nutshell, there is a threat of conflict between 3p49 and 4p11, and part of what Spinoza is attempting in 5p5d is to show that those two are consistent by using both of them in a single argument. Let us set that aside. We should also not be troubled by Spinoza's notion of 'imagining x *simpliciter*'. All he means by this is 'just imagining x itself, with no views about what caused it'. He equates this with 'imagining x as free', on the strength of his view that the belief in radical freedom is ignorance of the causes of our actions (see §40.4).

What remains in 5p5d is a plainly invalid inference from 3p49 to the

5. Or so Spinoza must mean. His words mean merely '. . . greater than towards necessary'.

conclusion that 'the greatest affect of all' is towards a thing we imagine as free. Spinoza does not try to justify the broadening move from 'love and hate' to 'affect', although 3p48,49 depended on special facts about the definitions of love and hate. But let that pass, for there is even worse trouble in the transition from p5 to p6, which says: 'To the extent that a mind understands all things as necessary, it has a greater power over affects. . . . ' This increased power is to come from the lessening of the affects which is produced by the belief that their objects were caused. There seems to be a slide from affect size to affect intensity (see §65), but that may not be important. What is crucial is the move from '. . . will lessen my affect towards Peter' to '. . . will lessen my affect'. If we are lavishly indulgent towards the sequence 3p48–49–5p5 we may credit it with showing that my belief that Peter was caused to act as he did will lessen the intensity of my emotion towards him, but we cannot extract the further conclusion that I shall then be in a less intense and upsetting emotional state altogether. The argument concerns the redistribution of emotions over a wider range of objects; it gives no promise of showing that beliefs about causes can make one less intensely emotional, and Spinoza's pretence to the contrary in 5p6d is not even prima facie supported by anything he has said. Here is a possibility: When I think of Peter deterministically, much of my hate is redirected towards his ancestors and schoolteachers; I have as great a total amount of hate as before, and now it is harder to control because it is wide-ranging and unfocussed. I don't believe this; but it is a coach-and-four which can be comfortably driven through the gap in Spinoza's argument.

2. The demonstrations aside, Spinoza is in any case wrong in holding that determinist thoughts tend to quell *all* affects. Fear is not calmed by the thought that if the feared event occurs it will be caused. And here is another example from my own experience. We saw lightning, heard thunder, and then noticed on the opposite rim of the canyon a pine tree, flanked by dark green neighbours, itself completely invested in golden flame. My thought 'That's what a divine miracle should look like' made me aware of my conviction that the tree was burning from natural causes; but that awareness did not lessen my joyful delight in the scene. Spinoza might say that that lies outside the scope of p6 because the emotion in question was not harmful or dangerous, but he is not entitled to that as a defence, for p6 clearly implies that the determinist thought will lessen *any* affect.

Still, some affects are reduced by causal thoughts about their objects. As Spinoza says, in an example which doesn't fit the point he is making but does fit mine: 'We see that unpleasure over some good which has perished is lessened as soon as the man who has lost it realizes that there was no way the good could have been kept.' (5p6s) I agree that there is something healing in the thought that a failure was not a near miss, this being something to which 'experience testifies' (p6s). It cannot be explained through the claim that every affect is diminished by thinking about the causes acting on its object.

3. But the most important truth buried in p6 has to do not with changing disappointment into resignation but rather with such changes as that of resentment into mere regret. In expounding this matter, I shall rely on some work by Strawson, in a version which I have developed and which has his assent.[6] Given that something has occurred which is welcome or unwelcome to me, my attitude towards it may be of either of two kinds. (a) I may adopt the 'objective attitude' of one who wants to understand what happened—to know what the mechanisms were—so as to raise or lower the chances of its happening again. (b) I may adopt a 'reactive attitude' such as gratitude or resentment. The objective attitude can be taken with respect to any event, including human actions; but human actions can, though they need not be, made the objects of reactive attitudes instead. For most of us, there seems to be an incompatibility between the two: while I am in a prudentially inquiring frame of mind about your benefit or harm to me, I cannot also feel true gratitude or resentment in respect of it. I don't know why. Probably it can't be explained until we can define 'reactive', which I have been unable to do. Still, the incompatibility exists, whatever the reason for it, and it can do philosophical work for us.

In the background of my use of it lies Strawson's view that praise and blame are rooted in feelings of moral approval or indignation, which in turn are vicarious analogues of gratitude and resentment. The general idea, simplified, is that for me to hold you morally accountable for how you treated Paul is for me to resent, on Paul's behalf, what you did to him.

Consider now the common belief that a person is not to blame for an action which was fully causally determined. There are respectable arguments for that, but I doubt if they really explain the prevalence of the belief. If they do, then we are left with no explanation for the fact that the impulse to blame someone for an action tends to fade not only in face of a cool, careful thought of the action as determined, but also in face of a cool, careful thought of it as not determined. Perhaps there are good arguments on both sides, and our concept of moral accountability is inconsistent. But I suggest a different and deeper explanation for the data. What we have here, I suggest, are not logical conflicts between propositions, but an incompatibility between two frames of mind—the reactive frame which

6. P. F. Strawson, *Freedom and Resentment and Other Essays* (London, 1974), the title essay; J. Bennett, 'Accountability', in Z. van Straaten (ed.), *Philosophical Subjects* (Oxford, 1980), pp. 14–47; Reply by Strawson, *ibid.*, pp. 260–266.

begets thoughts of moral accountability etc., and the objective one which generates questions about whether and how the action was caused. If this is right, then the mere truth of determinism is no challenge to our continued use of praise and blame. Whether we should retain praise and blame is a practical question—more like 'Should we continue with chamber music?' than like 'Should we retain quantum theory?' Like Strawson, I want to retain at least some reactive attitudes because I think that the prospect of being without any of them is horrid. To welcome this part of our natures, rather than trying to suppress it, is to choose to retain a degree of impulsive uncalculated response to one another; it is to refuse always to act and feel in the light of a considered view of the facts.

4. When Spinoza implies that every affect is diminished by the thought of its object as caused, what he says is too weak in one way, too strong in another. It is too weak in that the sort of emotional quelling he presumably has in mind can be done just by getting into the objective frame of mind: it is enough to ask whether the event was caused, even if the answer is 'No' or 'I don't know'. But what he says is too strong in that he applies it to all affects, whereas it really works only for the ones involving reactive attitudes. I have noted its failure with fear and delighted wonder. Let us now try it out on pity, an emotion which is specially worth studying if one wants to grasp the concept of a reactive attitude.

Pity is not reactive in Strawson's sense. For one thing it is a response to sufferings, passivities, whereas I take reactive attitudes to be responses to actions or attitudes or active dispositions—one is grateful to or angry with someone for what he does or is disposed to do, not for what he undergoes. Also, I understand reactive attitudes to be ones that civilized people would adopt only towards things they regarded as not merely sentient but personal. By that standard pity is not reactive: pity towards a sparrow with a broken wing is a proper response to suffering, and not sentimental or anthropomorphic. Indeed, pity is the minimal emotion—surprisingly little has to be present for it to be appropriate. Spinoza, oddly, defines it as an emotion towards 'another whom we imagine to be like us' (AD 18; see also 3p27s), which should mean an emotion towards a fellow human. That error cannot be explained away as a covert value-judgment, as though Spinoza were saying that pity ought to be directed only towards one's own kind; for he thinks that all pity is bad (4p50d).

My third clue to pity's not being reactive is its being perfectly compatible with objectivity of attitude. When I think about the bird's broken wing as the product of causes and as a subject for cure, the pity is not drained out of me. Indeed, in many cases when objectivity dislodges a negative reactive attitude, what the latter gives place to is, precisely, pity. So this is an emotion for which the technique offered in p6 will not work.

Spinoza thinks otherwise. He illustrates the p6 therapy first with resignation to loss and then with pity, thus:

No one pities infants because of their inability to speak, to walk, or to reason. . . . But if most people were born grown up, and only one or two were born infants, then everyone would pity the infants, because they would regard infancy not as a natural and necessary thing but as a defect of Nature. (p6s)

I submit that this is wrong. The reason why we do not find the infant's incapacities pitiable is that they do not in general involve suffering—and perhaps also because we know that the infant will grow out of them. Our knowing that the incapacities are natural and inevitable is irrelevant, as can be seen by considering our pity for someone who is dying in pain and fear. Even if such a manner of death were the universal lot, 'a natural and necessary thing' for all of us, would that evaporate our pity for actual people actually going through it? Not mine, and I suspect not yours either.

§79.   *Reactive attitudes in the* Ethics

1. We can command a clearer view of some broad aspects of Spinoza's thought by confronting him with Strawson.

To a philosopher who says 'If determinism is true we should stop blaming people' Strawson says, in effect: 'That assumes that since objectivity is always possible, reactive attitudes are always wrong.' For him, that puts an end to the question. He is sure that we should not try to empty ourselves of our reactive attitudes; acknowledging that they can impede the cool study of particular facts, he would have us be incompletely 'rational' in *that* sense in order to conduct ourselves rationally 'in light of an assessment of the gains and losses to human life, its enrichment or impoverishment'. Most people, if they accepted his diagnosis, would agree with his conclusion. But not Spinoza: he would say that on Strawson's diagnosis the retention of blame etc. involves a lessening in our efforts to understand the causes of actions; and Spinoza finds that unacceptable. Recall that for him error is a sort of ignorance, so that he has no sharp line between shutting out facts (the price Strawson will pay for reactivity) and believing falsely (the price nobody will pay). And we are reminded of this Spinozistic doctrine right in the middle of our present area, when in p5d Spinoza equates imagining a thing as uncaused with 'simply imagining it' while not knowing its causes.

But Spinoza does not rely on that theory of error for his opposition to anything that would deflect us from trying to understand our world. When he infers from 4p26,27 that 'An affect is bad or harmful only to the extent that it prevents the mind from being able to think' (5p9d), he argues invalidly; but he shows his commitment to intellect above all else—one which probably lay too deep in his mind for argument.

Few of us share that absolute commitment of Spinoza's, and Strawson plausibly suggests that those who do have not thoroughly imagined what our life would be like if they had their way.

Of course in particular cases reactivity may be especially harmful, and then good can be done by cultivating objectivity of attitude. But that refers to such harms as offending or depressing others, becoming ill, diverting energy from profitable ventures, and so on. This is not to endorse Spinoza's view that when an emotional state impedes one's thinking objectively, that *is harm* just in itself. Still, we can suppose that the more obvious and earthy harms were also in his mind, even if they find no place in his arguments.

2. Spinoza's intellectualism should make him more hostile to reactive kinds of feeling than he is to affects generally. And he does seem to have reactive feelings in his sights when, after condemning any affect which 'prevents the mind from being able to think', he concludes: 'And so that affect which determines the mind to contemplate many objects together is less harmful than another equally great affect which engages the mind solely in contemplating one or a few objects, so that it cannot think of others.' (p9d) This is about affects that shoulder thinking aside; but when Spinoza reverts to it in his list of therapeutic techniques (p20s at 293/13), he takes it to concern affects that can be lessened by thinking. That is, he sees a tussle between emotion and thought, in which either might be used as a lever against the other. That is exactly right for the reactive emotions. My angry resentment towards you does exclude my thinking objectively about you, and yet I can sometimes—*do* sometimes—quell my anger by deliberately setting myself to think objectively, causally, prudentially, about its object.

This prompts the thought that the concept of a reactive attitude might be found lurking, in some guise or other, in the pages of the *Ethics*. Was Spinoza subliminally aware of the line which Strawson draws and puts to such effective use?

Well, when he says that 'Because men consider themselves to be free, they have a greater love or hate towards one another than towards other things' (3p49s), and that therefore repentance and self-satisfaction 'are very violent because men believe themselves free' (3p51s at 179/25), he may be showing some awareness of the concept of a reactive feeling. As Strawson shows, it is common and natural for people to think that reactive feelings, above all others, require the belief that the object is not fully caused.

And some other remarks of Spinoza's, without mentioning freedom, suggest the antithesis between reactivity and the stance of coolly inquiring objectivity. He praises 'a judge who condemns a guilty man to death, not from hate or anger etc. but only from a love of the general welfare'

(4p63cs).[7] He says that a reasonable man 'tries above all to conceive things as they are in themselves, and to remove the obstacles to true cognition, like hate, anger, envy, mockery, pride, and others of that sort' (4p73s at 265/27). Above all, 3 Preface is full of the contrast between reactive and objective, as in the remark about 'those who prefer to curse or laugh at the affects and actions of men, rather than understand them' (138/6).

3. But the reactive/objective line is not to be found systematically present in the *Ethics*. There is a hint of it when Spinoza alludes to 'hate or anger *etc.*' and to those two together with 'mockery, pride, and others *of that sort*', as though he had some definite species of emotion in mind; but if he has, he does not produce it. The most likely vehicle for it would be the idea that some emotions essentially involve the thought that their object is free, but Spinoza defines only two of his affect kinds directly in that way (AD 26 and 27).

In 1 Appendix he ties praise and blame to the belief in freedom, which may be tantamount to putting them in the reactive category. But they appear only twice in the affect definitions (AD 30 and 31). It is interesting that the four emotion kinds which are defined directly or indirectly in terms of a belief in freedom, all have oneself as object. That may be evidence that Spinoza, in his thinking about the difference between reactive and objective attitudes, tended to focus on attitudes to his own behaviour, making less of the difference between (say) regret and resentment at others' conduct than of the difference between (say) regret and guilt over his own.

I find it surprising, incidentally, that he does not develop the idea that blame and praise express emotional attitudes. It is his *kind* of view, and in one place he entertains it. In Letter 78, replying to the question whether determinism implies that men are excusable for all their actions, Spinoza says that that depends on what 'they are excusable' means, and adds ironically that they are excusable if this means that 'God is not angry with them' (IV/327/4). I do not know why the link between blame and anger is not systematically worked out in the *Ethics*.

So we have at most four emotion kinds whose definitions reflect their reactive status. The definitions of favour and indignation (AD 19 and 20) give them no praise-blame force. Nor are anger and vengeance (AD 36 and 37) defined so as to give them a reactive status. Indeed, the objects of anger are not even confined to individuals thought of as personal. The definition of vengeance is also too broad: it counts me as feeling vengeful

---

7. Spinoza does not think that penal systems should be relinquished along with moral accountability. 'As to the claim that if this were granted then all wickedness would be excusable: what of it? For wicked men are no less to be feared, and no less pernicious, when they are necessarily wicked.' Letter 58 at IV/268/1.

towards you if I want to harm you because (I think that) you harmed me out of hostility towards me. I might fit that definiens because I want to kill you in sheer self-defence, my attitude towards you being perfectly objective and coolly prudent, and quite untouched by vengefulness ordinarily so-called. The definiens does include the word 'hate', but that does not bring reactiveness into the picture, as can be seen from looking at AD 7.

Finally, there is gratitude, Spinoza's definition of which sounds promising. Gratitude, he says, is 'a desire or eagerness of love, by which we try to benefit one who has benefited us from a like affect of love' (AD 34). But he links this with 3p39, which bases gratitude on prudence. putting it squarely in the domain of the objective attitude. In 4p71,s he contrasts the best sort of gratitude, of which only free men are capable, with the lower kind which ordinary people have towards one another. Despite his saying that the lower kind is mostly commercial and manipulative, he in fact describes both of them in self-interested terms; the primary contrast seems to be between sober judgments about long term interests on the one hand and, on the other, 'blind desire', i.e., immediate and thoughtless likes and dislikes, as though the lower kind of gratitude were not commercial enough! Whatever is going on here, the essentially reactive nature of gratitude is not being recognized unless the lower kind of gratitude is being treated as reactive and deplored for that reason.

§80.   *Love towards God*

1. To keep things orderly, I should relate Spinoza's list of therapeutic procedures, as given in p20s, to mine. Here is his list with references to his text, mostly supplied by Spinoza himself:

(a)   curing passive affects by making them active (p3,4)

(b)   separating and joining (p2)

(c)   (the immovable affect arising from reason) (p7)

(d)   taking a more comprehensive view of the causes (p8,9,11)

(e)   reordering the affects (p1,10; 'see also p12–14').

I have highlighted Spinoza's (b) and (a) and the procedure of reflecting on determinism (p5,6) which is omitted from his list, oddly enough, though (d) might be a pointer towards it. That leaves (c) and (e), which do not describe usable therapeutic procedures but merely express optimism about how much good such procedures can do.

I think that p9 should stand on its own, and that p8,11 should be grouped with p12–14 as a fairly unified addition to what p1,10 say about the reordering of affects. I shan't discuss p8,11–14 in detail, however, because I don't understand them. (Their topic is the joining of *images*, but they also use the phrase 'image or affect' and 'all the body's states, or images

of things': Spinoza is here having trouble like that discussed in §64.4.)
The more things a given affect is 'related' to, Spinoza seems to hold, the
more handles by which its owner can grasp it to bring it under control. Add
that an affect or image will have more such handles if it is 'related to
things we understand clearly and distinctly', and we can infer optimism
about the ultimate victory of reason over the harmful affects. I have
been unable to extract anything less vague from these materials.

The 'many images' theme runs through p8,11–14, and p14–20 are
about love towards God. One cannot avoid seeing p14—'The mind can
bring it about that all the body's states or images of things are related
to the idea of God'—as the link between the two groups of propositions;
which makes it odd that although p8 leads through p11 to p12 the thread
is broken there; and p13d reaches back to Part 2 for its only premiss,
while p14d mentions none of its immediate predecessors. I cannot pretend
to explain this oddity, for I confess to not understanding these propositions anyway.

2. If p14d shows anything, it is that to the extent that you have adequate
ideas your states *are* 'related to the idea of God', and p15d adds this argument: If you have adequate ideas then your states are related to the idea
of God (by p14), and you are pleased (by 3p53); from which it follows
by AD 6 that you love God. Strictly, AD 6 requires that you be in a
pleasant state while having the idea of *God as the cause of your pleasure*;
but perhaps Spinoza is entitled to that.

The big defect in this argument is its reliance on the unduly weak
account of love in AD 6. For a proper account of love, what is needed
is not merely a belief about a cause but a belief which is a cause (see
§63.6). But if Spinoza had built that into AD 6—'Love is pleasure caused
by the belief that some external thing has caused . . . '—he would be
unable to hook it into the other premises of p15d. In short, his conclusion
that reasonable people love God depends on giving 'love towards God'
an unacceptably thin meaning.

3. I need not comment on the unsurprising doctrines that this love for
God 'must engage the mind most' (p16) and 'cannot be tainted by envy
or jealousy' (p20). Nor is there any puzzle in Spinoza's arguing that God
has no passions, and—because they involve changes in level of perfection—
no pleasure or unpleasure either (p17). The reader may enjoy working
out why p18d is at once Spinozistic and spectacularly invalid, as is a similar
argument purporting to dissolve the problem of evil in p18s. The faulti-
ness of p19d has already been shown in §41.5.

4. I am sure that Spinoza 'loved God', i.e., took pleasure in the thought
of the universe's immensity, orderliness and richness. This went with his
love of understanding—the assiduous inquirer becomes devoted to his

subject matter—but it seems also to have arisen from a kind of vision, an awed *sense* of how wonderful it is that the whole of reality should form a single system. A glimpse of that vision can be gleaned from the closing paragraph of Isaac Bashevis Singer's story *The Spinoza of Market Street*. An elderly Spinoza scholar has just contracted a marriage of convenience with an ugly ungainly woman; she surprises him by coming to his bed, and, the storyteller says, 'What happened that night could be called a miracle'. Towards dawn Dr. Fischelson gazes out his window and thinks Spinozistically of the one substance, awed by the fact that it includes the galaxies, the heaving of Europe as World War I begins, and the tumult of his own heart.

It is a real vision, and for some people it is powerful. Spinoza was one such, and Dr. Fischelson another. I offer it no disrespect when I say that Spinoza has not shown that any fully reasonable person will feel its power and will thus 'love God'. The mind, as Hume said, has a great propensity to spread itself on external objects; Spinoza has spread himself on the rest of us, taking some of his own principal character traits and arguing wildly that the acquisition of them is a sure route to freedom and happiness.

§81.   *Hampshire's Spinoza*

1. I have done my best with everything in the *Ethics* that could possibly be called a technique for emotional control, and I am afraid that my account of these materials may look cheap and shallow when compared with what has been said on the topic by Stuart Hampshire. Running through his work, spread across three decades, there has been a strong implication that in Spinoza's pages we can find a coherent, unified, important and true theory about cognitive therapies for emotional troubles, whereas I have found only a scatter of truths, none completely under control and no two properly related to one another. Hampshire's Spinoza gives the impression of a deep, subtle thinker about psychotherapy, whereas mine had a few good intuitive insights into the psychopathology of everyday life but utterly failed to draw them together into a coherent whole. For my generation it was Hampshire who first made Spinoza accessible, and in the thirty years since then he has continued to be one of the most insightful and fertile writers on Spinoza's thought. Nothing that he writes is negligible; the clash between us on Spinozist psychotherapy is unignorable; and so I must criticise his account in defence of mine.

2. In his first work on Spinoza, Hampshire gives this account of how cognitive procedures are supposed by Spinoza to help our emotional lives:

The . . . method of salvation consists in making the patient more self-conscious, and in making him perceive the . . . struggle within himself to preserve his own internal adjustment and balance; he must be brought to realize that it is this continuous struggle which expresses itself in his pleasures and pains, desires and aversions.[8]

The part after the semicolon is not convincing: it is neither plausible nor Spinozistic to say that the cure will be effected by the person's coming to see the truth of Spinoza's general doctrine about self-preservation and its relation to pleasure and unpleasure. Nor does it help much to add that the person, as well as seeing the truth of the general doctrine, applies it to his own case by perceiving the struggle within himself. To be plausible as psychotherapy, or as exegesis of Spinoza, the account must make the cure depend on the person's coming to know certain specific things about his internal struggle. Hampshire does not here say what they are.

In his most recent writing on this topic, he again implies that a proper cure involves knowing certain general doctrines, and again brings in self-knowledge; but this time the picture is more complicated. We are now told that reasonableness will increase if and only if:

[a] Men are converted from egocentricity to detachment in their thought about themselves and about their relations to external things and persons. [b] This conversion depends upon their realizing that their innate drive to increase their power and liberty requires disciplined thought, and an assertion of independence. . . . [c] Once a man realizes the power of thought, and exercises this power, he begins to enjoy the exercise and to feel the power of understanding, which is a positive pleasure, as men enjoy the exercise of physical powers. [d] The drive for clear thinking and for understanding necessarily brings with it some self-knowledge and some degree of detachment from unconsidered and destructive passions.[9]

I protest at (a). No philosopher was less inclined than Spinoza to make any theoretical use of the notion of the first person singular. Hampshire admits that 'The contrast between the standpoint of the thinking subject . . . and the standpoint of the observer . . . is not to be found in Spinoza'; and he remarks, apparently about that contrast, 'I have added it as a gloss upon the notorious contrast within Spinoza's writing between the exhortation to correct the intellect and the simultaneous exhortation to abandon . . . notions of free will'.[10] This is excessively compressed and difficult to follow, but perhaps it can be unpacked so as to say something like what I have said about the 'notorious contrast' in §67.2. I see no prospect of using it to show that Spinozist psychotherapy involves the distinction between egocentricity and detachment in one's thought about oneself.

I don't understand (b), unless Hampshire really means by it only that the acquisition of greater power and liberty requires disciplined thought.

8. Hampshire, *Spinoza*, p. 141.

9. Hampshire, *Two Theories of Morality*, pp. 66f. Letters added.

10. *Ibid.*, pp. 76f.

In that case (b) amounts to the statement that to be helped by Spinozist therapy one must think that that is the way to be helped. That seems right, and Spinozist, but it does not take us far. The point (c) about the pleasure of thought as such belongs to that 'substitution of something pleasant for something unpleasant' technique which I discussed in §77.3. I stand by my opinion, there expressed, that it is not a weighty contribution by Spinoza to psychotherapy. That leaves (d). Its phrase 'detachment from . . . passions' echoes the theme of (a)—release from egocentricity—which Hampshire acknowledges is not Spinoza's. With that set aside, all we are left with is (d)'s attribution to Spinoza of the belief that if we are assiduous in our thinking, that will help us to take control of our emotions. Spinoza does indeed say such things. But this is hardly interesting in the absence of details about how thought can help us to achieve emotional self-control; and in the two works from which I have quoted, Hampshire offers no such details.

3. He does provide some, however, in a paper which comes chronologically between the other two:

Every passion that can be attributed to me is a pleasure or a pain combined with an idea of the cause of this pleasure or pain. There must therefore be an explanation of my having this idea about the cause of my pleasure or suffering. Suppose then that I am at all times asking myself the question—Is the sequence of ideas that has terminated in this idea a self-contained sequence that, by itself, completely explains my idea of the cause? In other words, was the conclusion reached by a rational process? Or must I mention ideas that are associated in my experience, but that are without intrinsic connection, in explaining my conclusion? Under these conditions of self-conscious reflection, I never affirm a proposition, or commit myself to a belief, without qualifying it as adequately or inadequately founded. If this condition were fulfilled, I could not be a victim of those passions that consist in the association of my pleasure or suffering with the idea of a particular transient thing, or person, in the common order of nature as its adequate cause.[11]

Hampshire assumes that when (for instance) I hate someone I have an unpleasant feeling associated with a belief about the person who causes it. I am to reform my emotional life by scrutinizing such beliefs about the objects of my emotions, asking of each whether it was arrived at rationally. If it wasn't, then the reform procedure requires me to do something with the belief—something which will free me from the feeling which it caused.

But what am I to do with the belief? If the answer is simply 'Lose it', then this is the 5p2 technique discussed in §76.2: If you have a bad emotion, relinquish the belief which caused it. Hampshire is presumably trying to stop short of that when he says that what has to be done, on recognition that the belief is ill-founded, is to not 'affirm' its content or 'commit myself' to it 'without qualifying it as inadequately founded'. Pre-

11. Hampshire, 'Spinoza and the Idea of Freedom', pp. 306f.

sumably, the therapeutic benefit of this is that if the belief which caused my emotion turns out to be poorly founded, I shall believe it less whole-heartedly and that will lessen its emotional impact.

That would work if the belief turned out to be so poorly supported that I seriously doubted its truth. Short of that, however, there is no therapeutic benefit to be got here. One might try Descartes's advice that we suspend judgment on any belief which is not perfectly secure, but Spinoza has shown that that advice cannot be followed (see §38.4). As for the effective therapy—I mean the discovery that the relevant belief has a good chance of being false—that is usually not applicable because few of our harmful emotions are based on false or highly questionable beliefs. In p4s, which may be what Hampshire has in mind, Spinoza brackets ill-foundedness with falsity by saying that we should conduct ourselves 'so that the mind may . . . think those things which it perceives clearly and distinctly, and with which it is fully satisfied, and so that the affect itself may be separated from the thought of an external cause and joined to true thoughts' (283/12). But the implication that 'the thought of an external cause' is not true is neither explained nor defended, and I see no reason to accept it.

4. A little further on in the same paper, Hampshire implies that harmful emotions will usually involve one false belief, namely, the belief that the object of one's emotion is its 'adequate cause':

To be angry is to be displeased and to be disposed to injure someone, together with the thought that he has been the cause of injury to me. When I consider my true interests as an active thinking being, and also examine a train of un-conscious associations that leads to the idea of him as the original cause of my displeasure, and recognize the inadequacy of the idea, the passion of anger dis-appears. When I realize the contributing causes of my displeasure in my own unconscious memories and consequent dispositions, the idea of an adequate external cause disappears, and there is nothing left to be angry with.[12]

This is reminiscent of p9—the lessening of an affect by taking into account more of its causes—except that now the emphasis is on its causes within oneself. I cannot think of anything in Spinoza's text which could be read in that way, nor am I convinced that it is true as psychology. I was once nearly destroyed by a persistent cancerous anger. My enemy's conduct angered me only because of facts about the sort of person I then was: I knew that at the time, but that knowledge did me no good. Saying to myself 'He is not the adequate cause of my anger' would not have helped me if I had meant merely 'The causes of my anger include factors other than his conduct'.

12. *Ibid.*, pp. 307f.

Why does Hampshire think otherwise? Well, in the passages I have quoted we find the phrases 'ideas that are associated in my experience . . . without intrinsic connection', 'the association of my [emotion] with the idea of a particular transient thing, or person', 'a train of unconscious associations that lead to the idea of him as the original cause of my displeasure'. Perhaps he is thinking of the phenomenon Spinoza reports in 3p15,16, namely, the establishment of certain emotional patterns by sheer coincidences—my dislike for a person who happens to resemble my enemy, my fondness for a town which never did me any good but where I chanced once to be happy, and so on (see §64.3). I doubt if this looms large in the psychopathology of everyday life. Also, when it does occur, I doubt that the diagnosing of it involves the rooting out of false or ill-founded beliefs, so much as the supplying of causal beliefs to fill a vacuum. And, finally, it is only Hampshire who proposes to put this phenomenon to work in psychotherapy: Spinoza uses 3p15,16 in depicting emotions as dangerous and unruly, but he does not try to turn them to account in his therapeutic proposals. If he thinks I can cure an emotion by discovering that I have it *per accidens* (as he puts it in 3p15), he is notably quiet about it.

In a later paper, Hampshire offers a different angle on the same idea that we can alter our emotional state by recognizing our own contribution to it. He contends that Spinoza's theory of emotion is modelled on the causal theories of sense perception which flourished in his day. We naively look at the world without realizing that our seeing is a causal transaction between ourselves and it; then we come to realize this, and we look again, and now the sensory impressions are the same and yet also different. Similarly, according to Hampshire's Spinoza, with the emotions:

Under the influence of a passion, we do not think of that passion as a psychophysical phenomenon issuing from a complication of causes, internal and external. We typically confuse our unexamined love or hatred of someone with a veridical perception of his amiability or hatefulness. We fall into a kind of naive realism in respect of the objects of our attitudes and sentiments, leaving our conceptions of the objects uncorrected by calm and persistent thought about complex causes.[13]

This is a striking idea, memorably expressed, but I don't believe it. A man in a passion does not typically think at all about the etiology of his state, but does he unthinkingly harbour false beliefs about it? The suggestion that we think of our hatreds as perceptions of hatefulness, though impressive, seems false.

Furthermore, this is supposed to help in emotional therapy, but Hampshire stops short of claiming that benefits will ensue from correcting our

---

13. Hampshire, 'A Kind of Materialism', p. 222.

'naive realism' about the objects of our emotions. Comparing someone who learns more about what caused his perception of the sun with someone who learns more about his anger towards a friend, he says about the latter:

When he reflects on how his belief about the external cause was formed, his original thought of a simple cause will be cancelled, as the primitive impression of the sun is cancelled; and his state of mind, and particularly his attitude to the offending person, will have changed also, merely as a consequence of this reflection. He may still have disagreeable feelings, and may recognize a tendency in himself to attribute these feelings to his friend's behaviour, just as the observer's first impression of the sun remains. But as his thoughts about the causes of his own feelings are corrected, the nature and direction of his emotions, and his consequent dispositions to act, will change also.[14]

Why? And how? Hampshire writes as though he has in mind here some definite thesis about how thoughts can act upon emotions, but apparently he doesn't, for he goes on to say: 'For his reflective thought about his own sentiment, and his reflective interpretation of its cause, and his identification of its object, always have to be included in any adequate account of his final psychophysical state.' That is all. It comes down to the trivial remark that any thinking I do makes a difference to my total mental state. There is no psychotherapeutic doctrine in that.

5. Hampshire has made a certain amount, much more judiciously than some other writers, of the comparison between Spinoza and Freud. In his first writing on Spinoza he offers an illuminating comparison, rightly emphasizing the fact that these two great thinkers were alike in holding that increased control over emotions is to be achieved not by moral effort but by informed medical intervention.[15] The familiarity of this view to those of us who are swept along in Freud's wake should not blind us to how radical and original Spinoza's approach was in his own time. And the two were alike in holding that knowledge of causes—and especially of the cognitive causes of emotional states—could not only guide therapy but could be therapy.[16]

14. *Ibid.*, pp. 223f.

15. Hampshire, *Spinoza*, pp. 141–4. The comparison between Freudian libido and Spinozist self-preservation is also interesting, though Hampshire apparently conflates the latter's official Spinozist form ('tendency') with its teleological converse ('drive').

16. And that in two different ways—through bringing health in its train and through being intrinsically valuable. We have seen Spinoza's emphasis on the latter—on knowledge as valuable for itself—and this is something he shared with Freud. 'Freud was, of course, convinced that psychoanalysis had a wholesome effect on the analysand. But while he provided us with the outline of the essentials of this process, which can be defined in terms of cognition, as making the uncon-

I am not sure whether Hampshire holds that Freud and Spinoza share the belief that mental health can be helped by bringing unconscious mental content into consciousness. That would be wrong, I think. The only thing Spinoza says about the difference between what we are conscious of and what we are not is that consciousness makes no causal difference (see AD 1, explanation, at 190/10); and in the therapeutic parts of Part 5 there is no reliance on a conscious/unconscious line. Perhaps Hampshire would agree. But his sketches of Spinoza's position use the term 'conscious' and its cognates rather a lot. He speaks of 'making the patient more self-conscious, . . . making him perceive the more or less unconscious struggle within himself'.[17] He credits Spinoza with having 'the outline of a psychopathology' which involves 'laws of unconscious memory'.[18] He says: 'The association of ideas [and] active reflection . . . are the two mechanisms by which thoughts are recombined and modified: they are the two levels of thinking, the one passive and largely unconscious, the other constituting actively directed, fully conscious thinking.'[19] He speaks of the 'fantasies and unconscious wishes and memories of a mentally disturbed man'.[20]

6. In Hampshire's later writings, however, there has been less about consciousness than about reflectiveness, i.e., thought about thought. He is of course interested only in conscious thoughts about one's own mental states, but he seems to distinguish a thought's being consciously present in my mind from its being a thought *about* my mind (see §44.6), rightly taking the notion of *conscious reflection* to combine two distinct concepts. I want to look at how Hampshire uses the concept of reflection in describing Spinoza's views.

Spinoza does imply that a person can alter his thoughts by thinking about them: Hampshire is right about that, but wrong—I shall argue—in what he makes of it.

He treats it as a thesis about 'psychic causality': my thoughts about my thoughts *cause* them to alter. Now look back over the list of psychotherapies in §80.1, remembering what the textual reality is in each case.

---

scious conscious, he never elaborated in theoretical terms his conviction of the wholesome effect of analysis in the form of the claim that it cures psychological illnesses, that it establishes mental health. He believed in the intrinsic desirability of knowing as much as possible: he was committed to the task of knowing the truth, facing the truth, seeing reality clearly.' Heinz Kohut, *The Restoration of the Self*, (New York, 1977), p. 64, quoted with omissions.

17. *Spinoza*, p. 141.

18. 'Spinoza and the Idea of Freedom', p. 306.

19. 'Spinoza's Theory of Human Freedom', p. 42.

20. *Two Theories of Morality*, p. 85.

The only one which shows much promise of fitting a causal pattern is the fifth—the only one I have been unable to understand.

More important than that, however, is Hampshire's treating this thesis about psychic causality as what primarily marks Spinoza off from 'the crass materialist',[21] and his saying: 'Spinoza held that there was a peculiar feature of psychic causality, which sets it apart from physical causality, namely, that a man's thought about the causes of his thoughts modifies the original thoughts. . . . I cannot think of a scientific determinist who has suggested, or who would accept, [this].'[22] It is strange to find Spinoza being credited with the view that psychic causality has any 'peculiar feature' which 'sets it apart from physical causality', and I cannot find anything true that Hampshire could mean by this. I have argued that Spinoza should hold that ideas have features which do not map systematically onto any features of physical things, namely, their representative contents; but the latter, just because they do not map onto the physical, must be irrelevant to the causal powers of ideas (see §51.5). Hampshire's apparent view that there are two distinct *causal* orders, one physical and one mental, seems to me deeply unSpinozist.

But Hampshire implies that it is not his view, and that he is working within the confines of 2p7, for he writes: 'I think that Spinoza thought that the . . . reflexive nature of human thought was associated with some still unknown complexity of physical structure.'[23] Yet he ends that paper by saying that in presenting Spinoza's views about the powers of reflexive thought he has 'been expanding 2p22'. The crucial point about 2p20–22 is that they offer an idea of every idea, systematically and across the board, irrespective of any facts about complexity of structure. Also, the sources of the 'ideas of ideas' doctrine in Spinoza's system utterly rule out the possibility that $I(I(x))$ should 'modify' or in any way act upon $I(x)$. If Hampshire holds onto the 'complexity of physical structure' theme, he should leave 'ideas of ideas' out of the story, and acknowledge that he has no textual basis for what he is saying.

I don't mean that he ought not to say it. If we set aside 2p20–22, but hold onto the main lines of Spinoza's thought including his parallelism, we can construct a Spinozist theory of reflective thought which answers to Hampshire's description. It goes something like this:[24]

21. 'A Kind of Materialism', p. 229.

22. 'Spinoza's Theory of Human Freedom', p. 45. See also 'Sincerity and Single-Mindedness', in Hampshire's *Freedom of Mind* (Oxford, 1972), especially p. 256.

23. 'A Kind of Materialism', p. 230.

24. I am partly guided here by D. M. Armstrong, *A Materialist Theory of the Mind* (London, 1968), ch. 15.

We drop the assumption that I(x) is in any useful sense a thought about x, or that it represents x. We tie the notion of thought *about* things to ideas *in*directly of them—e.g., my thoughts about your body, which correspond to states which your body causes in mine (see §37.3–5). Now, we suppose that my brain contains a subsystem which I shall call its Monitor. Events in the Monitor are caused by events elsewhere in the brain, and bear traces of what those other events are like; so events in the Monitor are physical 'images', in Spinoza's sense, of other brain events. Let x be a brain event outside the Monitor, and let y be its 'image' in the Monitor. Then I(y) is the idea directly of y and is an idea indirectly of x; although x is an inner and not an outer event, it relates to I(y) in the same way that a movement of yours relates to my idea indirectly of it. In each case, I have an idea directly of a bodily state of mine which is caused by and is qualitatively dependent on some other event. Furthermore, it is only because I have I(y) that I have a thought *about* x; for I(x) is merely the mental counterpart of x and is not, we are now supposing, a thought about x. Still, I(x) does exist in my mind, and I(y) can be regarded as being about it as well as being about x itself; and so I(y) is, in a way, an idea (of mine) indirectly about an idea of mine.

We can build into this theory both of the features which Hampshire wants and 2p20–22 do not allow. I may have thoughts about some of my thoughts but not all, because not all events in my body have 'images' in the Monitor. And my having I(y), my thought about I(x), may make a difference to I(x)—this being Hampshire's thesis that reflective thought can modify its subject matter. How can this be? Well, when y is caused to occur in the Monitor by the occurrence of x outside it, that causal transaction could make a difference to x, taking up some of its energy or the like, analogous to water's losing heat to the thermometer which is plunged into it. If so, then x is different from how it would have been if y had not occurred, and so, by the parallelism, I(x) is different from how it would have been if I(y) had not existed. That secures the power of reflective thought, and I don't see any other Spinozist way of doing it. Notice, though, that psychic causality is now being credited with having the supposedly 'peculiar feature' *because* physical causality has it! There is nothing here for a scientific materialist, however 'crass', to shy away from.

So again I conclude that Hampshire has not revealed an important truth the discovery of which can be credited to Spinoza. Although the broadly Spinozist theory of reflective thought which I have just constructed could have been built within the framework of the *Ethics*—with 2p20–22 dropped, and more attention paid to ideas 'indirectly of' things—it would be going too far to say that it is implicitly there or that Spinoza invented it without realizing that he had done so.

15   *The Last Three Doctrines*

Most of the faults in the *Ethics* occur while Spinoza is tackling real problems and are traceable to specific sources in the foundations of his thought. That makes his failures worth studying. But the final one-twentieth of the work, from 5p23 to the end, contains a failure of a different order—an unmitigated and seemingly unmotivated disaster. I would like to excuse myself from discussing it, but my adverse judgment on it should be defended. Also, a little can be learned from firmly grasping what is wrong with the core of it. I shall therefore reluctantly spend a chapter on it.

We have to confront three interlinked doctrines, starting with the astonishing thesis that part of the human mind is 'eternal' and 'remains' when the body is destroyed: p21–3, p29–31, p39, p40c. Next, there is some doctrine about what Spinoza calls 'the third kind of cognition'. This refers to the trio in 2p40s2: 'imagination', 'reason', and 'intuitive knowledge'—the third kind which is said to be even greater than reason. This theme occupies p24–28 and p31–33. Finally, Spinoza exclaims about 'the intellectual love of God' in p32–37 except p34. This theme does not hook into the 'love towards God' treated in p14–20. (Indeed, nowhere in the demonstrations of p21–38 does Spinoza invoke anything from p1–20.) The notion of 'love towards God' (§80) is bad enough, but what Spinoza says about the 'intellectual love of God' will be seen in §84 to be even worse. Notice the overlaps among the groups of propositions: p31 links the eternity of the mind with the third kind of cognition, and p32,33 link the latter with intellectually loving God.

§82. *The mind's eternity*

1. What Spinoza says about the mind as eternal depends on a certain distinction between the 'actual existence' of a body and its 'essence', and correspondingly between ideas which 'express the actual existence' of a body and ones which 'express its essence' (p23d). In this contrast my body's essence is just its nature, considered as a possibility. It exists eternally, i.e., necessarily and forever, although it is instantiated only contingently and briefly. My body came into existence in 1930, but its essence didn't, for there has always been the logical possibility of a body with just those features. It doesn't matter whether my body's essence is taken to comprise all its features or only some of them; the essence/accident distinction is not at work here.

Similarly, there is the essence of my mind, this too being an eternal possibility which was briefly actualized starting in 1930. Spinoza should say that the parallelism holds between essences as well as between existents; otherwise he would have to admit that parallelism *could* fail because some possibilities under one attribute have no counterparts under the other. That is ruled out by my account of 2p7s; so it is satisfactory to have Spinoza saying that the ideas of nonexistent particulars 'must be comprehended in God's idea in the same way as the essences of the particulars are contained in God's attributes' (2p8, quoted with omissions), and saying that this is explained by 2p7s. Although 2p8 is not perfectly clear, I think it must mean that there is a psychophysical parallelism between possibilities as well as between actualities.

2. Essences, then, are possibilities or ways things could be. And they are eternal: any truth of the form 'There is an F-type essence' is absolutely necessary. From this Spinoza infers that it is true at all times, because eternity in his sense entails sempiternity though it is not entailed by it.

So the essence of my mind is eternal. And Spinoza will argue that a *part* of my mind is eternal (p23,39) and even that *I* am eternal (p23s at 296/4)—this last inflation presumably being based on the later contention that if all goes well 'the part of the mind which perishes with the body is of no importance compared with what remains' (p38s).

3. Some commentators have supposed Spinoza to be saying only that the mind's essence is eternal, like all essences, and to be making this sound more dramatic than it is by giving the impression—and later saying outright—that *part* of the mind is eternal. Of course Spinoza did not really think that a thing's essence is a part of it, as though the whole thing were contructed by stirring together an essence and an instantiating ingredient (see §16.4); but it is perhaps believable that he should sometimes write as though a thing's having an eternal essence is its being eternal or having an eternal part.

I shall call this the 'symmetrical account' of the eternity doctrine, meaning that it applies evenhandedly to the mind and to the body: if that was why Spinoza said that the mind is eternal then he must have seen that he was committed to saying that the body is eternal also, since it too has an eternal essence. But what Spinoza says is asymmetrical: 'The human mind cannot be absolutely destroyed with the human body, but something of it remains which is eternal.' (p23) It has been contended that he has merely underexpressed his position, and would not have minded adding that if the mind is eternal then so is the body;[1] but that is too weak to rescue

---

1. Curley, *Spinoza's Metaphysics*, p. 142. The same line is taken in Friedman, 'An Overview of Spinoza's *Ethics*', pp. 78, 100.

the symmetrical account. If the appearance of asymmetry is to be explained as a mere result of understatement, then Spinoza must be willing to say: 'The human body is not absolutely destroyed with the human mind, but something of it remains which is eternal', and, indeed, 'The human body is not absolutely destroyed with the human *body*, but . . . etc.'. No-one has been willing to cram those sentences into his mouth.

That is one count against the symmetrical interpretation. It would be better to have a reading which does justice to the sharp asymmetry of the text—the fact that p23d draws a conclusion about the eternity of the mind from a premiss about the essence of the body.

It is also objectionable that the doctrine of the mind's eternity should be understood to be a mere truism (essences are eternal) decorated with a mistake (the suggestion that essences are parts). It would be more satisfying if we could find an interpretation which gives the argument thick roots in Spinoza's thinking and gives it a contentful conclusion.

The third objection to the symmetrical account is that it cannot explain—and indeed positively undercuts—Spinoza's view about the practical consequences of his doctrine of the mind's eternity. From the tame thesis that essences are eternal, what follows? Only what Leibniz inferred when writing to a friend about Spinoza's 'amusing view of the immortality of the soul': 'He thought that the Platonic idea of my being, which is doubtless as eternal as that of a circle or a triangle, is what properly constitutes our immortality, and that one should try to perfect oneself in every sort of virtue so as to leave behind at death that much more perfect an eternal essence or Platonic idea.'[2] Leibniz goes on to mock this position (not quite fairly, but never mind that). The crucial point is that the practical import Spinoza finds in his eternity doctrine is nothing like what Leibniz says it is. He never speaks of having a *good* eternal part of the mind, but rather of having a *large* one. And that is something which cannot be explained on the symmetrical account, and which is indeed found to be 'completely unintelligible' by one defender of that account.[3]

4. I now offer a different explanation of what underlies Spinoza's doctrine of the eternity of the mind. It does full justice to the asymmetry of the relevant text; it draws a nontrivial conclusion from deeply rooted Spinozistic doctrine; and it explains how Spinoza can have thought that my conduct can make a difference to how much of my mind is eternal. I am not defending him: on my interpretation of it, his eternity doctrine is certainly false. But I can make its parts hang together intelligibly, and

2. G. W. Leibniz, *Sämtliche Schriften und Briefe* II.1 (Darmstadt, 1926), p. 535.

3. Curley, *op. cit.*, p. 143.

can relate it to the whole text without having to explain away the asymmetrical bits.

The premiss of p23d concerns the eternal essence not of my mind but of my body. It is because my body has an eternal essence that my mind has an eternal part. To see why Spinoza should think this, we must remind ourselves of where he stands concerning what contents our thoughts can have, and what logical relations there are between a thought's nature and its content.

His most robust and plausible notion of thought content concerns thoughts indirectly of things—e.g., my thinking there are trees outside my window, which is the mental counterpart of a state which the trees caused my body to be in. These are irrelevant to my present topic, and I set them aside.

What remains are thoughts directly of states of one's body. The 'directly of' relation is not obviously representational at all—the mental counterpart of a cerebral episode is not what we ordinarily call a thought about that episode—but Spinoza does sometimes treat the 'directly of' relation as representational,[4] and in at least one context he *must* do so, namely, when he is considering thoughts whose content is necessarily true. Suppose that P is a logical truth, and that there occurs in my mind the thought that P; what can Spinoza say about this thought content? Presumably, it cannot have come indirectly from some realization outside my body of the fact that P: where necessarily true thoughts are in question, the 'indirectly of' relation is useless to us, and so we must turn to the 'directly of' relation. Spinoza must say that when I think that P (where P is a necessary truth), the proposition that P or some physical equivalent of it is realized or instantiated by my body, and my thought is the counterpart of that under the parallelism. This is not a good theory of necessarily true thoughts, but it is the only one Spinoza has room for, and I shall argue shortly that it is at work in p23d.

First, though, this point must be grasped: if x is a state of or fact about my body, then any transattribute feature of x which has to do with 'order and connection' must also be a feature of $I(x)$. For example $I(x)$ will be intermittent, or externally caused, or bad for me, if and only if x is also. Thus, if my body is gaining in health and strength, then the mental counterpart of that will be describable *both* as my mind's corresponding gain in health and strength *and* as my thought directly of my body's improvement.

Among these transattribute values of F which carry across from x to $I(x)$ is modal status. If x is an eternal truth about my body, then $I(x)$ — my thought of that eternal truth—must itself be an eternal item. Now,

---

4. For example in 2p7c, and in phrases in 3p11s and elsewhere about the mind's 'affirming of the body' that it exists, is moving upwards, and so on.

consider the proposition P which asserts the eternal truth that there could be an F body (where F is in fact the essence of my body). That is an eternal truth which is somehow realized in my body; and so under the parallelism there must be

> (a) an eternal truth *about* my mind, namely, that there could be an F* mind (where F* is in fact the essence of my mind).

And by Spinoza's doctrine of direct representation, there must also be

> (b) a thought *in* my mind, namely, that there could be an F body.

And the moral of my account of Spinoza's views about direct representation is that he cannot distinguish (a) from (b). That is, he is not in a position to distinguish the necessary truths which I think from the ones which are true of my mind. And so an item which is declared to be (a) eternal because it is an essence (of my mind) and corresponds to an essence (of my body) is also treated as (b) a bit of mental content, something *in* my mind, a *part* of my mind, because it is the thought of my body's essence.

Spinoza does not use the language of 'part' or 'contained in' in p23d. Rather, he says that the item in question is eternal and 'pertains to the essence of my mind'. But his later handling of the eternity doctrine clearly commits him to there being eternal parts of my mind, eternal items *in* it, and I submit that I have explained why he thinks so. In summary: Take a necessary truth about the body, note (a) the corresponding truth about the mind, and then redescribe it as (b) a thought in the mind. The upshot is that you have got a single item which is at once (a) eternal and (b) contained in the mind. Q.e.d.

5. The whole line of thought is wrong. It implies that there are no contingent truths of the form 'He has the thought that P' where P is a necessary truth; and any theory of thought which implies that is thereby condemned. Still, Spinoza's skimpy account of mental representation leaves him with no well-marked escape route, and we may wish to applaud him for not pretending to have one when really he hasn't. But we should deplore his failure to see that a theory of mental content which implies that the mind is eternal must be defective, and to be led by that to go back and reexamine his cognitive psychology.

And it looks even worse when we see how he draws his practical conclusion from it. The eternity doctrine as I have so far expounded it says that my mind has an eternal part because my body has an essence. It thus accords eternal parts to the minds of Dante and Shakespeare and to the most wretched person on earth, and provides no basis for discriminating among them. But later we find Spinoza saying that how much of your mind is eternal depends on how you conduct yourself intellectually: 'The mind is eternal to the extent that it conceives things under the aspect of eternity.' (p31s) I am not sure whether he means 'to the extent that it has true thoughts whose content is necessary' or rather 'to the extent that it has true thoughts of the form "It is necessary that P" '. But the details don't matter. Spinoza is clearly implying that how much of my mind is eternal depends on some facts about my conduct and my condition. Thus p39d says that a physically versatile person has 'a power of ordering and connecting the states of his body according to the order of the intellect', which makes it possible for him to 'have a mind whose greatest part is eternal'. This is a completely fresh doctrine. The original story makes no provision for my increasing how much of my mind is eternal, unless I can enlarge my body's essence, whatever that would mean. But now we are told that how much of my mind is eternal depends on what thinking I do, as though I could work at enlarging the eternal part of my mind.

This is dreadful, but not 'completely unintelligible': it flows smoothly from the very same doctrinal basis as does the original eternity argument of p23d. I interpreted the latter as resting on a spurious identification of (a) an eternal truth *about* the mind with (b) a certain thought *in* the mind: Spinoza starts with a genuine case of (a) and convinces himself that it is also a case of (b), whence he concludes that the very same item is (a) eternal and (b) part of the mind. But when drawing his practical conclusion he runs the identity in the other direction. He starts with genuine cases of (b), that is, genuine thoughts of necessary truths, these being mental episodes which come and go, and convinces himself that they are also cases of (a); whence he concludes that we can by intellectual effort increase the eternal parts of our minds. There is of course no direction in a true identity, but there is in a false one. Someone who thinks that Hobbes was Descartes may think that Hobbes was French or—running the identity the other way—that Descartes was English.

6. Spinoza runs his false identity first one way, then the other. This creates an impassable dilemma for him, and some of the odder aspects of this segment of the *Ethics* can be explained as his attempts to wriggle out of it. Here is the dilemma in a nutshell.

Since I gave up medical studies for philosophy I have had thoughts that P, where P is necessary, more often than before the switch and more often than I would have if I had stayed with medicine. Does my mind have a larger eternal part than it used to? and than it would have had if I had stayed on the medical path? One question concerns variation through time (= change), the other concerns variation across possible worlds (= evitability).

Spinoza should answer 'Yes' to both questions. He equates 'having a mind of which the greatest part is eternal' with being in a state of blessedness which, he says at the close of the work, is achievable only through 'great effort'. This concedes that it can be reached, and that one may fall short; so it must be subject to change, and must be evitable.

But he must answer 'No' to both questions. Most of his treatment of the eternal part of the mind assumes that the facts which determine how much of my mind is eternal are themselves eternal truths—true in all worlds and at all times, and thus inevitable and unchanging.

The split in Spinoza's position is unhealable. It is evident in his saying at the end of p20s that he has now 'completed everything which concerns this present life', and then several times in p21–42 talking about self-improvement. There is an attempt to hide the split in this curious passage:

For an easier explanation and better understanding of the things we wish to show, we shall consider the mind as if it were now beginning to be, and were now beginning to understand things under the aspect of eternity. . . . We may do this without danger of error, provided we are careful to draw our conclusions only from evident premisses. (p31s)

We are not told how our understanding will be aided by mixing falsehood with truth. Nor can we learn by seeing what work the falsehood does in what follows, since it does none. Still, mysterious as it is, the pretence that the mind has just come into existence has one revealing feature. Spinoza is committed to saying that how much of my mind is eternal depends on facts which

(i) always did obtain

(ii) always will obtain

(iii) would have obtained, however I had behaved,

and his pretence in p31s is addressed to (i) alone. I cannot see how it is supposed to *help* with (i), but my present point is that it does not touch (ii) or (iii), which are quite enough to imply that the possession of a mainly eternal mind cannot be achieved through effort. Whenever Spinoza tries to be candid about this consequence of his doctrine, he always does it in terms of (i). As well as the p31s pretence, there is the remark that 'the mind has eternally had the perfections' by virtue of which part of it is eternal (p33s), and the association of those perfections with an 'intellectual love of God' which Spinoza says 'is eternal' and 'has had no beginning' (p33,s). He does not say, as he should, that it also has no end and that it could not have been different from how it actually is, no matter how anybody had behaved.

§83. *Intuitive knowledge*

1. In 2p40s2 Spinoza presents three kinds of cognition, of which the first is empirical, the second involves reason, and then:

In addition to these two kinds of cognition, there is . . . a third kind, which we shall call intuitive knowledge. This kind of cognition proceeds from an adequate idea of the formal essence of certain attributes of God to an adequate cognition of the essences of things.

We are not helped to understand this by the relevant Part 2 propositions, since they only contrast the first kind of cognition with the other two, not the second with the third. Our only help comes from an ingenious example: three routes to the same solution of an arithmetical problem are said to involve, respectively, the three kinds of cognitive process. The problem is, given three numbers x, y and z, to find the number n such that $\frac{n}{z} = \frac{y}{x}$.

(i) One route to the solution relies, as Spinoza thinks all empirical thinking does, on memory and faith. By this 'first kind' of cognitive process one applies the rule $n = \frac{y \cdot z}{x}$ either because one has learned it at school and trusts the teacher, or has found it to work in simple cases and trusts it to hold for the rest.

(ii) The second route applies that same rule on the basis of having deduced it from mathematical fundamentals. That is the way of reason.

(iii) In the procedure which illustrates intuitive knowledge, the 'third kind' of cognition, we do not use any rule, but rather 'We infer the fourth number from the ratio which we see at a glance [*uno intuitu*] that the first number has to the second'; or, in the Dutch version, which probably reflects an earlier state of the Latin work: 'We need to think only of the particular ratio of the first two numbers, not of the universal property of proportional numbers.' So much for what Spinoza says about the 'third kind'. But what does he mean?

He means two things at once, corresponding to two strands in the meaning of 'intuitive' and its cognates in the seventeenth century and long before and after.

2. One of them is vividly present when Locke distinguishes intuition from demonstration.[5] A demonstration takes you from premises to a conclusion, where you cannot see straight off that it follows, but you can see that each step in the argument is valid. The acts of the mind in which the validity of those steps is recognized are intuitions. The contrast, then, is between an intellectual step and an intellectual walk. That Spinoza is using

5. *Essay* IV.ii.1–3.

'intuitive' to carry this emphasis is suggested by the phrase about what we see 'at a glance'. But notice that we infer something *from* what we see at a glance: the third kind of cognition, though it is not long drawn out, is still inferential.[6]

3. That first strand in the traditional meaning of 'intuition' concerns what an intuition is like. The other strand has to do with the objects of intuition. Philosophers have used 'intuition' to refer to mental episodes in which one has a cognition of a particular, or to the general capacity for cognizing particulars. For example: 'Ockham held that the mind could be concerned directly with the particular by means of intuitions. Intuitive knowledge is a direct knowledge of a thing or its existence.'[7] When we read Kant saying that 'Intuition takes place only in so far as the object is given to us',[8] we are not merely depending on his translator's choice of 'intuition' to render the German *Anschauung*; for in a Latin work Kant uses *intuitus* for the same purpose.

Spinoza takes intuitive knowledge to have this second feature as well, for in 5p36cs he contrasts the second and third kinds of cognition as 'universal' and as 'of particular things' respectively (303/17,19). Also, the Dutch version of the arithmetical example in 2p40s2 says that in reaching the solution of the problem by the third route we 'think only of the particular ratio . . . and not of the universal property'. Since a ratio is itself a universal, this is not happily put, but we can see what Spinoza is getting at: in this third route to the solution we think only about these particular pairs of numbers, not detouring through a thought about pairs of numbers in general. Notice also that this list of kinds of cognition starts with an offer to list intellectual processes in which 'we form universal notions': Spinoza presents two species of 'the first kind', which, though not inherently universal, can generate universal notions in a manner he explains; then he describes 'the second kind', reason, which is inherently universal; and then he stops. The 'third kind', intuitive knowledge, is added as a sort of cognition but not as a source of universal notions.

So much for the surroundings. Does Spinoza's initial description of intuitive knowledge show that it is supposed to be of particulars? Well, the crucial phrase is 'an adequate cognition of the essences of things'. If in this phrase 'adequate' means 'complete', and if a thing's essence is here taken to be its whole nature, then intuitive knowledge involves a grasp of the whole natures of particular things. Spinoza does sometimes use 'essence'

6. For more on that, and other helps, see Parkinson, *Spinoza's Theory of Knowledge*, ch. 9.

7. D. W. Hamlyn, 'Epistemology, History of', in Edwards, vol. 3 at p. 16.

8. Kant, *Critique of Pure Reason*, A 19.

in that inclusive fashion, and sometimes uses 'adequate' to mean 'complete', as in the phrase 'adequate cause'.

But the thought of x's complete nature is not the same as a thought about x. Suppose that F is the complete nature of an individual person living on the far side of our galaxy, and that by sheer coincidence I have a thought involving the concept of F: 'It would be nice'—I think to myself—'if there were an F person.' (Of course we cannot have such rich concepts as that of F, but we must pretend that we can in pretending that intuitive knowledge is possible.) Is it not clear that that thought is not about the actual F person? My thought fits him, but it is not about him.

That seems right. I think we should accept it, just so long as we can explain what *would* make my thought be about the actual F person. Kant gave some answer to that, when he said that (i) our capacity for being cognitively in touch with particulars depends on (ii) our being causally acted on by the particulars, or, in his terminology, that (i) our faculty of intuition is (ii) a sensible (= passive) one. So my thought involving the concept F is not about the F person unless he helped to cause it. In developing this Kantian idea, Kripke has shown that it frees us not only to say that an F-involving thought is not necessarily about the F person, but also that a thought may be about x although almost nothing in its conceptual content fits x: we could be almost totally wrong about Homer, and yet our thoughts would be wrong thoughts *about Homer.*

By the Kantian standard, there can be no *a priori* thought about any particular. He holds that our intuition must be sensible, i.e., passive, i.e., dependent on causal influence from the outside, and that puts him in conflict with Spinoza's view that some knowledge of particulars is *a priori*, i.e., involves only adequate ideas. Kant is surely right. But he should not have expressed his view as a thesis about *human* intuition, allowing that some beings might have a faculty of 'active' or 'intellectual' intuition; because really it follows from an analysis of the concept of 'thought of x', the notion of cognitive contact with a particular.

Anyway, there are two suggested notions of what a thought about a particular is: a thought of a complete individual nature, descriptively packed full but tied to the particular only by being true of it; and a thought which is suitably caused by the particular, though perhaps not containing much descriptive truth about it. Spinoza must be working with the former notion, which is not really a notion of thought about a particular at all. But he took it to be so. He was not the man to be clear about how thinking of a complete individual nature differs from thinking of an individual. Presumably 2p8,c constitute an attempt to treat that difference seriously,[9]

---

9. The Kantian insight is perfectly used by Spinoza in *Metaphysical Thoughts* in an argument first against polytheism (I/253/3) and then for pantheism (262/7).

but Spinoza's near-blindness to it explains several crucial turns in the *Ethics*: especially his assumption of the identity of indiscernibles, implying that different individuals must have different natures (§17.2), and his doctrine about harmony through similarity (§69.2). If Spinoza had read Gueroult's phrase about the third kind of cognition as involving 'ideas of *things themselves*—real, particular things, captured in their eternal essences',[10] he would have nodded agreement, being as oblivious as Gueroult evidently was to the difference between a thing and the whole truth about it. He made it easier for himself to overlook this by concentrating on 'things' in respect of which the difference is nonexistent or unclear, such as numbers and geometrical figures.

4. Not that it matters. 'Intuitive knowledge' is supposed to take us to thoughts of complete natures of particular things; and this is impossible, by any reasonable or any Spinozistic standards, even if it is not supposed to take us to thoughts of the particular things themselves. For intuitive knowledge deals only in adequate ideas, and an idea of the whole nature of a real thing could not be adequate in my mind, i.e., caused wholly from within, unless my body contained the thing in question or a perfect duplicate of it. Objection: 'You are resting too much on the "caused from inside" aspect of adequacy, and not enough on adequate ideas as pertaining to the "common properties" of things.' In reply to this I summon Spinoza to my aid: he rightly says that no set of common properties can constitute the essence of any particular thing (2p37).

5. And there is worse to come, for late in Part 5 he associates intuitive knowledge with a heightened awareness not only of 'things' but also of oneself and of God. Two of these are linked in the proposition that 'the more we understand particular things, the more we understand God' (p24), and another two here: 'Insofar as our mind knows itself and the body under the aspect of eternity, it necessarily has cognition of God' (p30), and again when Spinoza allows himself the inference '. . . accompanied by the idea of oneself, and consequently by the idea of God' (p32d).

Just twice he brings all three objects of intuitive knowledge together in a single sentence, and each sentence is negative. In p39s we are told about the person who 'like an infant' has 'a mind which considered solely in itself is conscious of almost nothing of itself, or of God, or of things'; and in his very last scholium Spinoza says that 'the ignorant man . . . lives as if he knew neither himself nor God nor things' (p42s). These remarks look interesting, but if we press hard for an understanding we find that there is less in them than meets the eye. For example, we may be inclined to agree that an infant lacks a concept of self, an ability to make judgments of the form 'I . . .'; but if we look to the text to learn how Spinoza explains

10. Gueroult, vol. 2, p. 417.

this and why he believes it, all we find is this cure for the infant condition:

> In this life we try to bring it about that the infant's body is capable of a great many things and related to a mind very much conscious of itself, of God, and of things, so that whatever is related to its memory or imagination is of almost no importance in comparison with the intellect. (p39s at 305/28, quoted with omissions).

The second sentence of this, saying that we try to bring children up so that what they observe and remember is 'of almost no importance' compared with their *a priori* reasonings, shows that we are not in the presence of someone whose views about the infant condition should seriously interest us.

Nor does Spinoza explain how self-consciousness relates to anything presented earlier in the *Ethics*. He gives two conditionals which have it in the antecedent; but for it to be explained we need it in an (affirmative) consequent, and that happens only once: 'The more each of us is able to achieve in this [third] kind of cognition, the better he is conscious of himself and of God.' (31s) For a conditional to throw light on its consequent, it needs a more luminous antecedent than that.

6. Having looked at what happens *in* intuitive knowledge, and what it takes us *to*, let us consider what it starts *from*. Spinoza says that it takes one to an adequate cognition of the essences of things 'from an adequate idea of the formal essence of certain attributes of God', which in 5p25d is simplified to 'an adequate idea of certain attributes of God'. Have we an adequate idea of any attributes of God? In p31d Spinoza says that we have, on the strength of 2p45–47 which conclude that everyone who has ideas of any particular thing must have an 'adequate and perfect' cognition of 'God's eternal and infinite essence'. Clearly, these propositions are using 'cognition of God's essence' and kindred phrases in a drastically impoverished sense which spreads thinly over every sentient being—nothing in the demonstrations confines them to humans. This ought to embarrass the commentators on intuitive knowledge who stress the 'adequate cognition of God' from which it starts: can they really think that what is special to intuitive knowledge is its kicking off from something which humans share with lizards? But the emphasis on the starting point is theirs, not Spinoza's: he stresses only the nature of the cognitive process, and its end-point. The knowledge of God which he does emphasize late in Part 5 does not underlie the third kind of cognition but emerges from it. In p24,25 he treats intuitive knowledge as a route to cognition of particular things, and *through* that to cognition of God. This is rammed home at the end of p36cs, where intuitive knowledge is praised as superior to the Part 1 demonstration of pantheism: although the latter is cogent, it 'still does not affect our mind as much as when this is inferred from the very essence of any particular thing which we say depends on God'. Murky as this is, it shows intuitive knowledge being highlighted not because of what it comes from but because of what it leads to—namely, a cognition of particular things which can give us an especially powerful hold on the truth that all things are in God.

§84.   *The intellectual love of God*

1. Intuitive knowledge is supposed to be greater, finer, higher, than the mere exercise of reason; but we are not clearly told why. Two of the merits Spinoza claims for the third kind of cognition are shared with the second: each is confined to adequate ideas and is thus active rather than passive (p38), and each contributes to the eternity of the mind. In the obscure depths of p31d Spinoza seems to be reserving the latter merit for intuitive knowledge alone; but his heart is not in it, for in p40c he says that 'the eternal part of the mind is the intellect, through which alone we are said to act (by 3p3)', and contrasts that with the perishable part of us, namely 'the imagination'. This inescapably ties the mind's eternity to all its active or *a priori* procedures, reasoning as well as intuitive knowledge.

Intuitive knowledge is made to outrank reason when Spinoza says that 'the mind's greatest virtue is understanding things by the third kind of cognition' (p25). But this is inferred from the thesis that 'The more we understand particular things, the more we understand God' (p24), which is supposed to give intuitive knowledge a special privilege, since it is the kind of *a priori* cognition that has particular things as objects. Really, we have seen, its objects are not particulars but only their essences. Even apart from that the argument fails, however, because p24 comes straight from pantheism: it is only because particular things are caused by God that understanding them is understanding God. But the properties of things are also caused by God, according to Spinoza, and so the more we understand *them* the more we understand God! His argument for giving the palm to intuitive knowledge is matched by another, no worse, which awards it to reason.

Just once he explicitly alleges that intuitive knowledge is superior to reason. That is in p36cs where he says that his Part 1 arguments give us a less firm hold on God than we are given by inferring pantheism from the cognition of particular things to which we are led in intuitive knowledge; which shows the third kind of cognition to be 'more powerful' than the second. Apparently we are to accept that minds are in general more strongly affected by cognitions arising from the 'very essence' of particular things than by merely 'universal cognitions', but Spinoza does not say why. Nor does he explain *how* the proposition that 'all things depend on God' is to be 'inferred from the very essence of any particular thing which we say depends on God'. Perhaps he is relying on his thesis that the more we understand particular things the more we understand God, forgetting that he inferred this from pantheism and so ought not to be impressed by the power of an argument for pantheism which has it as a premiss.

2. That contrast between the second and third kinds of cognition immediately follows a diffuse panegyric upon 'men's intellectual love of God'. The connection of *that* with intuitive knowledge may be meant to give the latter its special value. Anyway, 'the intellectual love of God' should be looked at.

Because the mind's greatest virtue involves intuitive knowledge (p25), Spinoza concludes that the latter gives rise to 'the greatest satisfaction of mind there can be' (p27). From that he further argues—with details that I shall excuse myself from presenting—that intuitive knowledge involves pleasure accompanied by the idea of God as cause (p32), which in p32c is characterized as the 'intellectual love of God'. It seems that ordinary nonintellectual love is for visible and tangible things, and that intuitive knowledge, since it has no commerce with the senses, can only be associated with a kind of love which is not related to anything empirically given—a kind Spinoza calls 'intellectual'. That lame explanation is based on his saying that this love towards God is intellectual because we have it 'not insofar as we imagine God to be present, but insofar as we understand God to be eternal'. To amplify that into a positive account of intellectual love would presumably require a real understanding of what intuitive knowledge is.

Since intellectual love is a species of pleasure (p32c), and God 'is not affected with pleasure' (p17), it follows that God cannot have intellectual love. Yet Spinoza does credit God with having it—towards God (p35) and towards men (p36,c). He contrives this result by sleight of hand in p35d, where he says that God 'enjoys [*gaudet*] infinite perfections', and treats that as sufficient for the attribution to God of intellectual love, though the latter has been defined in terms of pleasure [*laetitia*] which is explicitly denied to God.

One is at first taken aback by Spinoza's assertion that God's self-love is to be identified both with God's love for men and with men's love for God (p36c). This is boringly derived from pantheism: since there is only God, what men do is done by God, and what is aimed at (the whole of) God is aimed at man. That drains most of the expected content out of the notion of God's love towards men. But then it was bound to be unlike what we ordinarily call 'love', given how impersonal Spinoza's God is. Our topic is the universe's 'love' towards men and towards *it*self.

The intellectual love of God is declared in p33 to be eternal, and in p34c to be the only kind of love that has that privilege. I shall not expound the details, as the burden of error and confusion has become unbearable.

3. The benefits of intuitive knowledge might be expected to concern freedom; and Spinoza gestures in that direction, tying the term 'blessed' to 'free' on the one hand and to intuitive knowledge and intellectual love towards God on the other. Not that there is much of this in his text. In 4p54s he uses the phrase 'be free and enjoy the life of the blessed'. Early in 5 Preface he promises to show 'what freedom of mind or blessedness is', and in the final scholium he claims to have done so. In between, however, all we get concerning freedom is a skimpy passing remark late in p10s, an implication early in p41s about what freedom is not, and the claim that 'Our salvation or blessedness or freedom consists . . . in a constant and eternal love towards God, or in God's love towards men' (p36cs).

These offerings are so jejune that we cannot even tell whether they involve the kind of freedom that Spinoza theorizes about in Part 4. Let us set freedom aside for a while, and look at blessedness.

Spinoza wants 'blessedness' to stand for the most elevated and desirable state one could possibly be in: 'If pleasure consists in the passage to a greater perfection, blessedness must surely consist in the fact that the mind is endowed with perfection itself' (p33s)—a remark which contrasts sadly with the coolly intelligent and ironical discussion of 'perfection' in 4 Preface (see §67.4). Since blessedness stands on such a pedestal, it is not surprising to find it being linked with intuitive knowledge and the intellectual love of God—see p31s and p42,d, and also the odd linking of blessedness with 'the intuitive *cognition* of God' in 4 Appendix 4. None of these links helps us to understand blessedness, because each ties it to items which we do not independently understand.

4. A fortiori, these materials do not throw light on how late Part 5 relates to freedom in Part 4. Despite Spinoza's implication that what comes after 5p20 does not concern 'this life', I think he means it to fit with Part 4 into one coherent moral doctrine, but he does not work hard at showing how they fit together. The only place where he runs them in a single harness is his final scholium. Contrasting the ignorant man with the wise one, here is what Spinoza says about the former:

Not only is the ignorant man [a] troubled in many ways by external causes, and [b] unable ever to possess true peace of mind, but he also [c] lives as if he knew neither himself nor God nor things; and [d] as soon as he ceases to be acted on he ceases to be. (p42s)

Clauses (a) and (b) seem to come straight out of Parts 3 and 4 and early 5. Clause (c) is an addition which I have discussed in §83.5. Clause (d) may be only a rhetorical way of saying that the unfree man depends heavily on his environment, but this way of saying it is shocking. Ever since 3p4 Spinoza has insisted that dependence on the outside world is dangerous, because that is where harm can come from; he has always implied that if only we could cease to be acted on we could be sure of surviving, whereas now he is saying that if ignorant people cease to be acted on that will drive them out of existence. I cannot guess how he saw clause (d): he is now writing in so lax and slippery a fashion as to defeat reasonable conjecture about his meaning.

That was the 5p42s description of the ignorant man. One might expect the contrasting description of the wise man to say that he (a) is not troubled, (b) does have satisfaction, (c) does know God etc., and (d) is not dependent on external causes for his survival. Spinoza does say something like that, but two of the clauses are heated up by an injection of the doctrine of the mind's eternity:

> On the other hand, the wise man—to the extent that he is considered as such—[a] is hardly troubled in spirit, but [c] being *by a certain eternal necessity* conscious of himself and of God and of things, [d] he *never ceases to be*, but [b] always possesses true peace of mind. (p42s, italics mine)

Apparently Spinoza is trying to bring doctrines from late Part 5 into the sort of bondage/freedom contrast that he deploys at length in Part 4. But he does not work at it. The disparate elements are merely thrown together in a single paragraph without being coherently interrelated.

§85. *A judgment on the last three doctrines*

1. I don't think that the final three doctrines can be rescued. The only attempts at complete salvage that I have encountered have been unintelligible to me and poorly related to what Spinoza actually wrote. They have thus doubly failed to present this part of the *Ethics* as something from which we can learn, and for me that is crucial. The courtly deference which pretends that Spinoza is always or usually right, under some rescuing interpretation, is one thing; it is quite another to look to him, as I have throughout this book, as a teacher, one who can help us to see things which we might not have seen for ourselves. That is showing him a deeper respect, but also holding him to a more demanding standard. By that high standard, the second half of Part 5 is negligible. After three centuries of failure to profit from it, the time has come to admit that this part of the *Ethics* has nothing to teach us and is pretty certainly worthless.

2. Hampshire's treatment of the doctrine of the eternity of the mind is interesting. He deals with it sympathetically from a long way off, and confesses defeat when he come close. On the one hand:

> We feel and know that we are eternal in so far as we conceive things *sub specie aeternitatis*; for we then know our ideas to be eternal truths, and so we know that we are in our thought 'playing the immortal as far as is possible for us', in Aristotle's phrase. In our intellectual life, at the more successful moments of completely disinterested, logical thought, we have these glimpses of the possibility of living, not as

finite and perishing modes of Nature, but identified or 'united' with God or Nature as a whole.[11]

On the other hand:

It cannot be claimed that we can easily understand what exactly Spinoza meant when he wrote [5p23]: certainly part of the explanation is to be found in [5p31d]. It seems—but this must be conjectural—that we sometimes have experiences of complete and intuitive understanding, and that on such occasions we feel and know ourselves to be mentally united or identified with the eternal order of Nature; so far we know ourselves to be, in respect of that part of the life of our minds, eternal.

After a further sentence elaborating this, Hampshire concludes:

But everyone must be left further to interpret these propositions as he can, or perhaps to confess that at this point he finds himself beyond the limits of literal understanding; it would be the work of a much longer study to show exactly where the limits of understanding may be expected to fall when we try to talk of the eternity of the human mind.

I contend that instead of implying that Spinoza has brought us 'beyond the limits of literal understanding' and that this is acceptable because it is inherent in his chosen topic, we should say openly that Spinoza is talking nonsense and that there is no reason for us to put up with it.[12]

3. The other admirable writer on Spinoza who has been fully sympathetic to the final three doctrines in the *Ethics* is Pollock. He wrongly thinks that eternity is not taken by Spinoza to entail sempiternity and is much too indulgent on points of detail. But much of his discussion is good, and I like the fact that although his principal judgment on this material is favourable he sometimes shows unease.

For example, he is worried about whether the second half of Part 5 shows Spinoza to be a mystic. He clears him of that charge on the grounds that Spinoza's reasons for holding the mind to be eternal are like unmystical Aristotle's reasons for *his* doctrine of immortality: 'But there is unquestionably something of an exalted and mystical temper in his expressions; and it seems possible enough that, but for his scientific training in the school of Descartes, he might have been a mystic indeed. If this be so, Descartes has one claim the more to the gratitude of mankind.'[13]

11. Hampshire, *Spinoza*, p. 175.

12. I do not understand, and cannot connect with Spinoza's text, Hampshire's later more sympathetic account of the eternity doctrine, *Two Theories of Morality*, p. 95.

13. Pollock, *Spinoza*, p. 303. Parkinson in 'Being and Knowledge in Spinoza' also points out that Spinoza's language is unmystical, but allows that there may be a mystical impulse in the background.

It is also useful—though not in a way Pollock can have intended—that he puts two crucial questions with exemplary firmness and clarity, and answers them on Spinoza's behalf in an abjectly feeble manner. One concerns what the practical upshot of the eternity doctrine is:

If we turn Spinoza's thought into a guide for action, . . . what is the outcome? Even that which true and fearless men have preached through all the generations to unheeding ears. Seek the truth, fear not and spare not: this first, this for its own sake, this only; and the truth itself is your reward, a reward not measured by length of days nor by any reckoning of men.[14]

The other question is: What is the bottom line? Pollock puts this superbly:

[Spinoza's] doctrine of the eternity of the mind must remain one of the most brilliant endeavours of speculative philosophy, and it throws a sort of poetical glow over the formality of his exposition. We have already said that it has a sufficiently certain practical lesson. But still we linger over it, seeking for some expression which may so give us the central idea that we can accept and use it for ourselves, some concentration of the commanding thought without the precarious dialectical form in which it is clothed.[15]

The phrase 'a sort of poetical glow' is exactly right. And the last sentence nicely expresses the proper wish to be told, straightforwardly and in a nutshell, what this last stretch of the *Ethics* amounts to. 'If the task were still to attempt, it might be a hard one', writes Pollock, but fortunately the nutshell account has already been given: 'The essence of Spinoza's thought is already secured for us. . . . M. Renan has expressed it in the perfectly chosen words . . . : *Reason leads Death in triumph, and the work done for Reason is done for eternity.*' When a commentator as shrewd as Pollock is reduced to such babbling by his desire to praise the final stretch of the *Ethics*, that is further evidence that this material is valueless. Worse, it is dangerous: it is rubbish which causes others to write rubbish.

4. Why did Spinoza write it? Throughout the rest of the *Ethics* we have not had to ask such questions. We have been tracking and criticising Spinoza as he has tackled profoundly important questions, some of them discovered by him, and even when he has been immersed in errors, we have been able to see why. But late in Part 5 the errors are not committed in the honourable service of a recognizably worthwhile philosophical project. I have shown that the doctrine of the eternity of the mind—construed as having teeth in it, not merely as the boring thesis that everything has an eternal essence—has support deep in Spinoza's thought; but I cannot believe that he accepts it just because he is committed to it by his theory of direct mental representation. Clearly, he *wants* this final trio of doctrines. Why?

14. Pollock, *op. cit.*, p. 302.

15. *Ibid.*, p. 308.

Perhaps he was trying to capture in his own terms some doctrines of others—e.g., Aristotle's views about immortality. If so, we should still have to ask why. When Spinoza captures a lot of Judaeo-Christian theology in his own terms, he can reasonably think that he is defending himself against a powerful enemy without having to turn aside from his own philosophical line of thought. But if late Part 5 is a capture of Aristotelianism, what are we to think? That Spinoza has gone enormously out of his way to protect his flank against an attack from *that* quarter? It is hardly credible. And he surely could not have thought that any critic would be disarmed by seeing in p23 a sufficient downpayment on the *Christian* doctrine of life after death.

Perhaps he was after all terrified of extinction, and convinced himself—through a scatter of perverse arguments and hunger for the conclusion—that he had earned immortality. Or perhaps Pollock's suspicion of mysticism was right. That was Broad's view: he said that the final doctrines are the 'philosophic expression of certain religious and mystical experiences which Spinoza and many others have enjoyed and which seem supremely important to those who have had them'.[16]

On either conjecture, Spinoza is sadly failing to live up to his own principles. To argue for things because you hope they are true is too obviously anti-Spinozist to need further comment. But the other diagnosis is also an indictment. Whatever mystical experiences Spinoza had, he ought to have written them off as *experientia vaga*—the mental side of a swirl in the cloud of particles constituting a human body. To accord them the dignity of important news about the whole of reality should have been unthinkable for him. Perhaps it was. Perhaps Spinoza basically viewed late Part 5 not as telling the truth but rather as giving a stern verbal expression to some ecstatic, uncontrolled, indescribable feelings. That may be what Broad was suggesting—'the philosophic expression of certain experiences'. If that is right, then Spinoza in late Part 5 is using the materials of intellectual inquiry for cosmetic purposes, and this should be beneath him.

Either way, it looks as though some passive affect—of fear or hope or excitement—clung stubbornly to the man and overcame his reason. Those of us who love and admire Spinoza's philosophical work should in sad silence avert our eyes from the second half of Part 5. I wanted to do so in this book; but I would have had to say why, and could hardly offer my judgment on 5p23–42 without defending it. I have hated writing this chapter, and have scruples and fears about publishing it. But it defends a negative judgment which is important if true and will be liberating if it is believed.

16. Broad, *Five Types of Ethical Theory*, p. 15. See also Hubbeling, 'The Logical and Experiential Roots of Spinoza's Mysticism'.

Bibliography

The following list gives the writings on Spinoza which I have found most valuable. Since I have not systematically searched the journals, there is doubtless good material which I do not know; so exclusion does not necessarily express a negative judgment. As regards English translations of the *Ethics*: the version by Elwes should not be used; the version by White and Stirling, now out of print, is also highly defective; the rendering by Samuel Shirley (Hackett Publishing Company) improves on all its predecessors, and is thoroughly usable for low-pressure study of the work; but for serious scholarly or philosophical research the version in E. M. Curley's *The Collected Works of Spinoza,* vol. 1 (Princeton University Press, 1985) is indispensable. It is less fluent and pleasing than the Shirley version, but it sets a standard of accuracy—a real mirroring of the Latin in the English—to which the other does not aspire.

Richard E. Aquila, 'The Identity of Thought and Object in Spinoza', *Journal of the History of Philosophy* vol. 16 (1978), pp. 271–288.

Albert G.A. Balz, *Idea and Essence in the Philosophies of Hobbes and Spinoza* (New York, 1967), first published 1917.

H. Barker, 'Notes on the Second Part of Spinoza's *Ethics*', *Mind* vol. 47 (1938), reprinted in Kashap, pp. 101–167.

José Benardete, 'Spinozistic Anomalies', Kennington, pp. 53–71.

Lothar Bickel, 'On Relationships between Psychoanalysis and a Dynamic Psychology', reprinted in Hessing, pp. 81–89.

David Bidney, *The Psychology and Ethics of Spinoza*, 2nd edn., (New York, 1962).

C.D. Broad, *Five Types of Ethical Theory* (London, 1930), ch.1.

Edward Caird, *Spinoza* (Edinburgh, 1888).

William Charlton, 'Spinoza's Monism', *Philosophical Review* vol. 90 (1981), pp. 503–529.

E.M. Curley, 'Descartes, Spinoza and the Ethics of Belief', Mandelbaum, pp. 159–189.

E.M. Curley, 'Experience in Spinoza's Theory of Knowledge', Grene, pp. 25–59.

E.M. Curley, *Spinoza's Metaphysics: An Essay in Interpretation* (Cambridge, Mass., 1969).

E.M. Curley, 'Spinoza's Moral Philosophy', Grene, pp. 354–376.

Raphael Demos, 'Spinoza's Doctrine of Privation', *Philosophy* vol. 8 (1933), reprinted in Kashap, pp. 276–288.

Alan Donagan, 'Essence and the Distinction of Attributes in Spinoza's Metaphysics', Grene, pp. 164–181.

Alan Donagan, 'Spinoza's Dualism', Kennington, pp. 89–102.

Alan Donagan, 'Spinoza's Proof of Immortality', Grene, pp. 241–258.

Willis Doney, 'Spinoza on Philosophical Skepticism', *The Monist* vol. 55 (1971), reprinted in Mandelbaum, pp. 139–157.

François Duchesneau, 'Du modèle cartésien au modèle spinoziste de l'être vivant', *Canadian Journal of Philosophy* vol. 4 (1974), pp. 539–562.

Paul D. Eisenberg, 'Is Spinoza an Ethical Naturalist?', Hessing, pp. 145–164.

Guttorm, Fløistad, 'Spinoza's Theory of Knowledge in the *Ethics*', *Inquiry* vol. 12 (1969), reprinted in Grene, pp. 101–127, and in Kashap, pp. 249–275.

William K. Frankena, 'Spinoza on the Knowledge of Good and Evil', *Philosophia* vol. 7 (1977), pp. 15–44.

William K. Frankena, 'Spinoza's "New Morality": Notes on Book IV', Mandelbaum, pp. 85–100.

Joel Friedman, 'An Overview of Spinoza's *Ethics*', *Synthese* vol. 37 (1968), pp. 67–106.

Joel Friedman, 'Spinoza's Denial of Free Will in Man and God', in Jon Wetlesen (ed.), *Spinoza's Philosophy of Man* (Oslo, 1977), pp. 51–84.

Moltke, S. Gram, 'Spinoza, Substance, and Predication', *Theoria* vol. 34 (1968), pp. 222–244.

Michel Gueret, André Robinet, and Paul Tombeur, *Spinoza: Ethica, concordances, index, listes de fréquences, tables comparatives,* (Louvain-la-Neuve, 1977).

BIBLIOGRAPHY

H.F. Hallett, *Aeternitas, a Spinozistic Study* (Oxford, 1930).

H.F. Hallett, 'On a Reputed Equivoque in the Philosophy of Spinoza', *The Review of Metaphysics*, vol. 3 (1949-50), reprinted in Kashap, pp. 168–188.

Stuart Hampshire, 'A Kind of Materialsm', *Proceedings of the American Philosophical Association* 1969, reprinted in Hampshire's *Freedom of Mind* (Oxford, 1972), pp. 210–231.

Stuart Hampshire, 'The Explanation of Thought', in Joseph H. Smith (ed.), *Thought, Consciousness, and Reality* (New Haven, 1977), pp. 3–23.

Stuart Hampshire, *Spinoza* (London, 1951).

Stuart Hampshire, 'Spinoza and the Idea of Freedom', *Proceedings of the British Academy* 1960, reprinted in Grene, pp. 297–317, in Kashap, and in Hampshire's *Freedom of Mind* (Oxford, 1972).

Stuart Hampshire, 'Spinoza's Theory of Human Freedom', *The Monist* vol. 55 (1971), reprinted in Mandelbaum, pp. 35–47.

Stuart Hampshire, *Two Theories of Morality* (Oxford, 1977).

C.L. Hardin, 'Spinoza on Immortality and time', Shahan, pp. 129–138.

Francis S. Haserot, 'Spinoza and the Status of Universals', *The Philosophical Review* vol. 59 (1950), reprinted in Kashap, pp. 43–67.

Francis S. Haserot, 'Spinoza's Definition of Attribute', *The Philosophical Review* vol. 62 (1953), reprinted in Kashap, pp. 28–42.

Michael Hooker, 'The Deductive Character of Spinoza's Metaphysics', Kennington, pp. 17–34.

H.G. Hubbeling, 'The Logical and Experiential Roots of Spinoza's Mysticism', Hessing, pp. 323–329.

Charles Jarrett, 'The Logical Structure of Spinoza's *Ethics*, Part 1', *Synthese* vol. 37 (1978), pp. 15–65.

Harold H. Joachim, *A Study of the Ethics of Spinoza* (Oxford, 1901)

Hans Jonas, 'Spinoza and the Theory of Organism', *Journal of the History of Philosophy* vol. 3 (1965), reprinted in Grene, pp. 259–278.

George L. Kline, 'On the Infinity of Spinoza's Attributes', Hessing, pp. 342–346.

Martha Kneale, 'Eternity and Sempiternity', *Proceedings of the Aristotelian Society* vol. 69 (1968-9), reprinted in Grene, pp. 227–240.

David Lachterman, 'The Physics of Spinoza's *Ethics*', Shahan, pp. 71–111.

Louis E. Loeb, *From Descartes to Hume* (Ithaca, 1981).

J.J. MacIntosh, 'Spinoza's Epistemological Views', in G.N.A. Vesey (ed.), *Reason and Reality* (London, 1972).

Wallace Matson, 'Death and Destruction in Spinoza's Ethics', *Inquiry* vol. 20 (1969), pp. 403–417.

Wallace Matson, 'Steps Towards Spinozism', *Revue internationale de philosophie* 119-120 (1977), pp. 69–83.

Wallace Matson, 'Spinoza's Theory of Mind', *The Monist* vol. 55 (1971), reprinted in Mandelbaum, pp. 49–60.

Thomas Nagel, 'Panpsychism', in his *Mortal Questions* (New York, 1979).

Jerome Neu, *Emotion, Thought, and Therapy* (London, 1977).

Douglas Odegard, 'The Body Identical with the Human Mind: A Problem in Spinoza's Philosophy', *The Monist* vol. 55 (1971), reprinted in Mandelbaum, pp. 61–83.

G.H.R. Parkinson, 'Being and Knowledge in Spinoza', in J.G. van der Bend (ed.), *Spinoza on Knowing, Being and Freedom* (Assen, 1974), pp. 24–40.

G.H.R. Parkinson, 'Hegel, Pantheism, and Spinoza', *Journal of the History of Ideas* vol. 38 (1955), pp. 449–459.

G.H.R. Parkinson, 'Spinoza on the Power and Freedom of Man', *The Monist* vol. 55 (1971), reprinted in Mandelbaum, pp. 7–33.

G.H.R. Parkinson, 'Spinoza's Conception of the Rational Act', *Studia Leibnitiana Supplementa* vol. 20 (1981), pp. 1–19.

G.H.R. Parkinson, *Spinoza's Theory of Knowledge* (Oxford, 1954).

G.H.R. Parkinson, ' "Truth is its Own Standard": Aspects of Spinoza's Theory of Truth', Shahan, pp. 35–55.

Frederick Pollock, *Spinoza, his Life and Philosophy* (London, 1880), reprinted by the Reprint Library.

Daisie Radner, 'Spinoza's Theory of Ideas', *Philosophical Review* vol. 80 (1971), pp. 338–359.

Leon Roth, *Spinoza* (London, 1929).

A.J. Watt, 'The Causality of God in Spinoza's Philosphy', *Canadian Journal of Philosophy* vol. 2 (1972), pp. 171–197.

BIBLIOGRAPHY

Margaret D. Wilson, 'Objects, Ideas, and "Minds": Comments on Spinoza's Theory of Mind', Kennington, pp. 103–120.

H.A. Wolfson, *The Philosophy of Spinoza* (New York, 1934).

INDEX OF PERSONS

INDEX OF REFERENCES

PART 1

PART 2

PART 4

PART 5